wild cape cod free by nature

john and pamela king

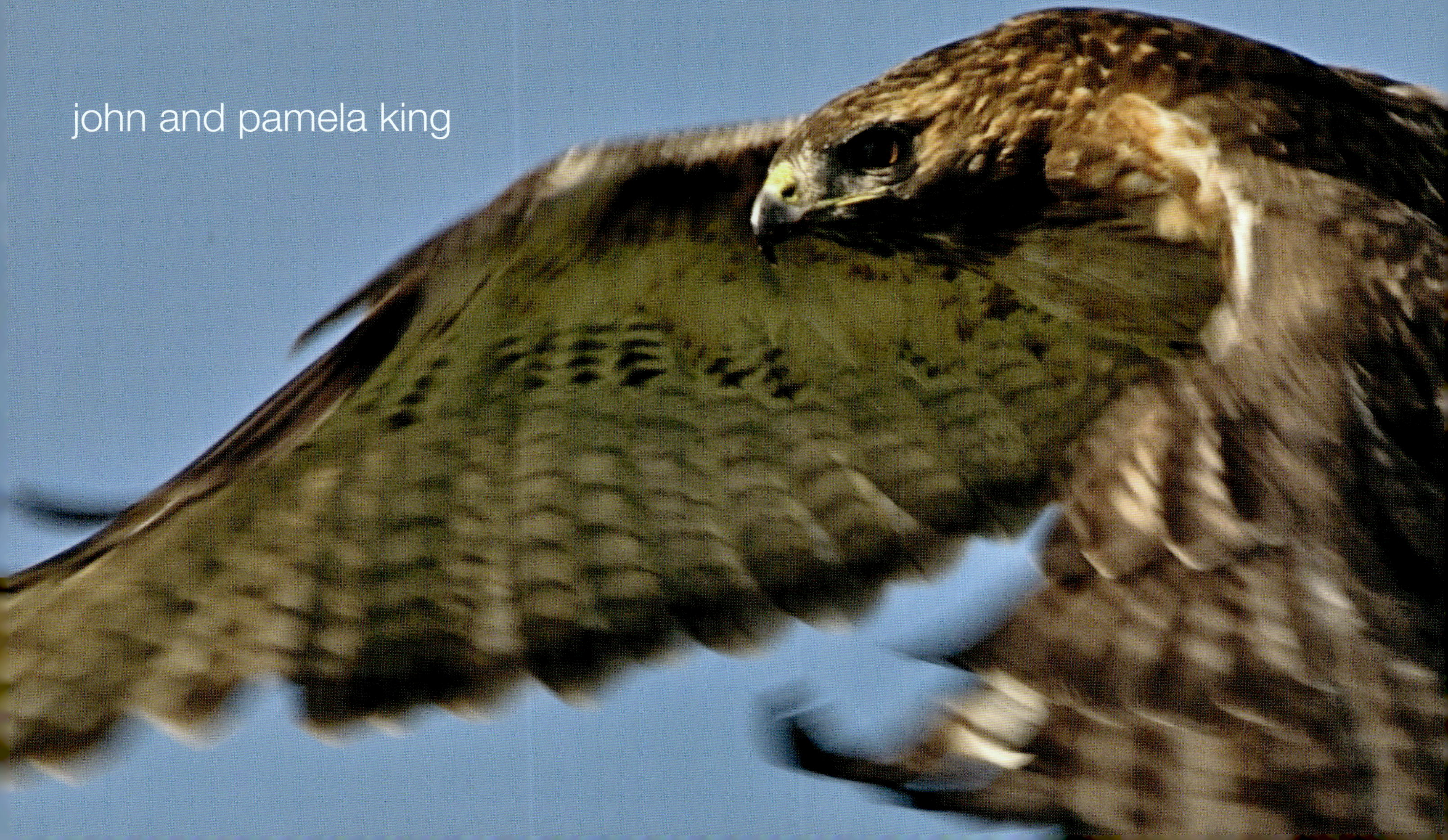

This book is dedicated to the memories of Robert Verity Clem and Louisa Russell: Two extraordinary people who showed the way for those who treasure and want to protect the wild side of Cape Cod.

Other Schiffer Books on Related Subjects:

Birds of Cape Cod & the Islands, 978-0-7643-2461-6, $45.00

New England's Natural Wonders: An Explorer's Guide, 978-0-7643-3983-7, $34.99

The Cape Cod National Seashore: A Photographic Adventure and Guide, 978-0-7643-3995-0, $24.99

Library of Congress Control Number: 2012937783

Type set in Helvetica Lt.

ISBN: 978-0-7643-4197-7
Printed in China

Published by Schiffer Publishing, Ltd.
4880 Lower Valley Road
Atglen, PA 19310
Phone: (610) 593-1777; Fax: (610) 593-2002
E-mail: Info@schifferbooks.com

In Europe, Schiffer books are distributed by
Bushwood Books
6 Marksbury Ave.
Kew Gardens
Surrey TW9 4JF England
Phone: 44 (0) 20 8392 8585; Fax: 44 (0) 20 8392 9876
E-mail: info@bushwoodbooks.co.uk
Website: www.bushwoodbooks.co.uk

contents

preface

Comparatively speaking, Cape Cod has been in existence for only a tiny heartbeat of planetary time. And if today's climatologists are correct in their assessment of current warming trends, the day when most of Cape Cod will disappear under the sea is only another geological heartbeat away.

So it is possible that twenty-first-century inhabitants may be among the last human beings to enjoy the Cape as we now know it. Thrusting eastward into the Atlantic Ocean to a distance of forty miles from the Massachusetts mainland, Cape Cod is home to a people who make their living at battle with the natural elements at sea, or in serving the legions of summer visitors who flock to Cape Cod to enjoy warm sandy beaches and charming seaside New England. A handful of our families can trace their roots back more than 300 years, to the first European settlers who found their way to the Cape in search of opportunity and a better life by the sea. How fitting that these settlers—and those that followed—made their homes on a spit of land that itself is but a stubborn product of the last great movement of ice in the waning days of the Pleistocene Era.

Scientists continue to gather data and interpret the evidence as they try to explain the genesis of Cape Cod and the plants, trees, and animals that live here. But this much is certain: Cape Cod is the hearty offspring of ice age glaciers and the continual shaping and reshaping forces of the North Atlantic ocean. It's birth stands out as a dramatic last act in the formation of the modern North American continent. The wild landscapes, plant, and animal life on Cape Cod offer a unique opportunity to view this land in a way that is often overlooked.

Much of the wildlife that inhabits Cape Cod finds its way here for respite on age-old migratory journeys, just as it has for millennia and long before Cape Cod was formed. In a quest to stay near their food sources as the seasons change, these species include wonderful populations of migratory birds, marine mammals (including whales), and various sea and insect life that migrate along the coastal regions of North America. The Cape is also home to other wild creatures often unseen by its visitors, even though these animals have learned to live in close proximity to human beings.

This book seeks to provide the reader with a rare Cape visitor experience—to imagine Cape Cod before human habitation by witnessing its vibrant wild flora and fauna. Our story is told through the images we have photographed over the past four years since returning to live full time on Cape Cod. We have organized our photographs to provide the reader with a view of the big picture through a sampling of landscapes representative of the Cape's geography, together with our best efforts at capturing some of the wilderness around us through the four distinct seasons that Cape Cod experiences. Though each season is well represented, you will notice more images from the active seasons of summer and fall since warmer ocean temperatures off of the Cape provide a backdrop for peak migrations. We chronicle the very large, like the whales—down to the very small, like insects, shellfish, and plants. We also have added images of some of our favorite trees; they are rare here and deserve to be imagined in their primordial setting.

It is an impossible task to provide a complete photographic record of the wild species and the landscapes of Cape Cod in a single volume. Therefore, we have attempted to provide some dramatic examples designed to inspire the reader to get outside and look at Cape Cod through the lens of a raw and wonderful wilderness that just so happens to have humans living nearby.

–John & Pamela King, Chatham, Massachusetts

acknowledgments

The authors are grateful for the encouragement and support from our friends and family, especially our children Spencer and Mia who believed we could follow through, and our friends Mark Delorey and Lynn Van Norman, who enthusiastically provided ideas on the wild locations of Cape Cod and in some cases even guided us to them.

We would also like to thank Tim Vorhees for agreeing to showcase his talent and beautiful images in our work, Gareth Glaser for his editing prowess, and Tracy Anderson for her essential creative contributions in organizing and preparing this book.

- lighthouse beach, chatham
- chatham
- chatham bar
- oyster river, chatham
- ryder's cove, chatham
- frost fish creek, chatham
- harwich
- little pleasant bay, orleans
- nauset beach, orleans
- kent's point, orleans
- nickerson state park, brewster
- first encounter beach, eastham
- eastham
- fort hill, eastham
- wellfleet
- wellfleet bay wildlife sanctuary
- marconi station, wellfleet
- cedar swamp, wellfleet
- truro
- cape cod national seashore, truro
- pamet river, truro
- provincetown
- cape cod national seashore, provincetown

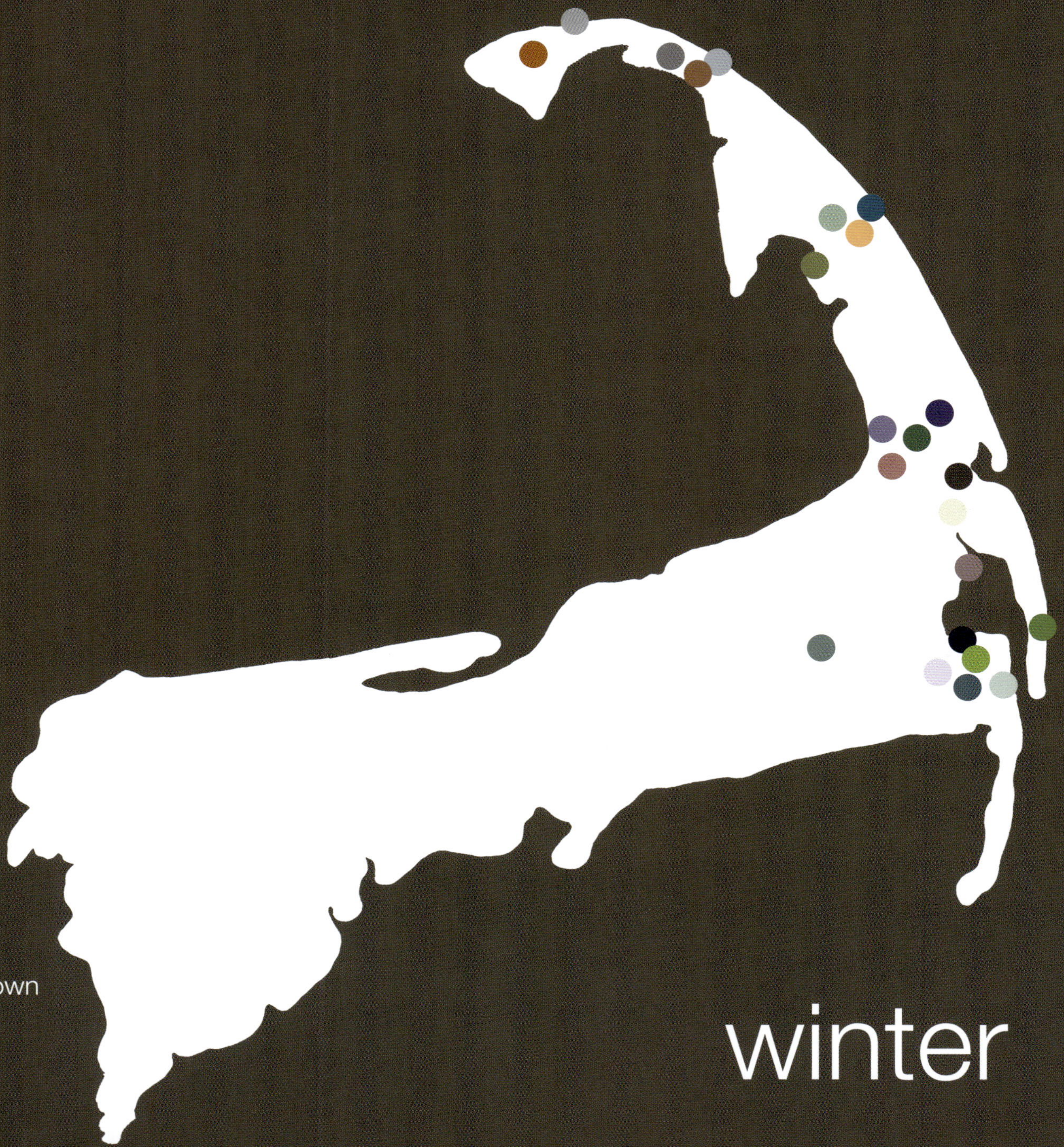

winter

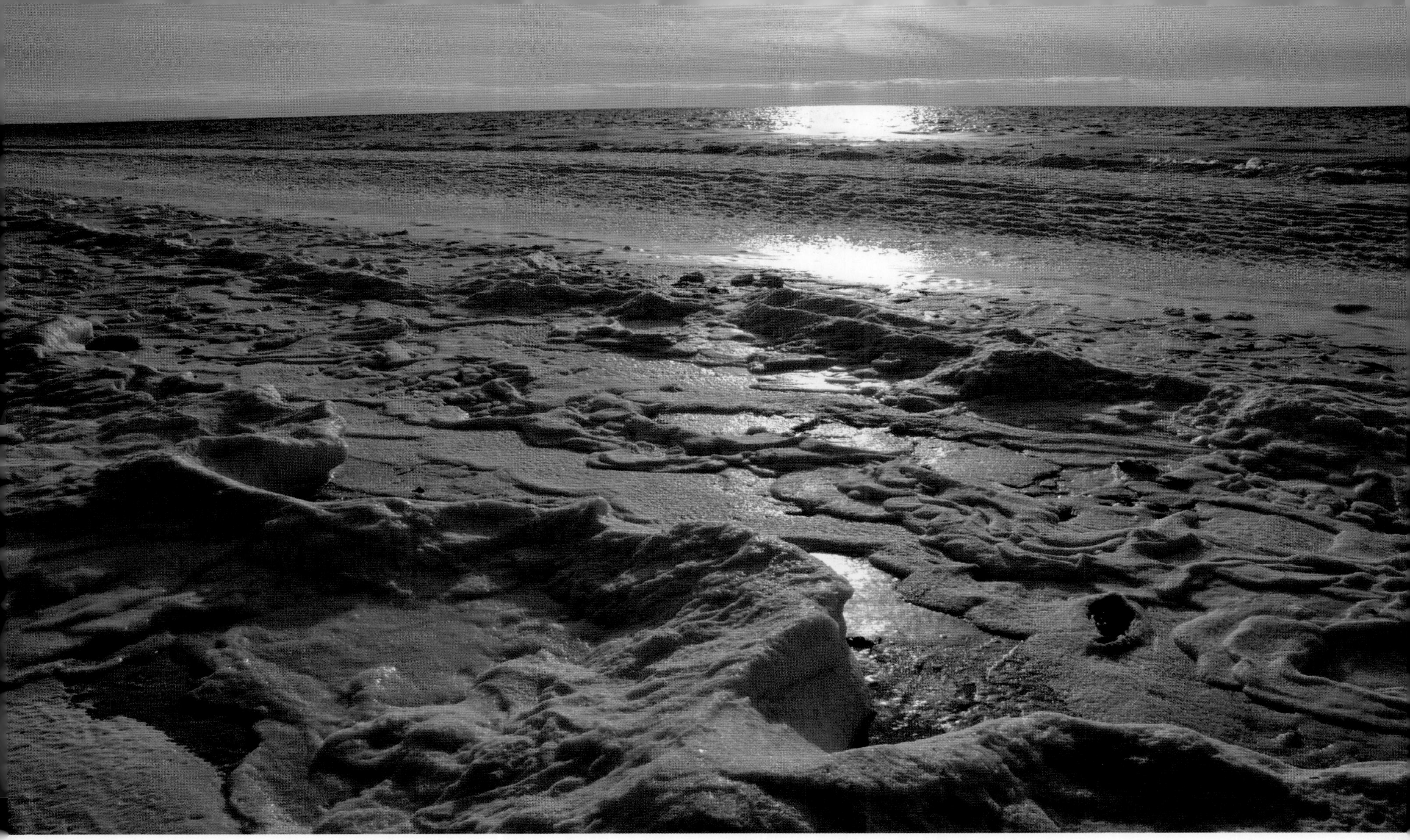

snow foam | first encounter beach, eastham

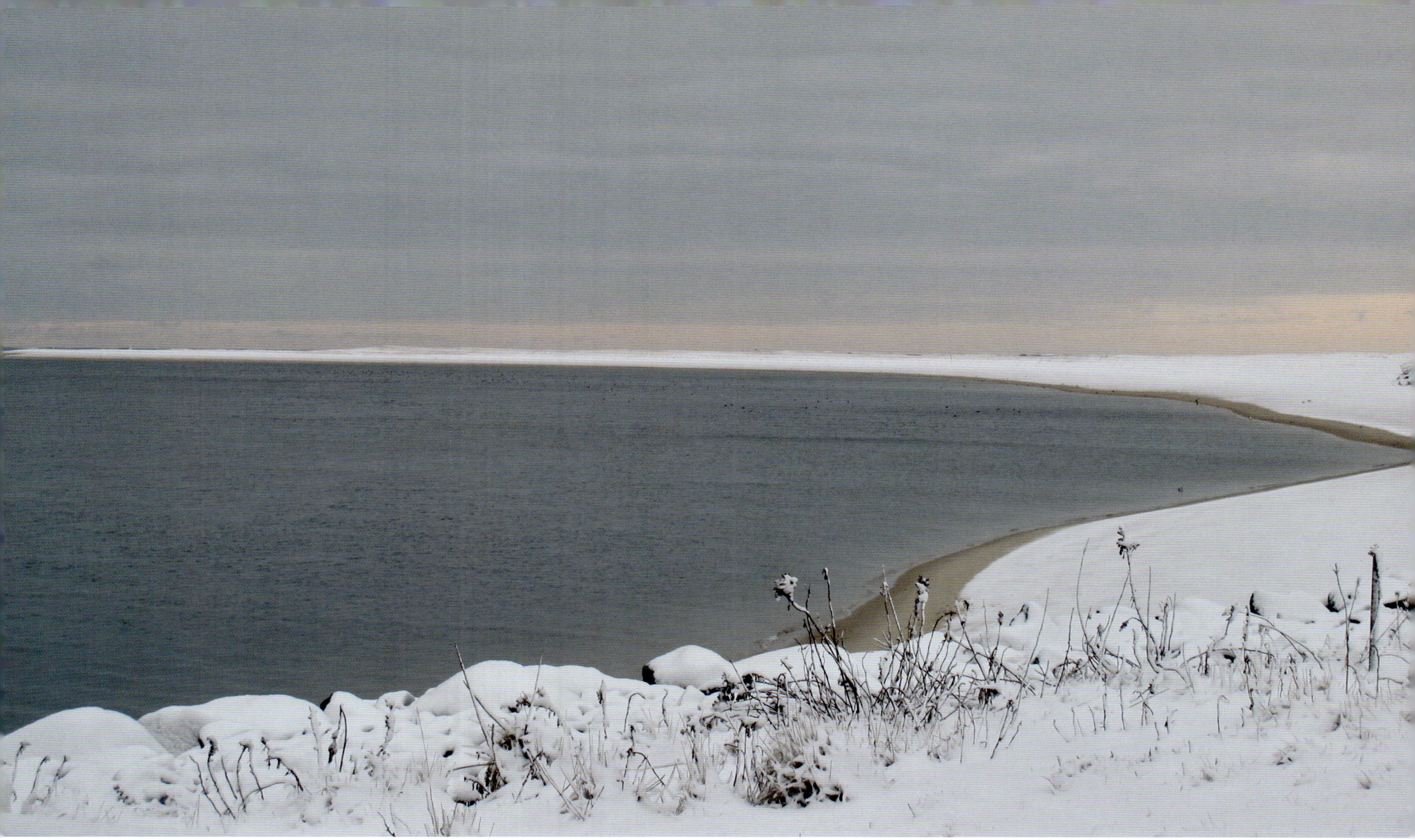

winter whites | lighthouse beach, chatham

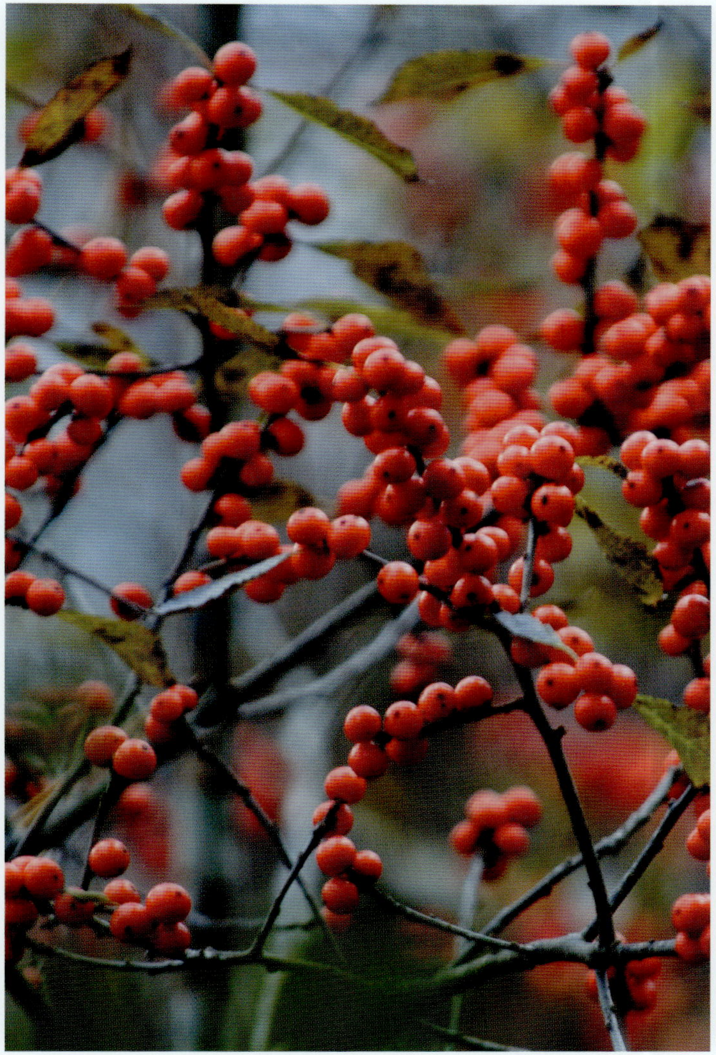

winter ripe

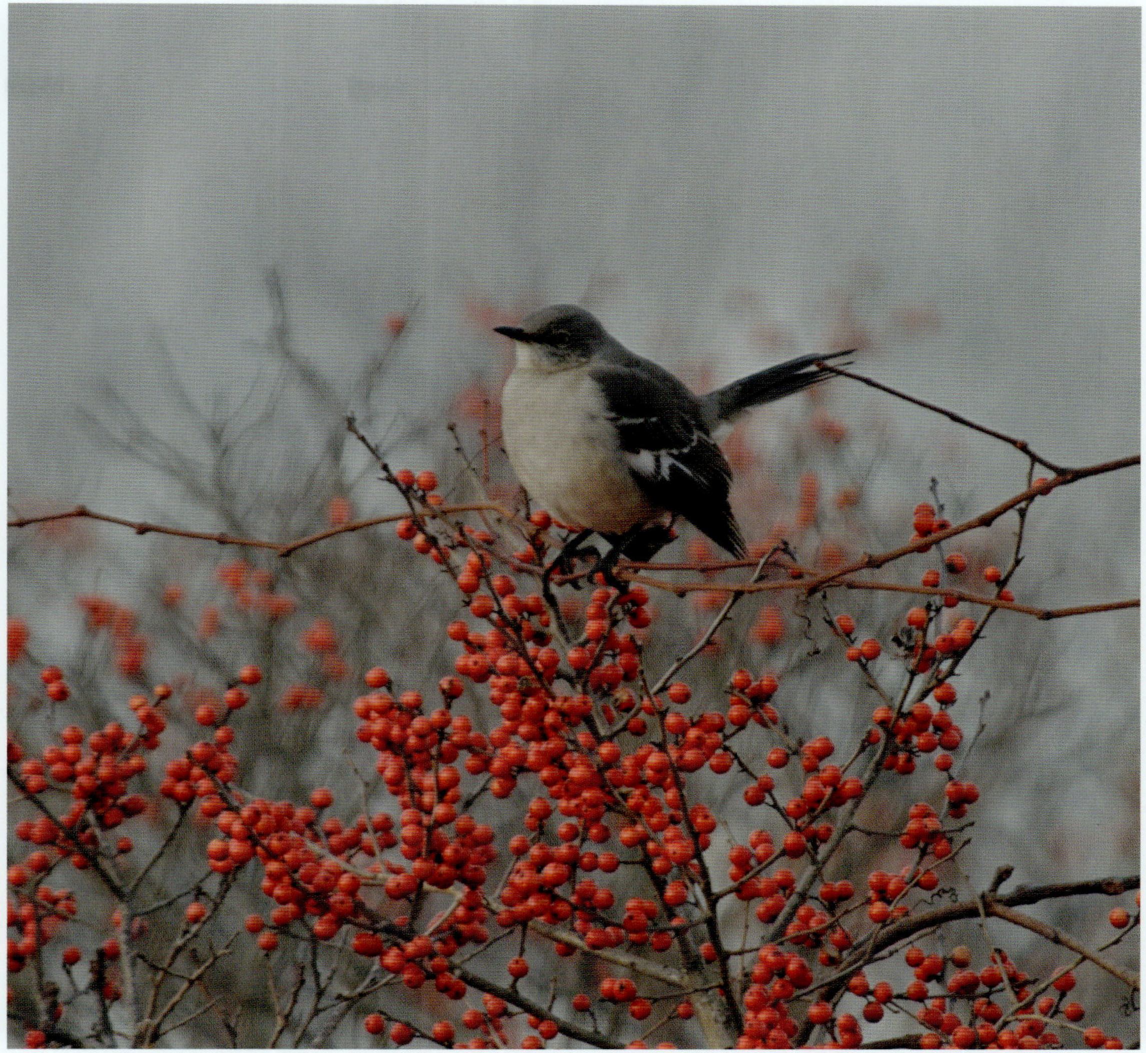

a christmas wish

winterberries and mockingbird,
truro

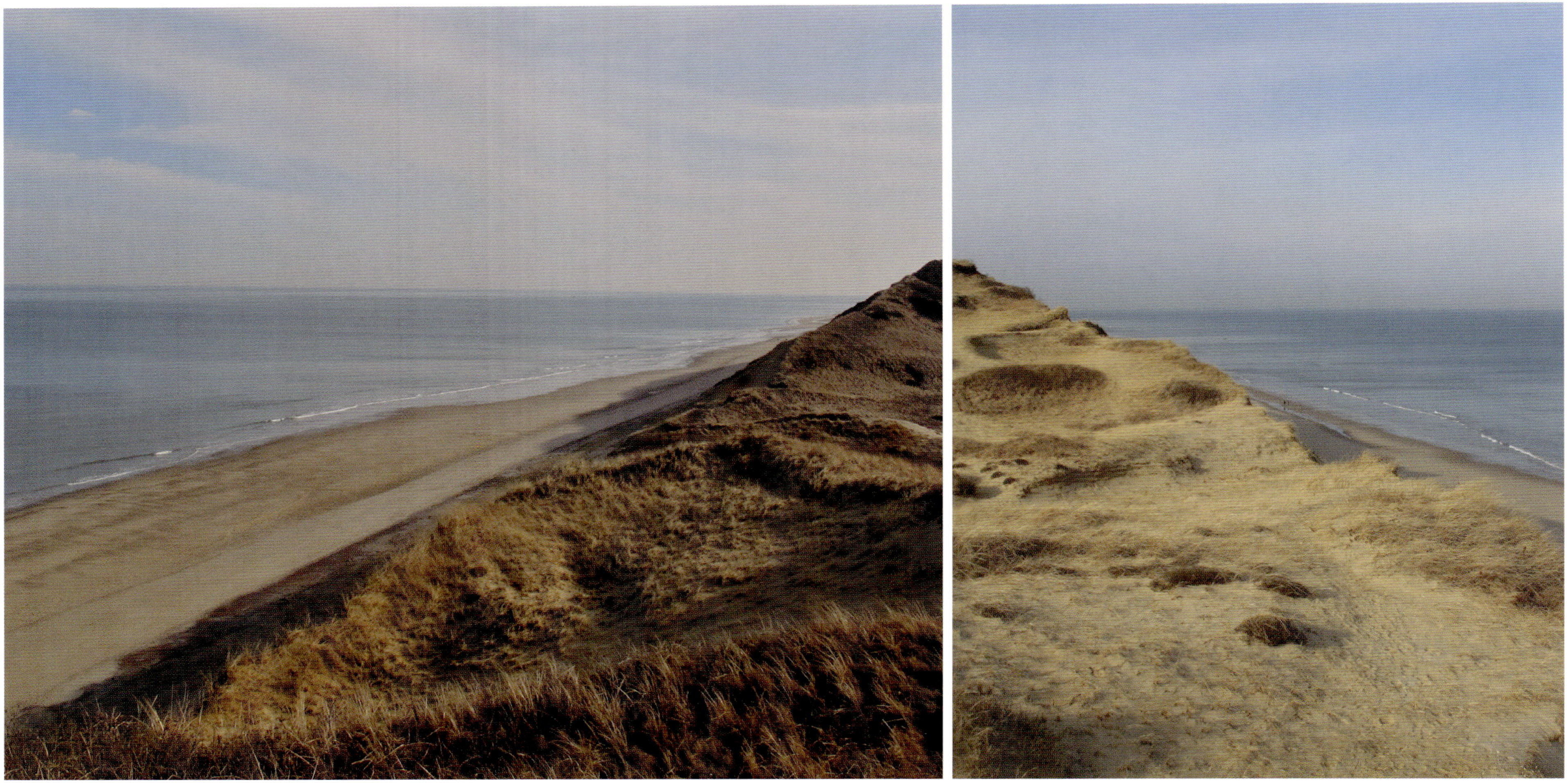

both sides of the equation

sand dunes,
truro

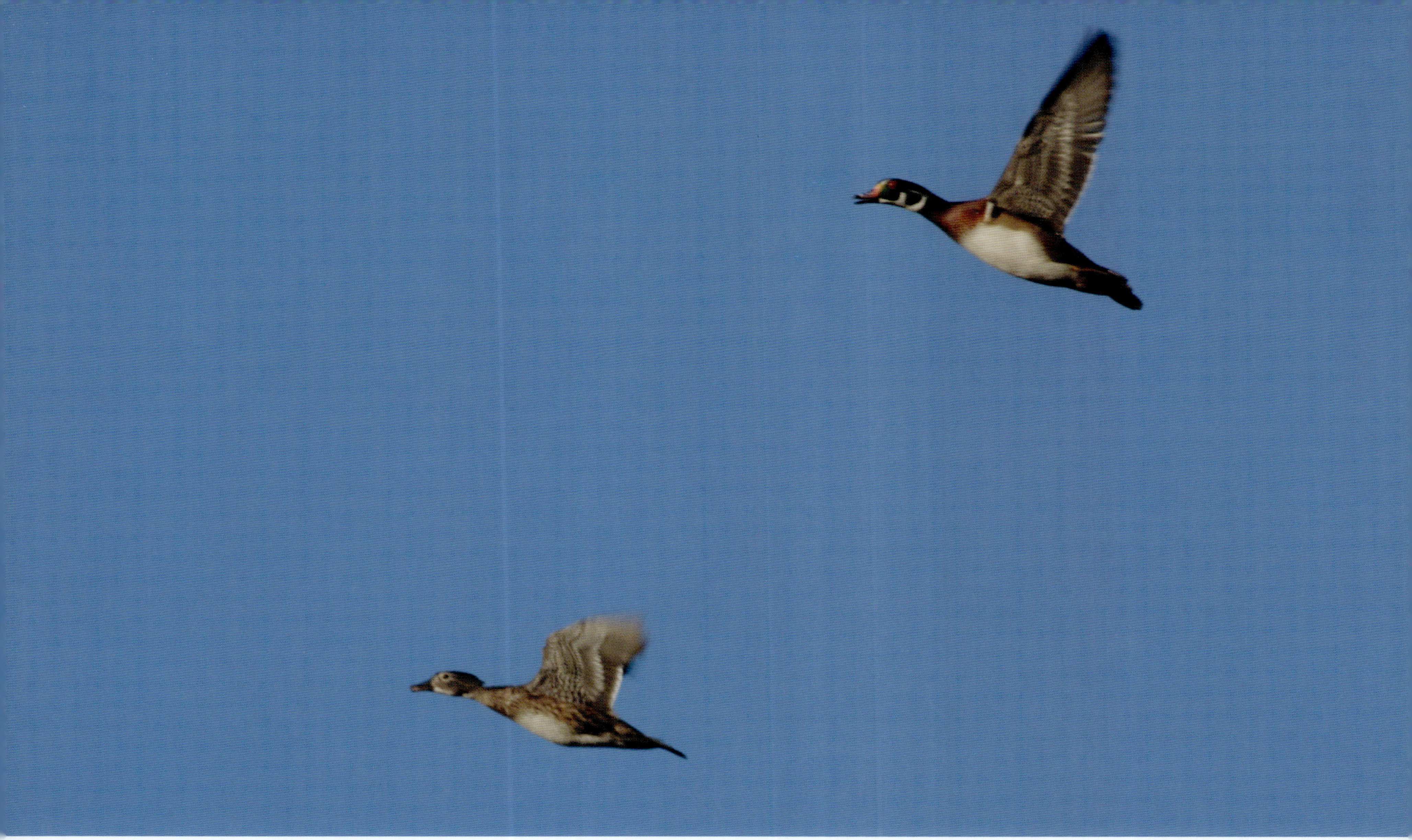

paired

wood ducks,
nickerson state park, brewster

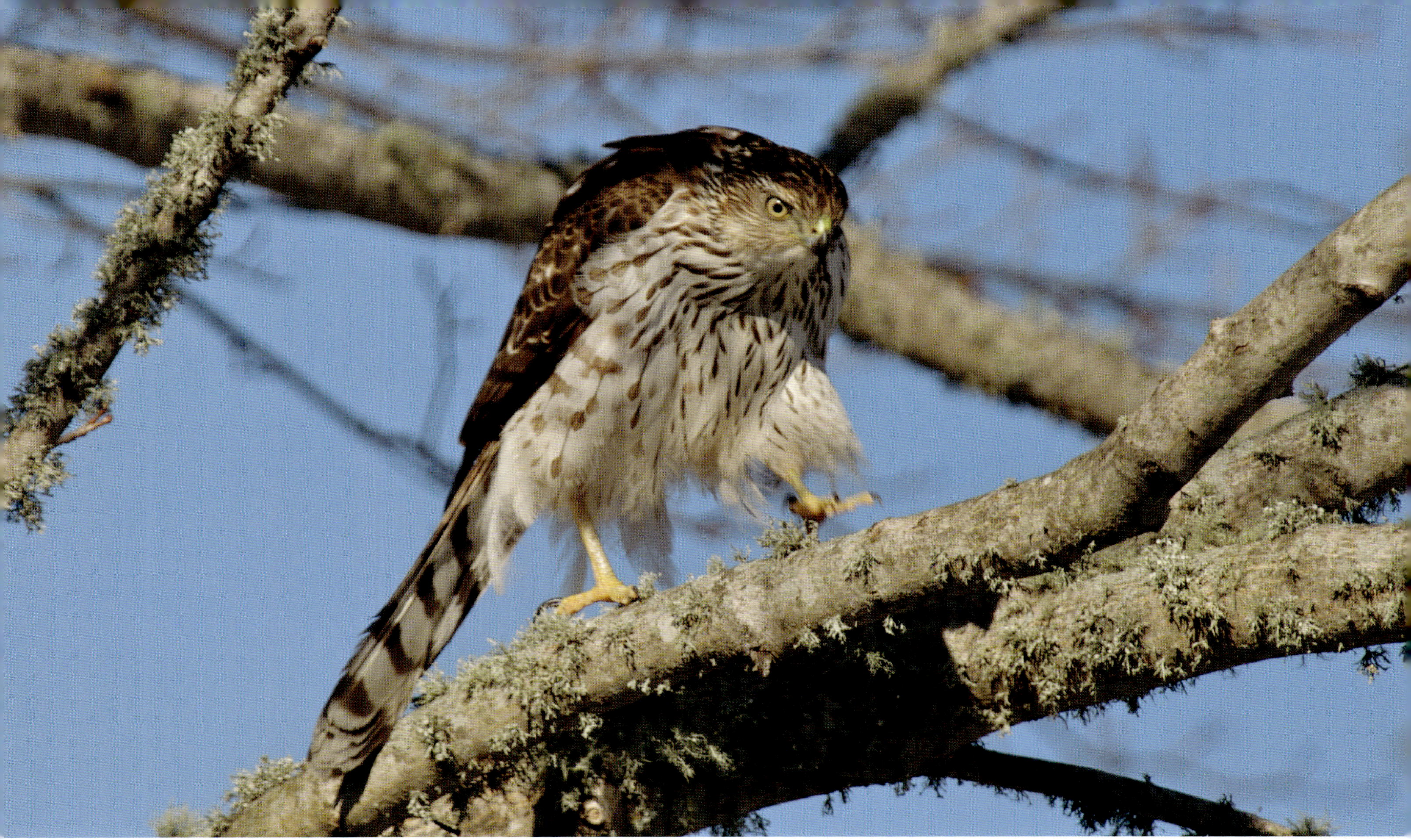

stalking hawk

young cooper's hawk, chatham

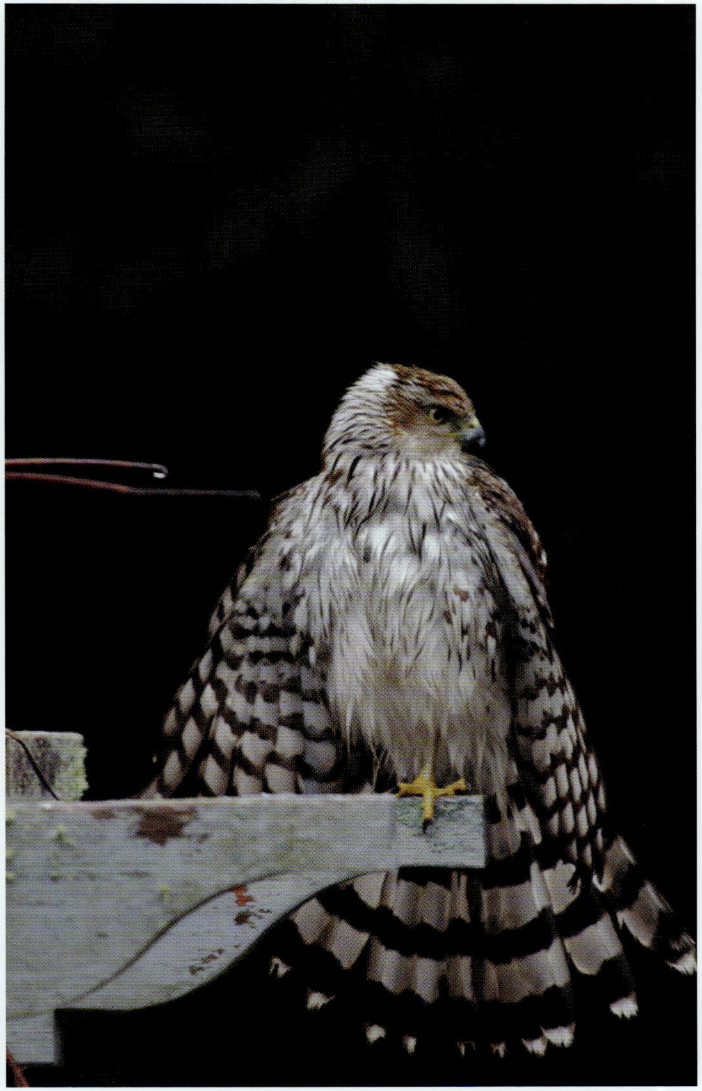

drying out

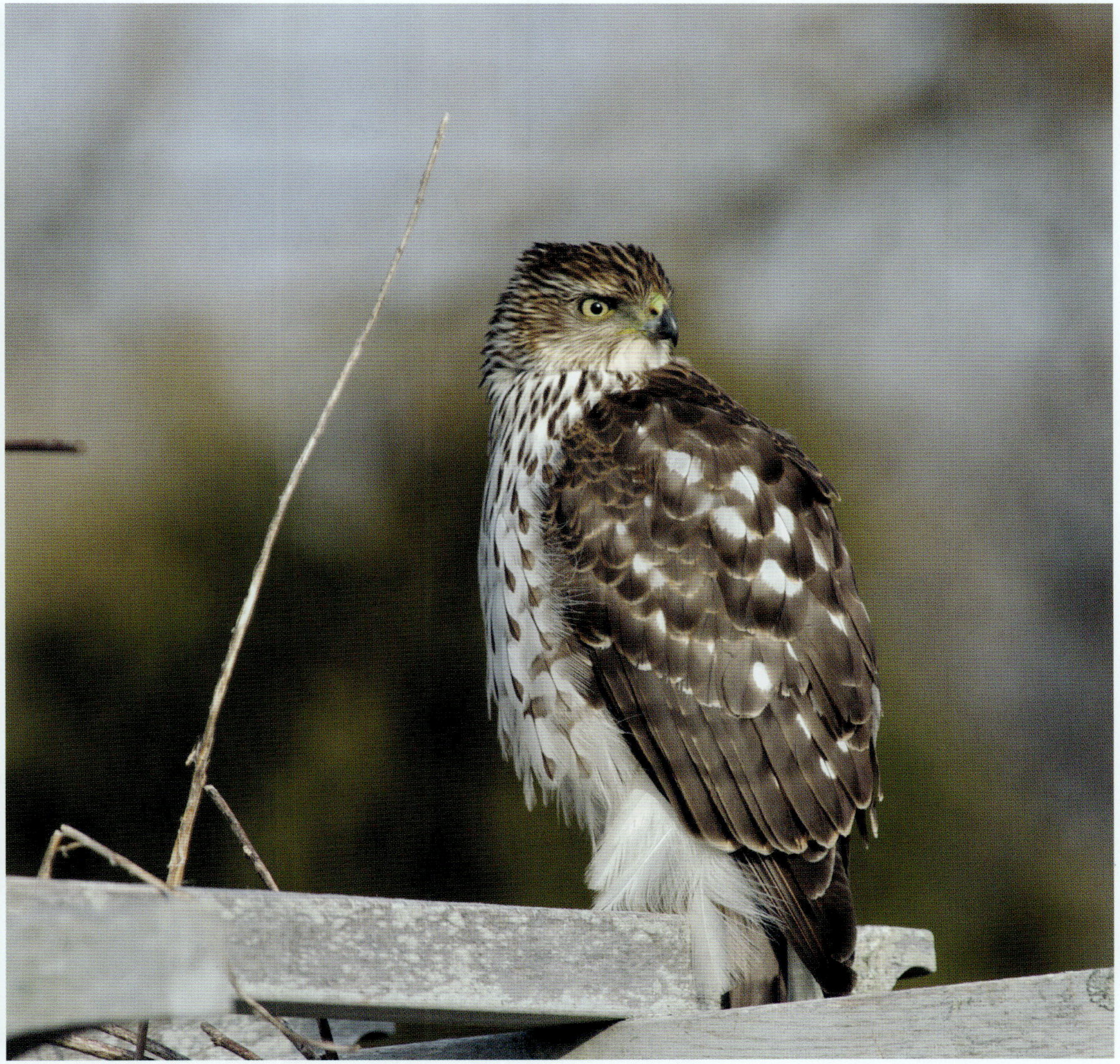

poised

cooper's hawk,
chatham

cool reflection

little cliff pond,
nickerson state park, brewster

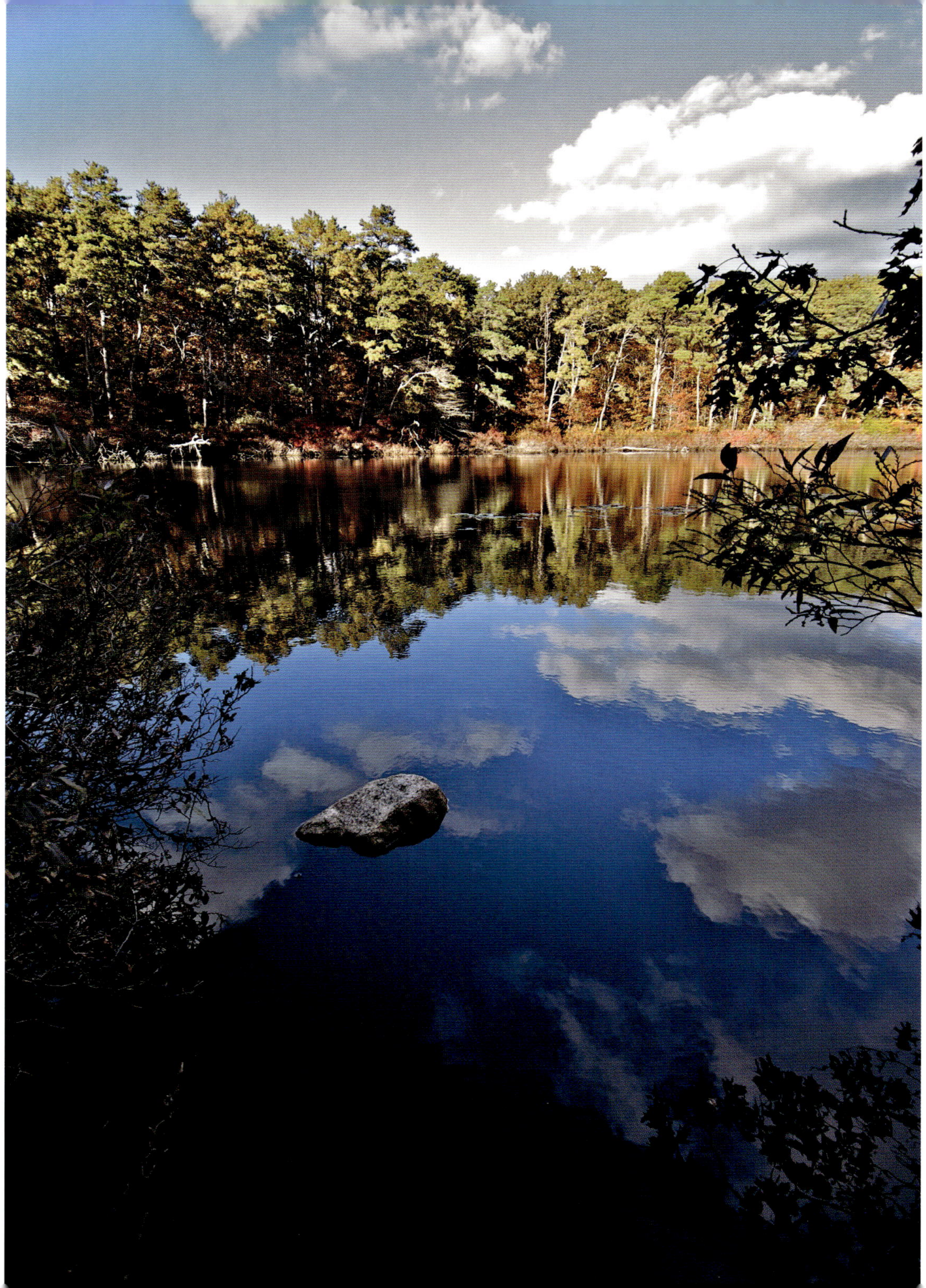

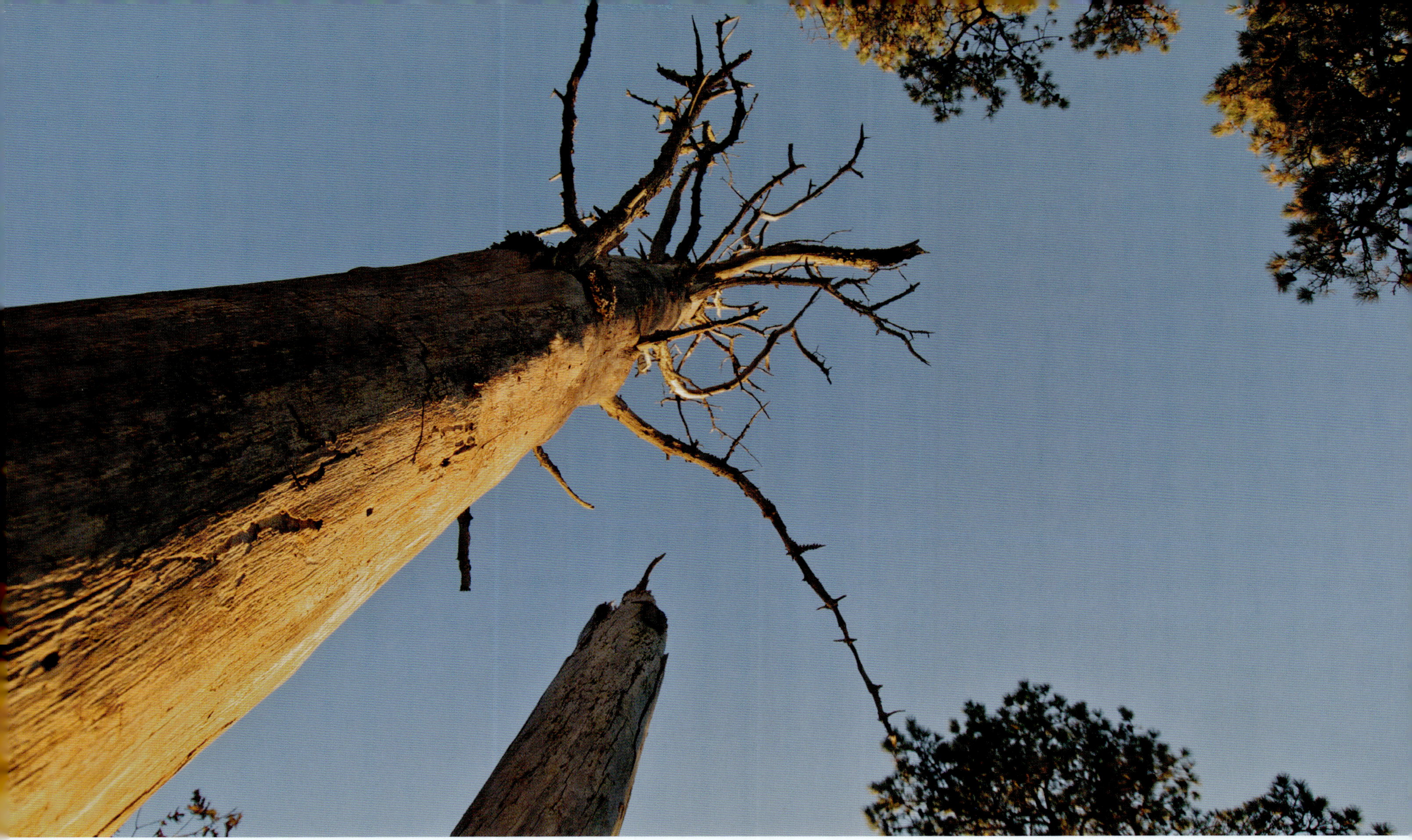

woodpecker's dream | nickerson state park, brewster

cape cod national seashore, provincetown

next page: northern harriers at the moors

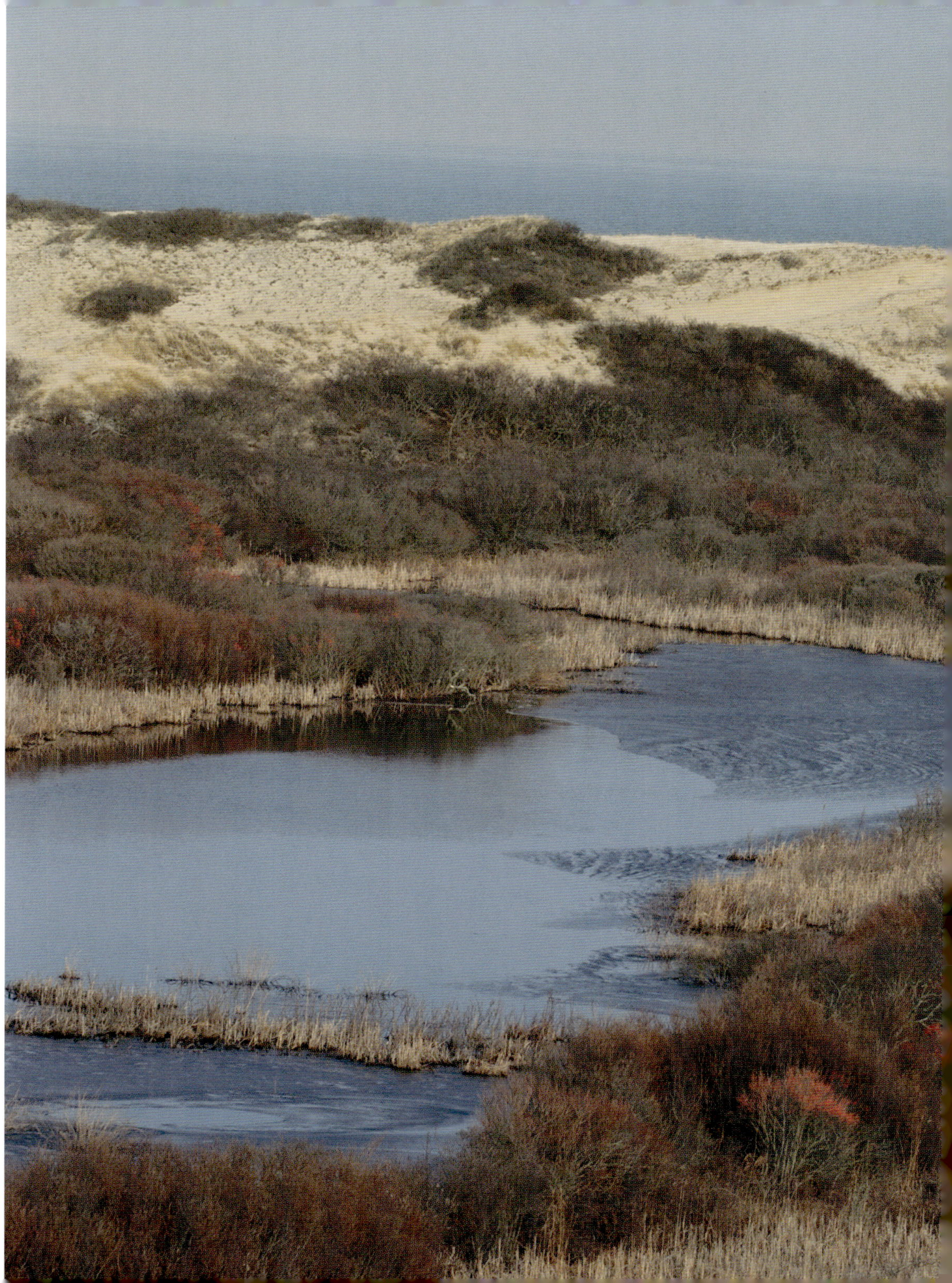

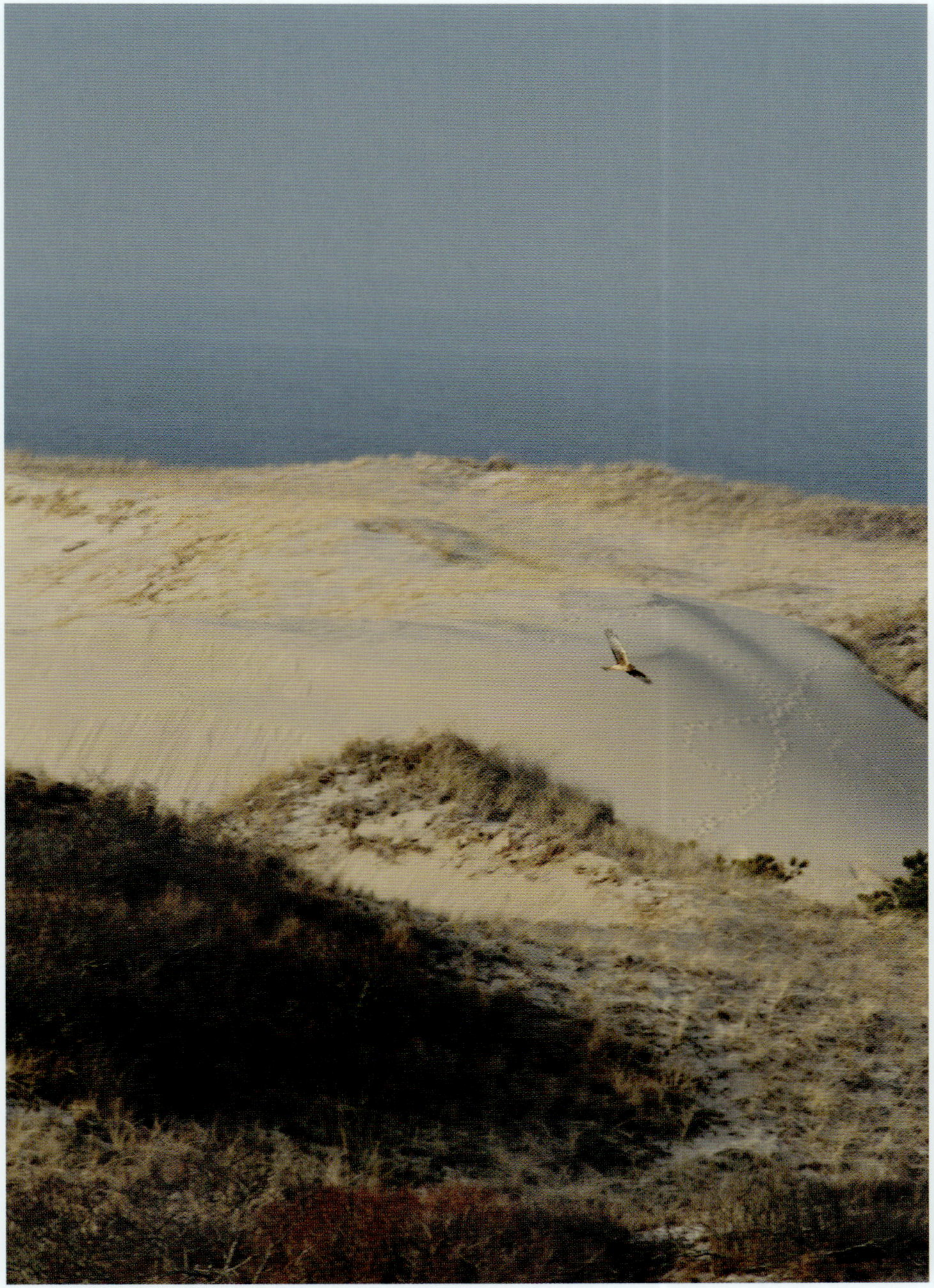

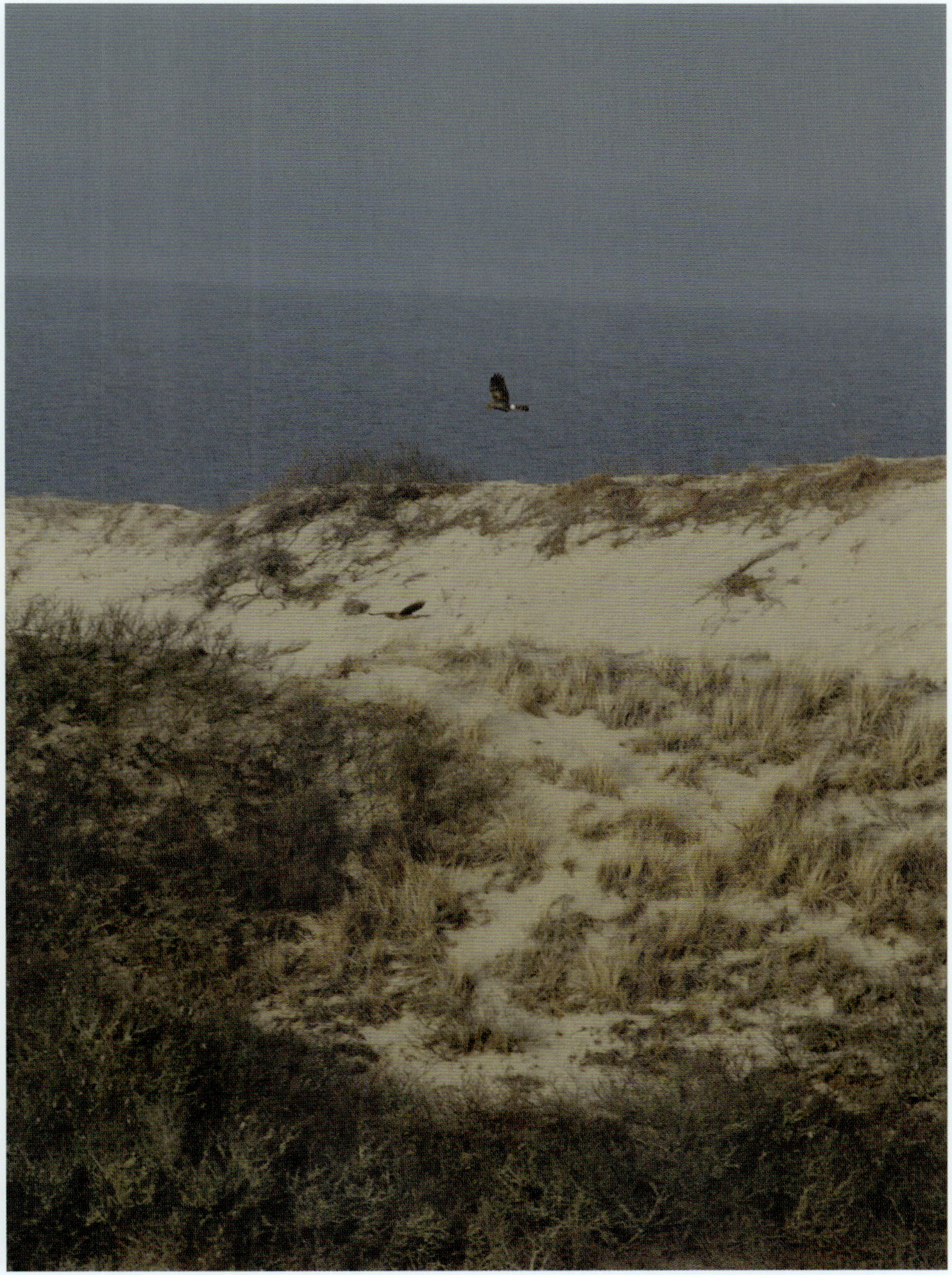

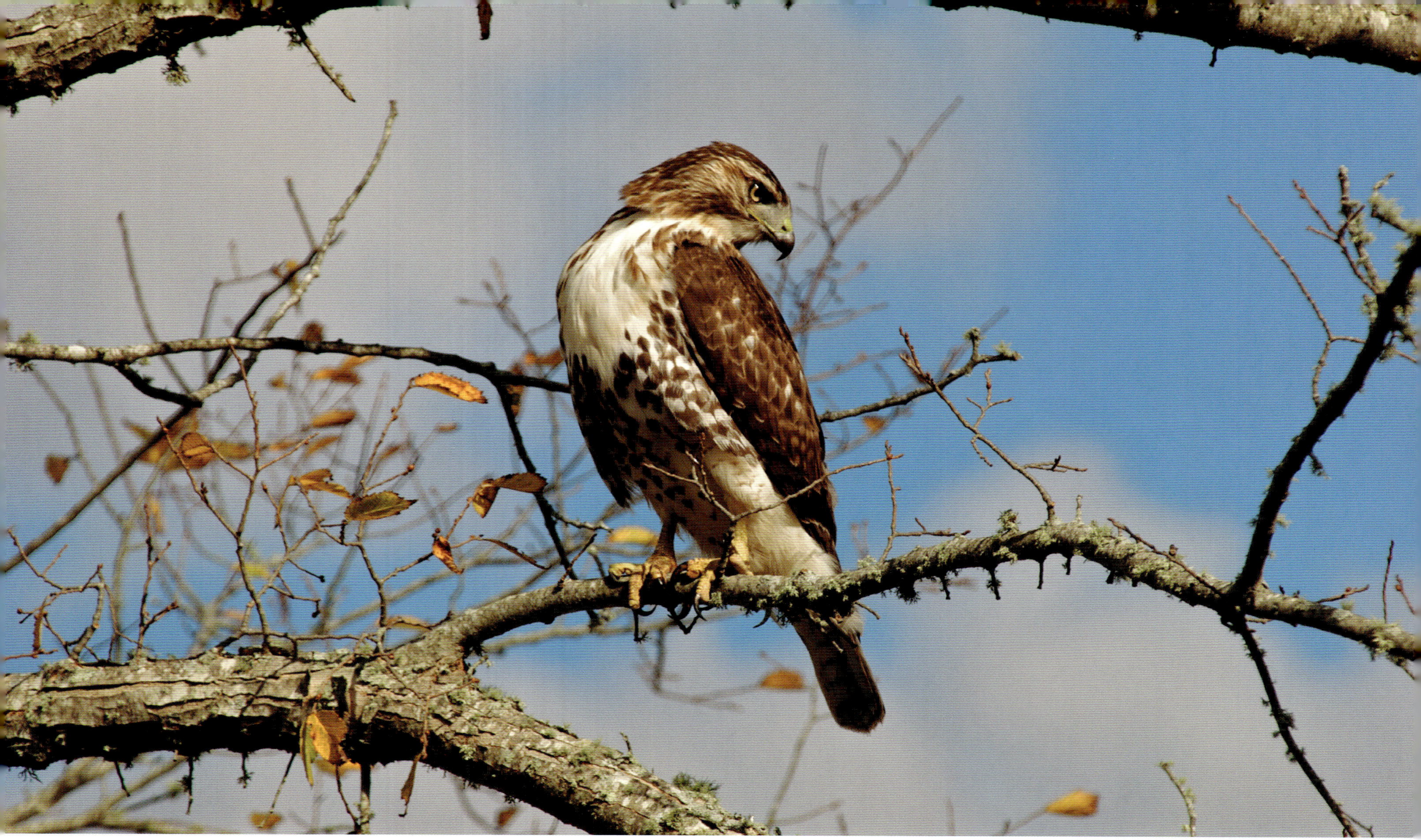

golden grip

young red-tailed hawk,
harwich

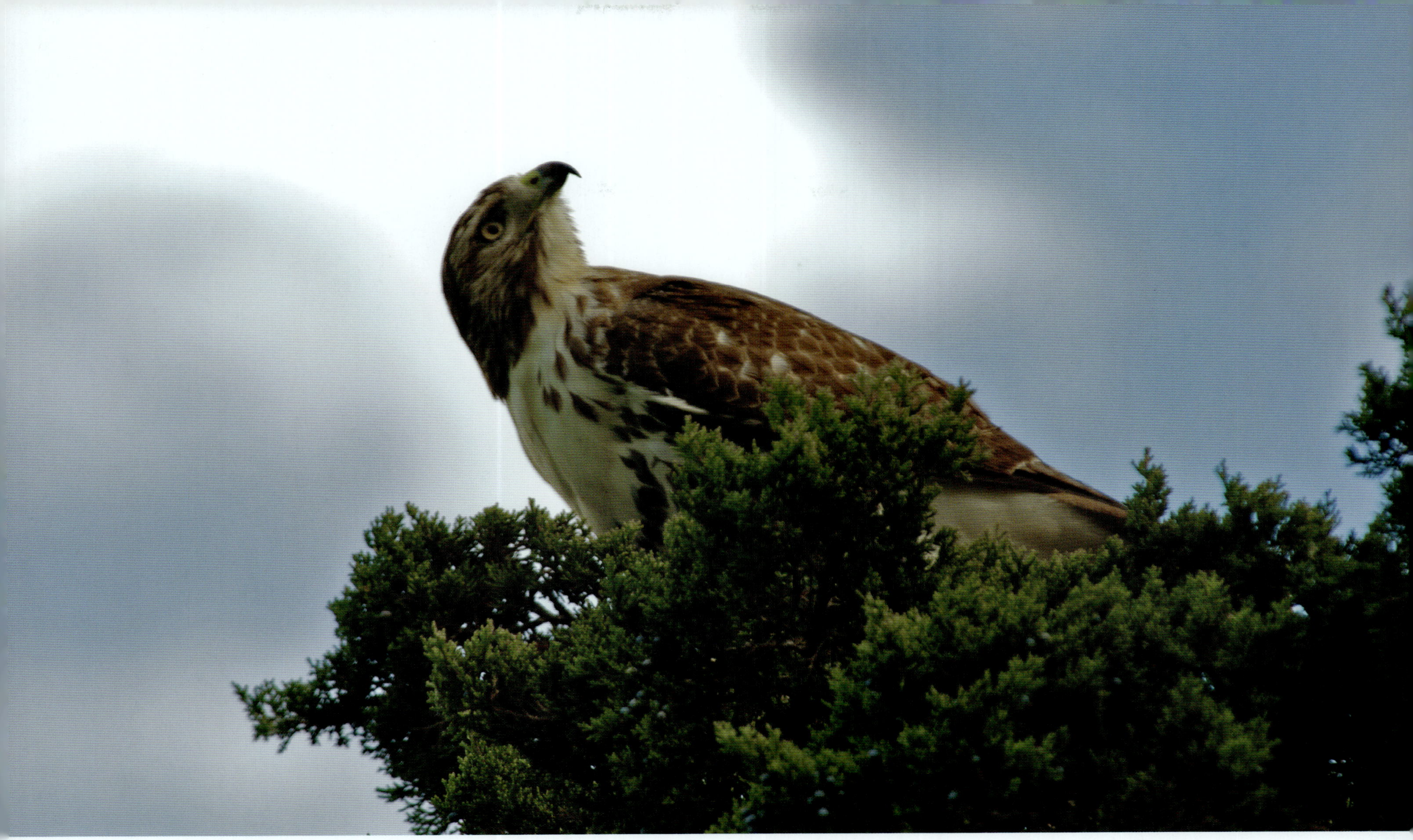

a penny for your thoughts

young red-tailed hawk,
harwich

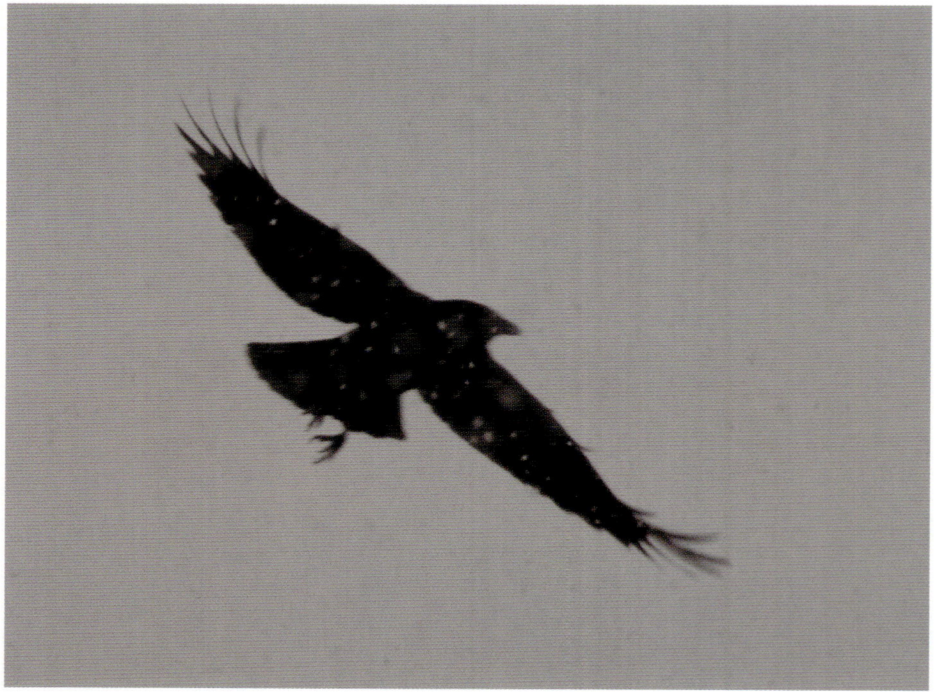

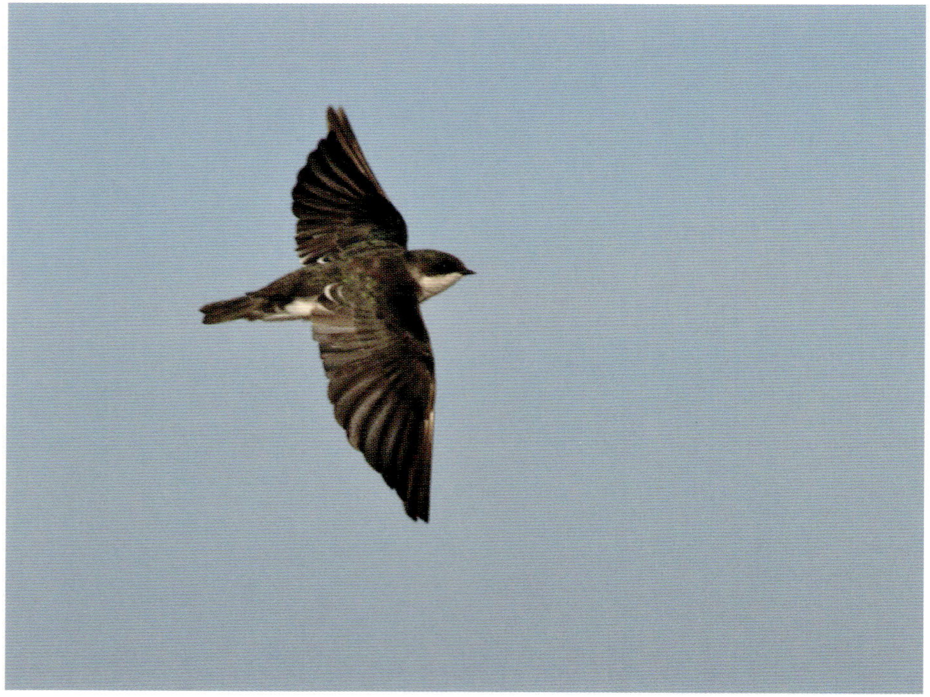

crow and tree swallow,
chatham

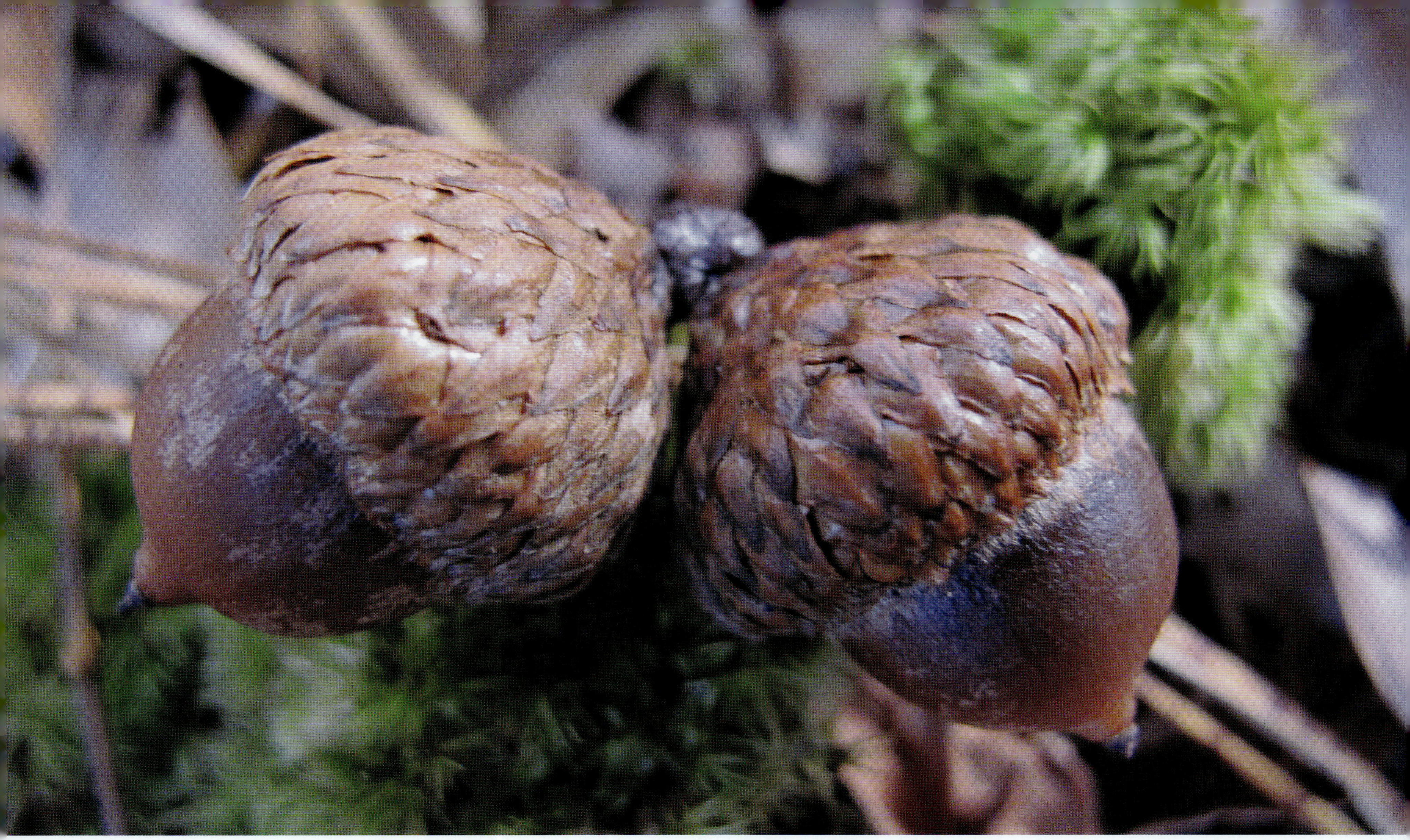

oak acorns,
eastham

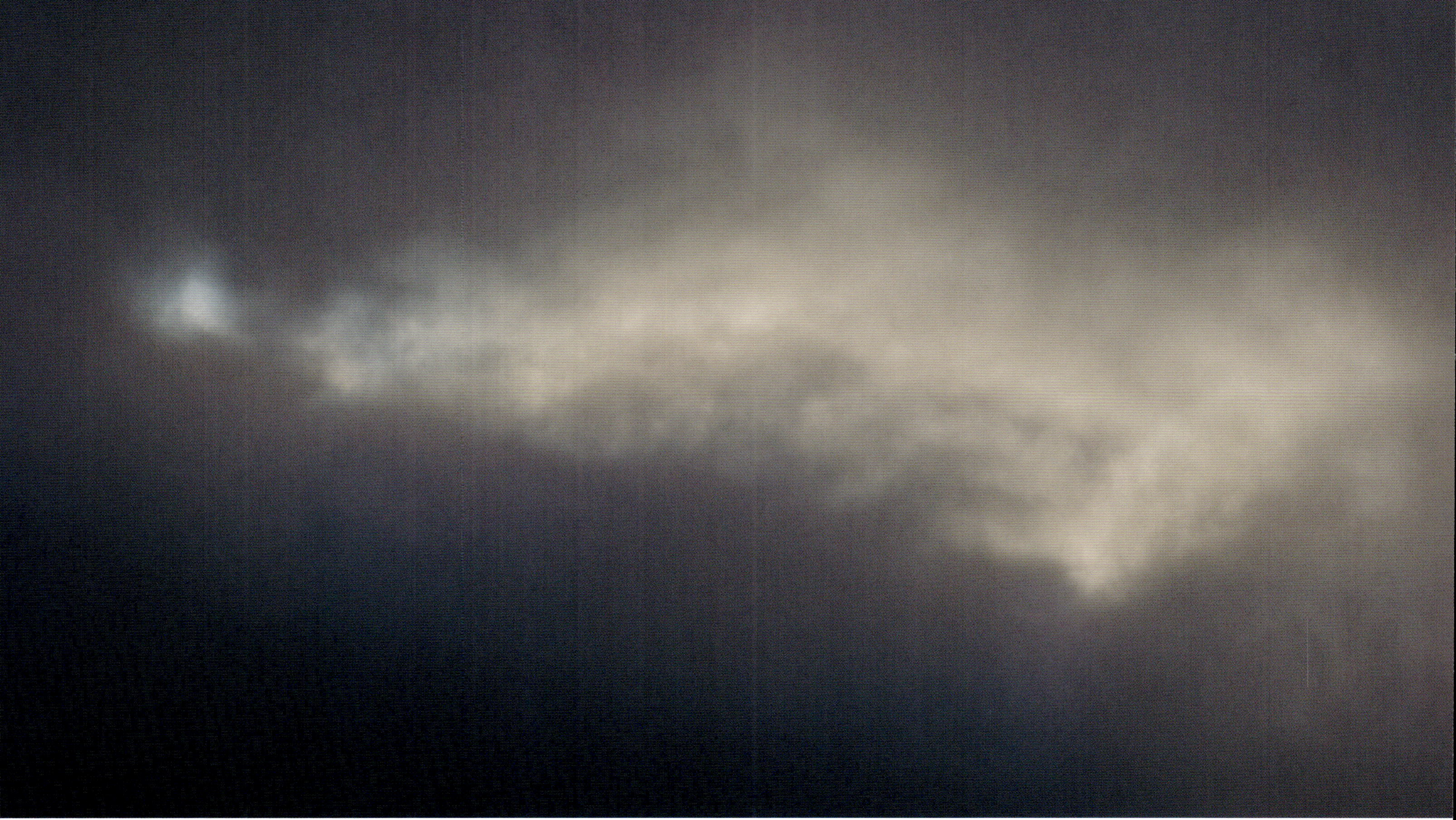

nor’easter brewing

northeast storm clouds, chatham

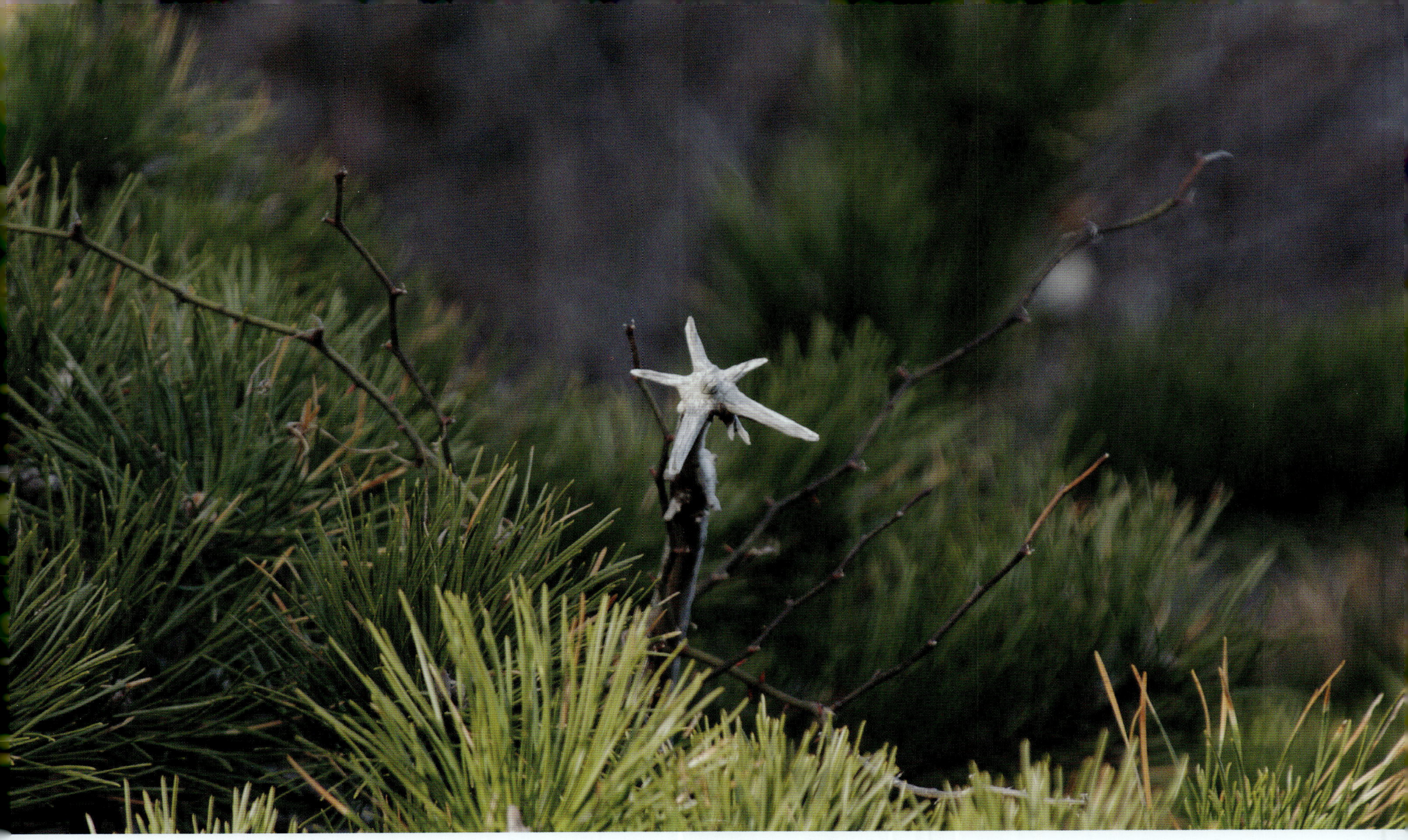

driftwood “star” on briar,
truro

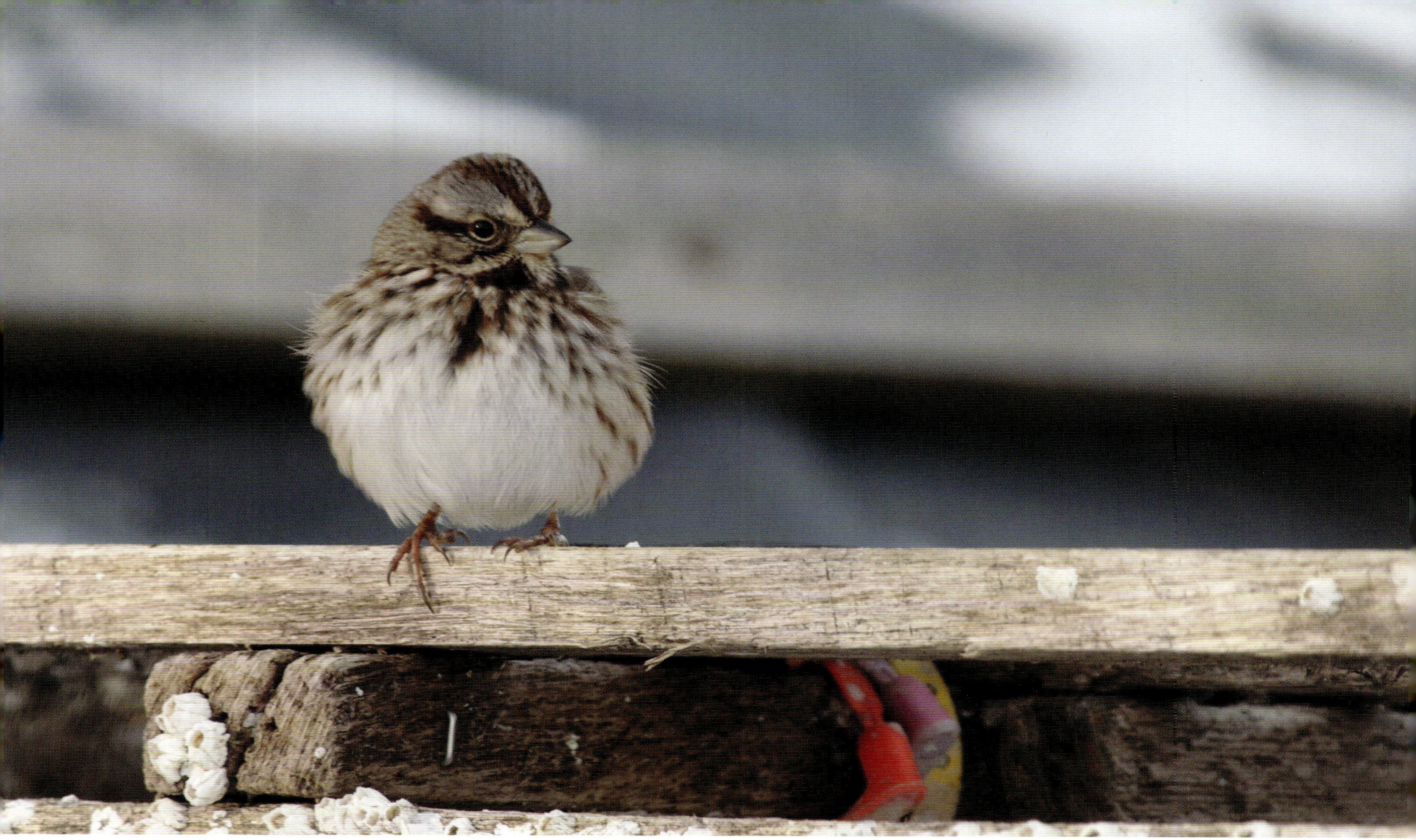

all fluffed up and no place to go

song sparrow,
chatham

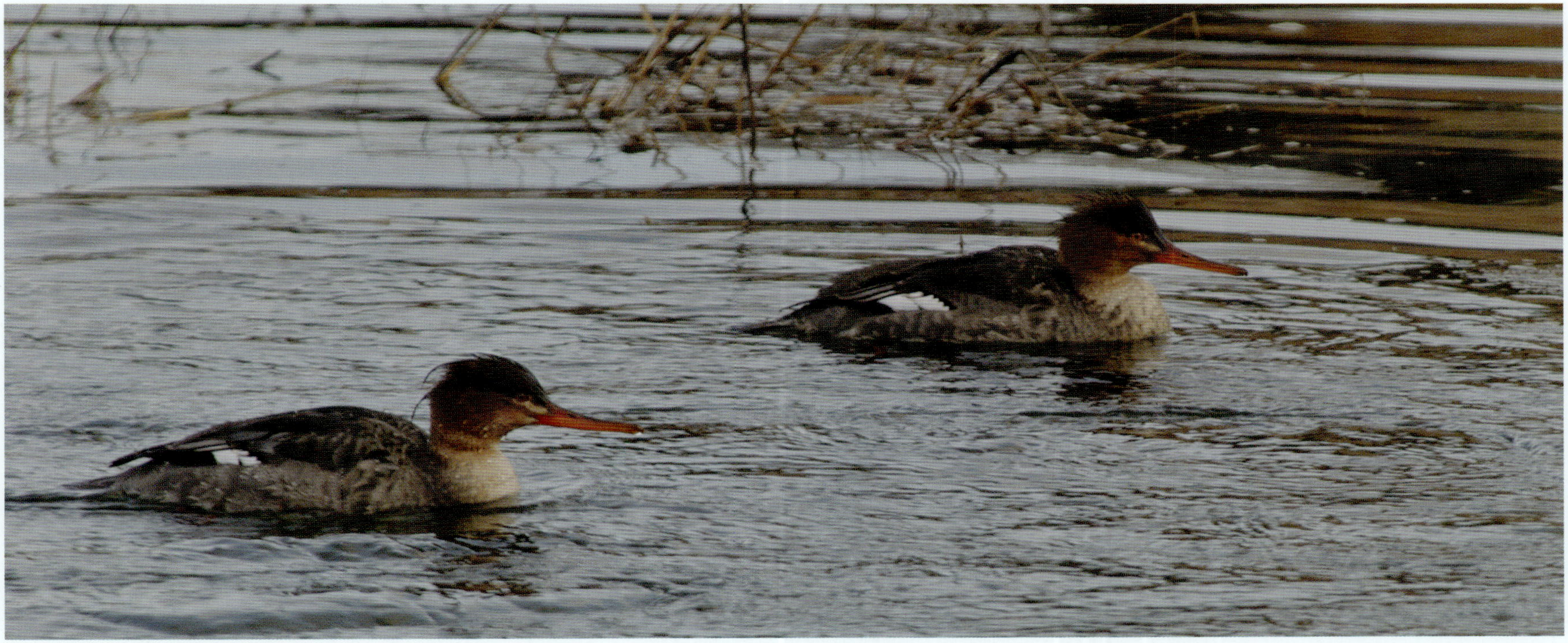

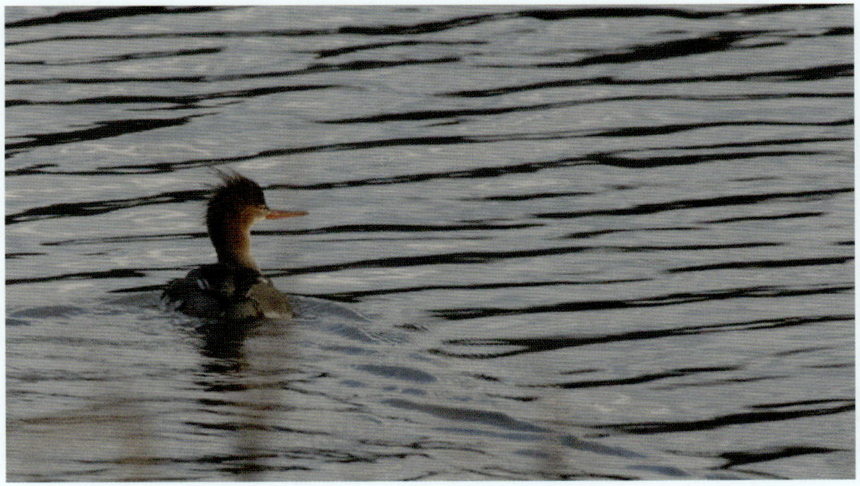

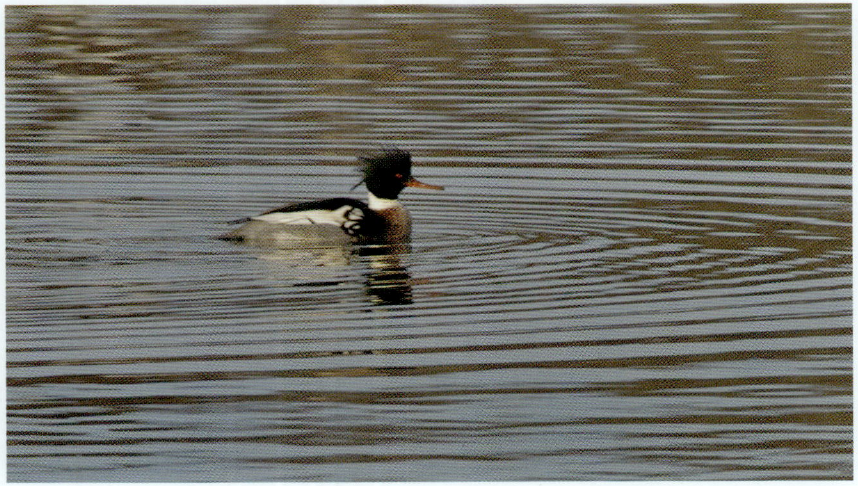

meandering mergansers

red-breasted mergansers,
little pleasant bay, orleans

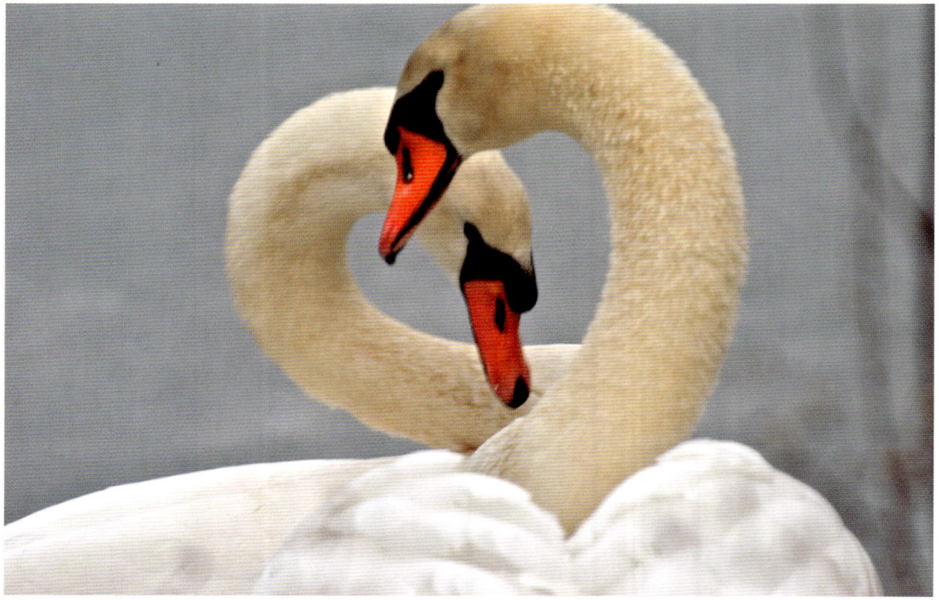

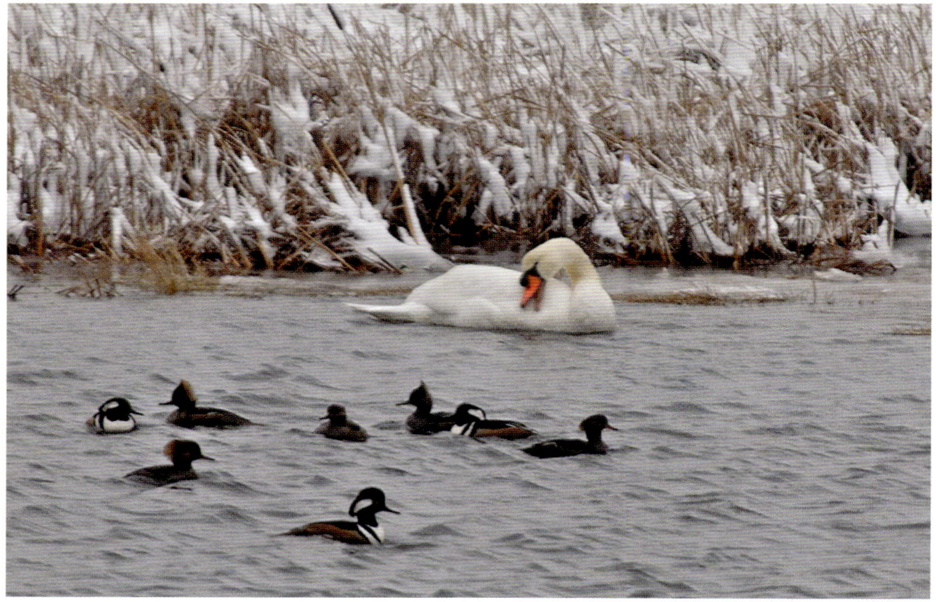

mute swans and hooded mergansers,
frost fish creek, chatham

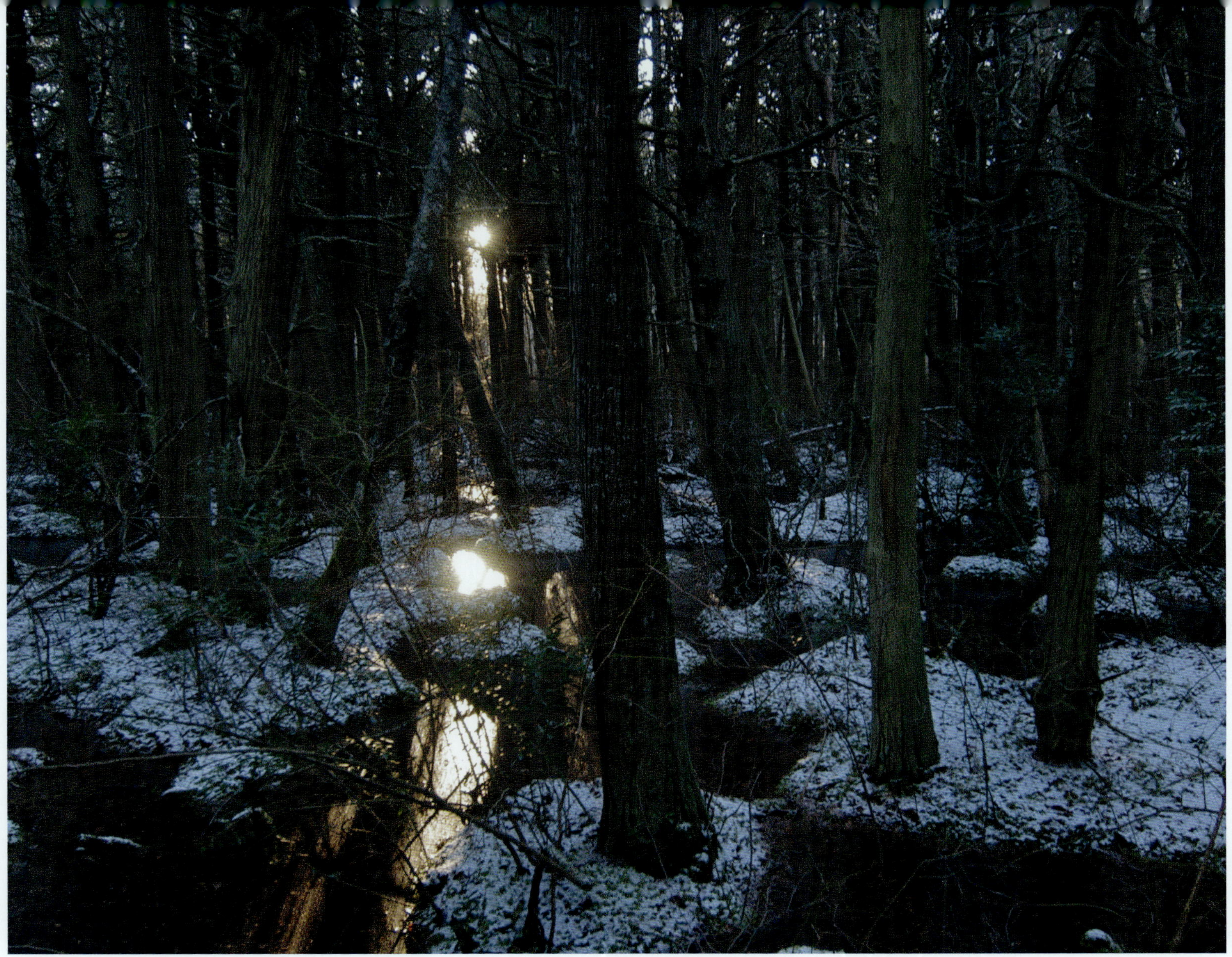

winter solstice

cedar swamp,
wellfleet

perched

white-breasted nuthatch,
chatham

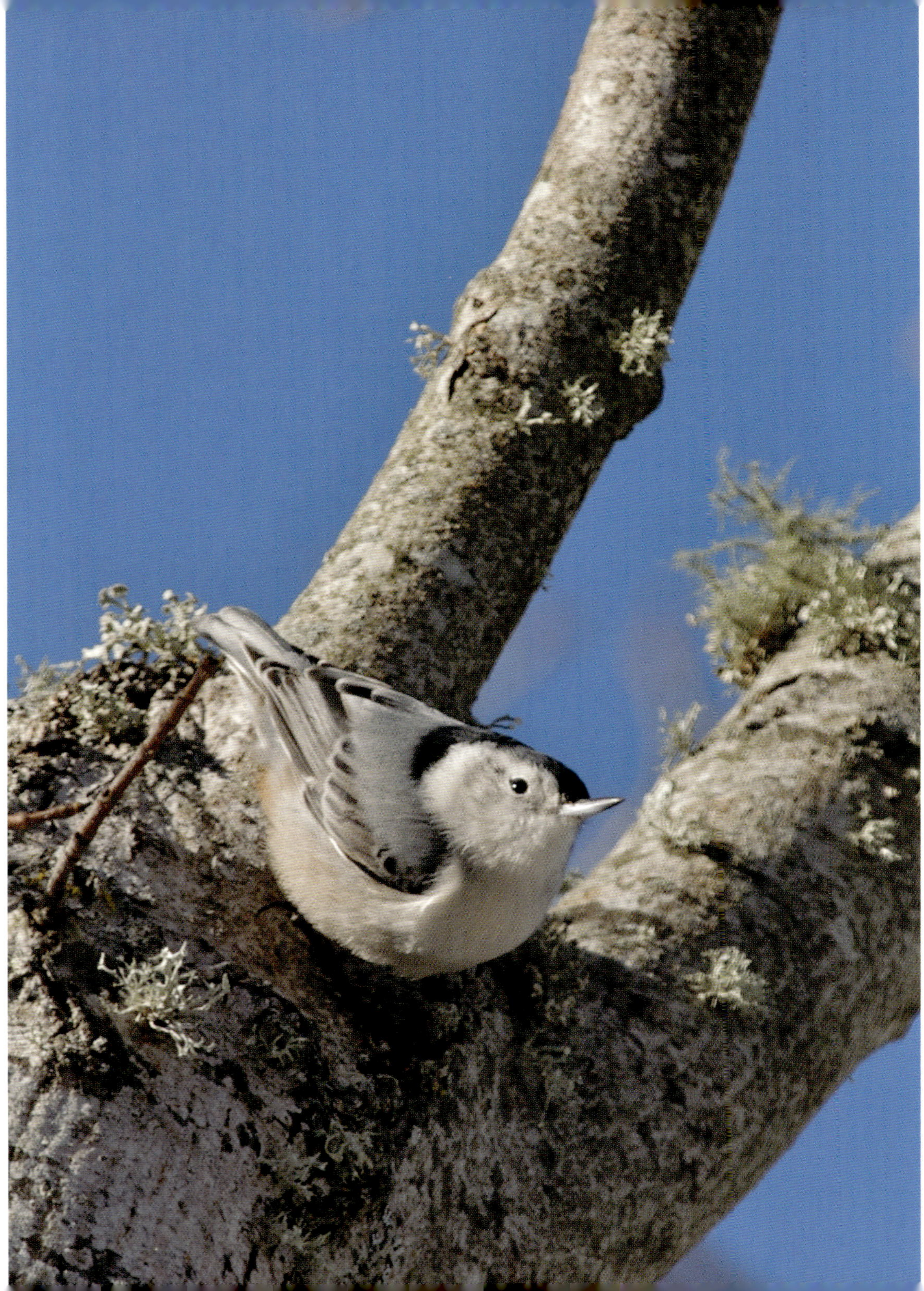

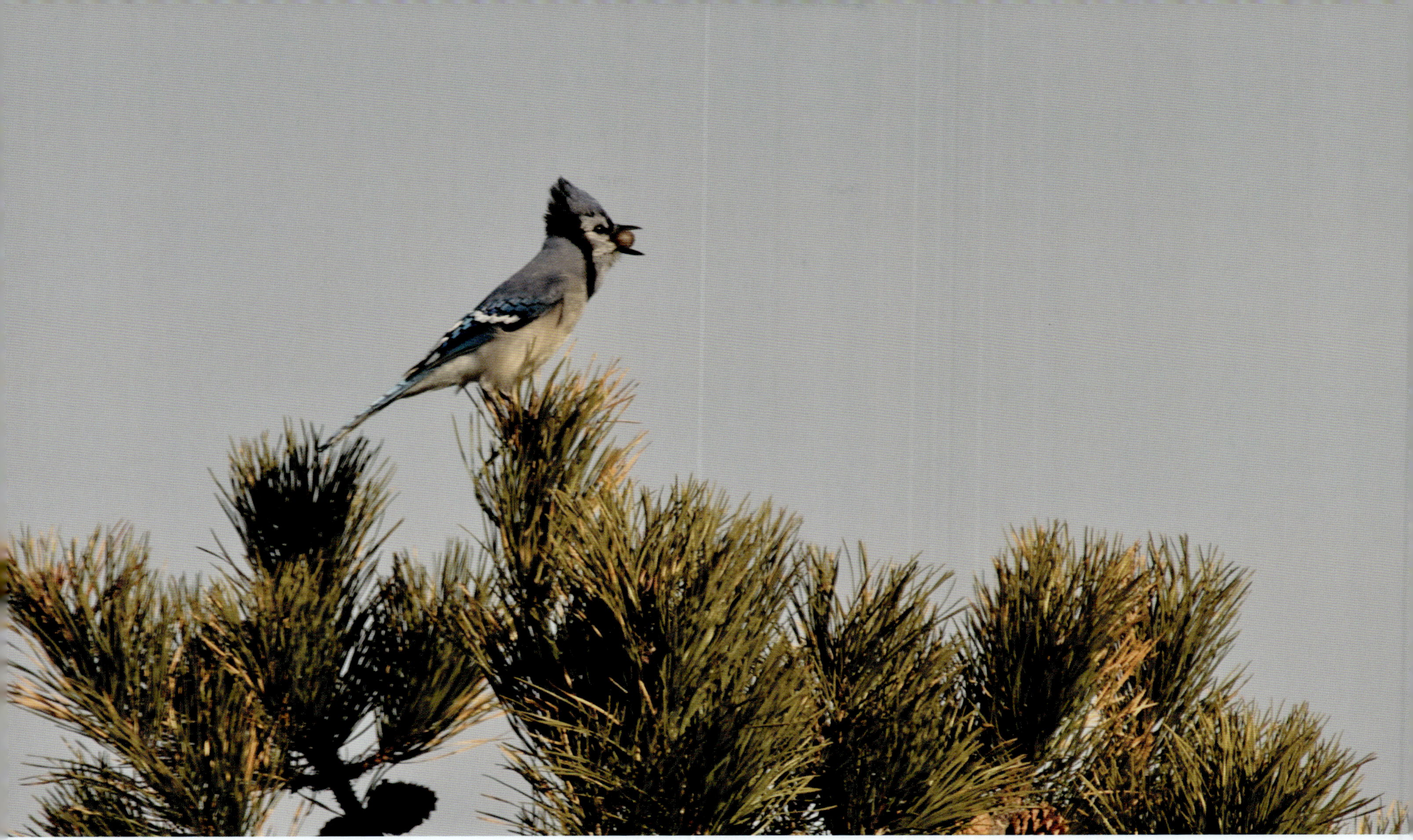

bluejay with berry,
truro

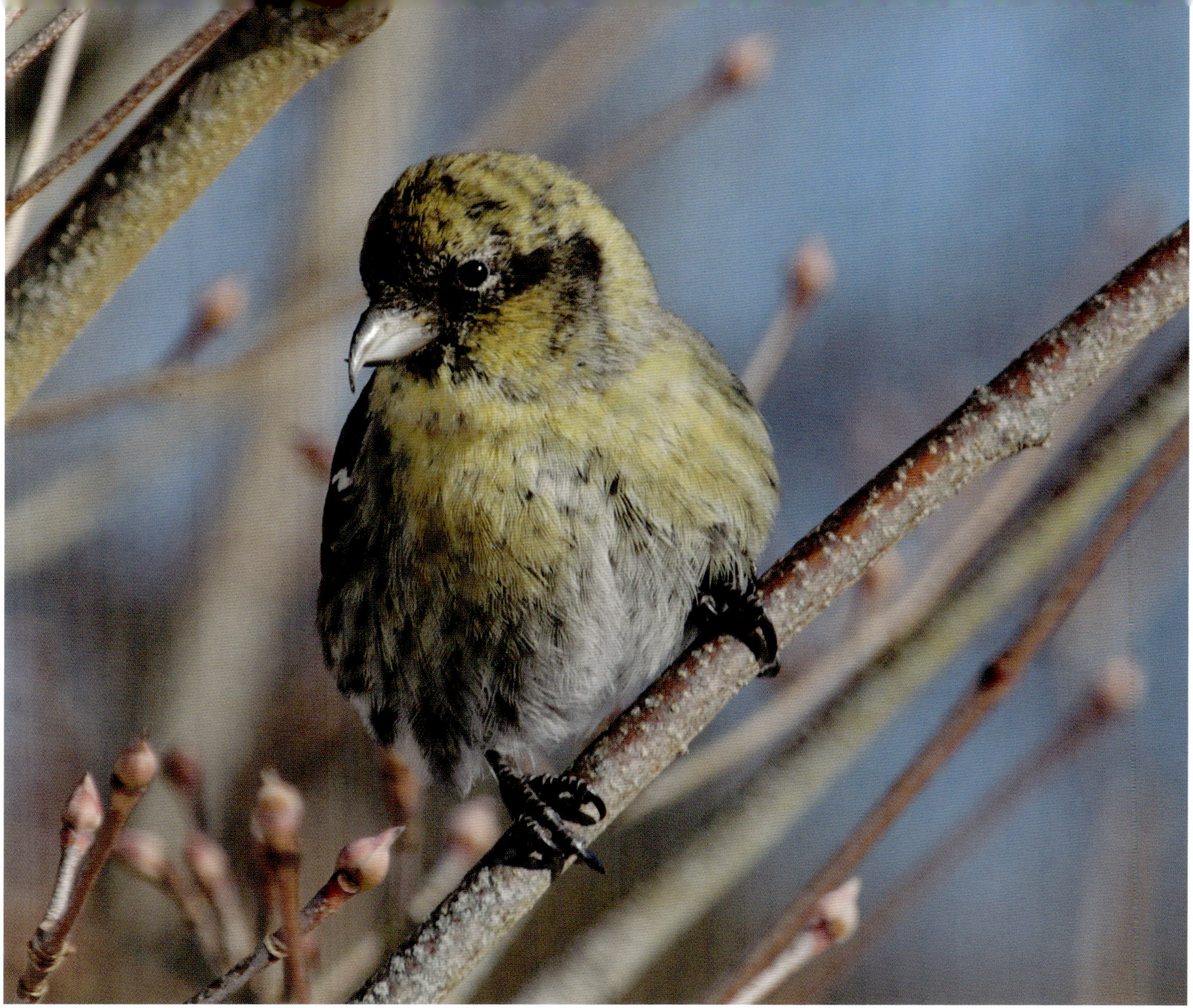

guest appearance

white winged crossbill,
chatham

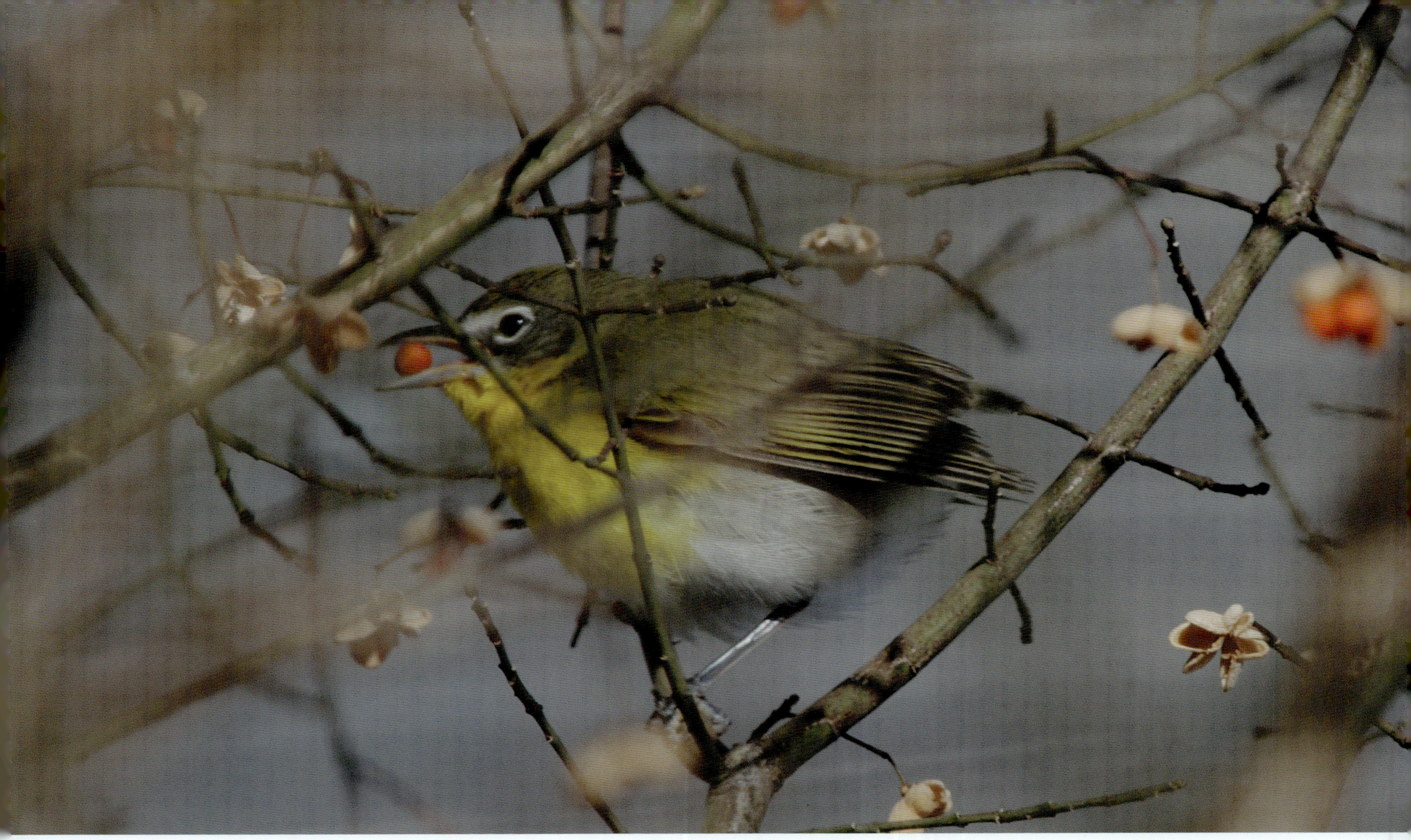

yellow breasted chat,
chatham

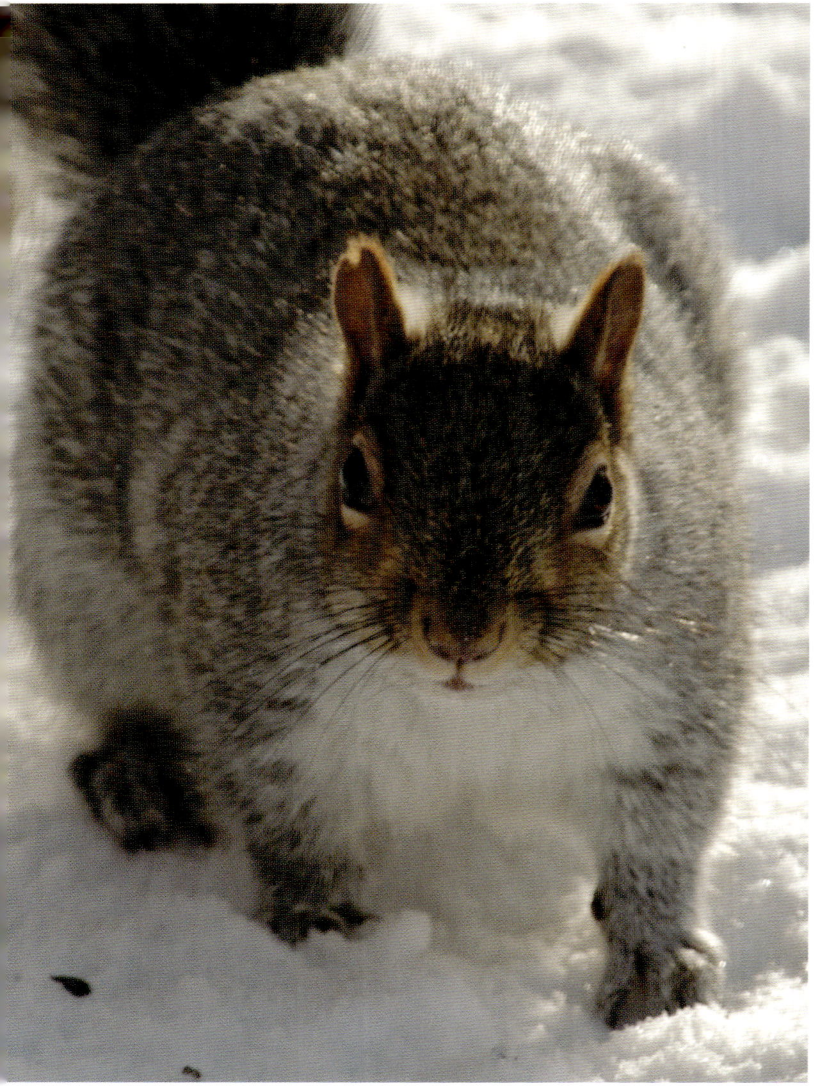

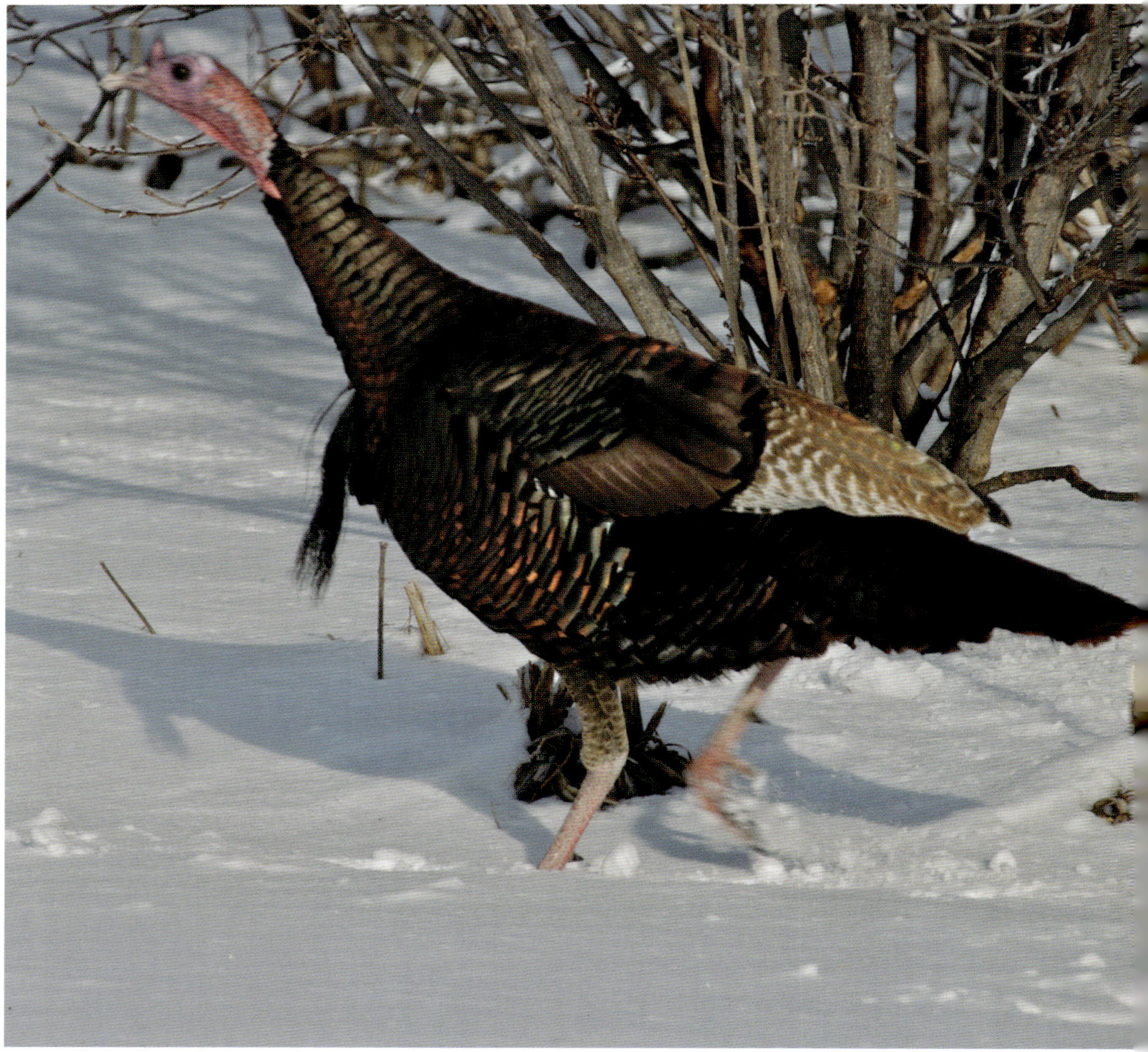

running wild

squirrel and tom turkey,
chatham

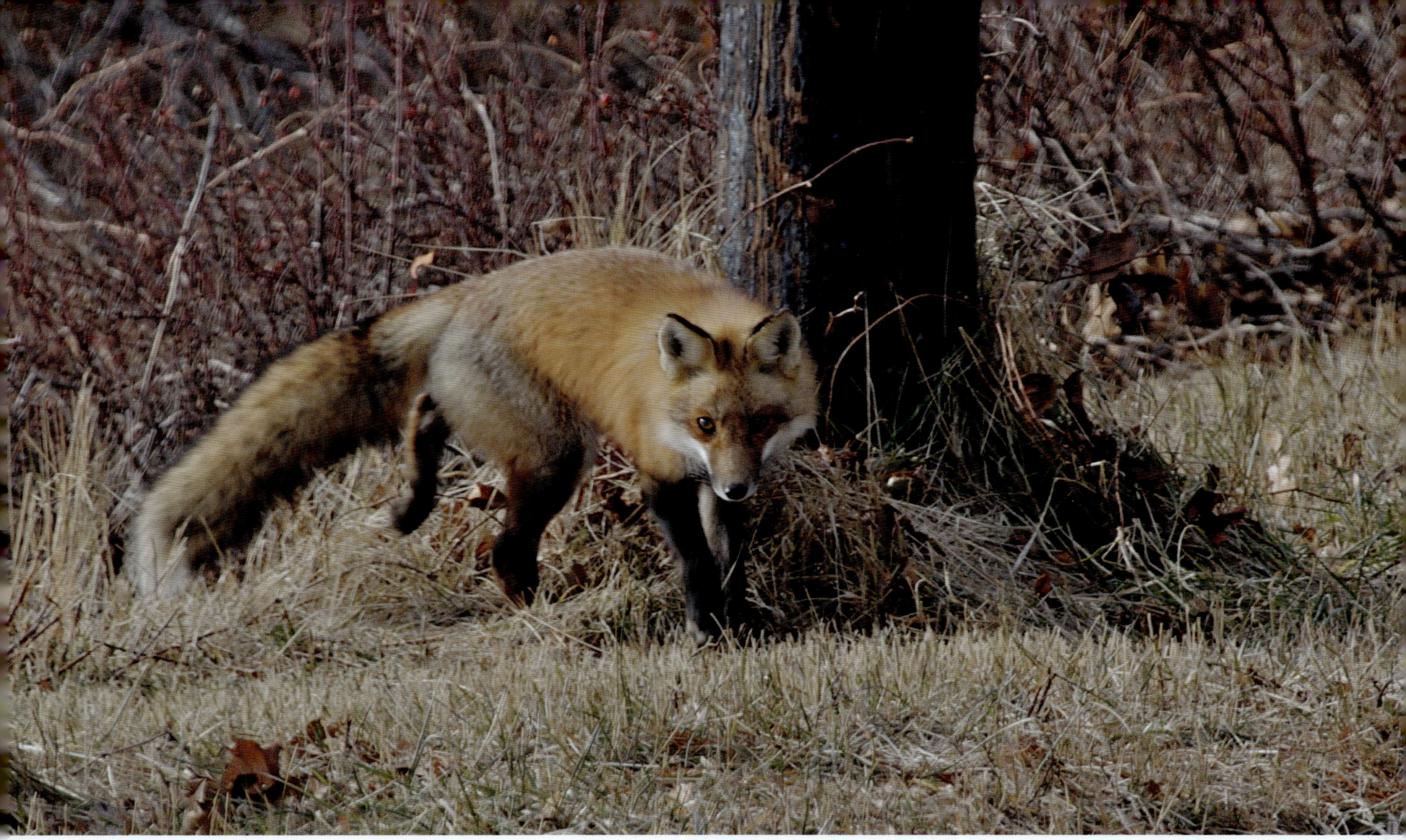

fox trot

red fox,
wellfleet

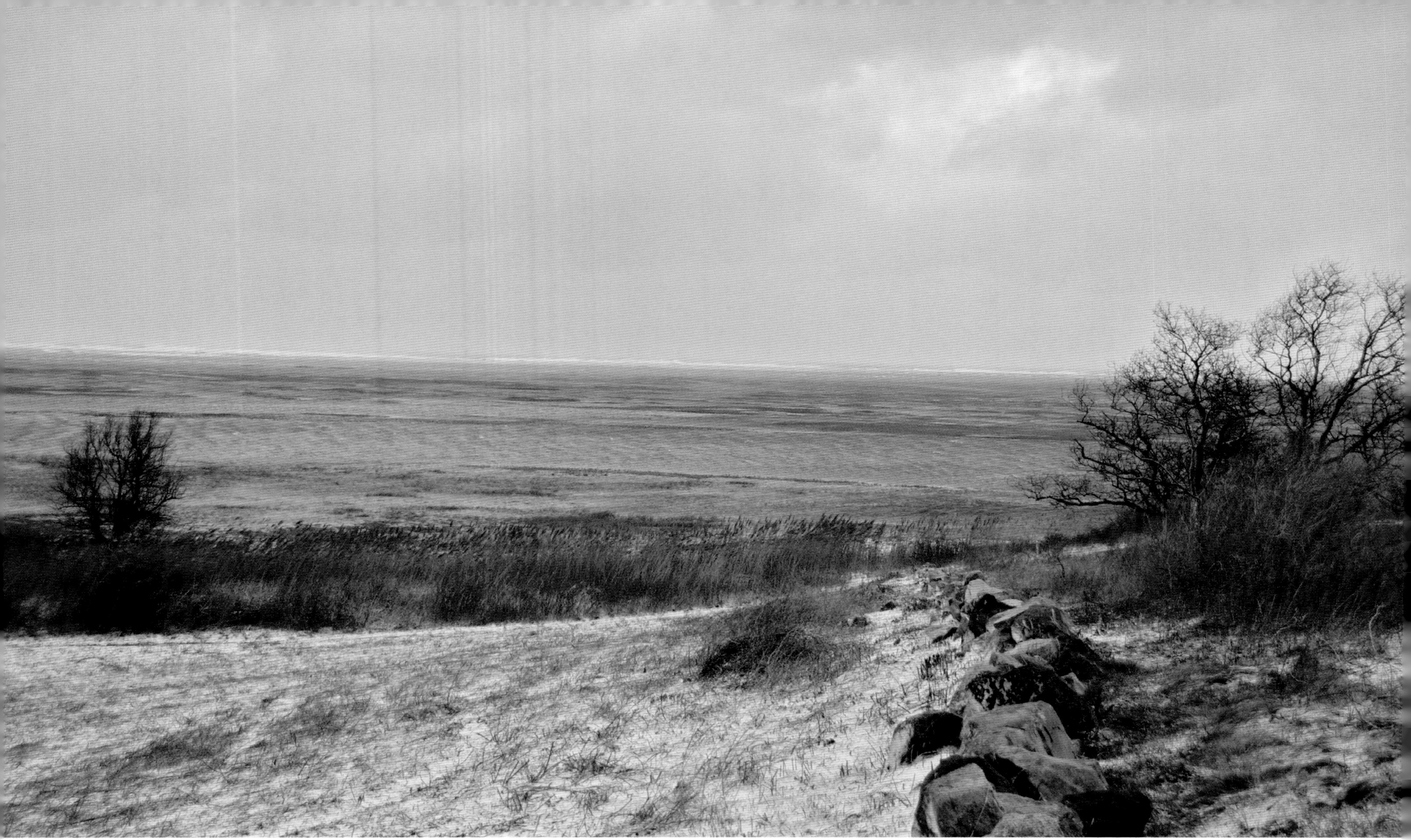

seaside dusting

fort hill,
eastham

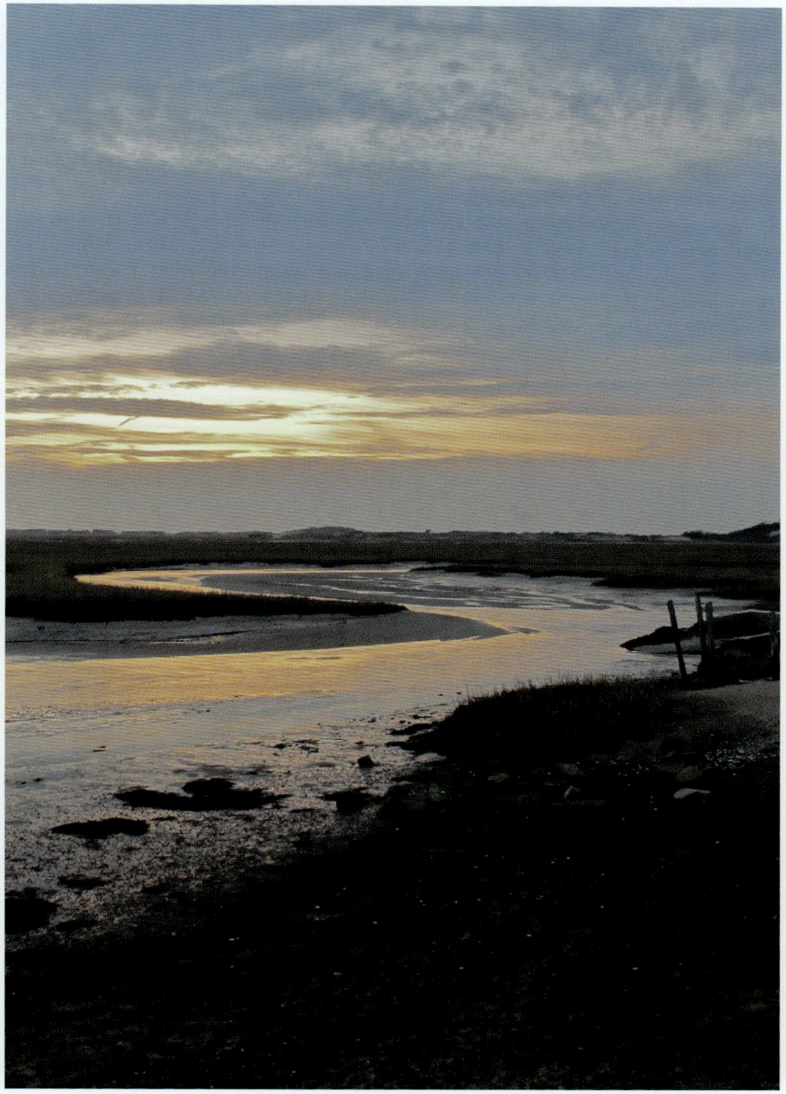

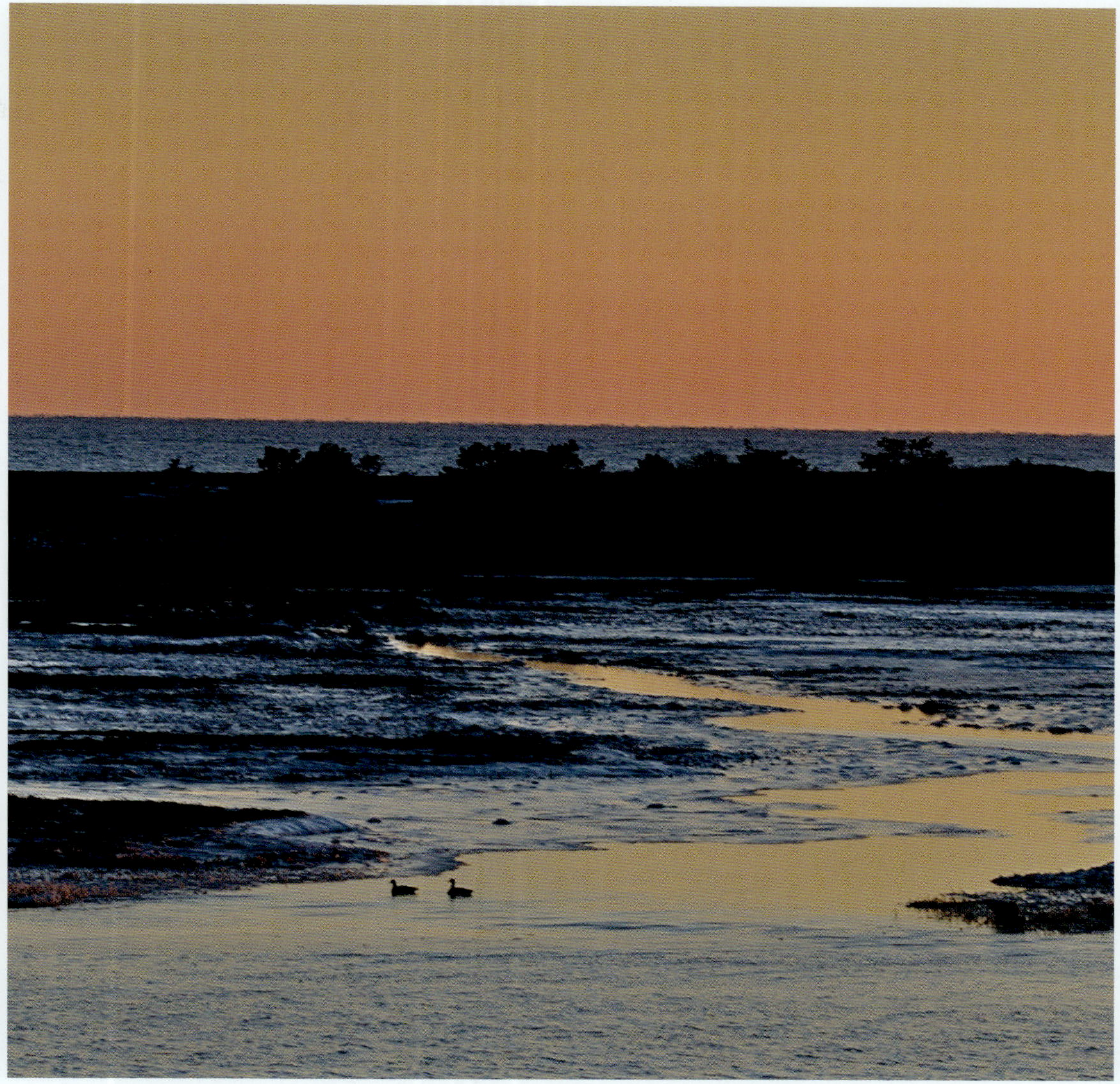

sun setting, provincetown and oyster river, chatham

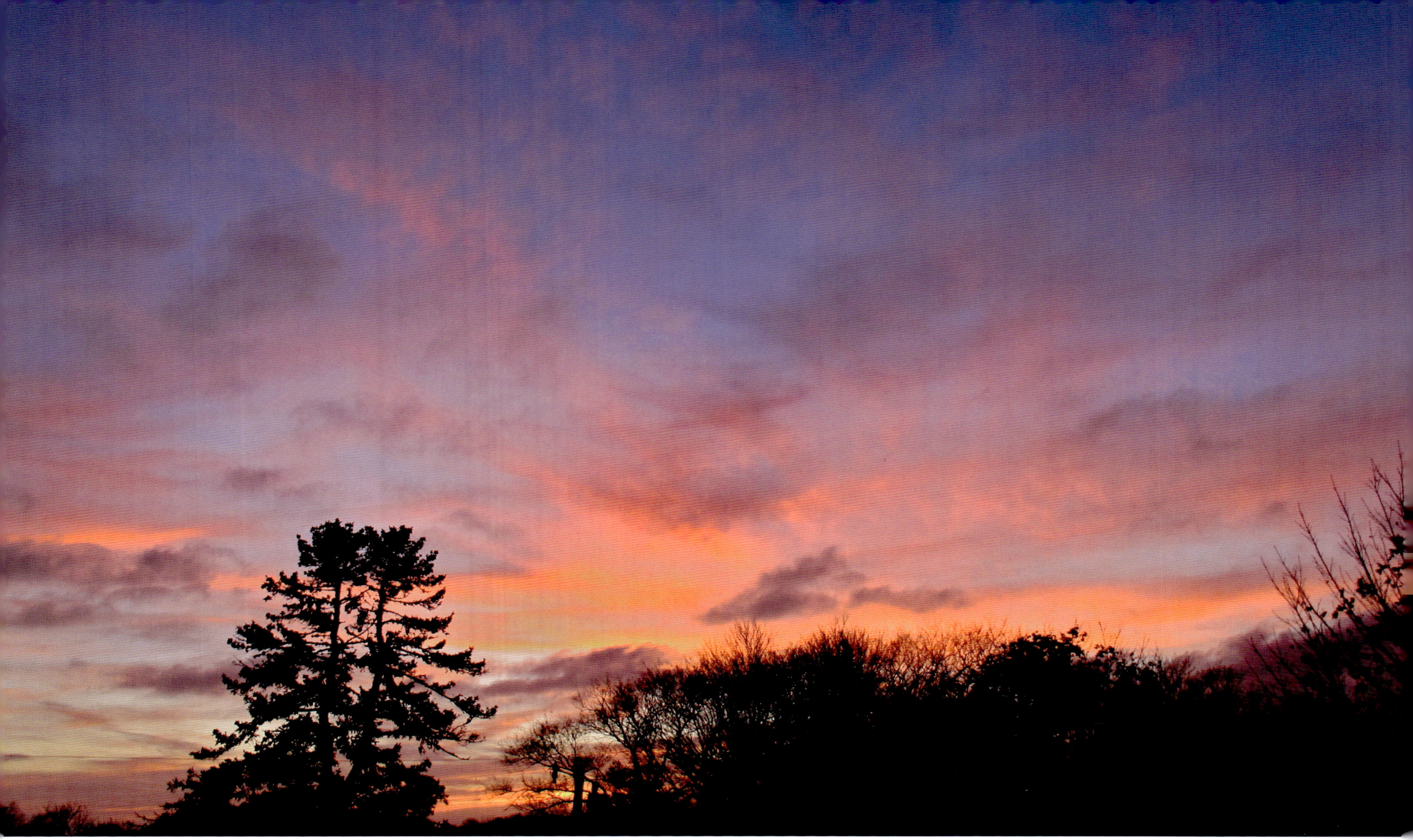

rooftop view

sunset, chatham

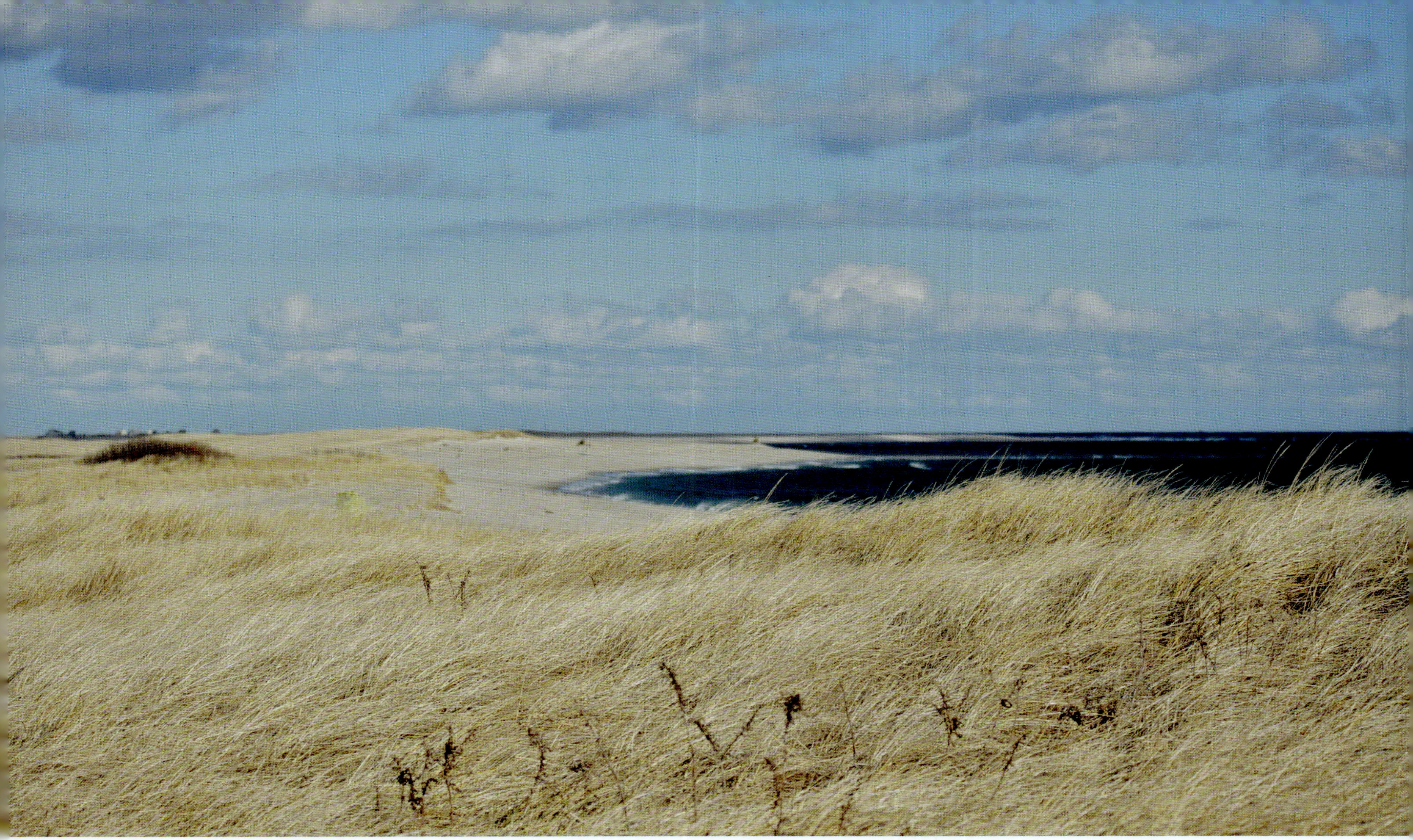

winter palette

south beach,
chatham

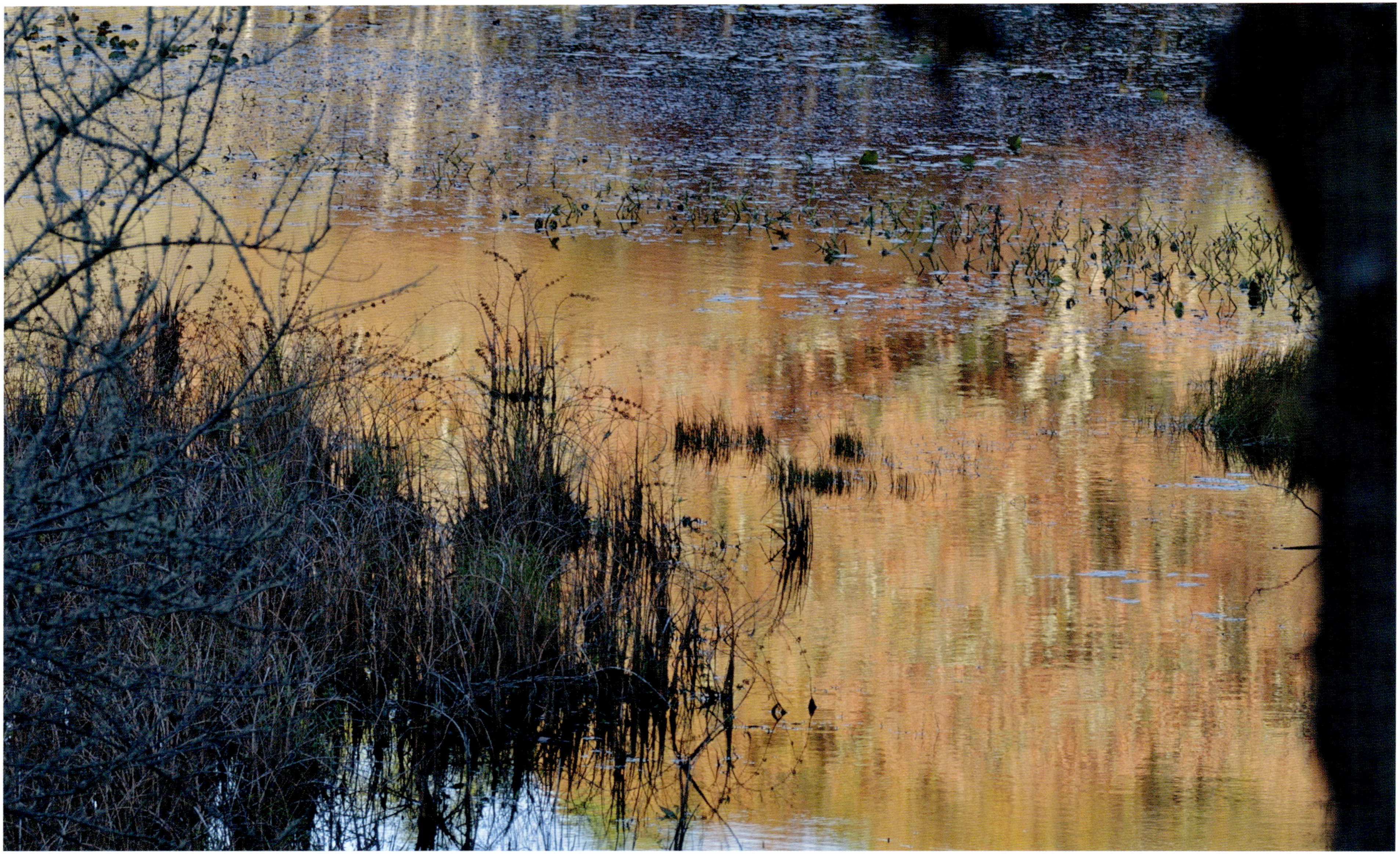

nature's renoir

nickerson state park,
brewster

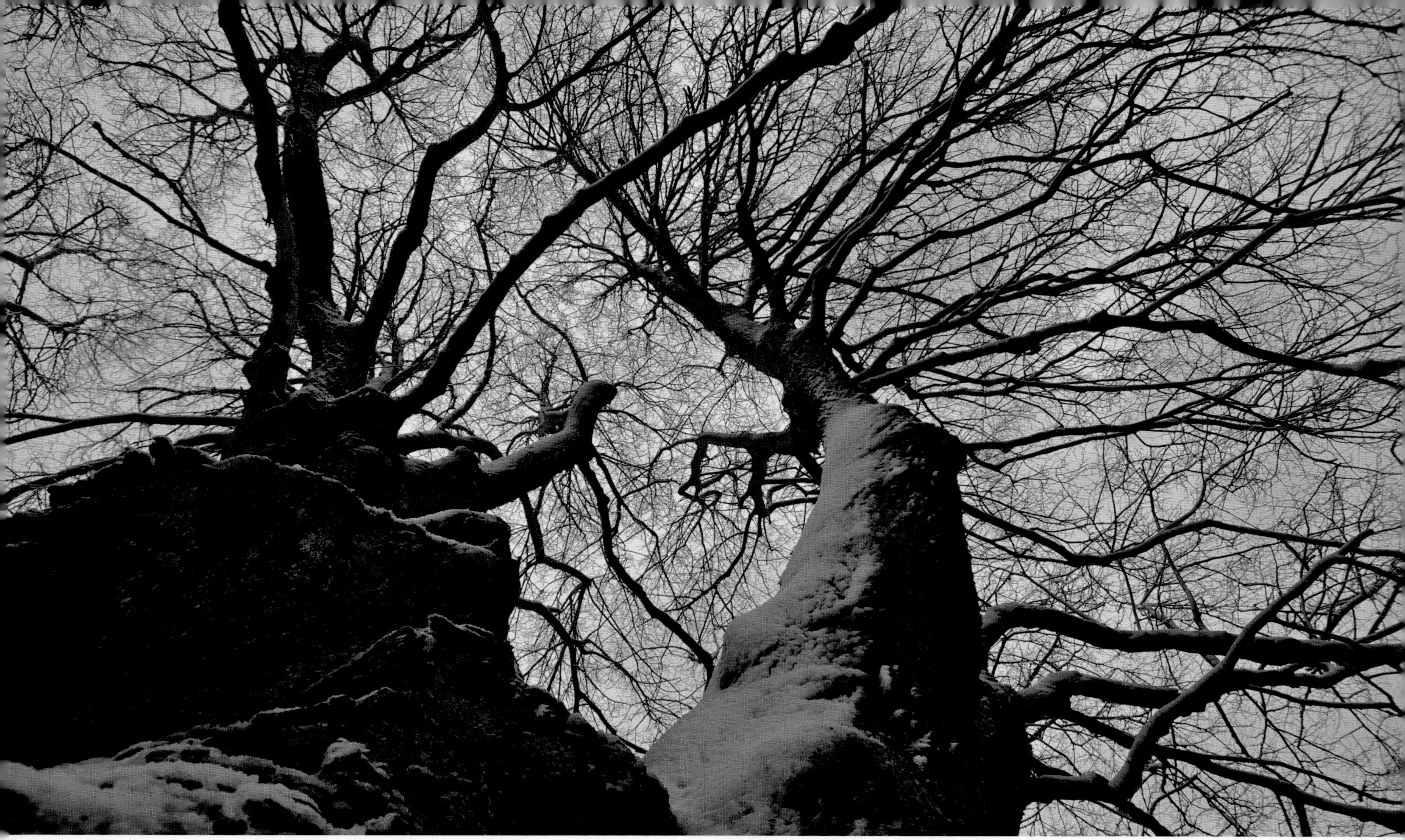

solstice sentinel

old bass wood,
chatham

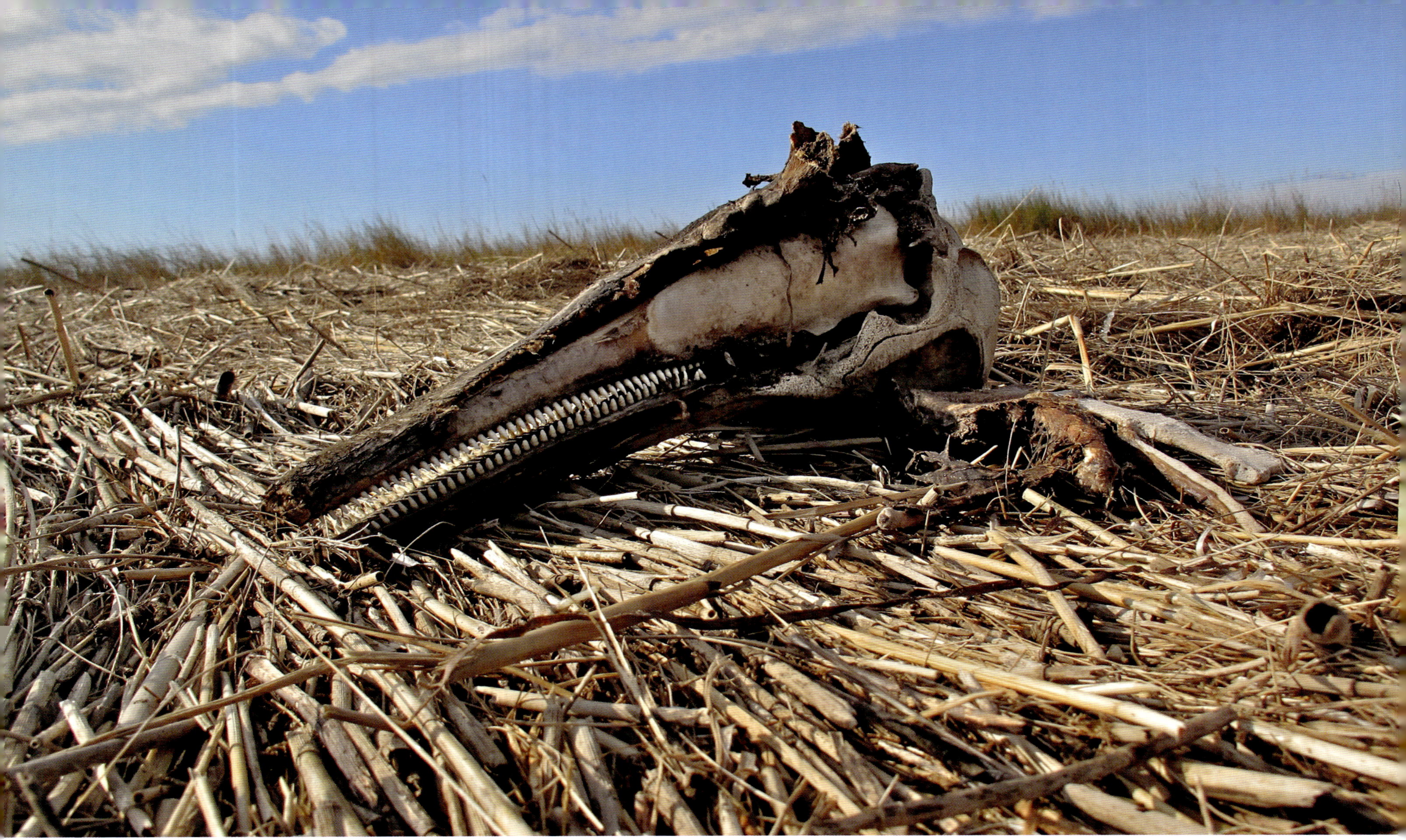

washed up

dolphin skull,
wellfleet bay wildlife sanctuary

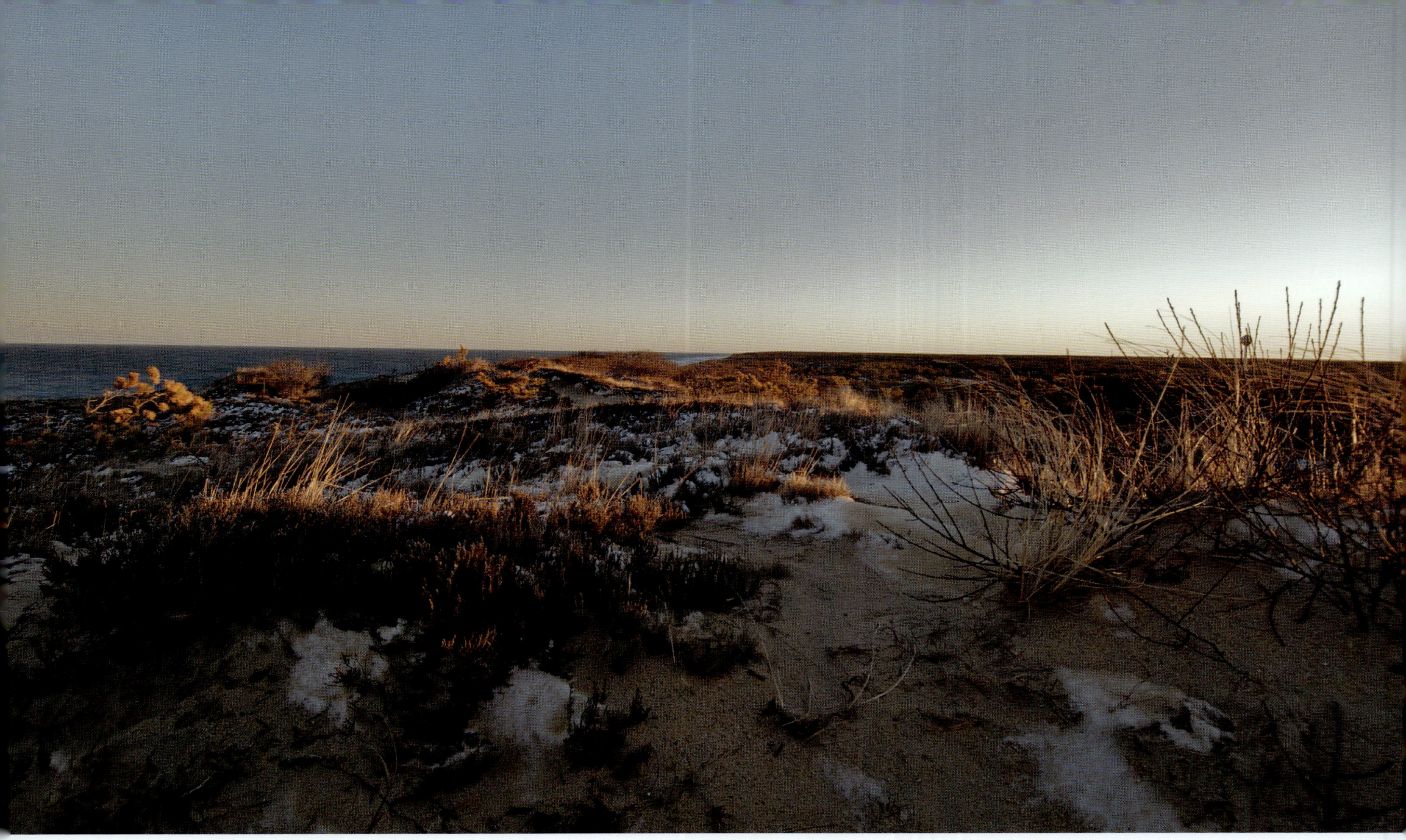

last light

cape cod national seashore
at marconi station, wellfleet

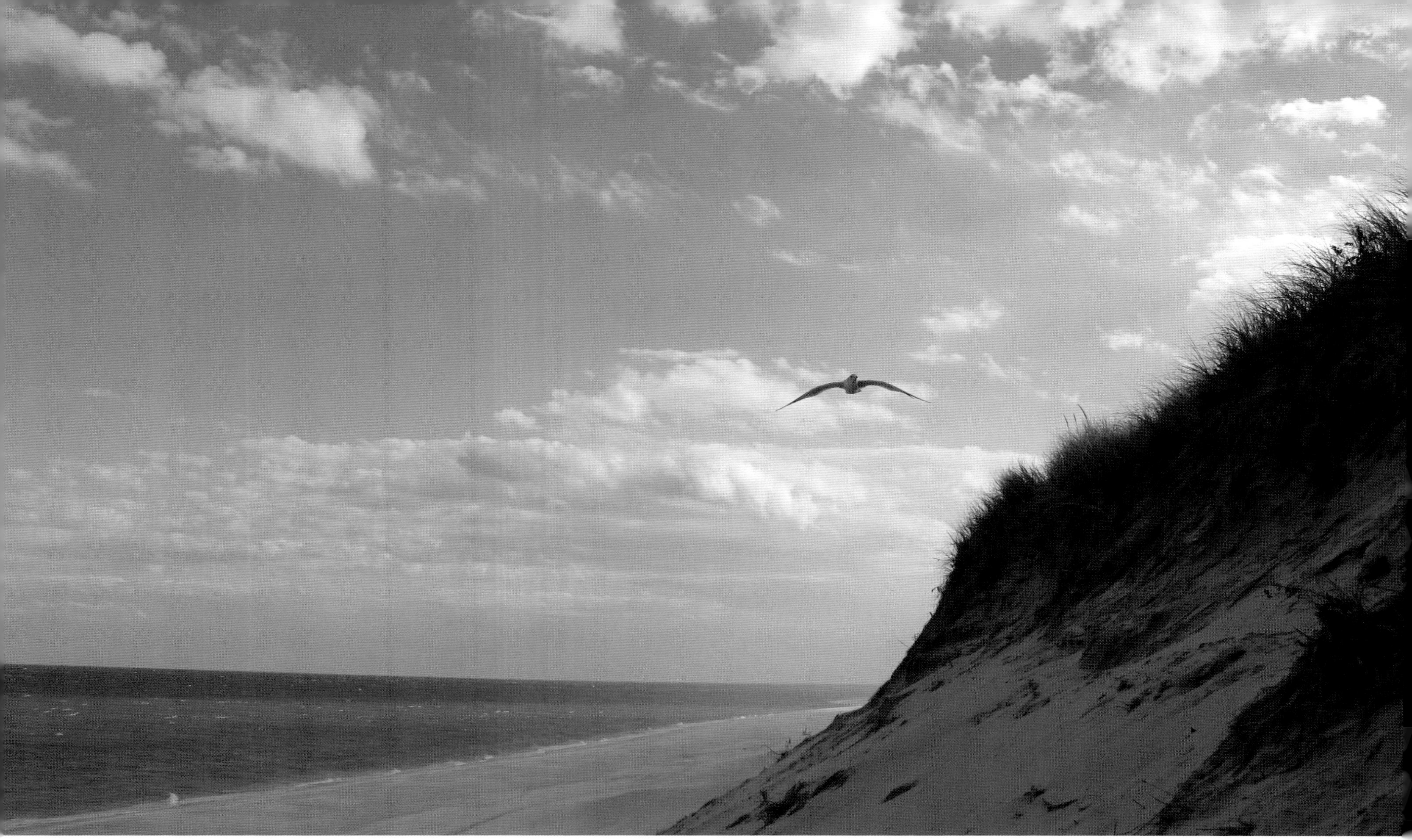

flight plan

cape cod national seashore,
truro

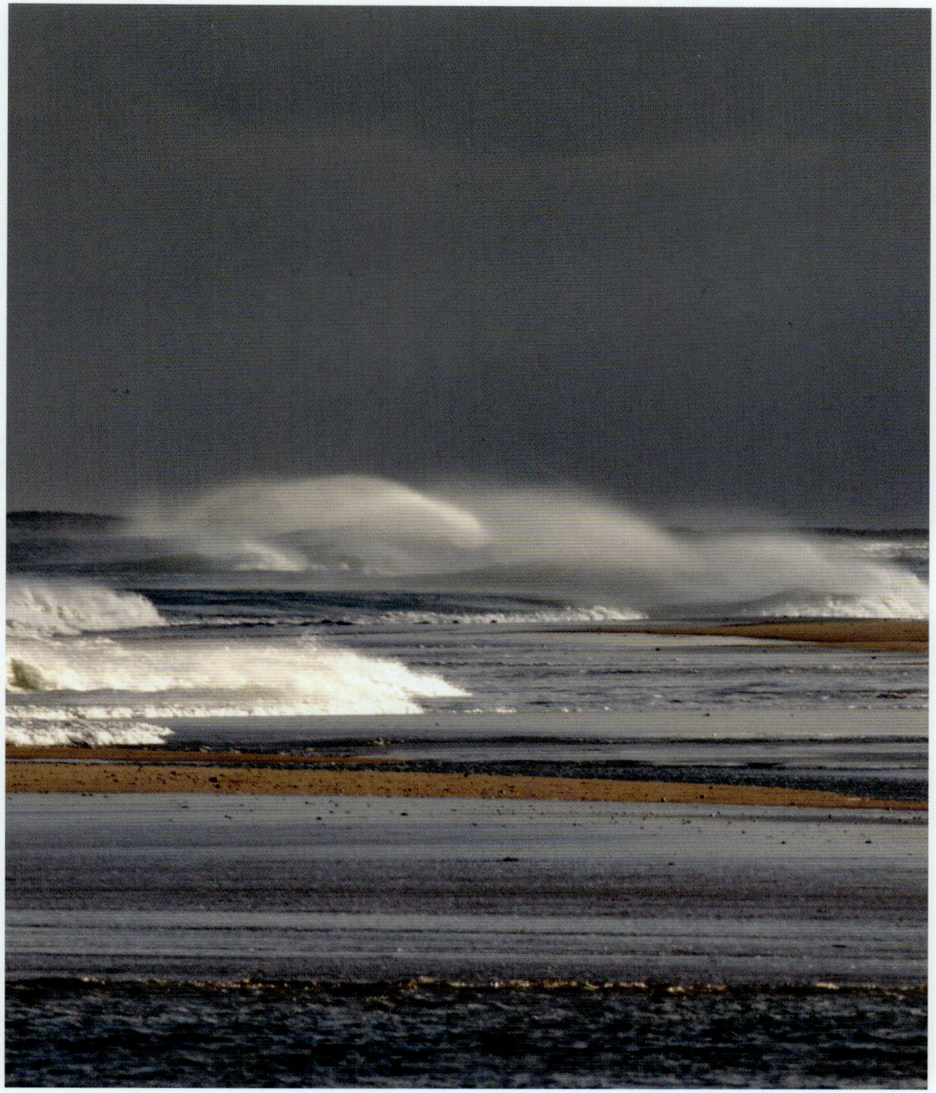

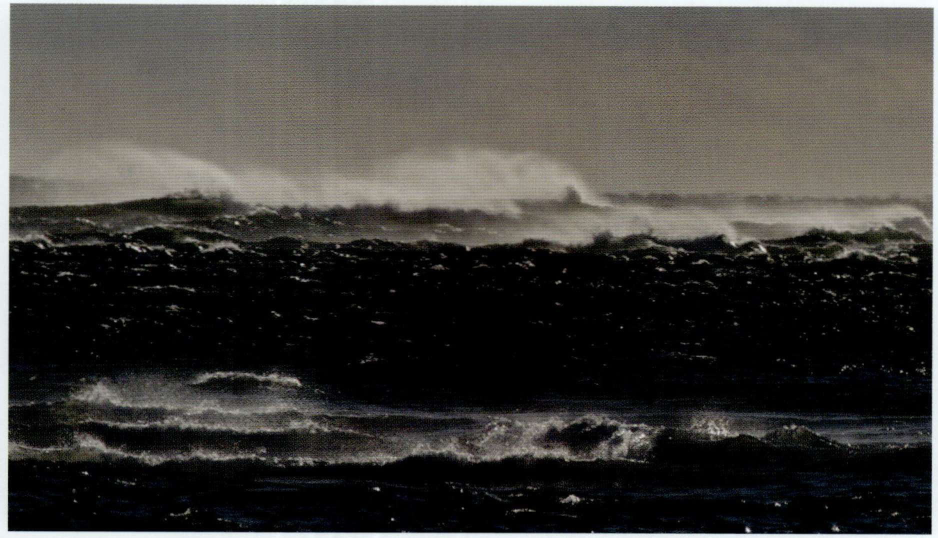

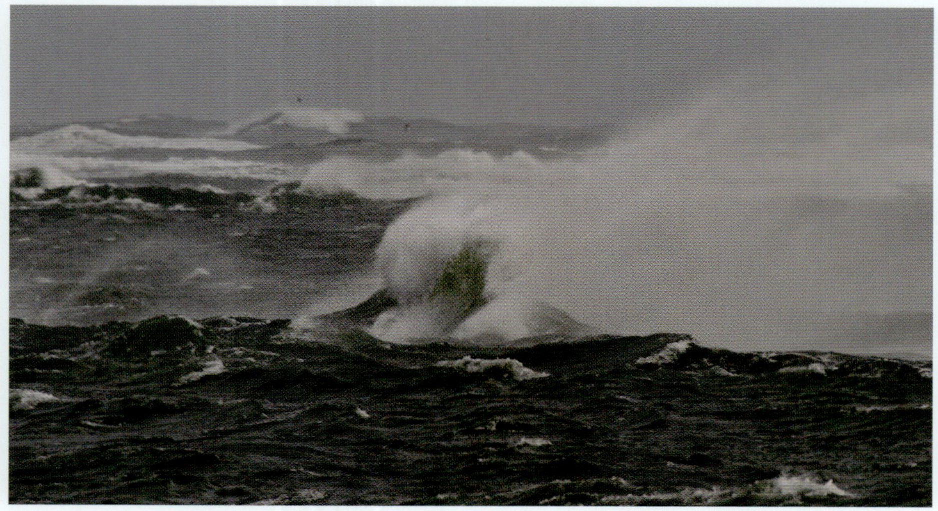

windy winter wrath

left: nauset beach, orleans
right: chatham bar

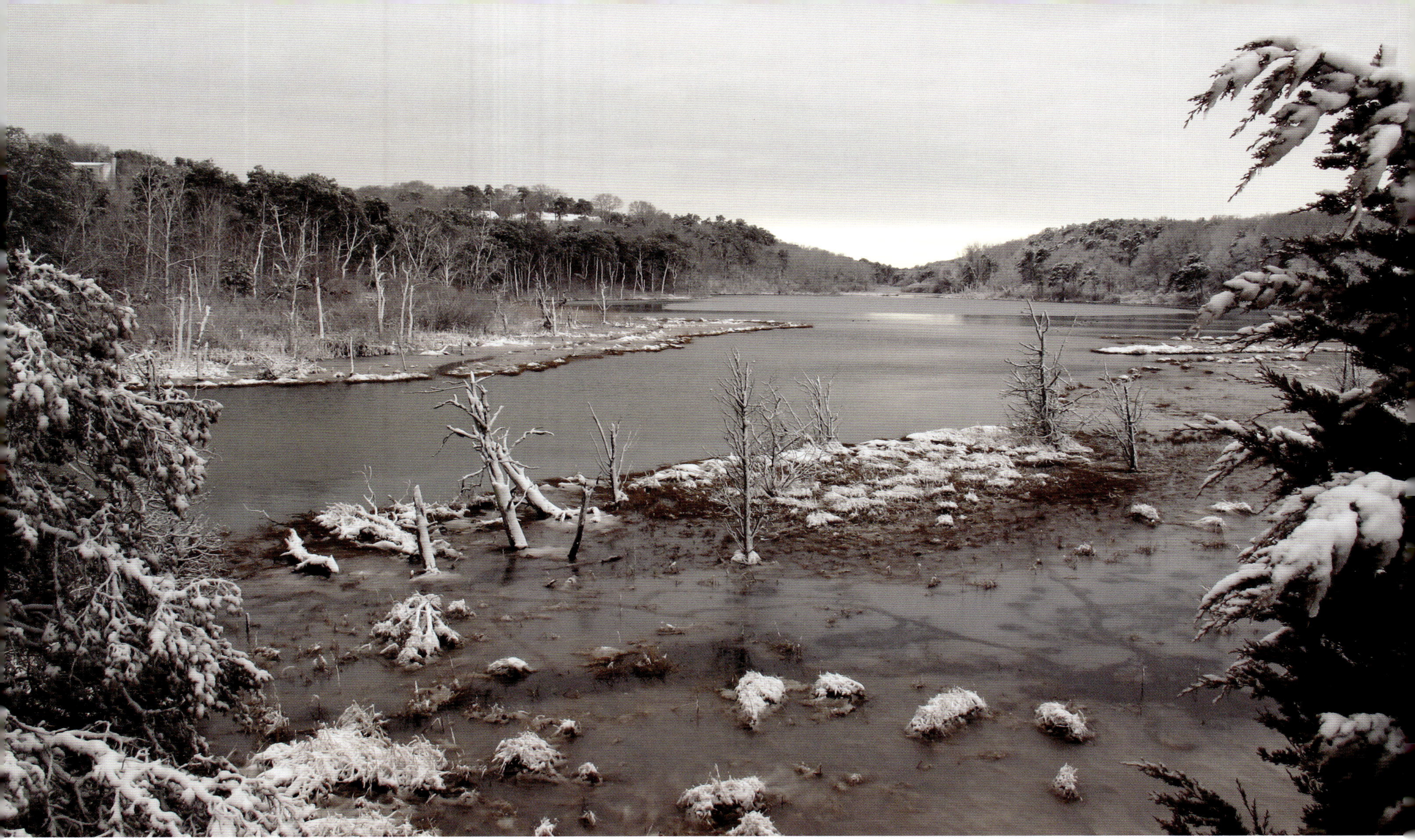

frozen divide

monomoyick river,
chatham/harwich

- atlantic ocean, off outer cape cod
- off chatham
- powder hole, monomoy national wildlife refuge
- morris island, monomoy national wildlife refuge
- south beach, chatham
- chatham

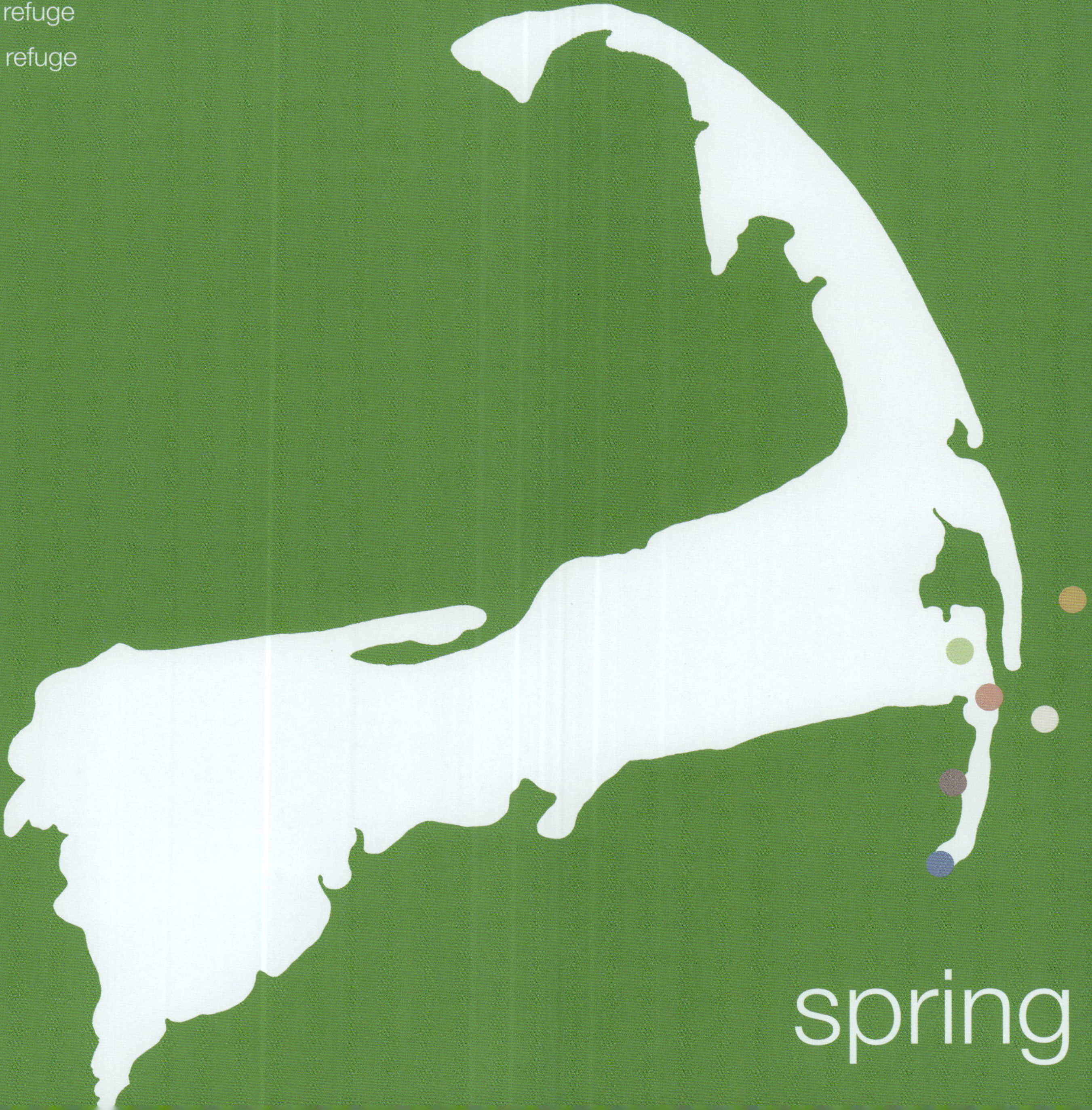

spring

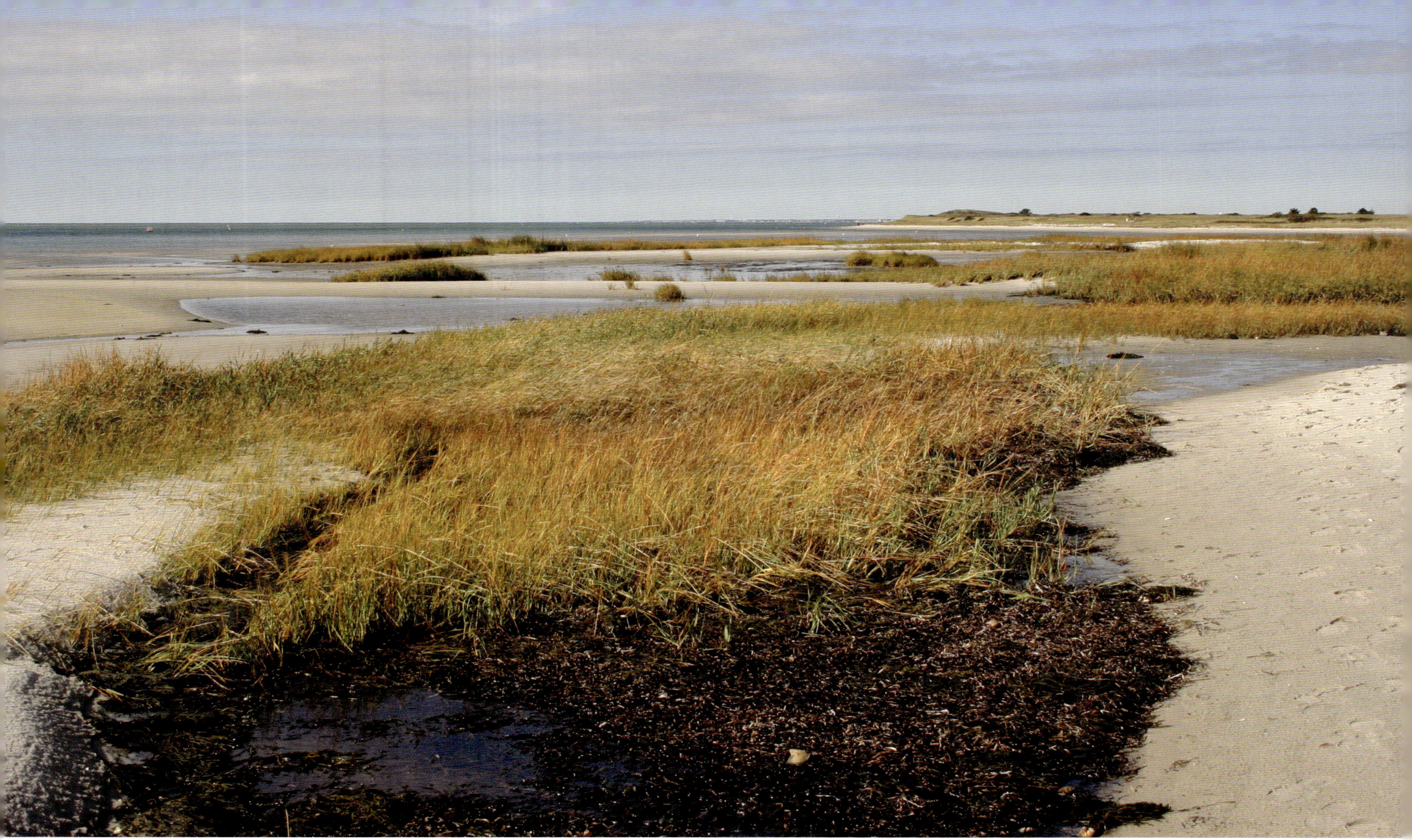

wild flatlands

morris island at low
tide, monomoy national wildlife refuge

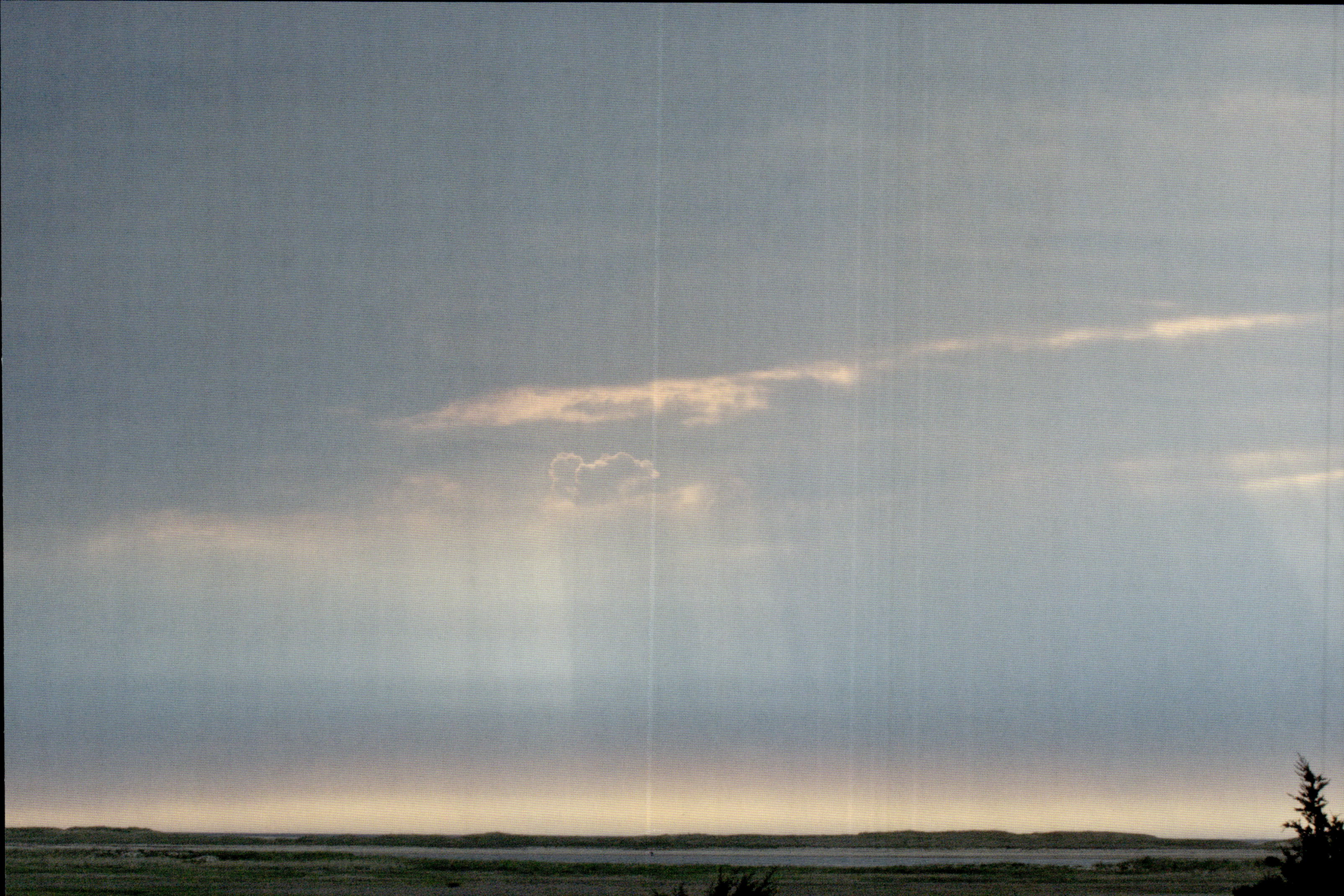

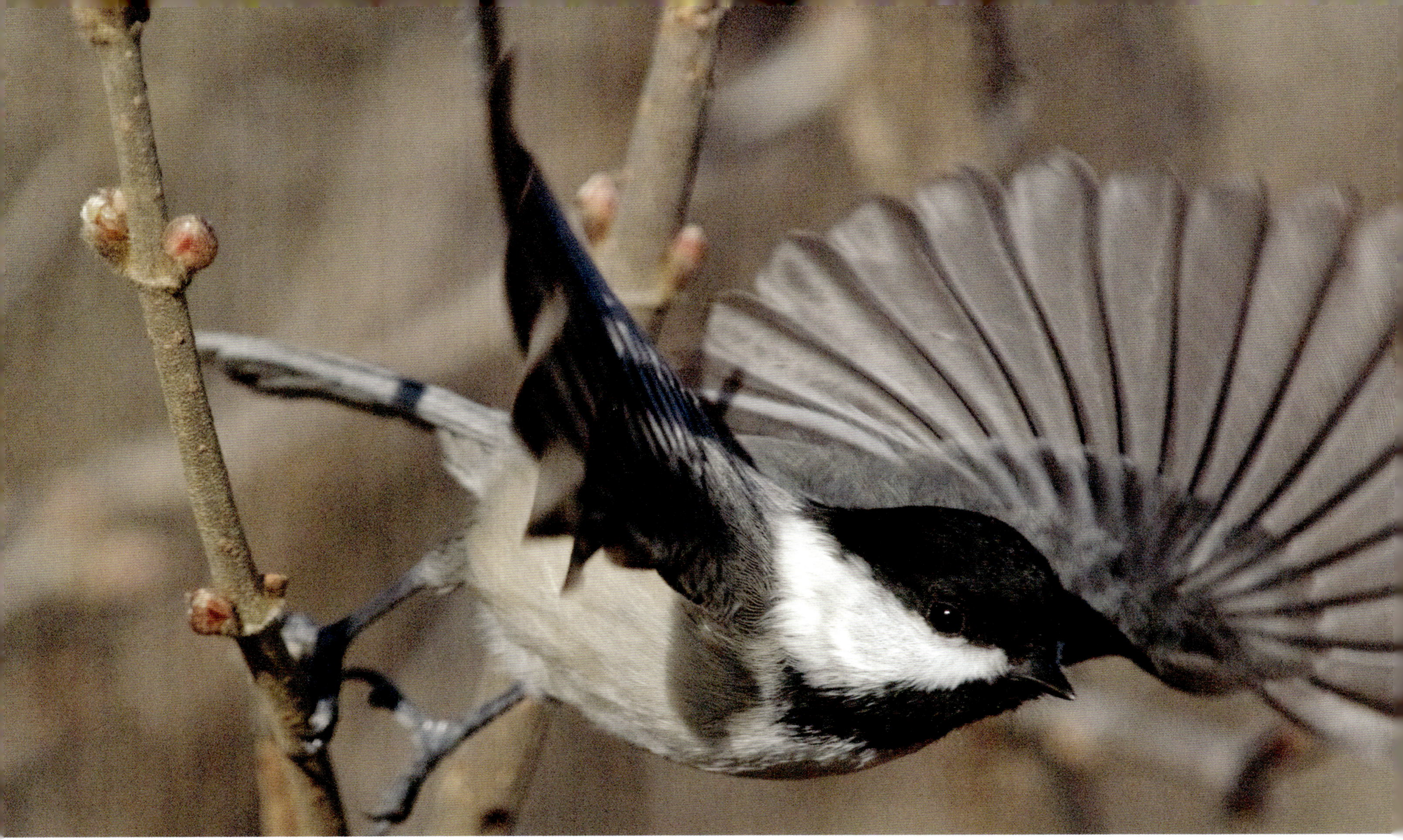

black capped chickadee,
chatham

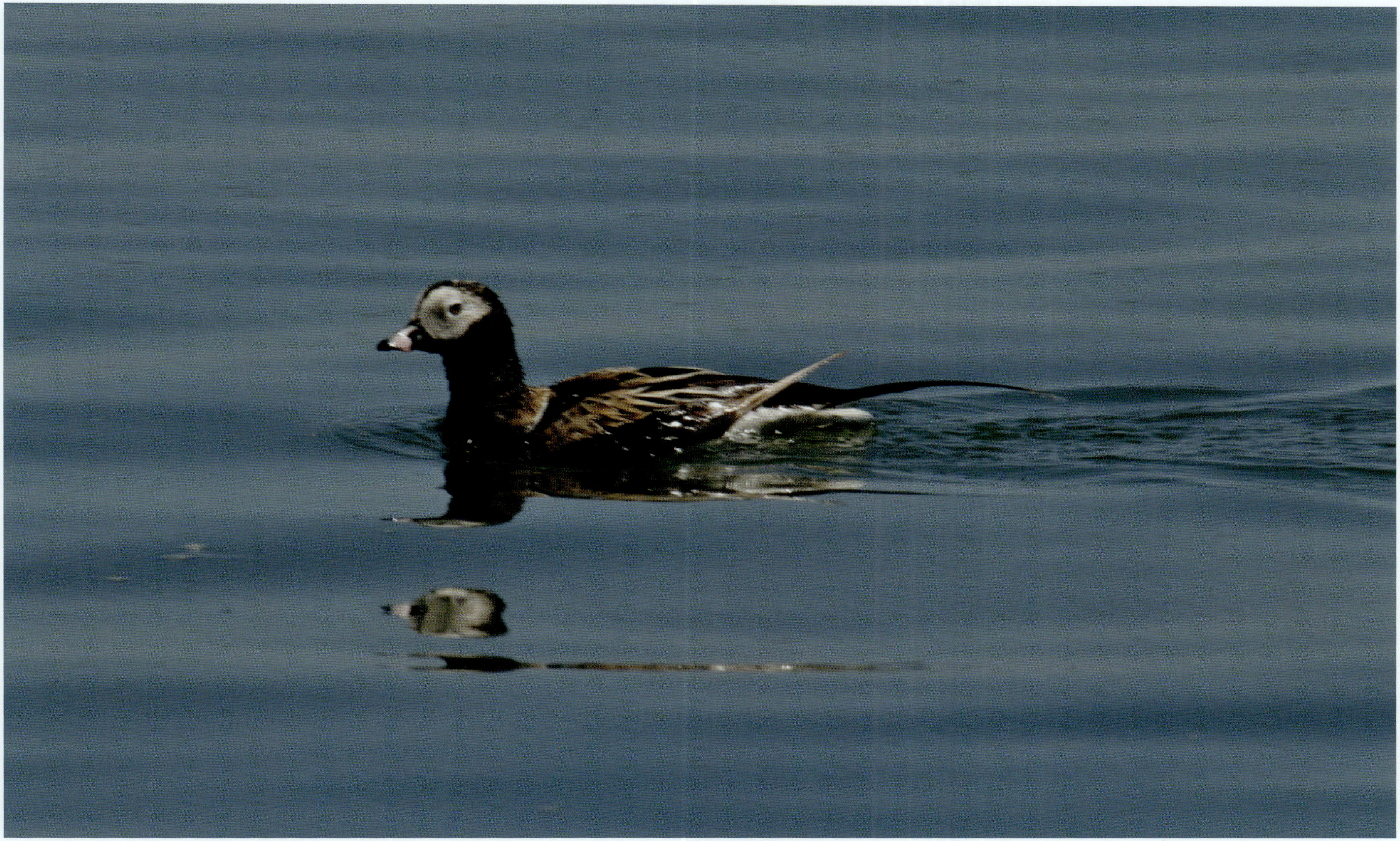

long-tailed duck,
monomoy national wildlife refuge

osprey, morris island,
monomoy national wildlife refuge

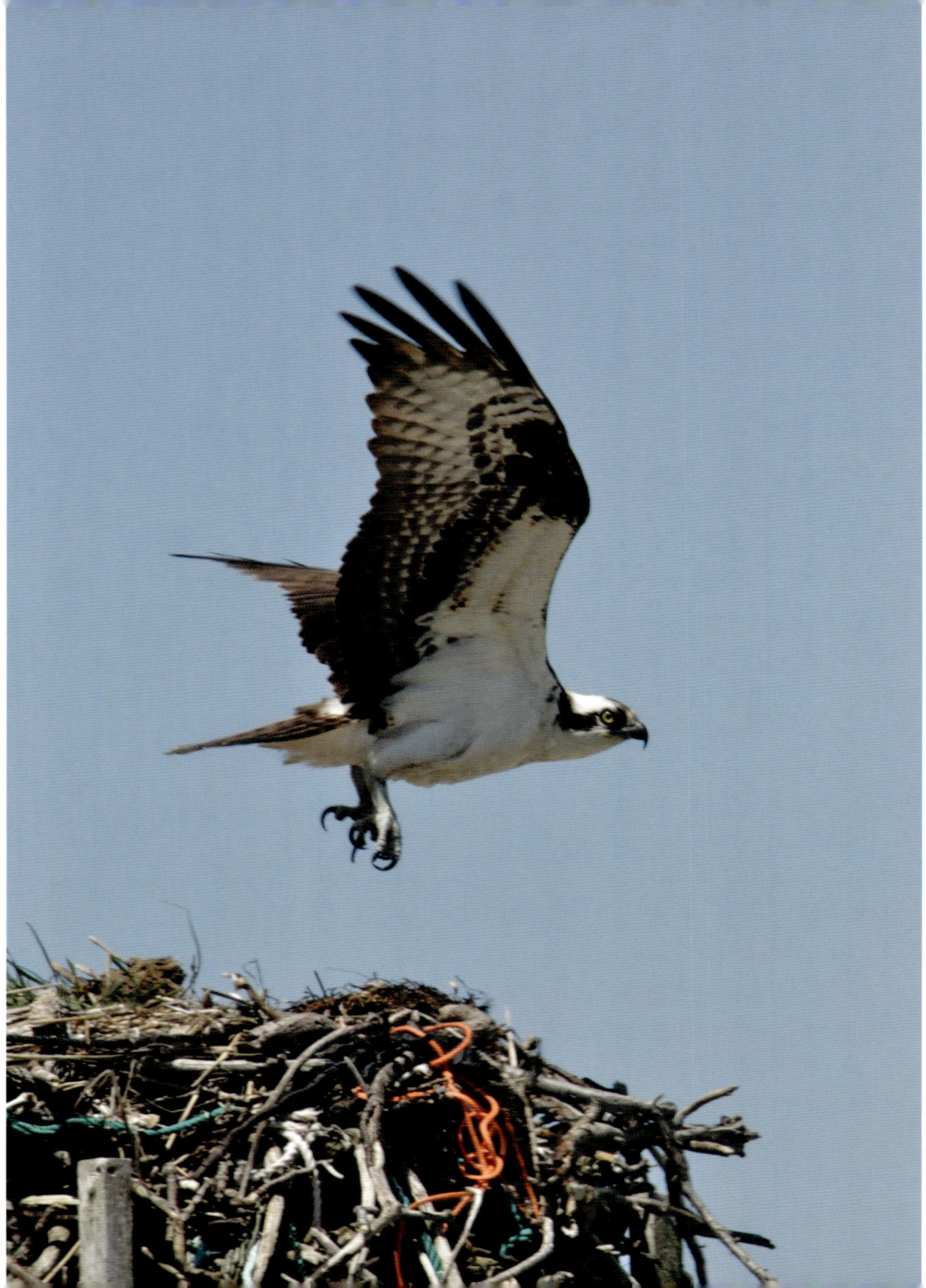

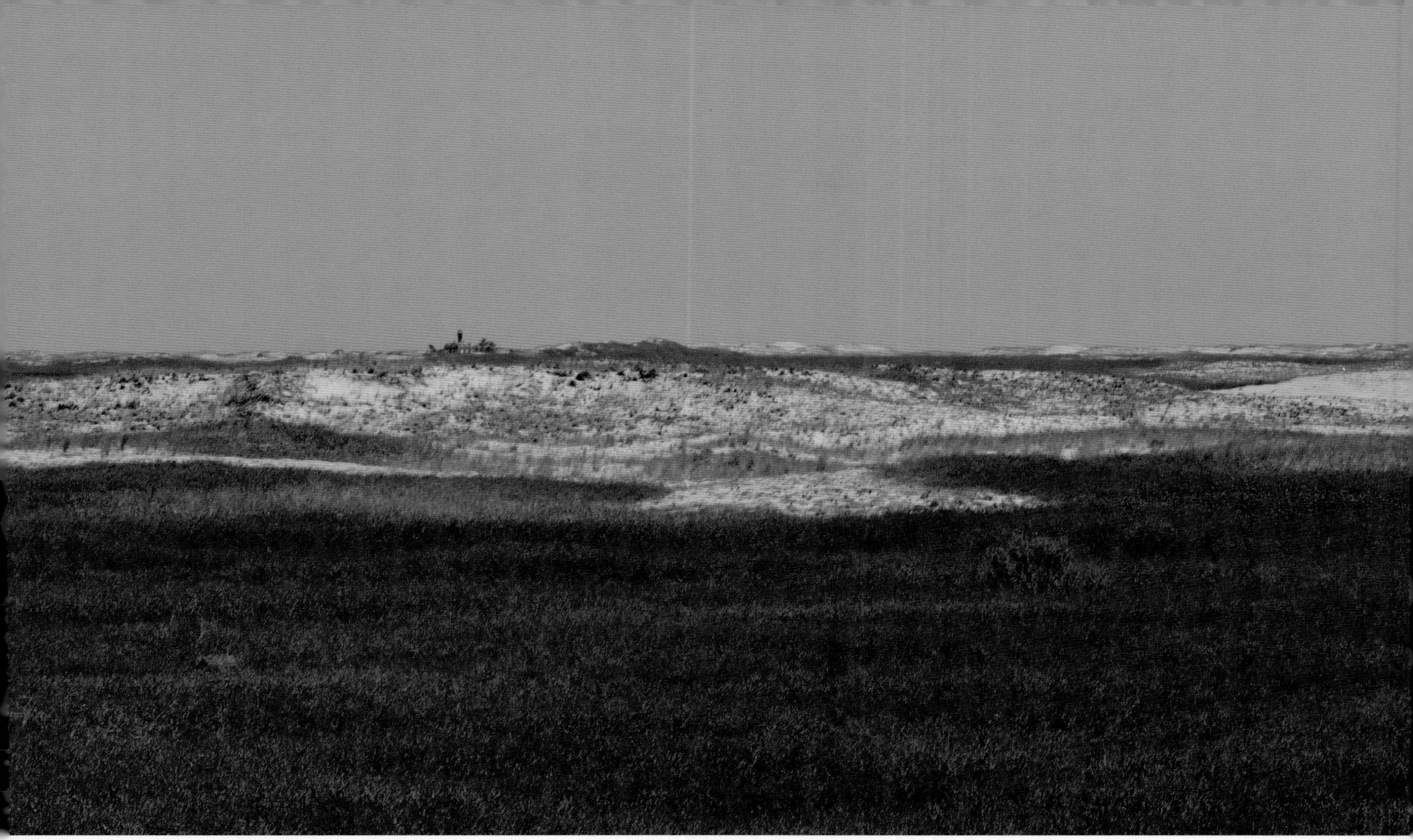

cold spring | powder hole, monomoy national wildlife refuge

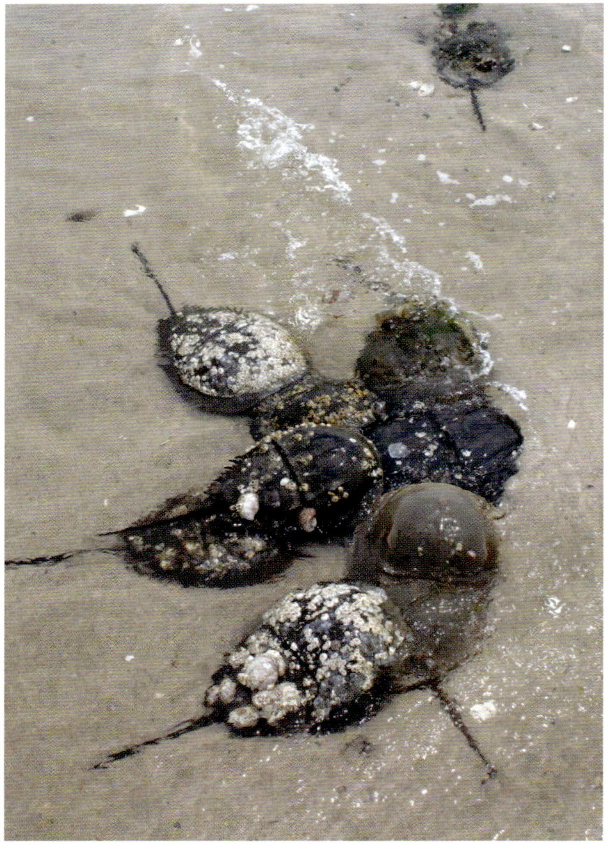

ancient spawning

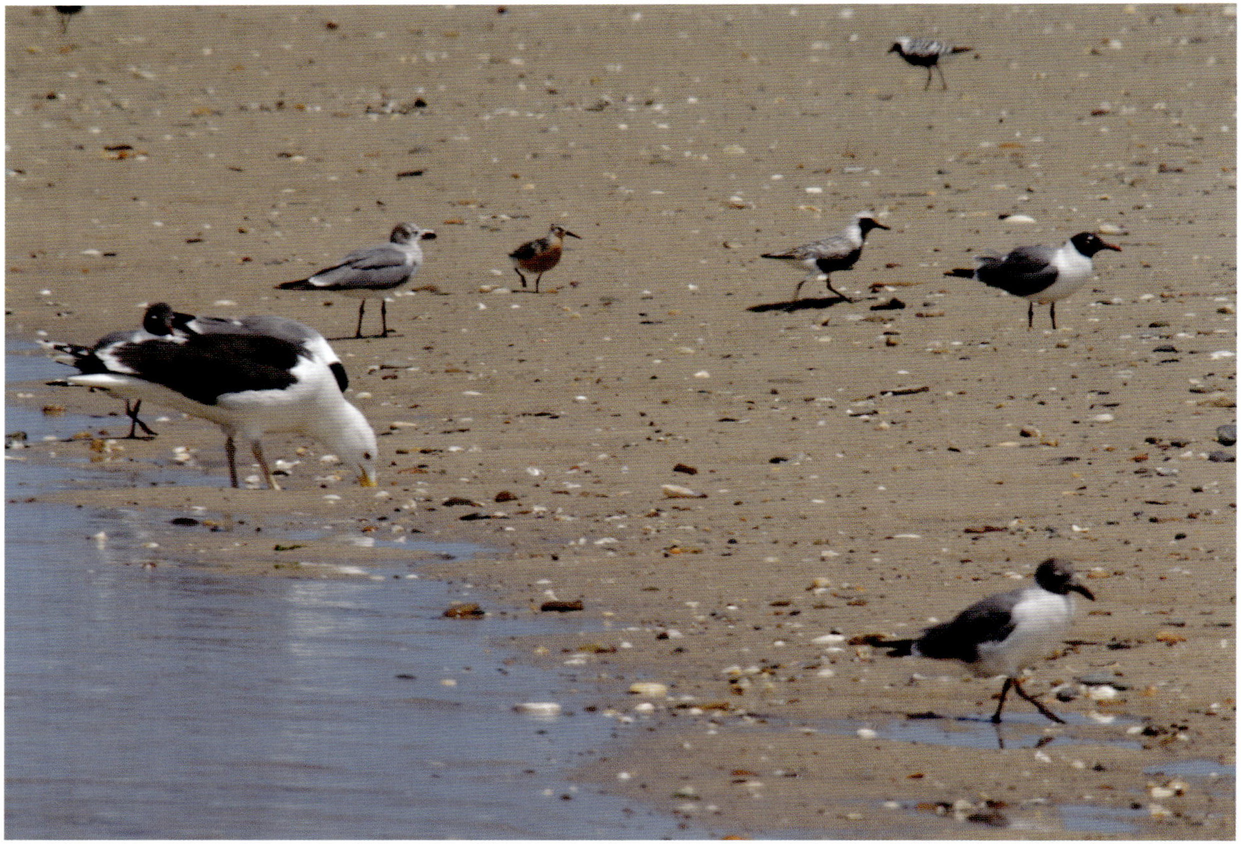

knot's landing

left: mating horseshoe crabs

right: feeding red knot and friends, south beach, chatham

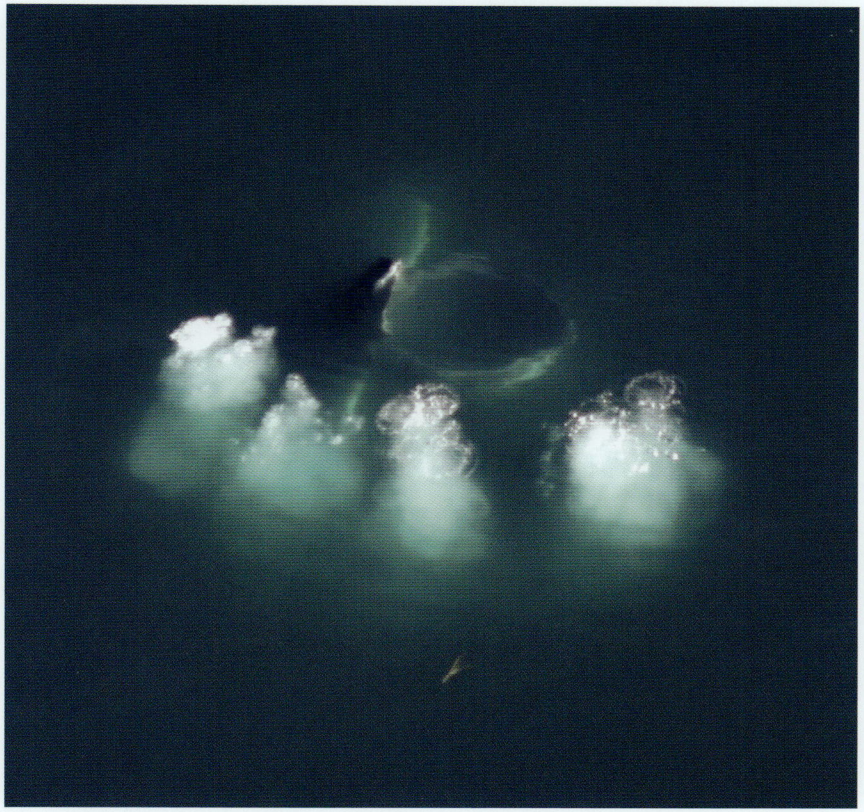

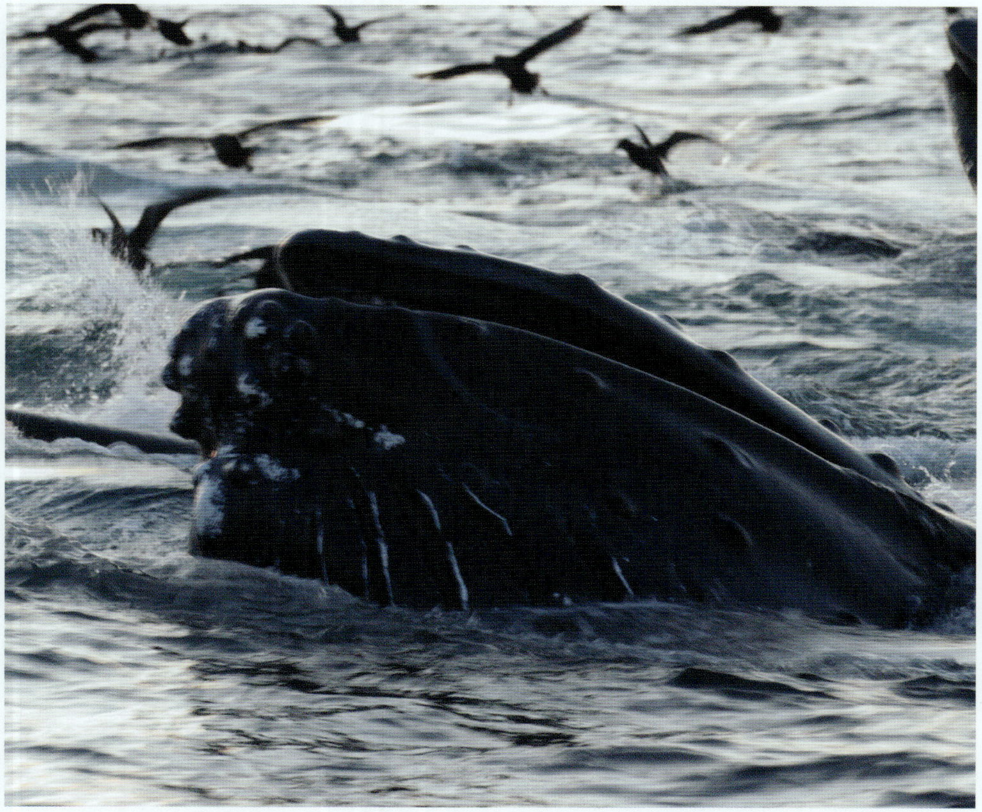

herding the feed

humpback whales bubble netting,
atlantic ocean, off outer cape

left: photo courtesy of tim vorhees

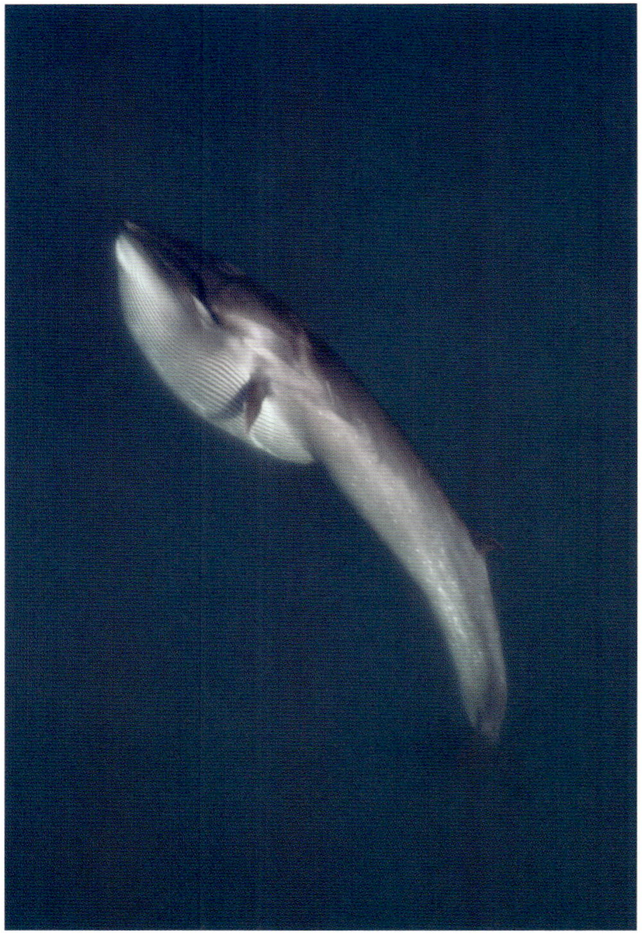

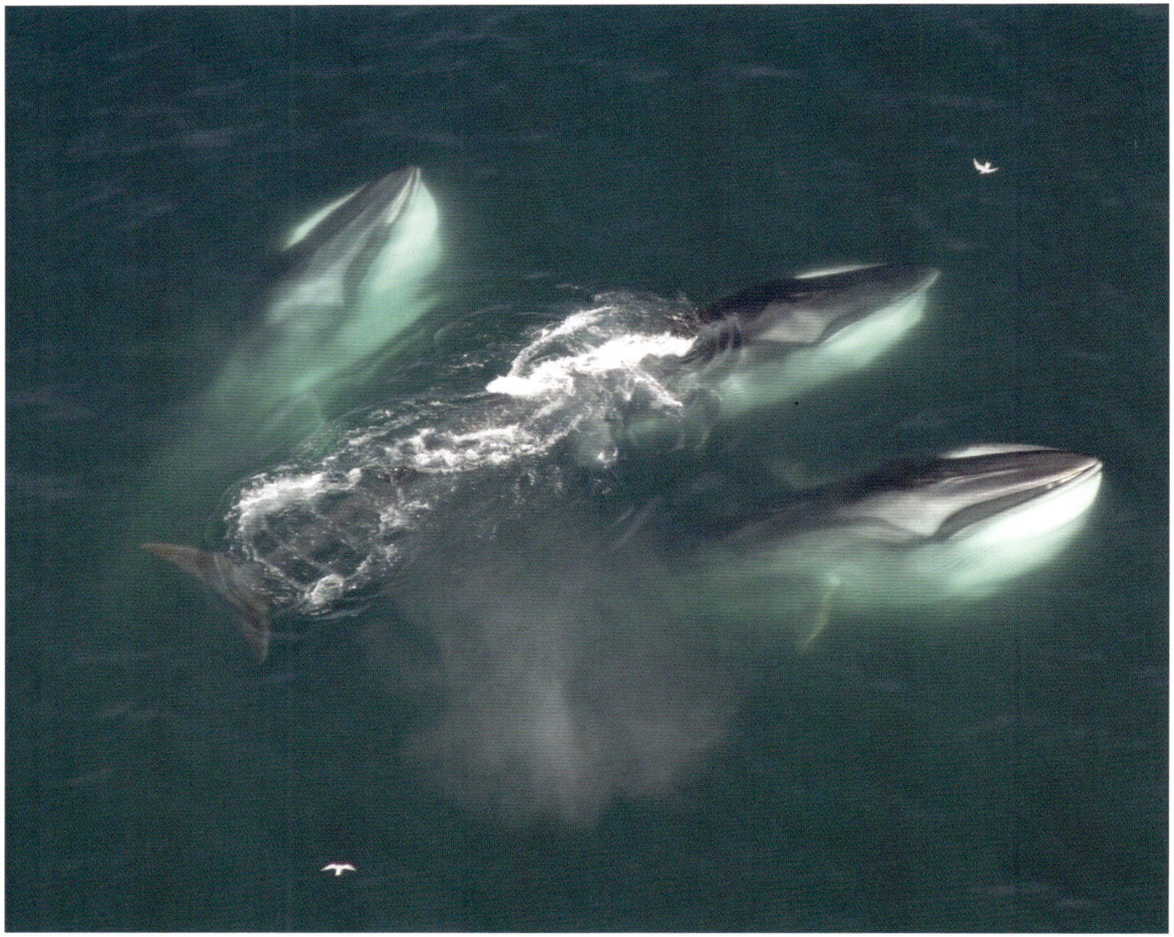

giants feed

fin whales feeding, atlantic ocean,
off outer cape

photos courtesy of tim vorhees

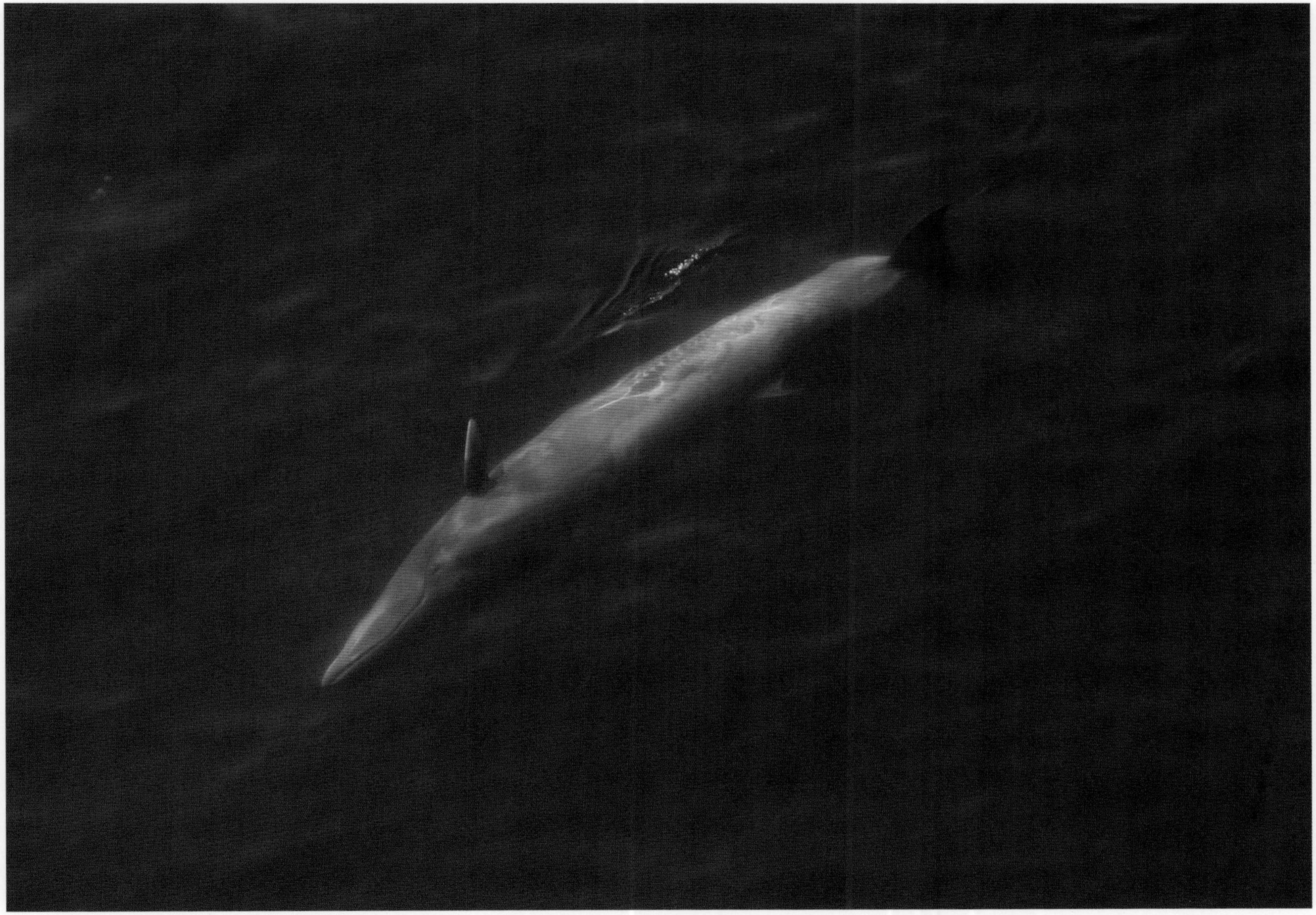

greyhound of the sea

sei whale, atlantic ocean,
off outer cape

photo courtesy of tim vorhees

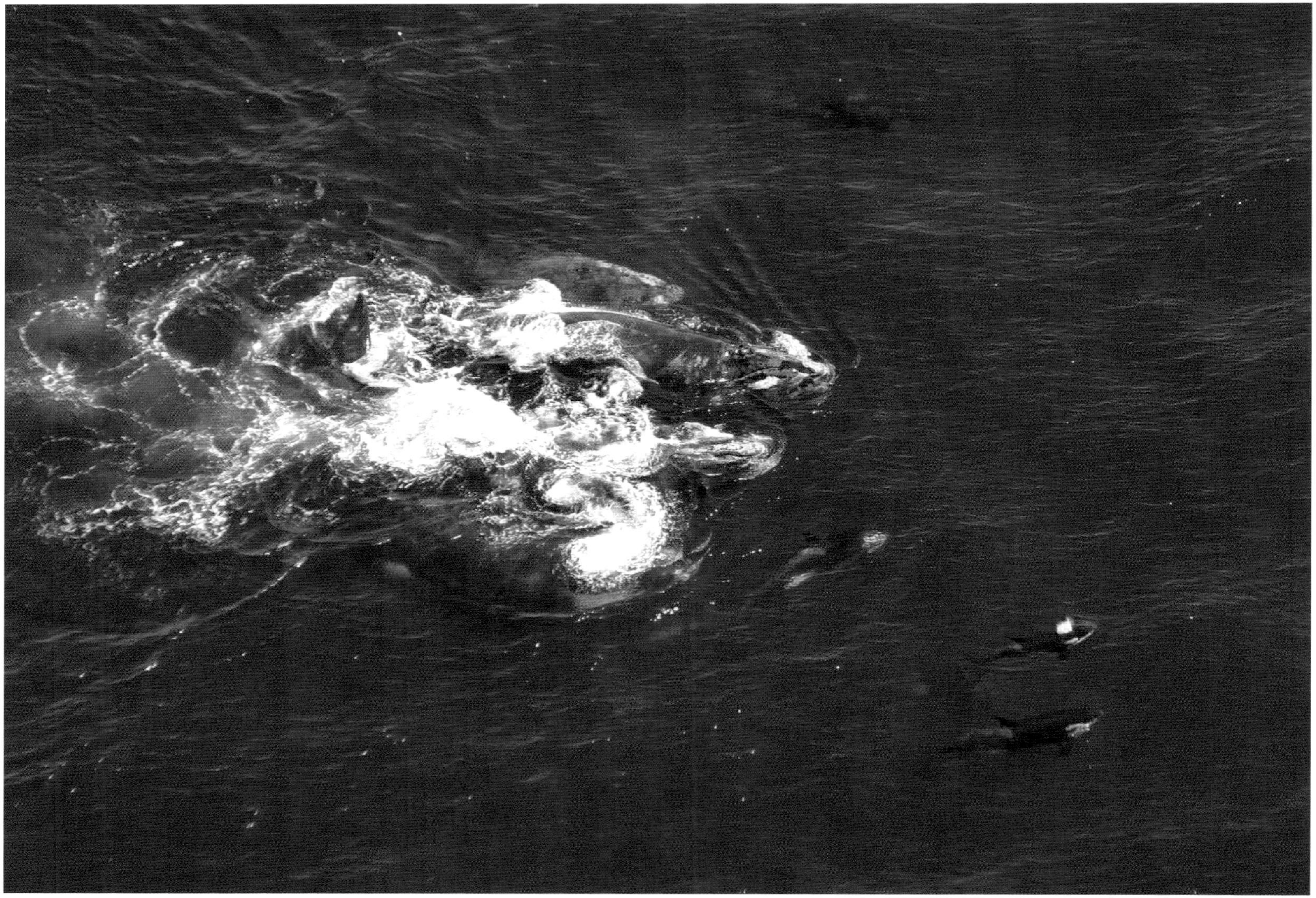

killer circle

northern right whales, atlantic ocean,
off outer cape

photo courtesy of tim vorhees

mighty vegans

basking sharks,
atlantic ocean, off outer cape

photo courtesy of tim vorhees

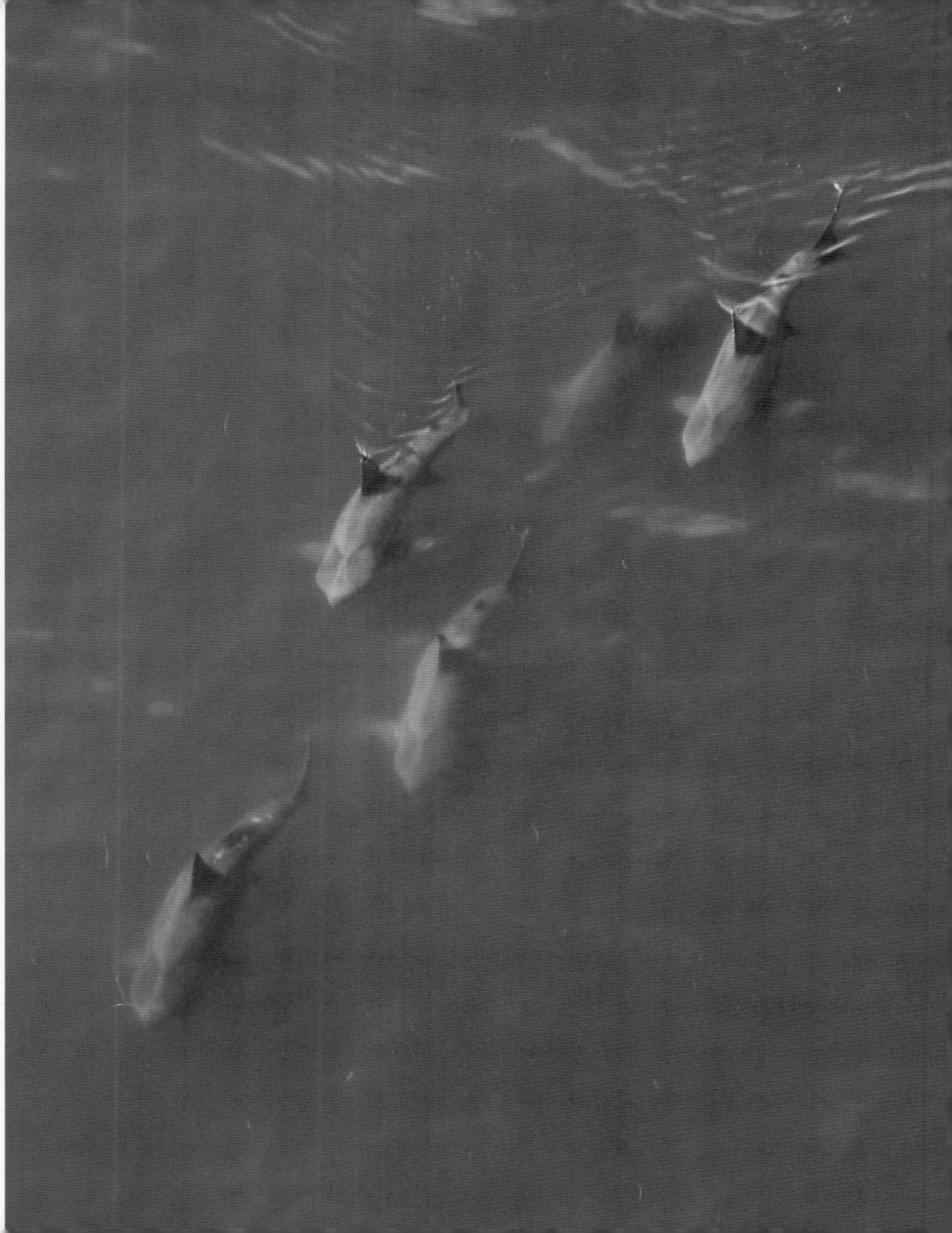

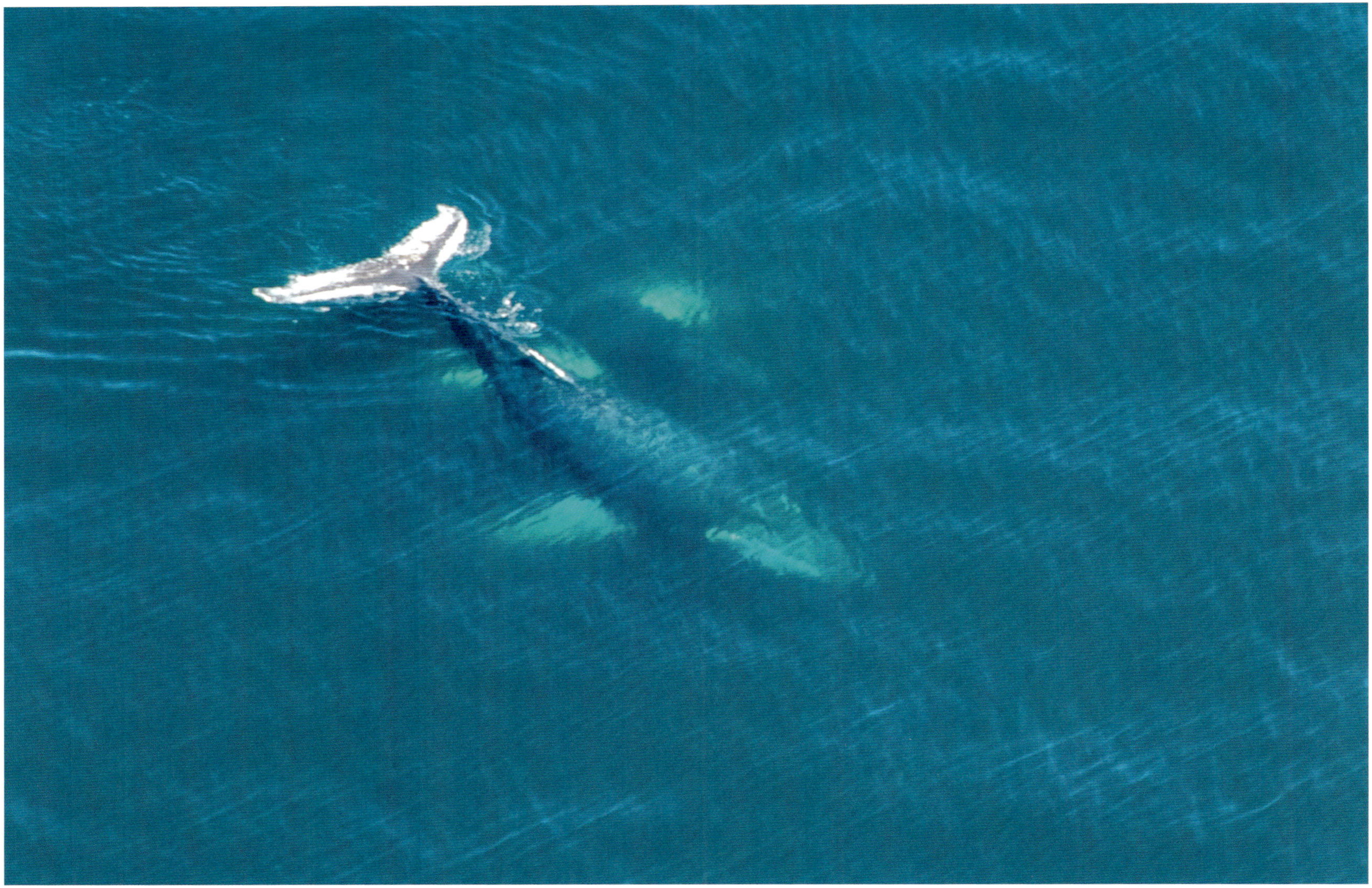

ripple effect

humpback whale with calf, atlantic ocean, off coast guard beach, eastham

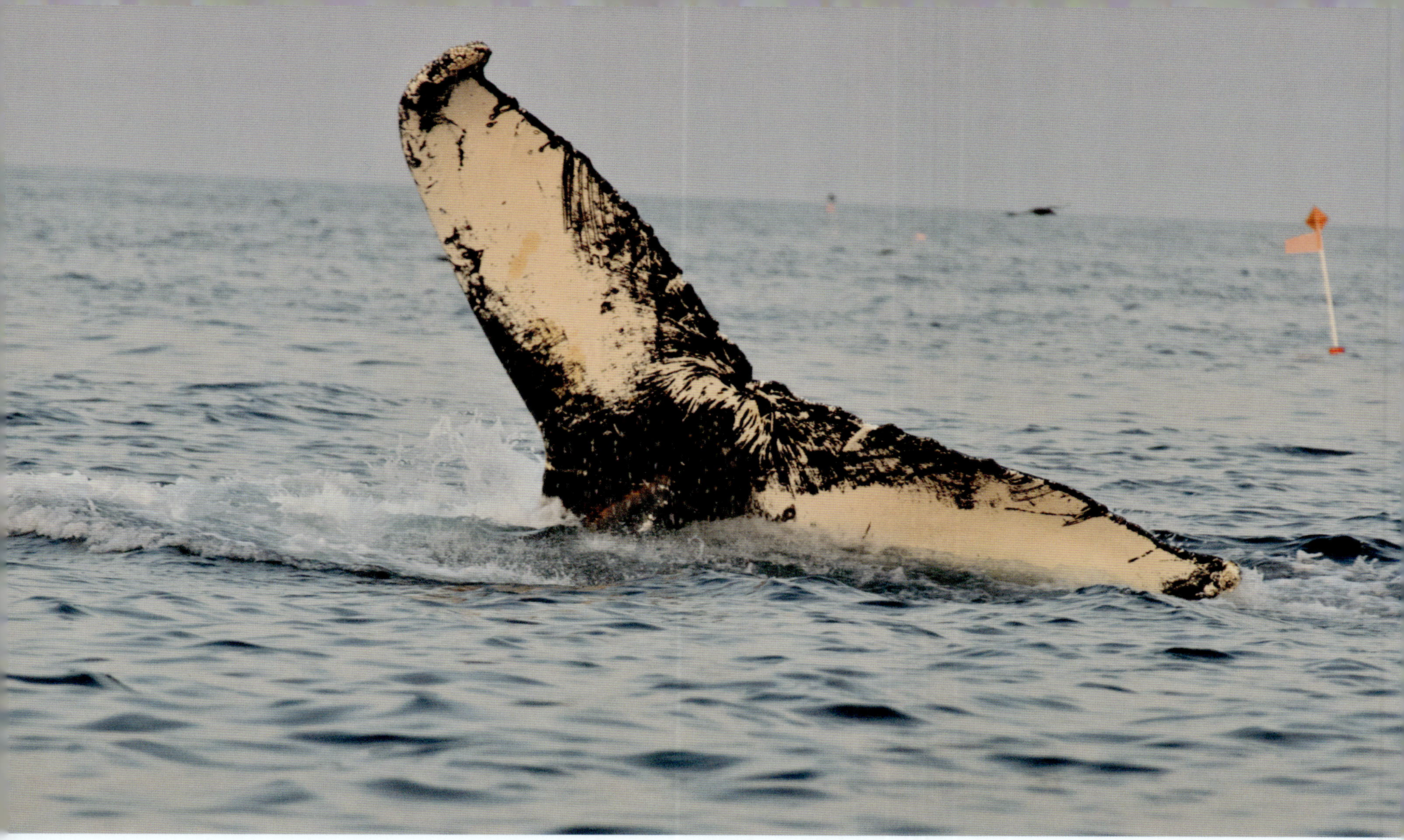

tail light

humpback whale at summer solstice, off chatham

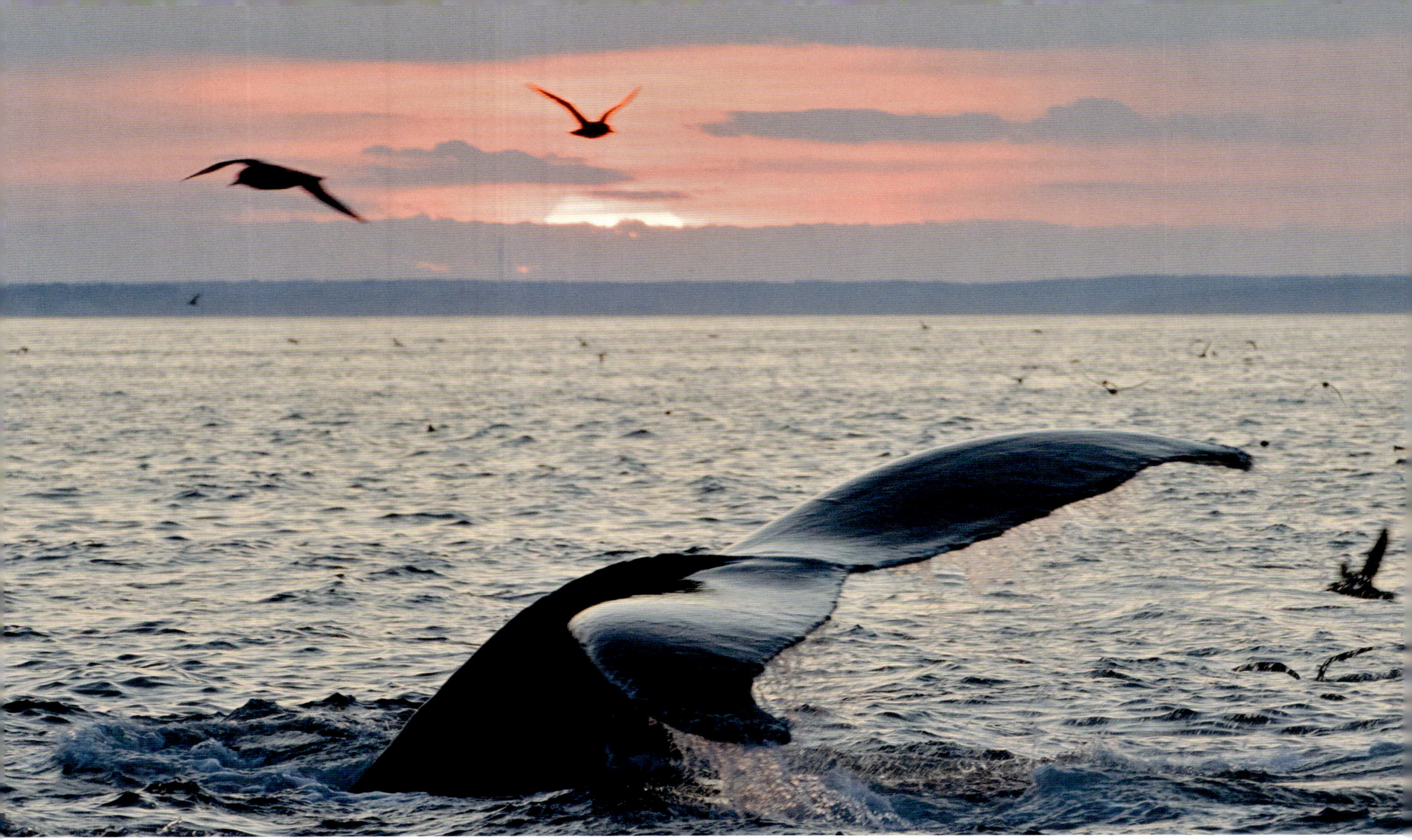

sunset dive

humpback whale at summer solstice, off chatham

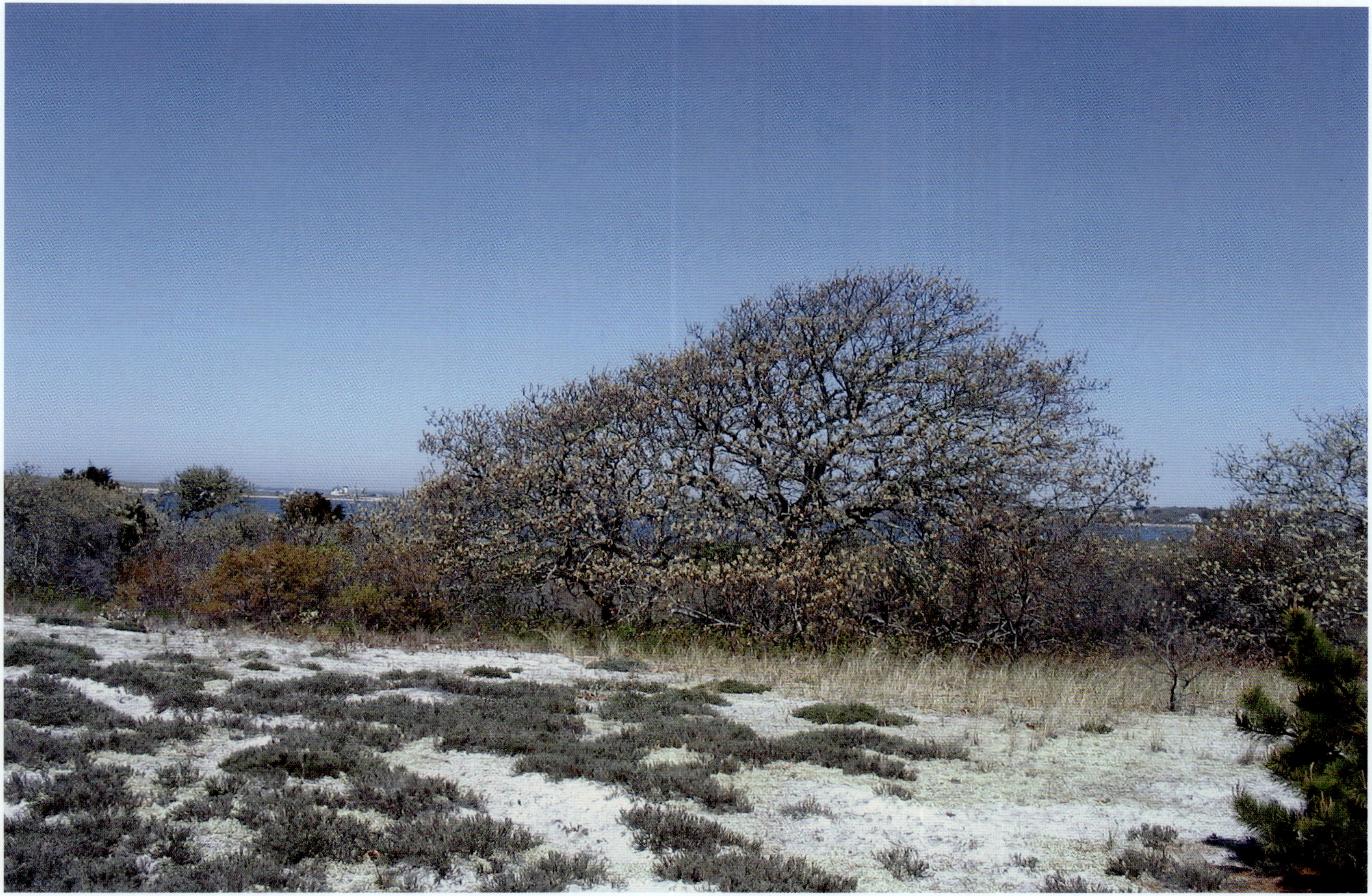

cobalt spring

morris island,
monomoy national wildlife refuge

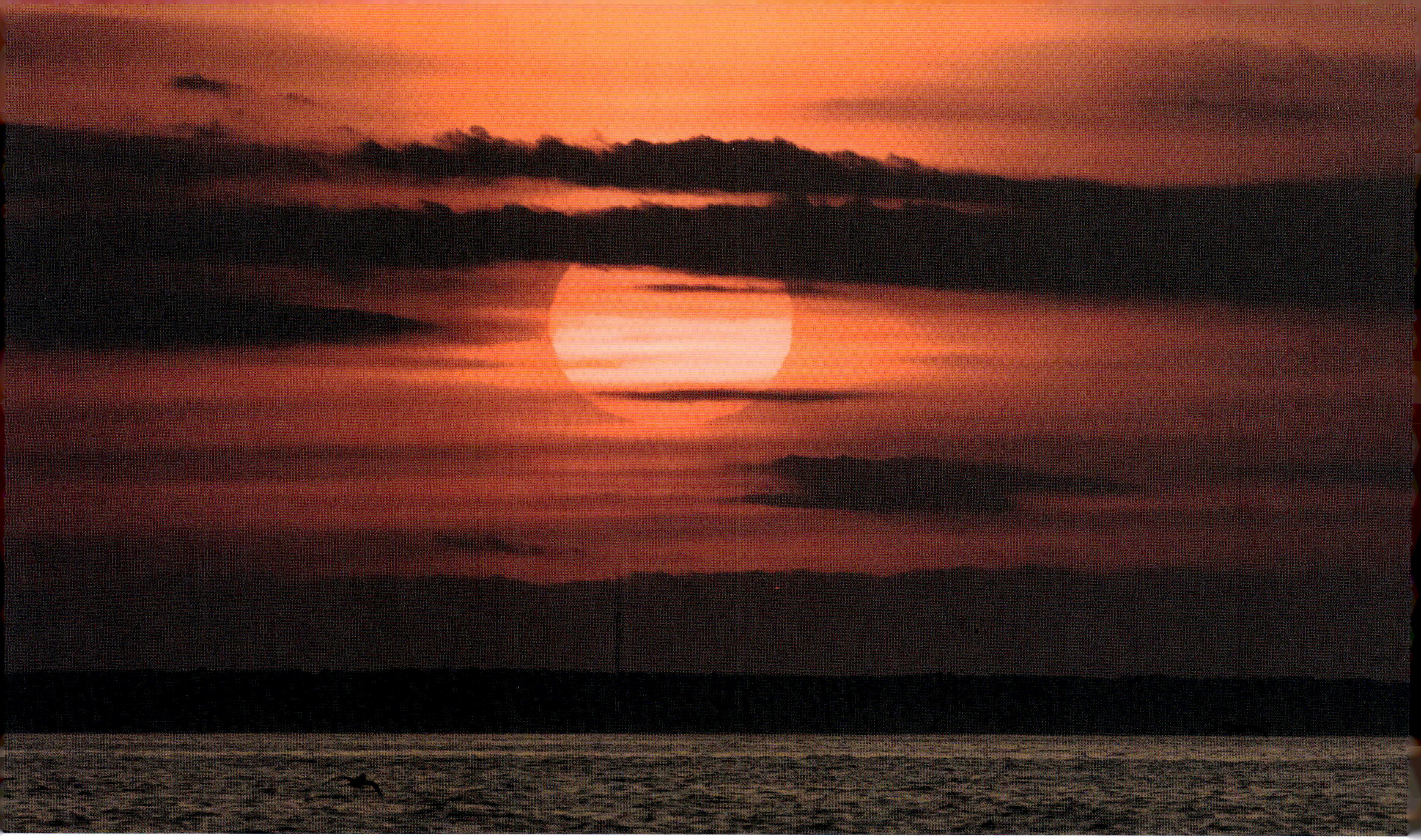

longest day

summer solstice sunset, off chatham

- north beach island, chatham
- off chatham
- powder hole, monomoy national wildlife refuge
- monomoy national wildlife refuge
- south beach, chatham
- pleasant bay, chatham
- tern island, chatham

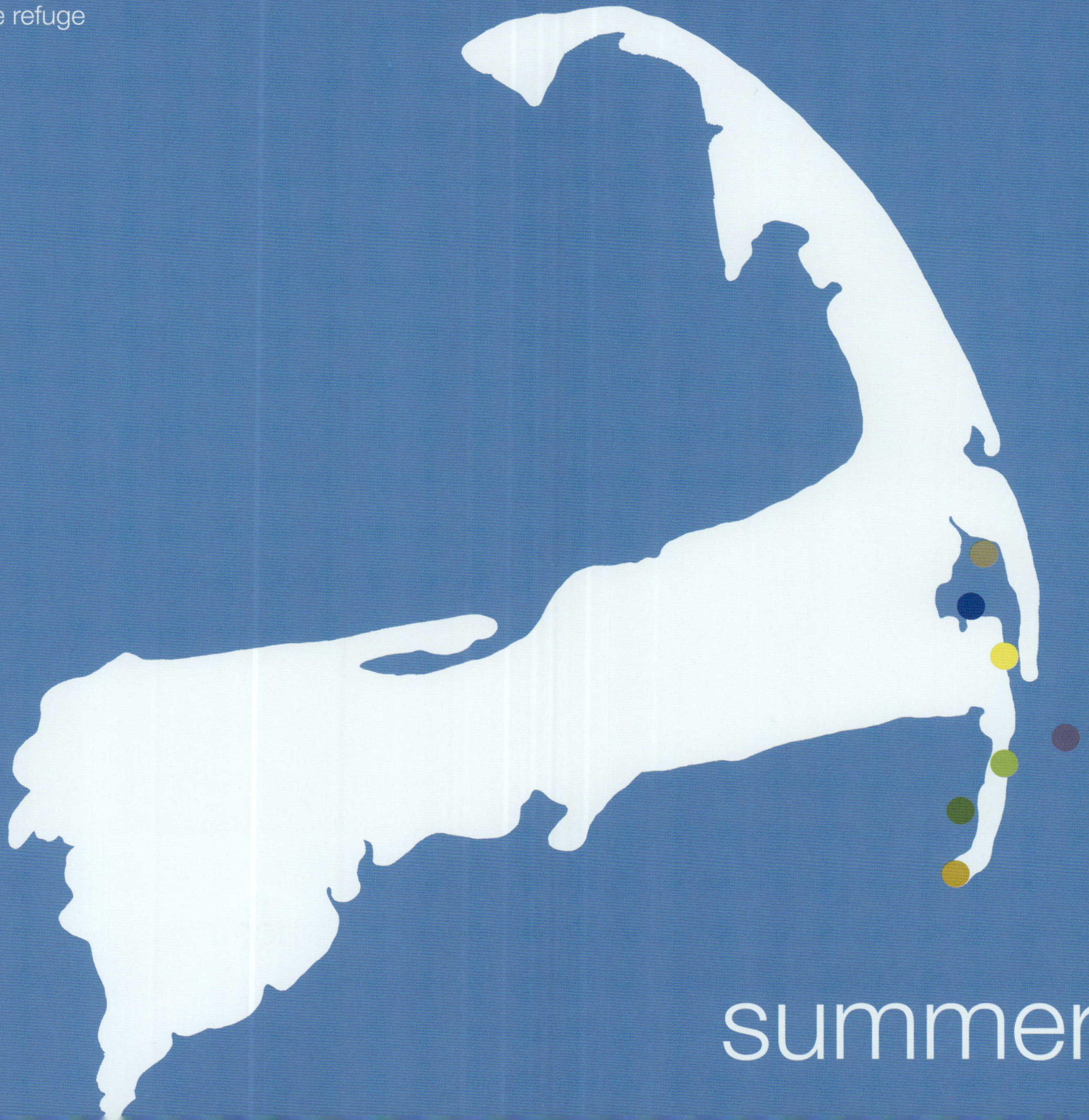

summer

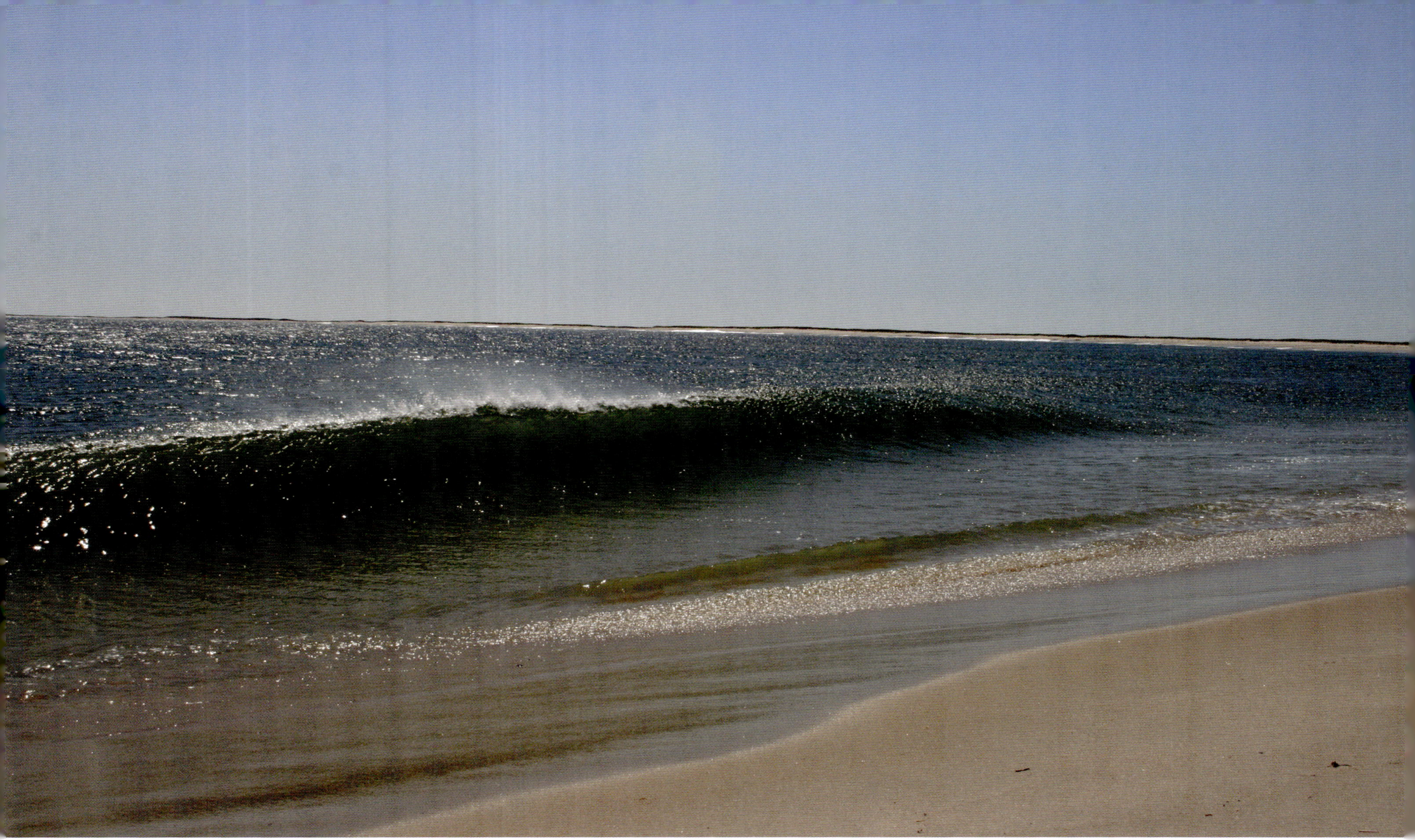

summer surf

south beach,
chatham

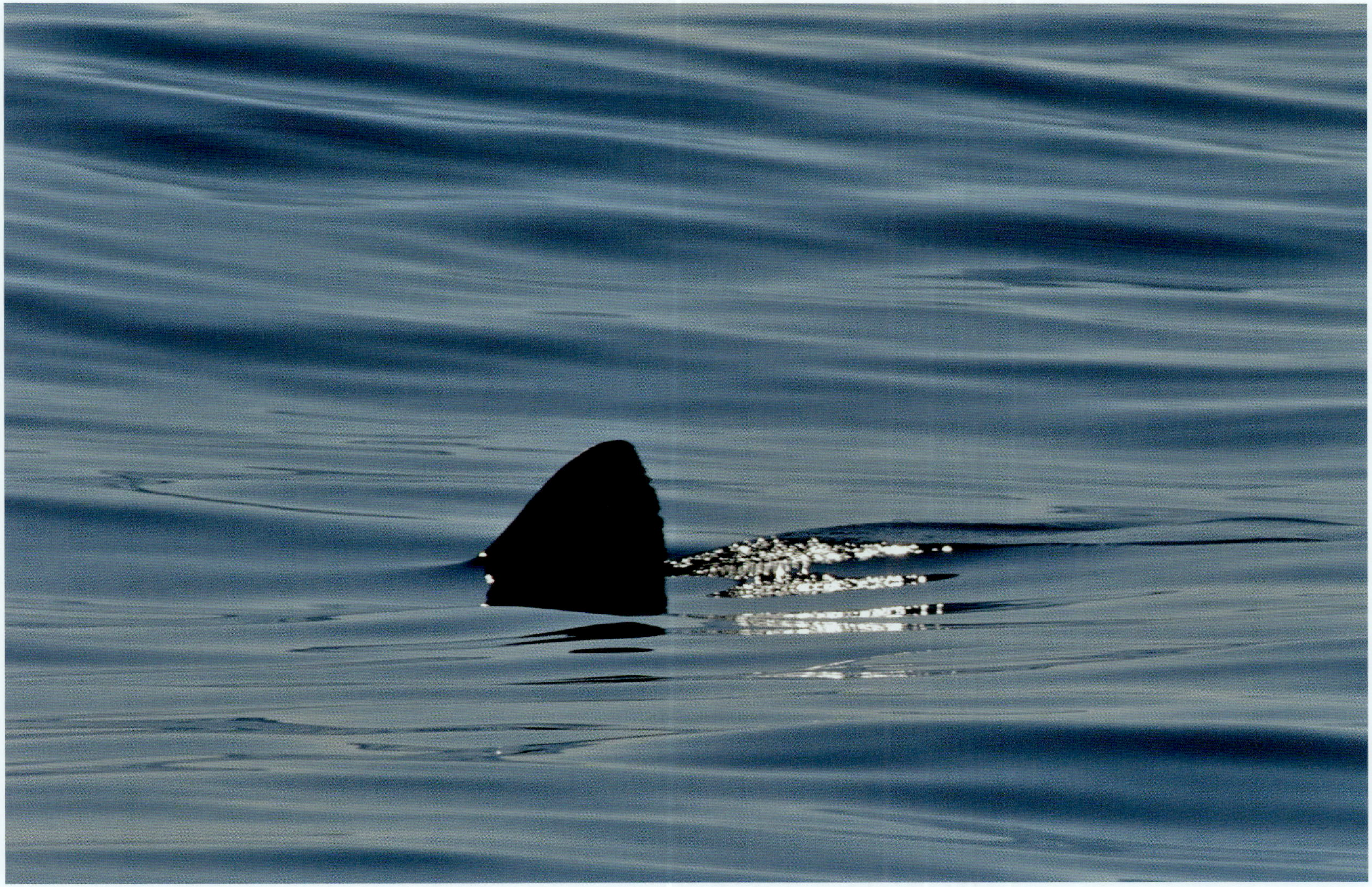

glistening fin

basking shark, off chatham

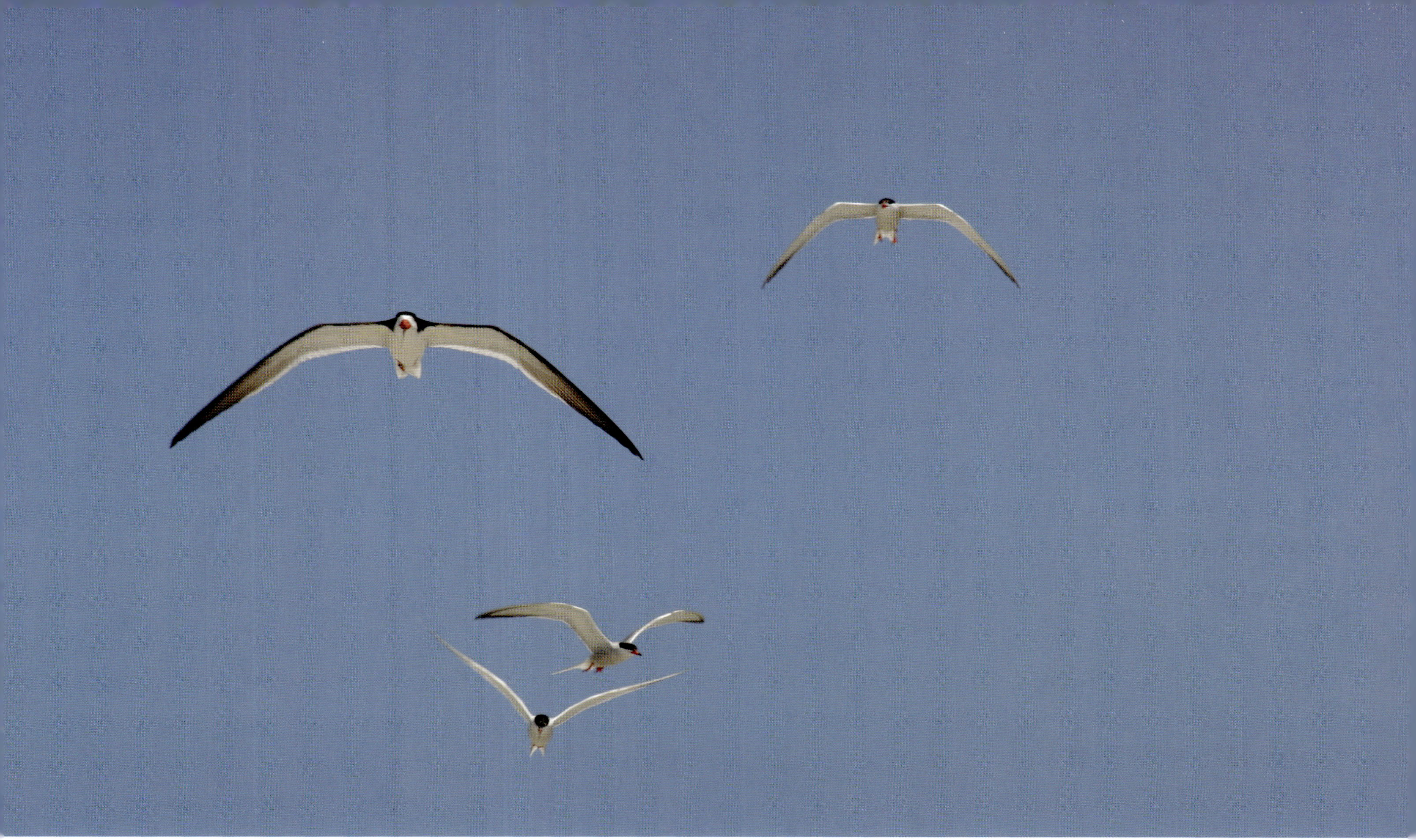

flight pattern

black skimmer with terns,
monomoy national wildlife refuge

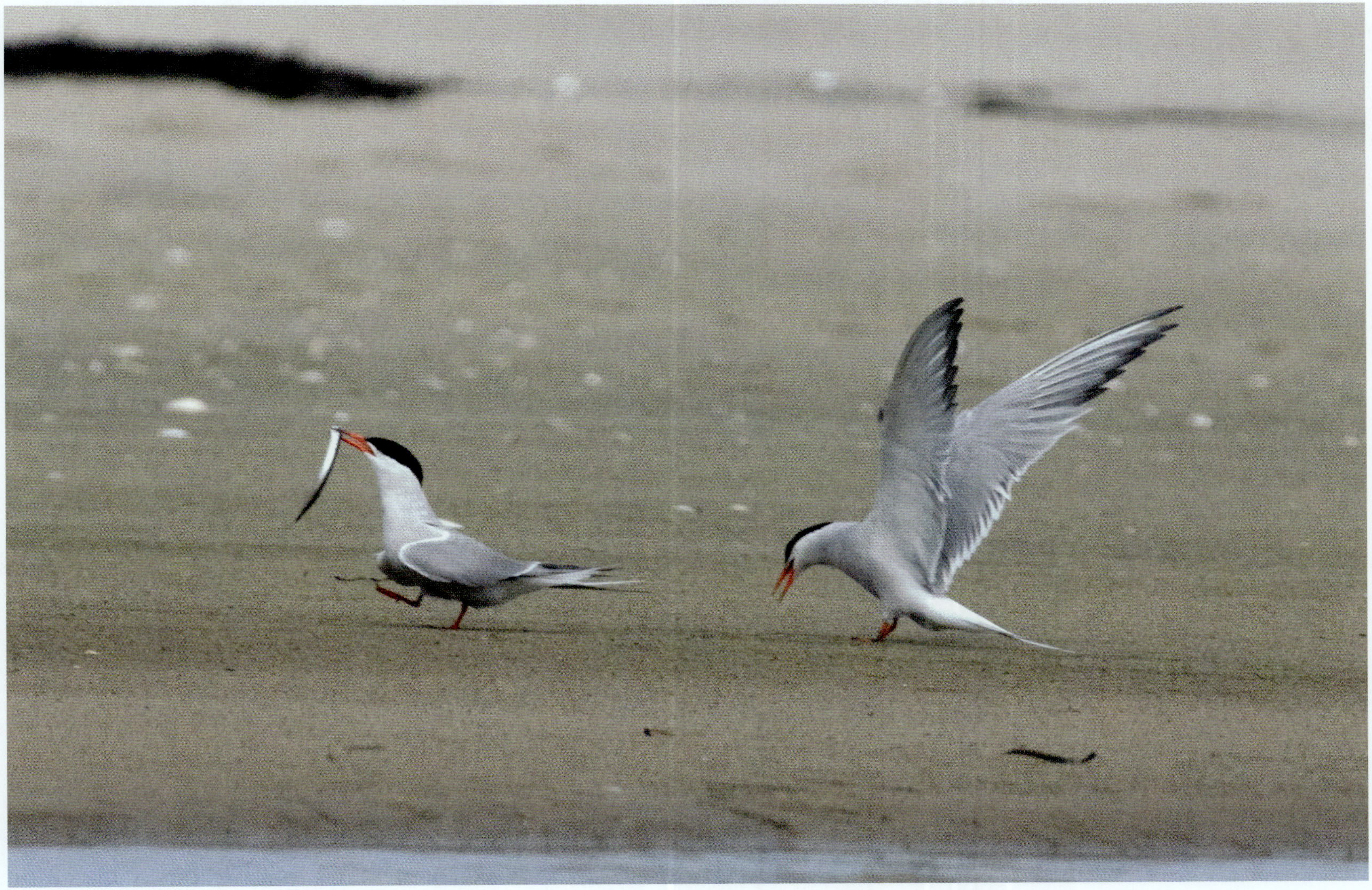

pas de deux

common terns,
north beach island, chatham

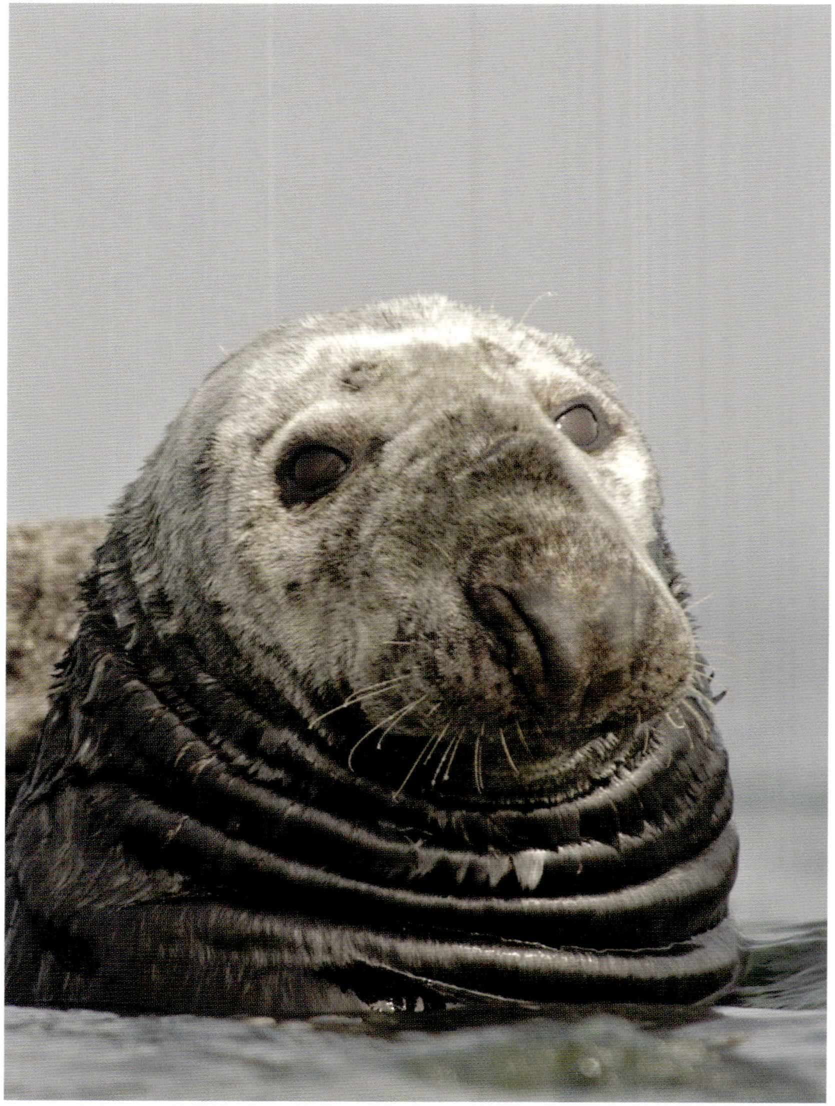

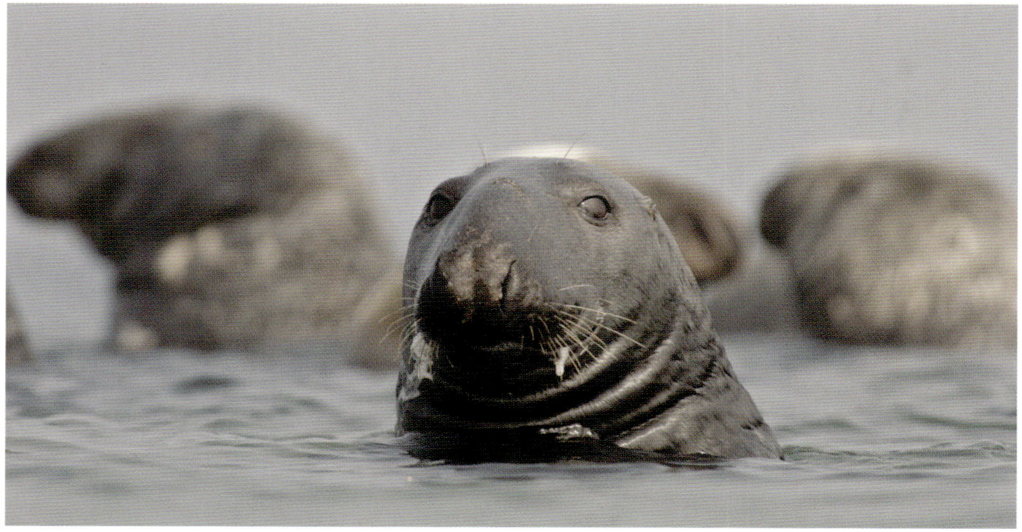

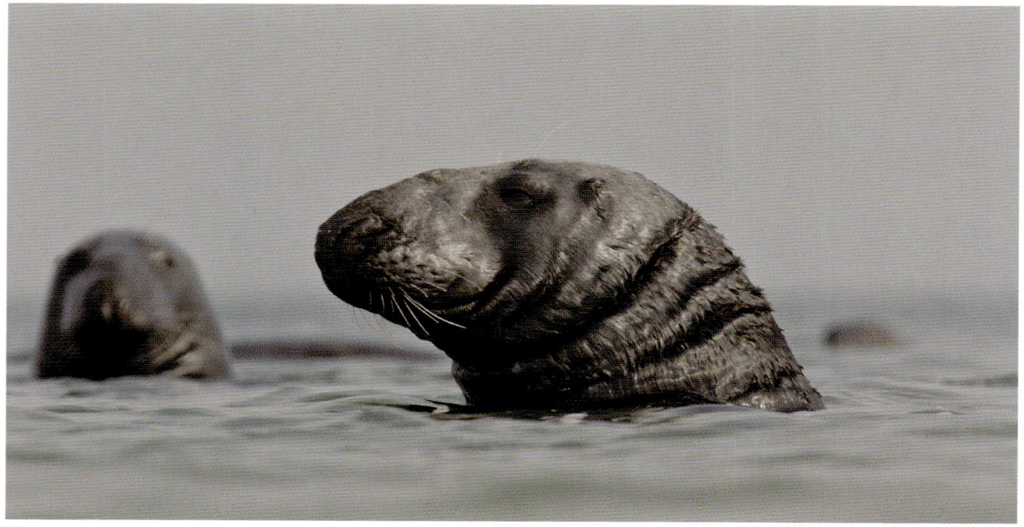

portraits

grey seals, pleasant bay,
chatham

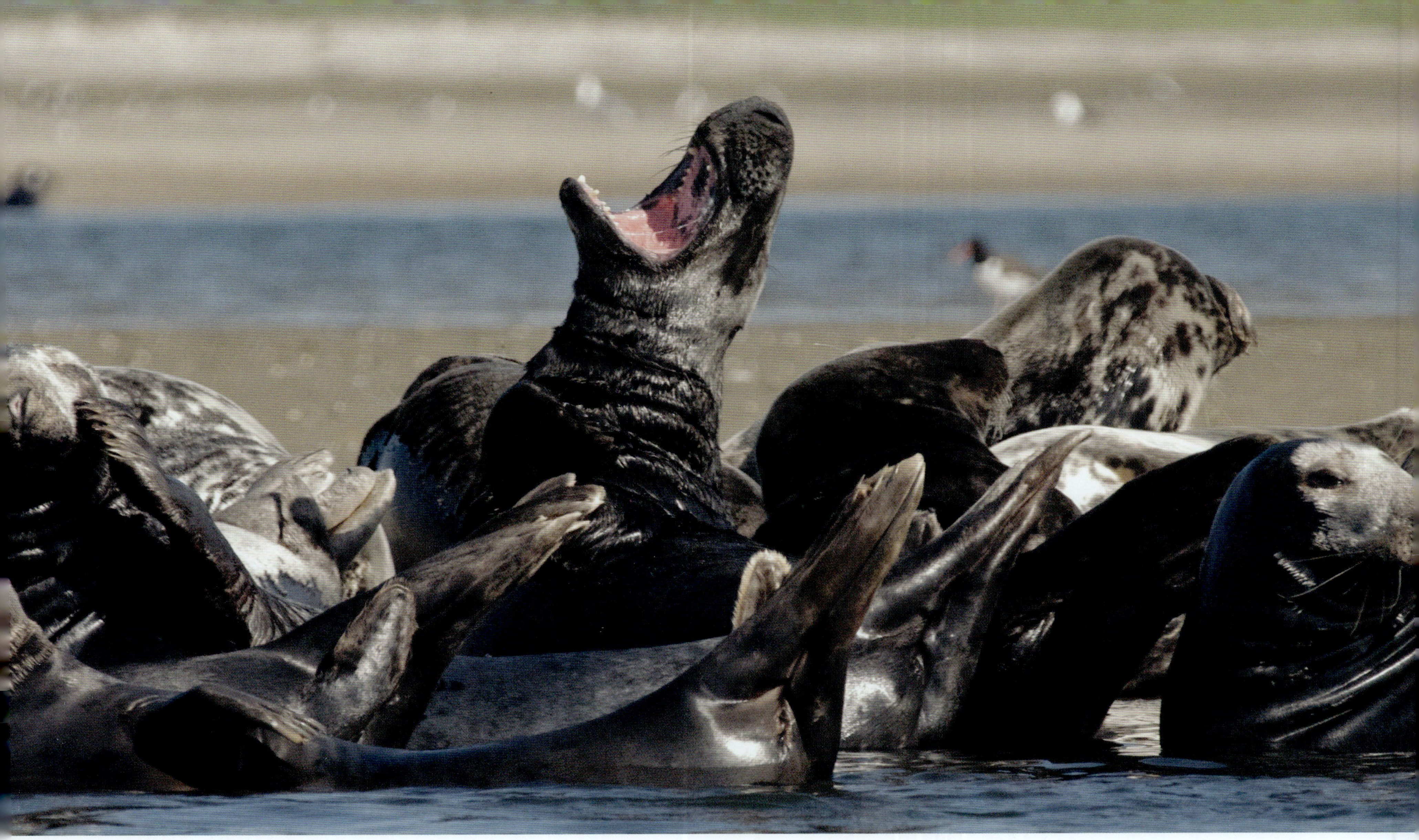

primal scream

grey seals, tern island, chatham

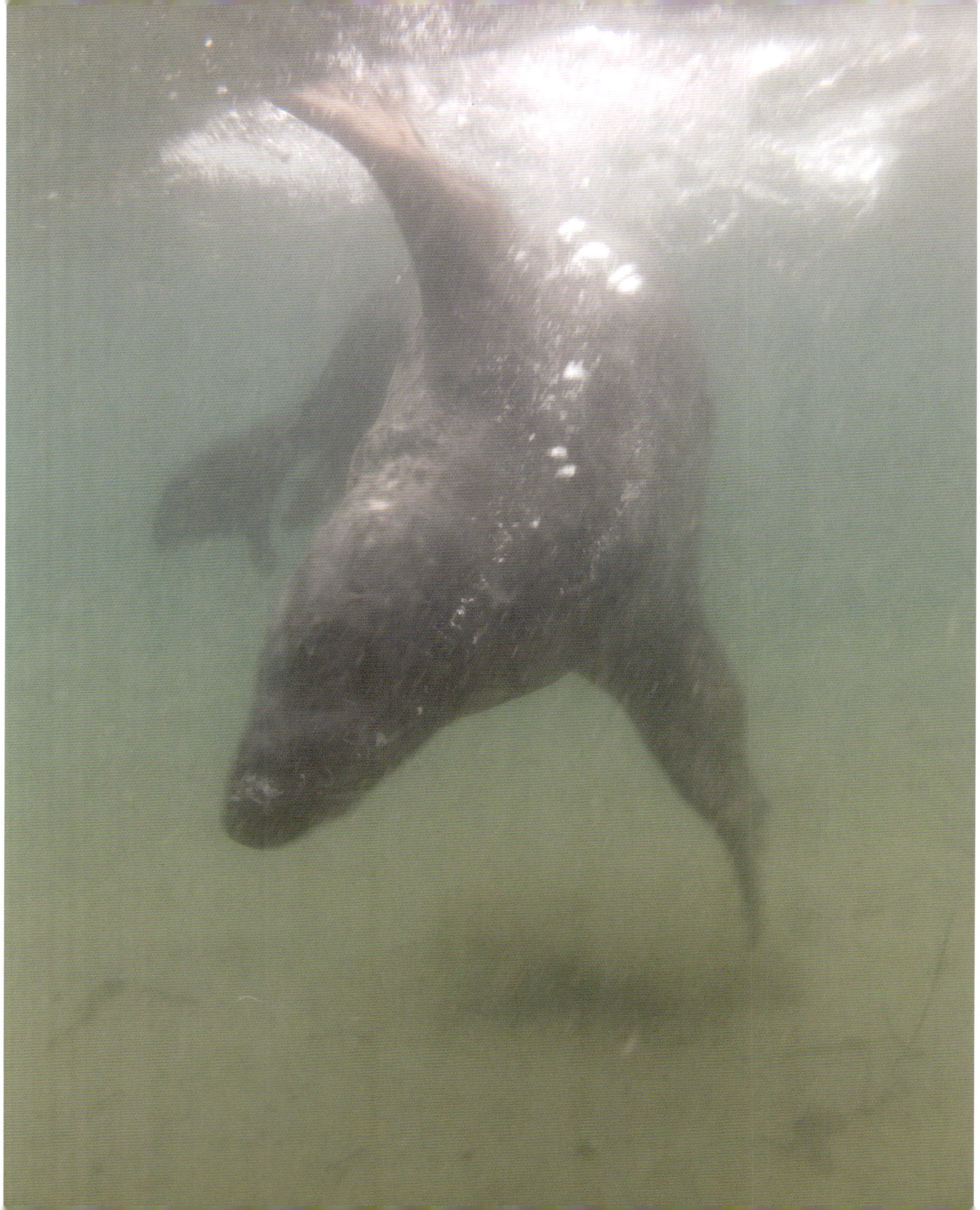

female grey seal, pleasant bay,
chatham

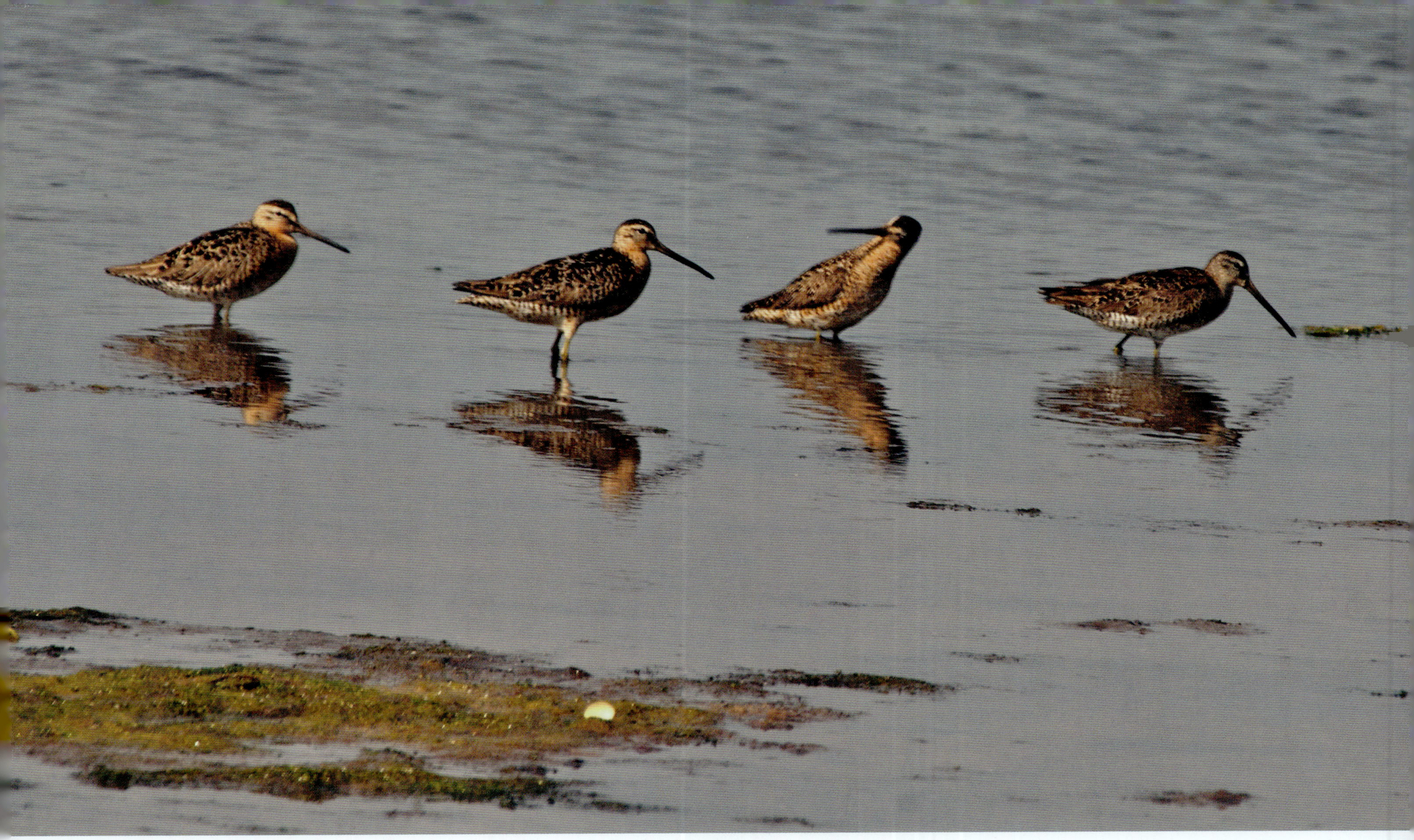

short billed dowitchers, north beach island, chatham

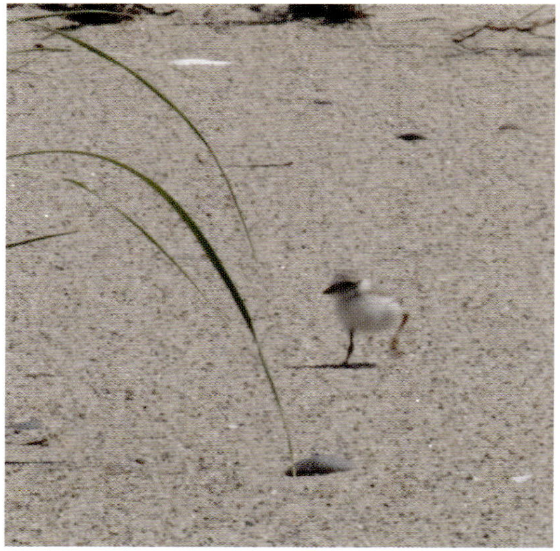 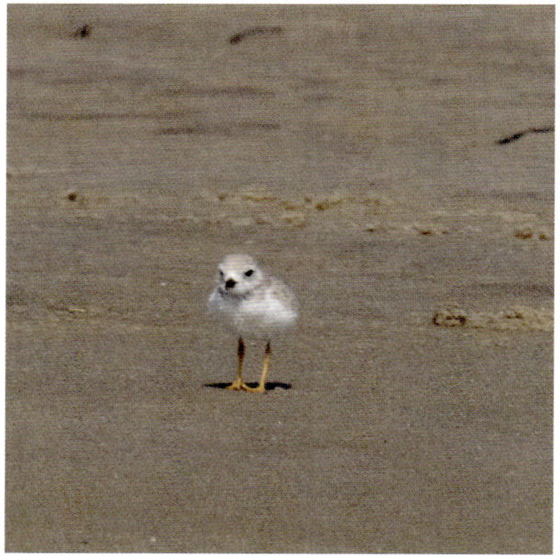 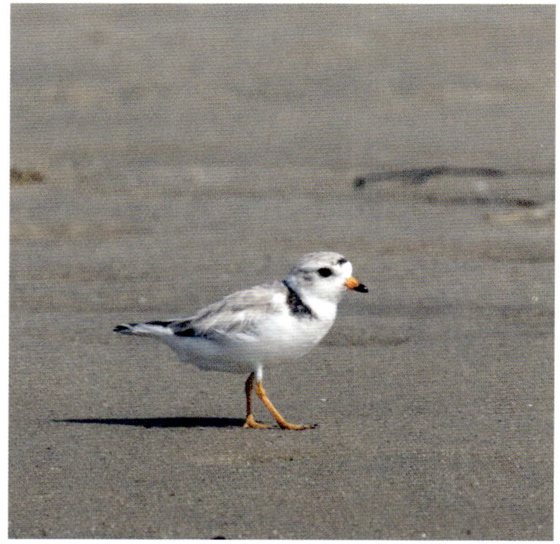

they grow up so fast

piping plovers, south beach, chatham

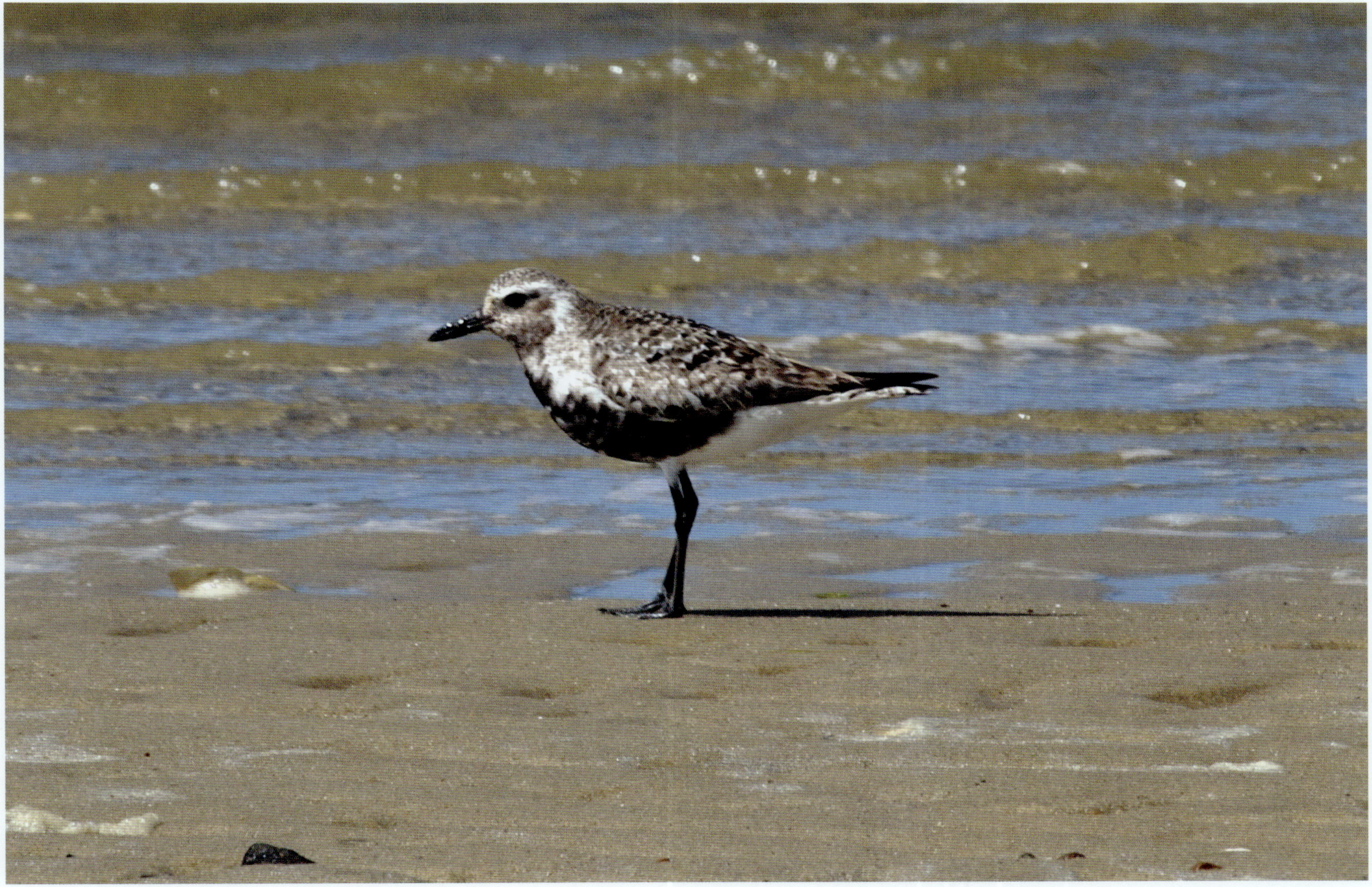

black bellied plover,
monomoy national wildlife refuge

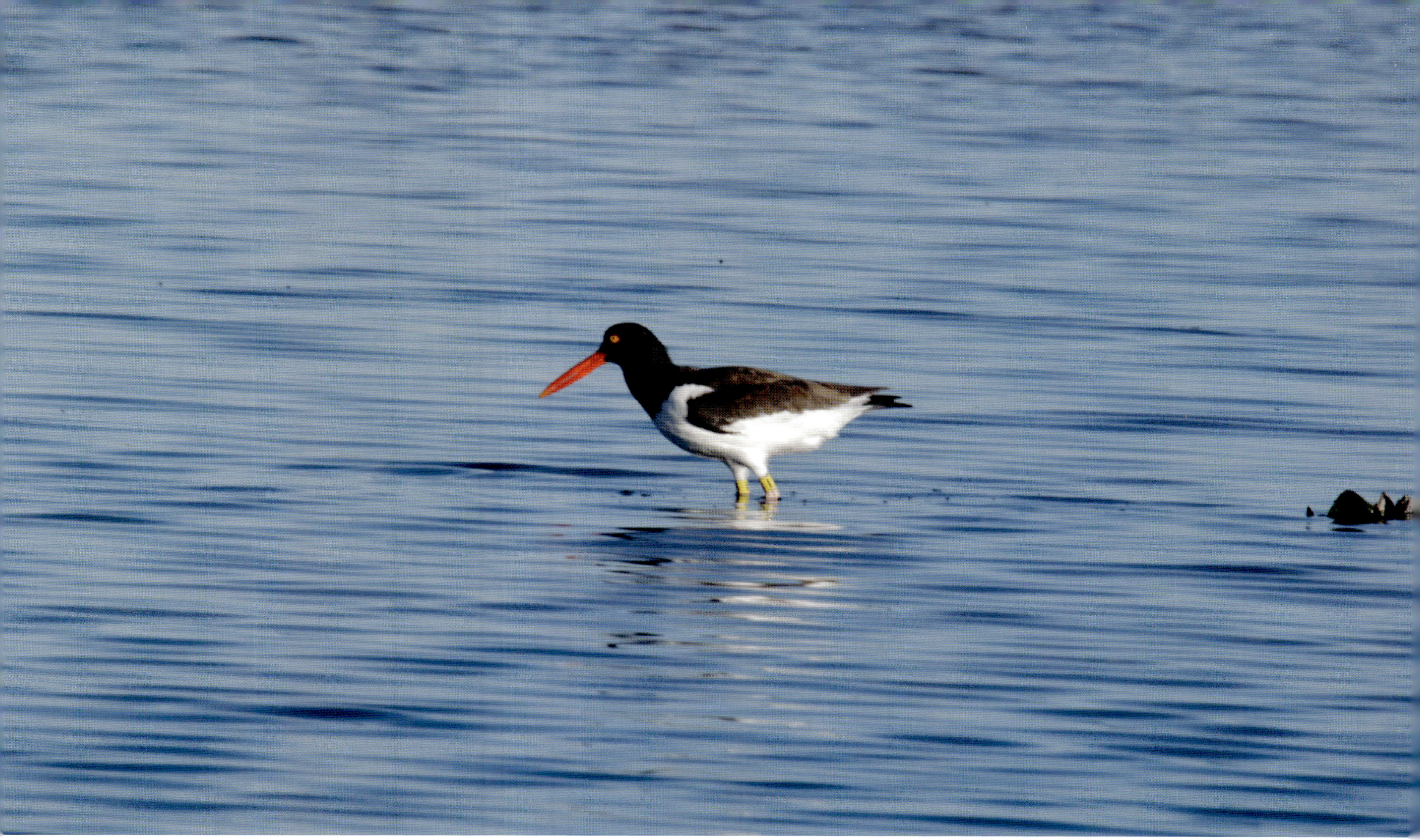

oystercatcher, tern island, chatham

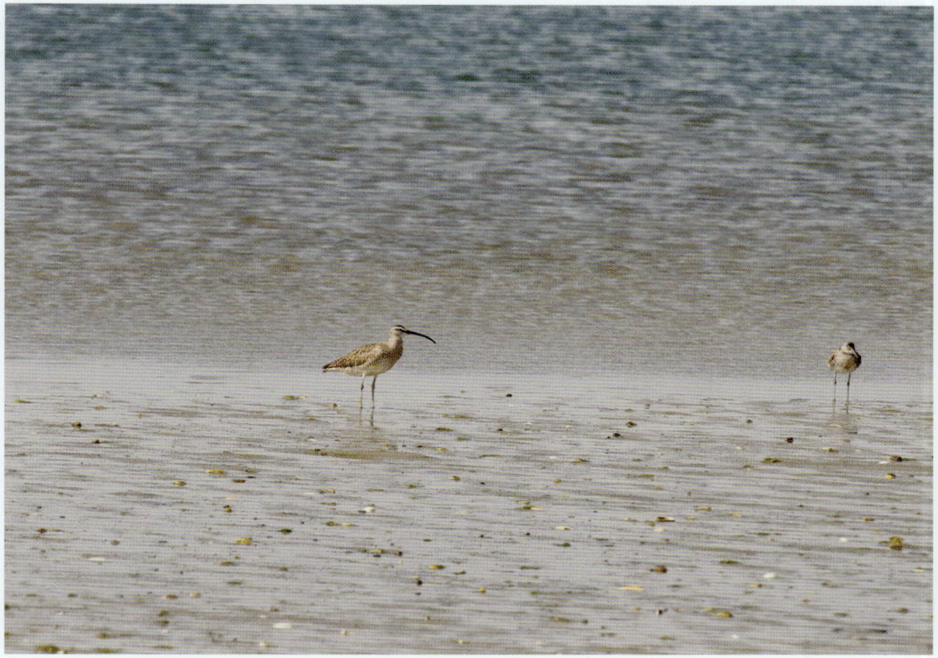

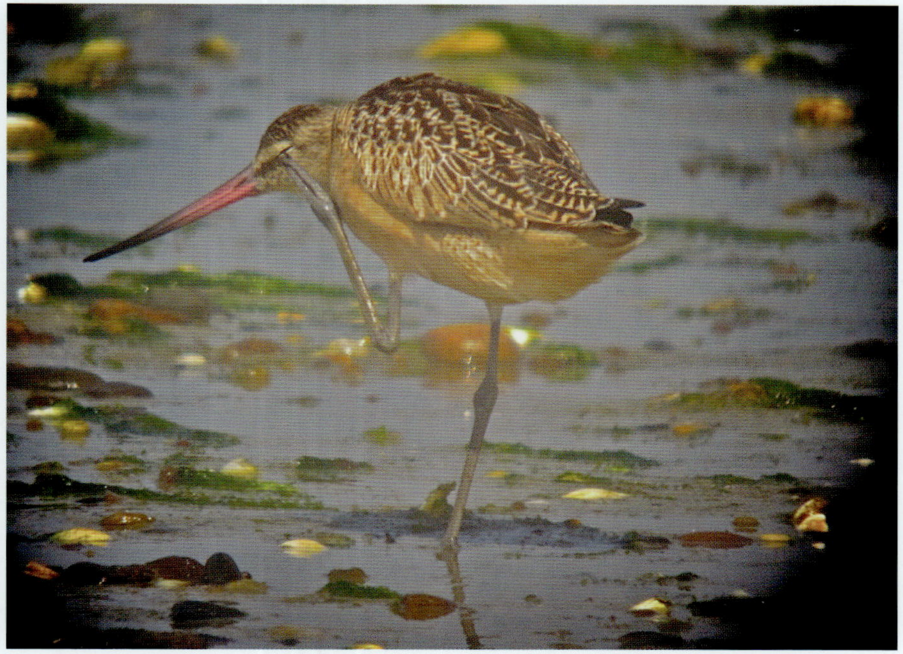

long distance travelers

left: whimbrel

right: hudsonian godwit, south beach, chatham

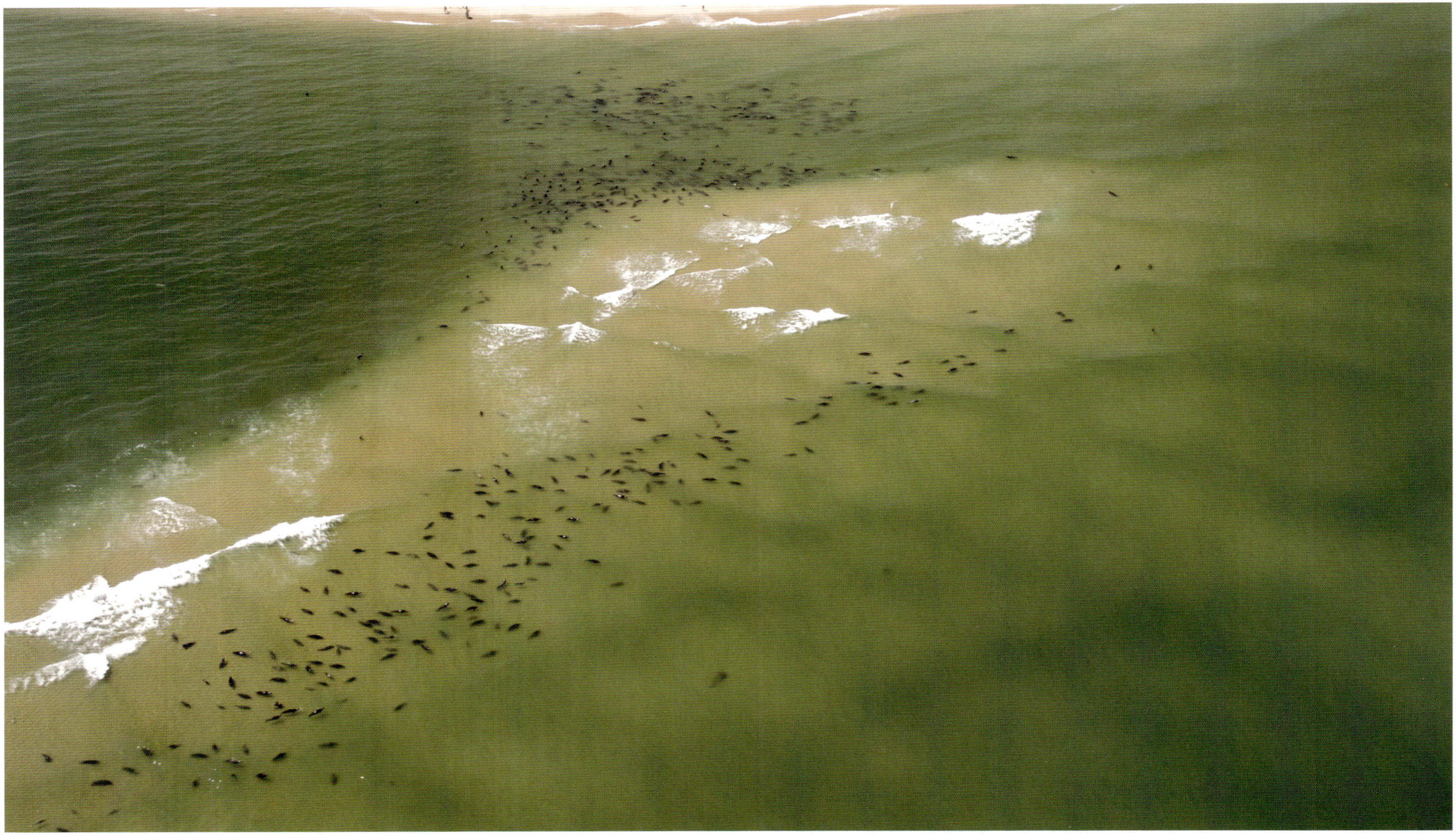

seals gather off chatham bar

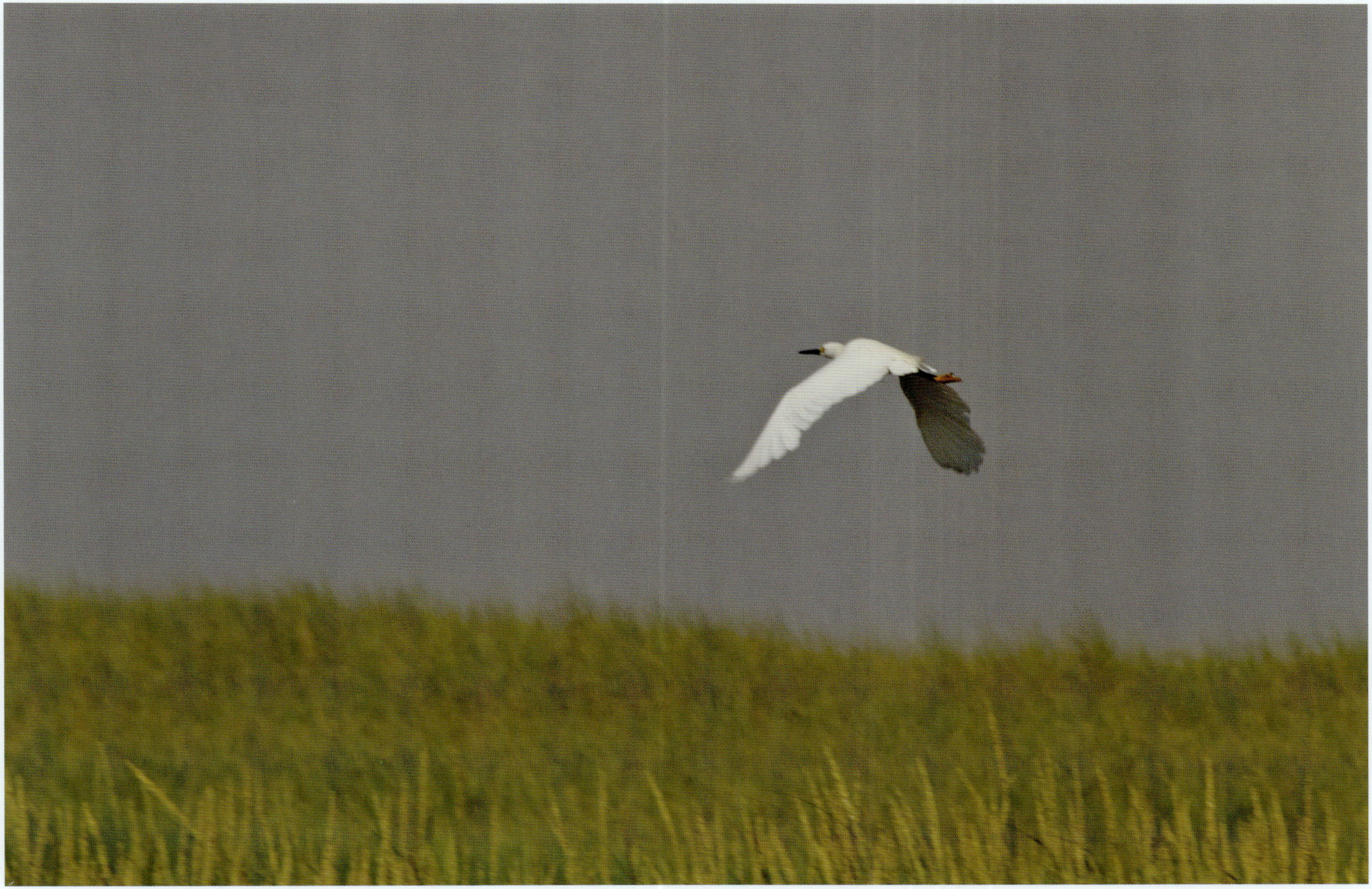

snowy egret, south beach, chatham

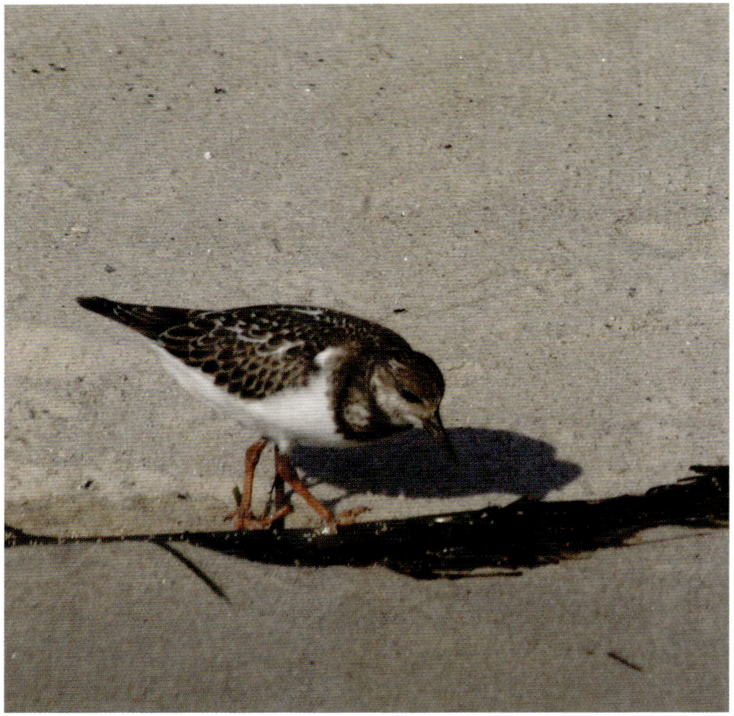

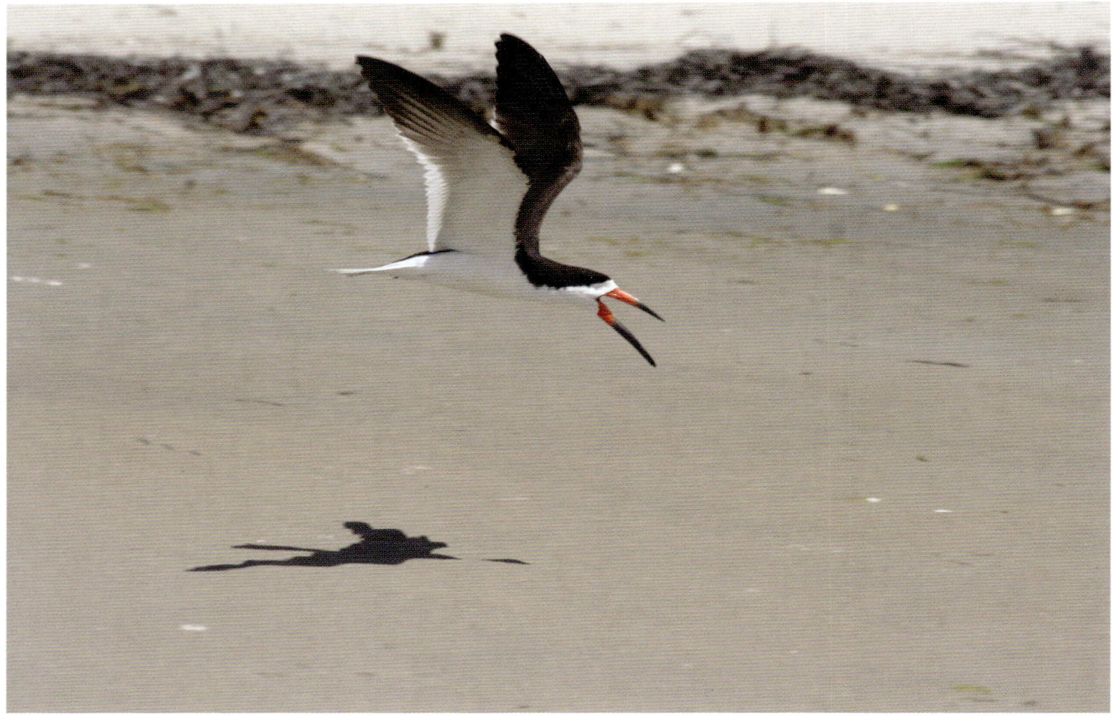

feeding

left: ruddy turnstone

right: black skimmer,
monomoy national wildlife refuge

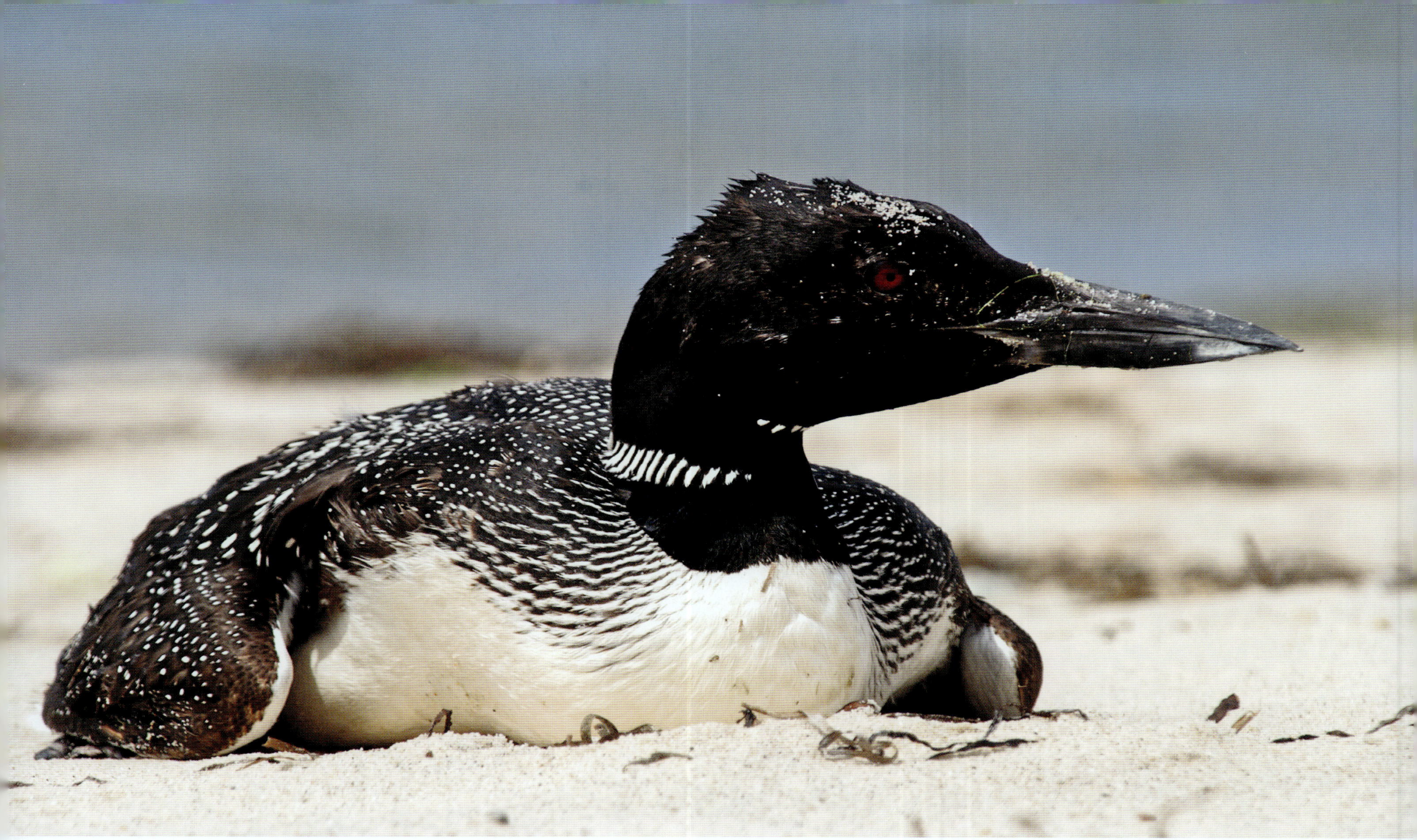

respite | common loon,
monomoy national wildlife refuge

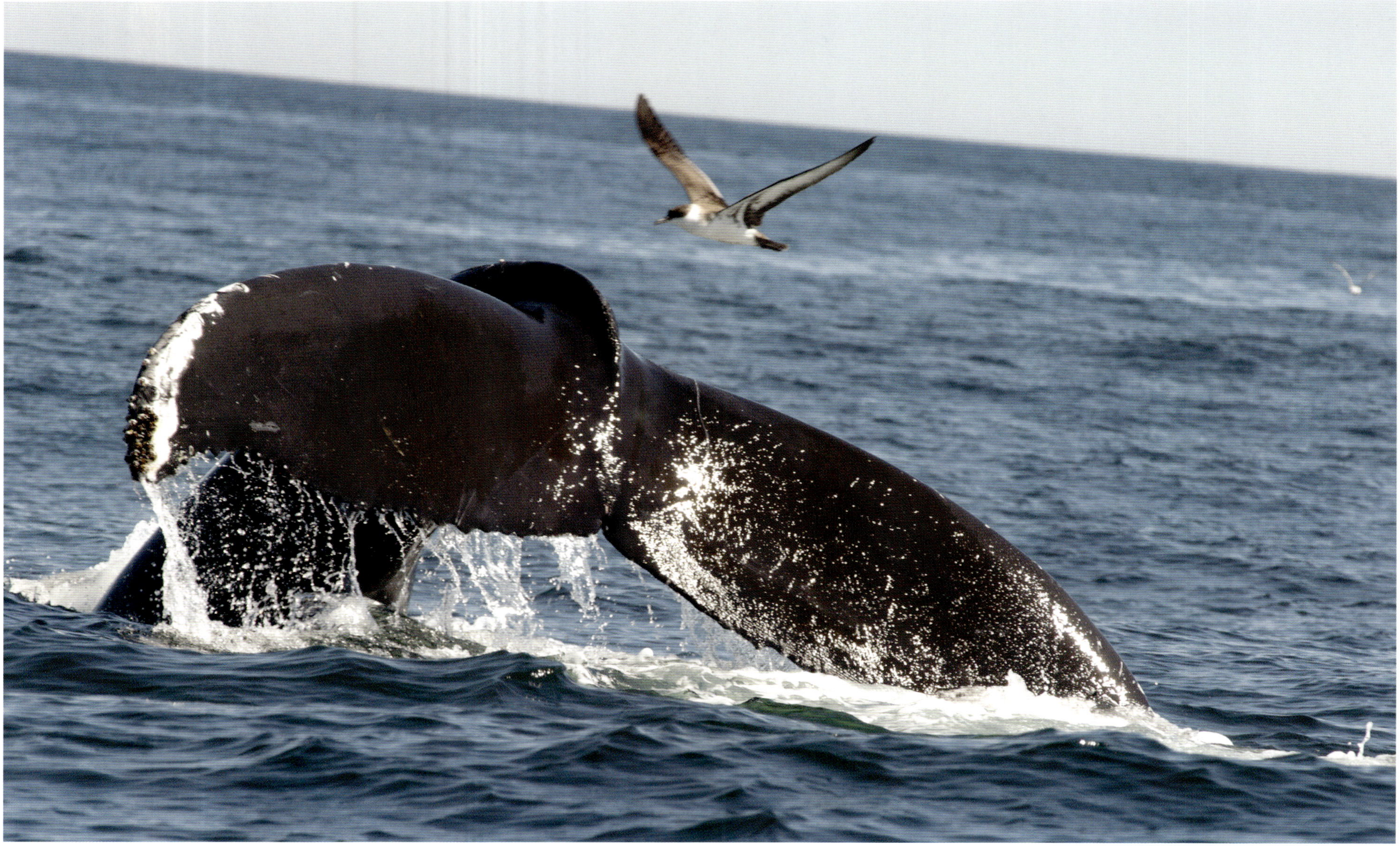

humpback and greater shearwater,
off chatham

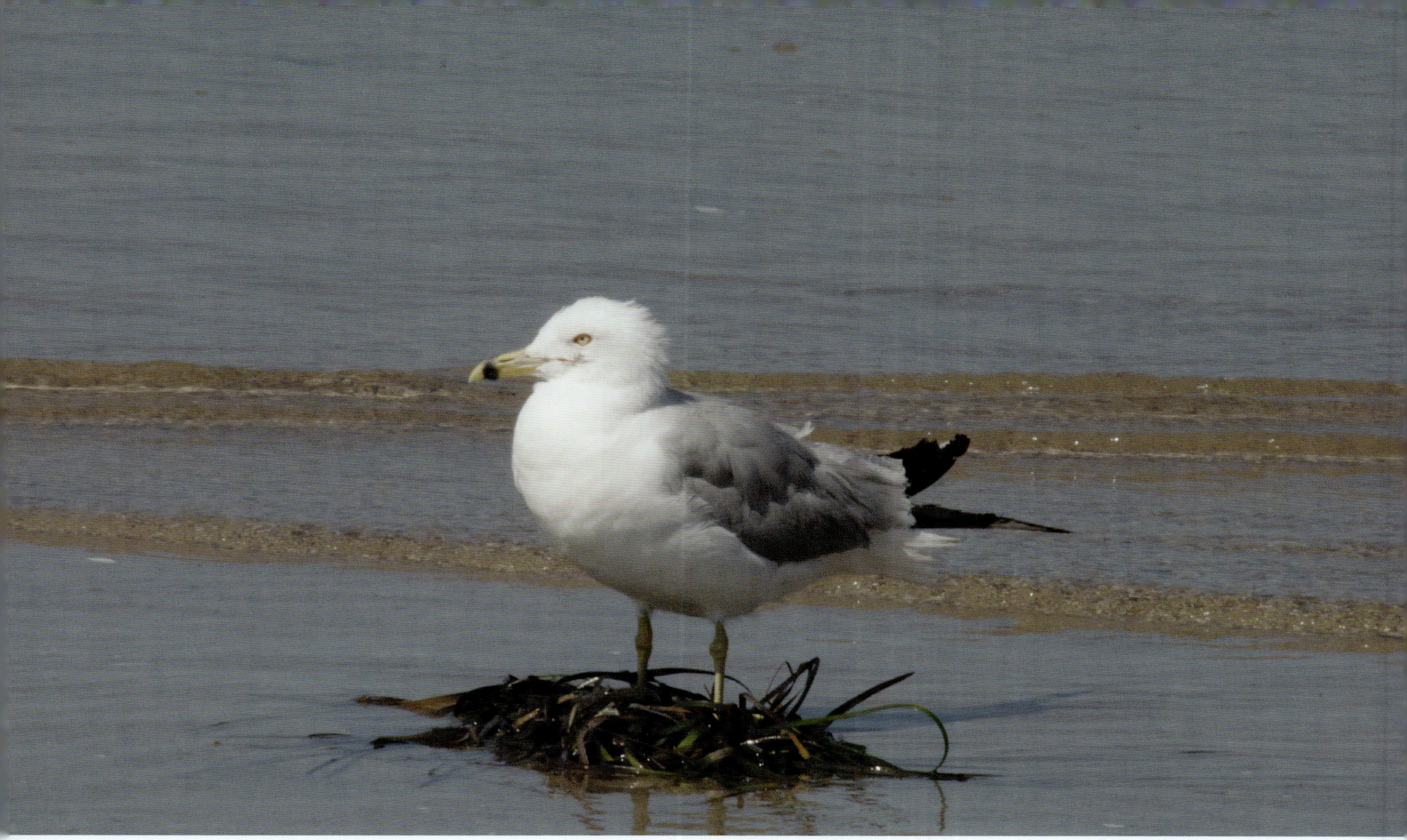

sea nest

ringed billed gull,
north beach island, chatham

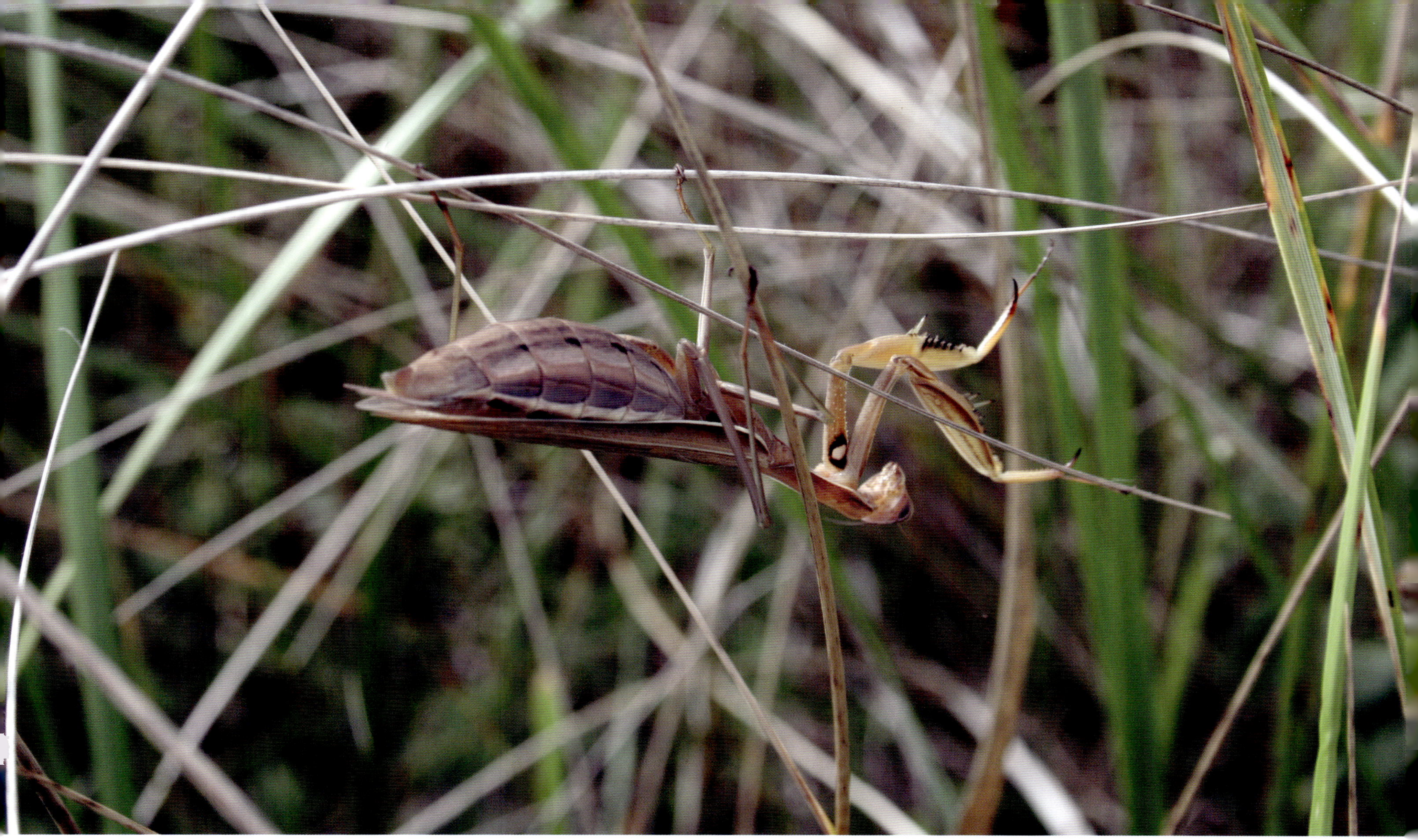

under cover

praying mantis,
north beach island, chatham

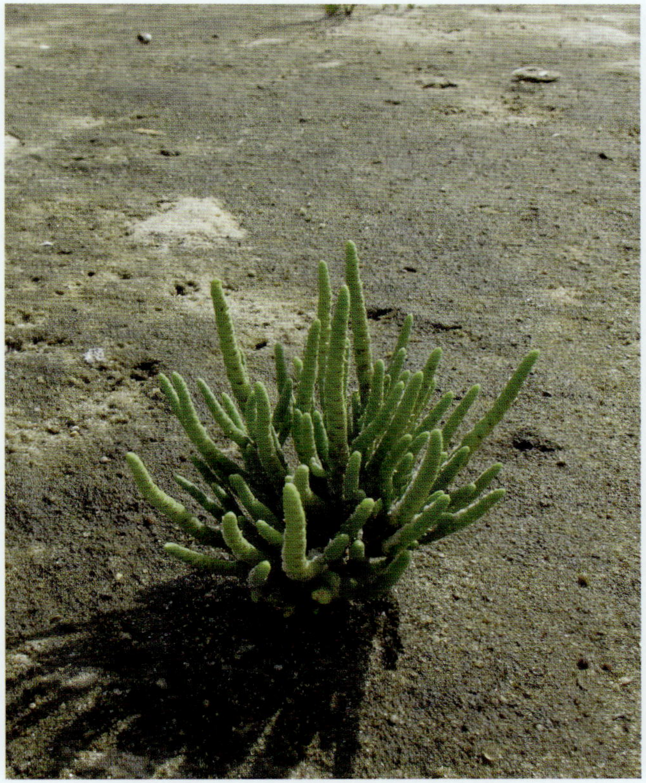 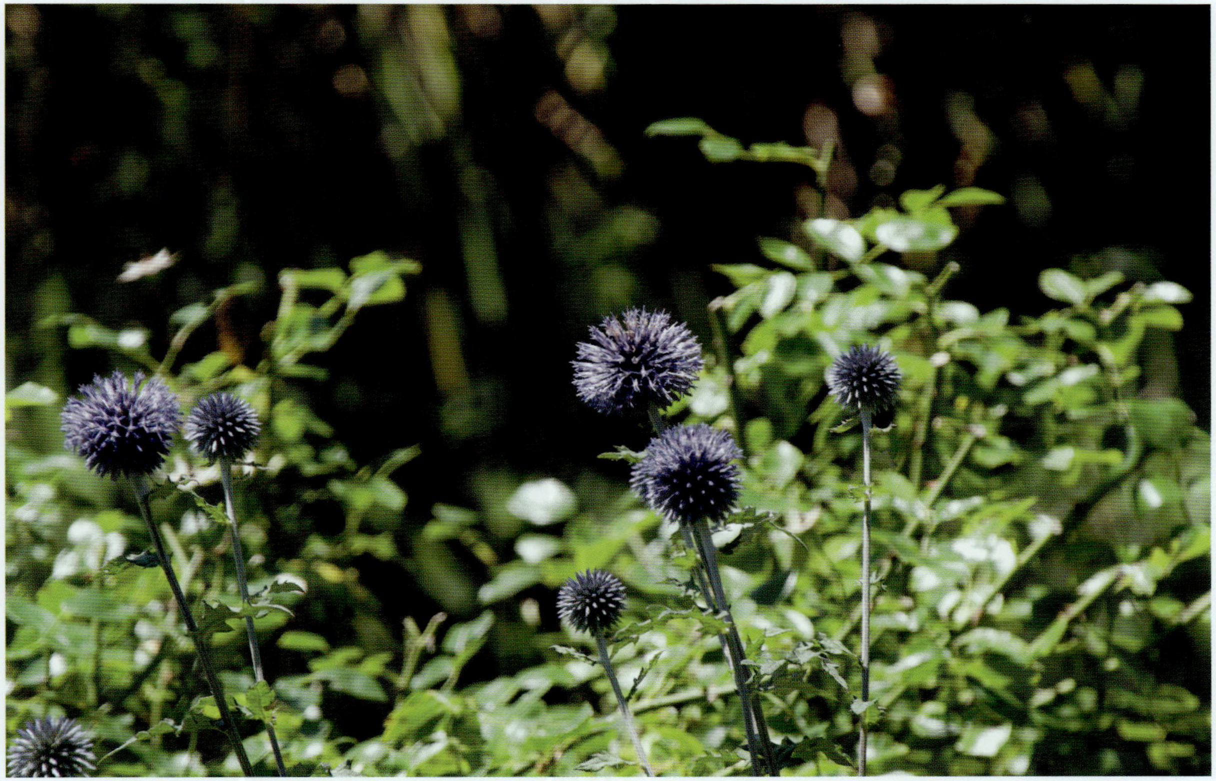

surf and turf

pickleweed and thistle,
chatham

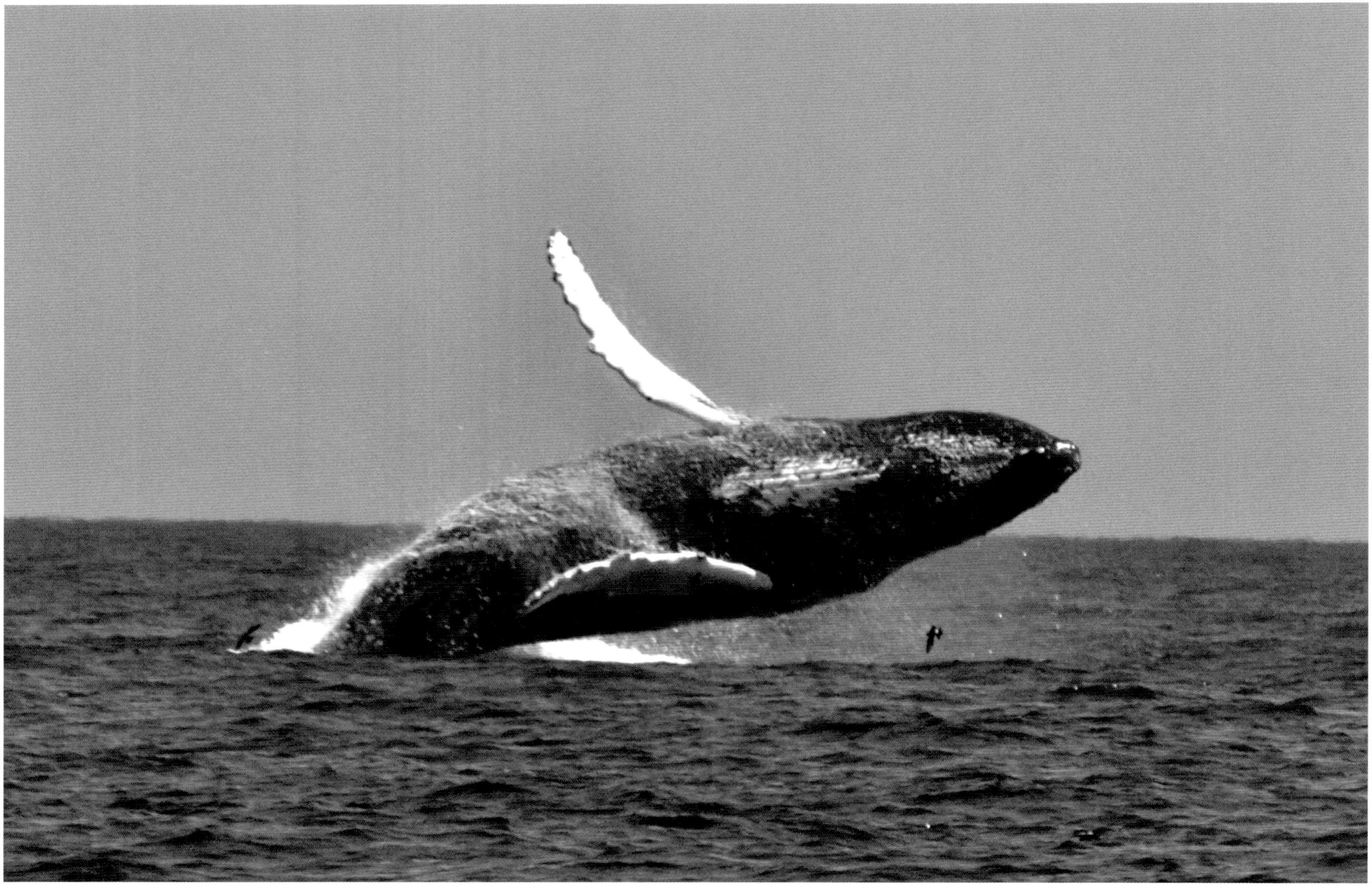

full breach

humpback whale, off chatham

moonwalk

humpback whale,
off chatham

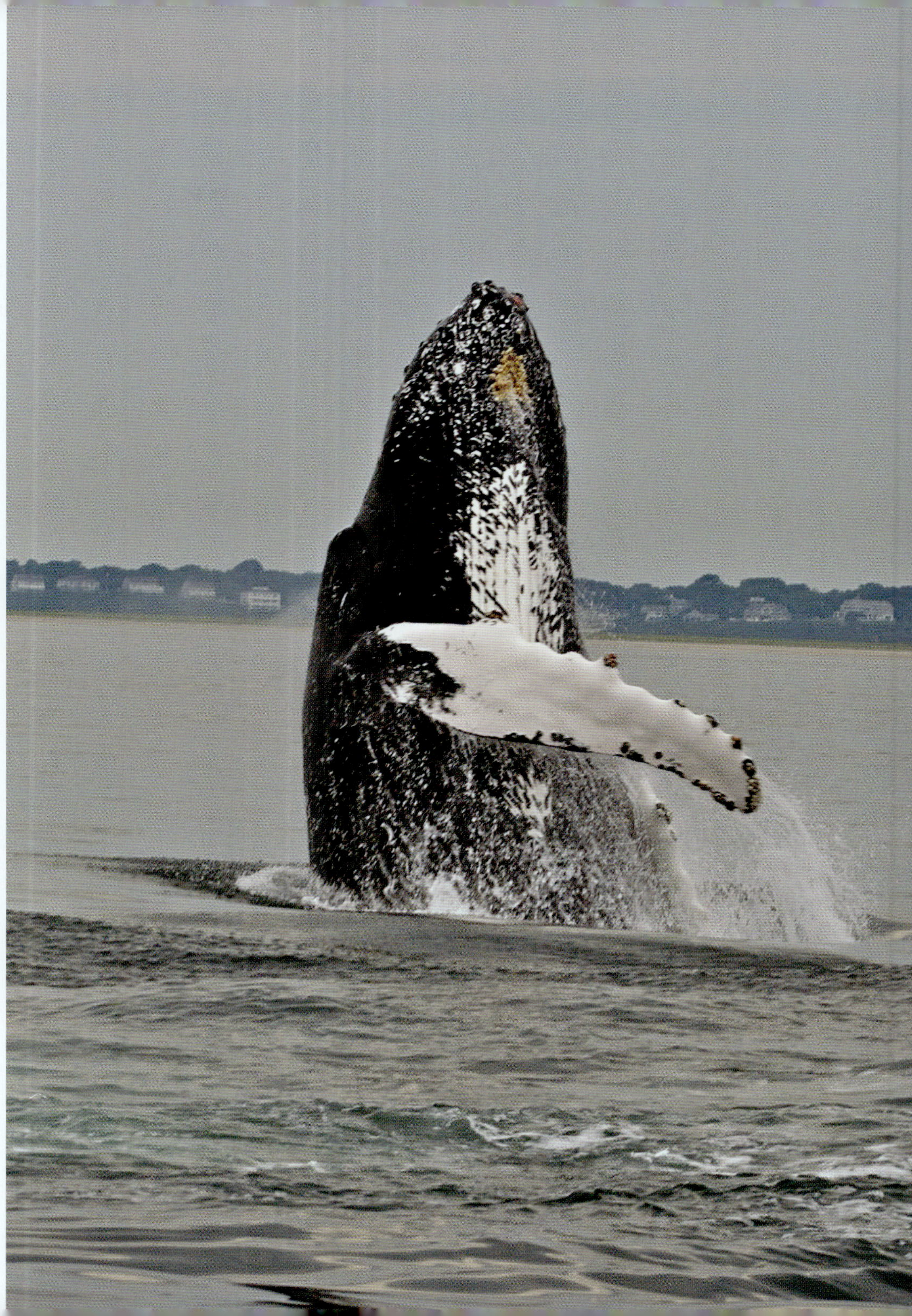

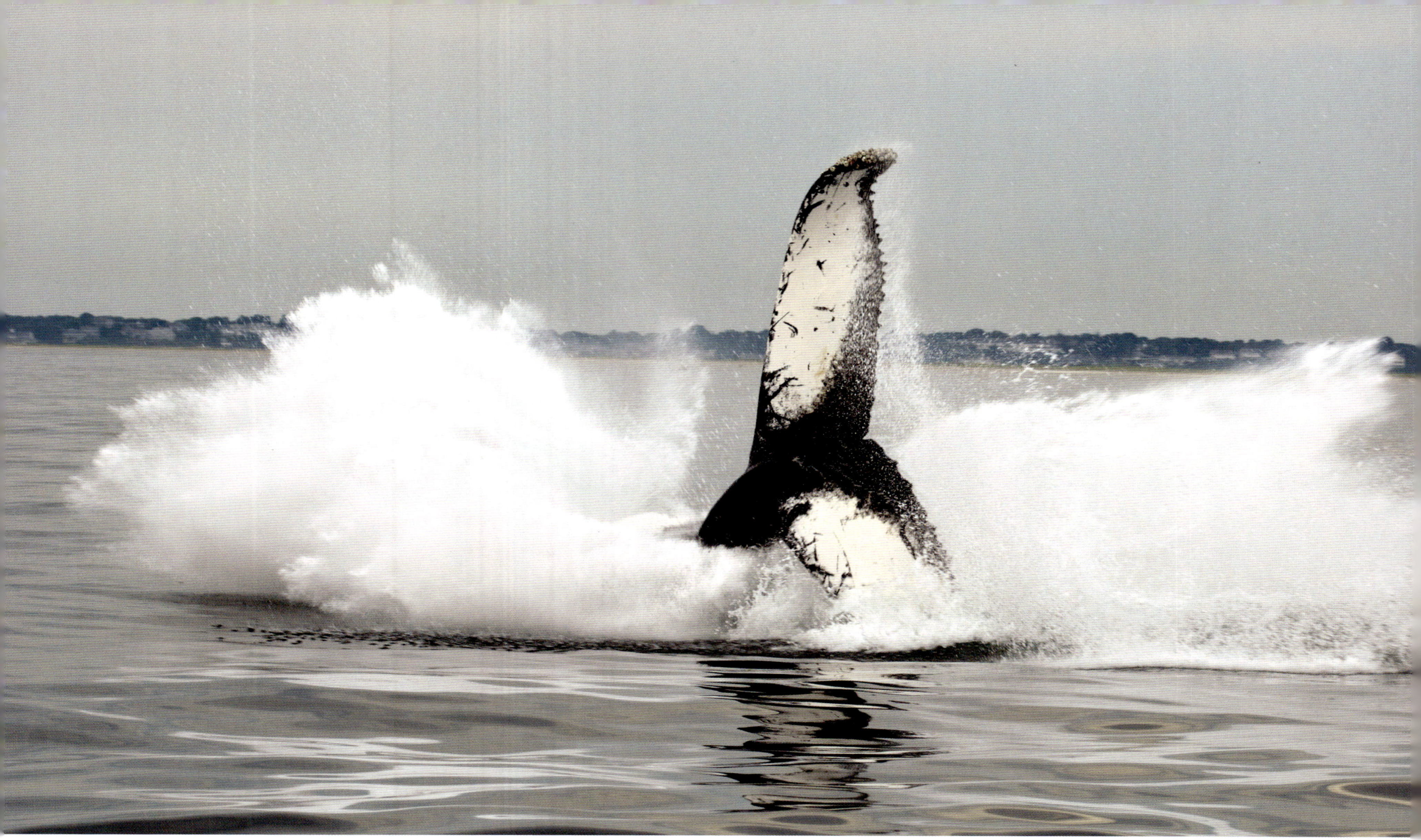

humpback whale,
off chatham

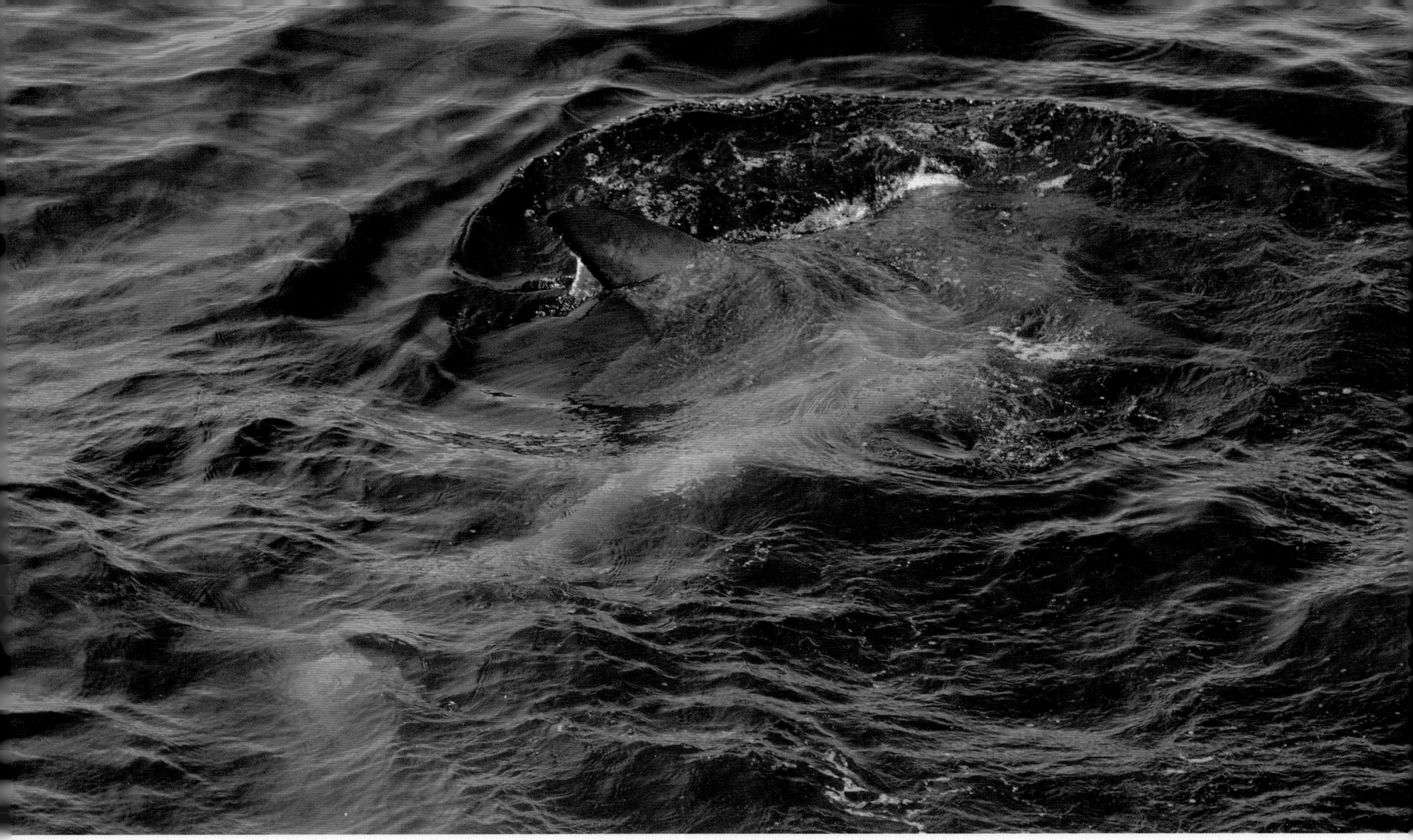

white shark, shark alley,
off south beach, chatham

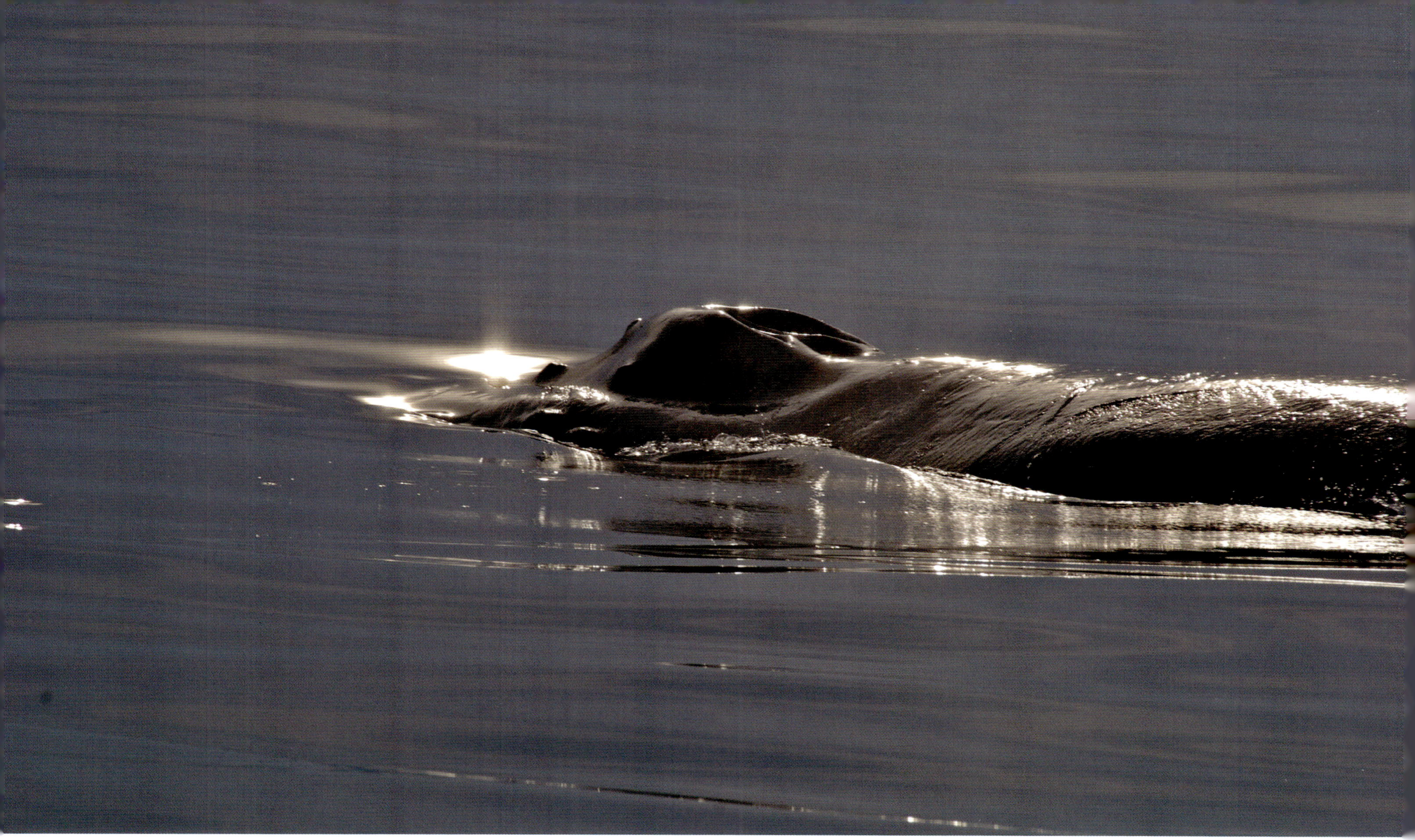

“logging” at sunset

humpback whale,
off chatham

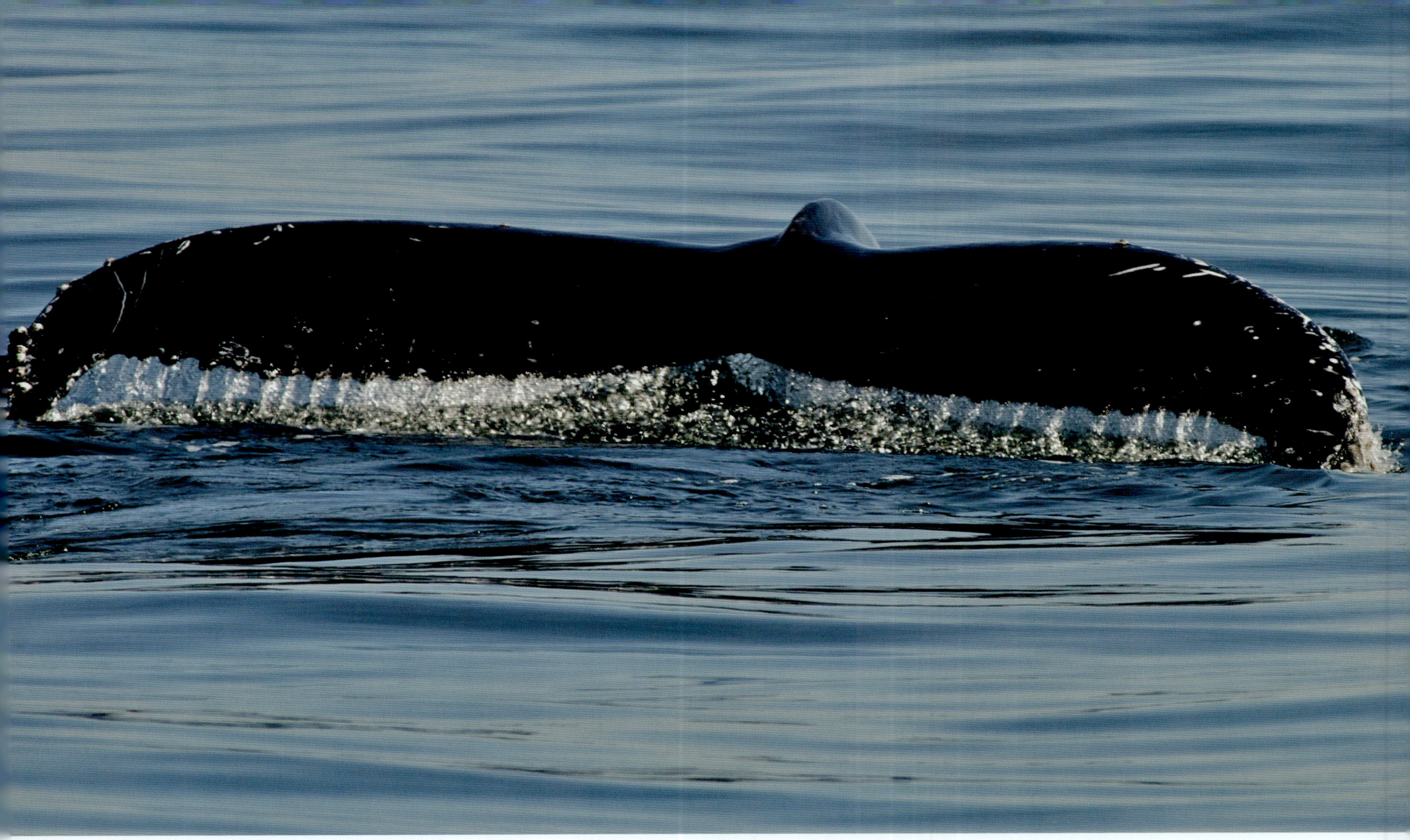

cascade

humpback whale,
off chatham

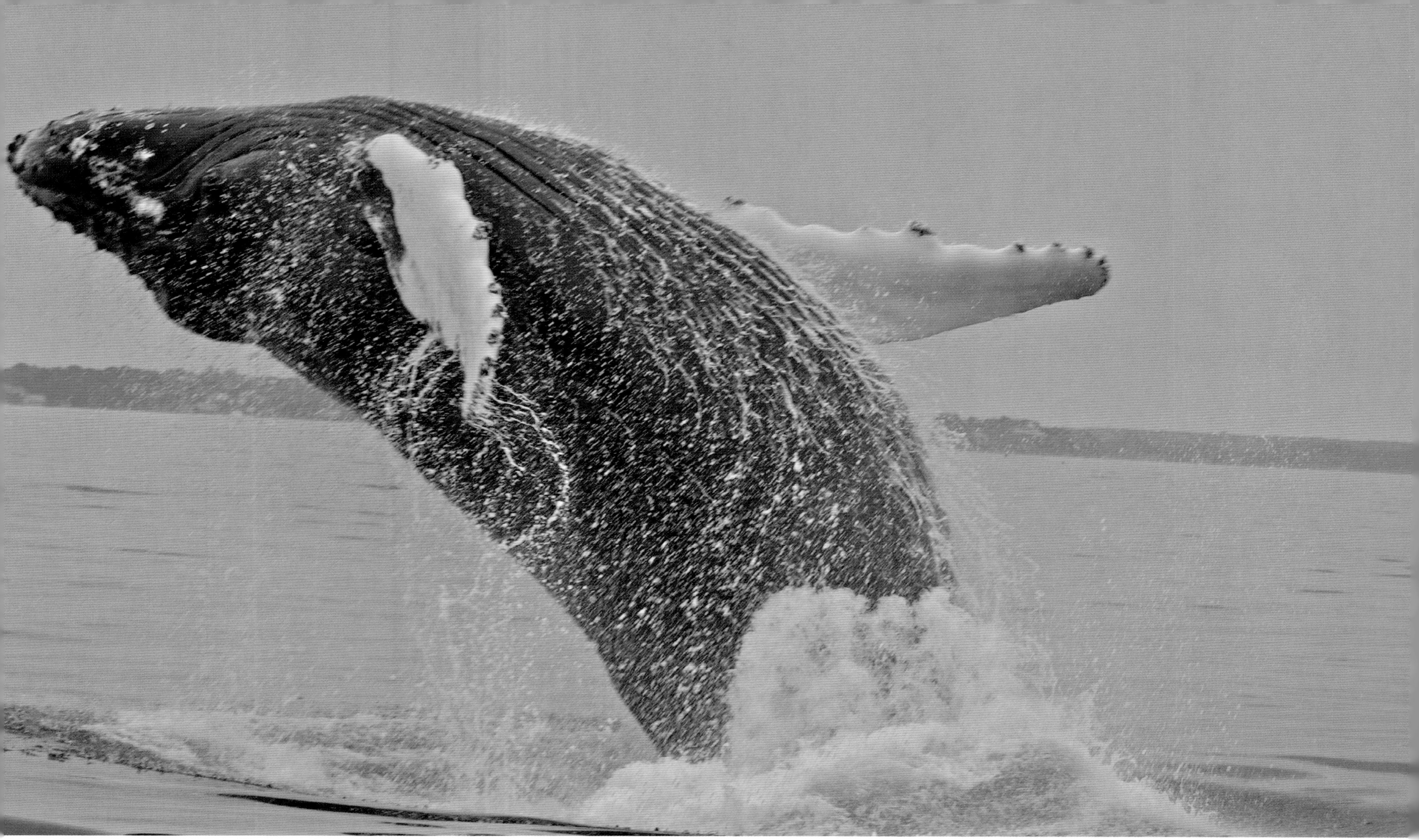

mighty arc

humpback whale,
off chatham

airborne

humpback whale (springboard's calf), off chatham

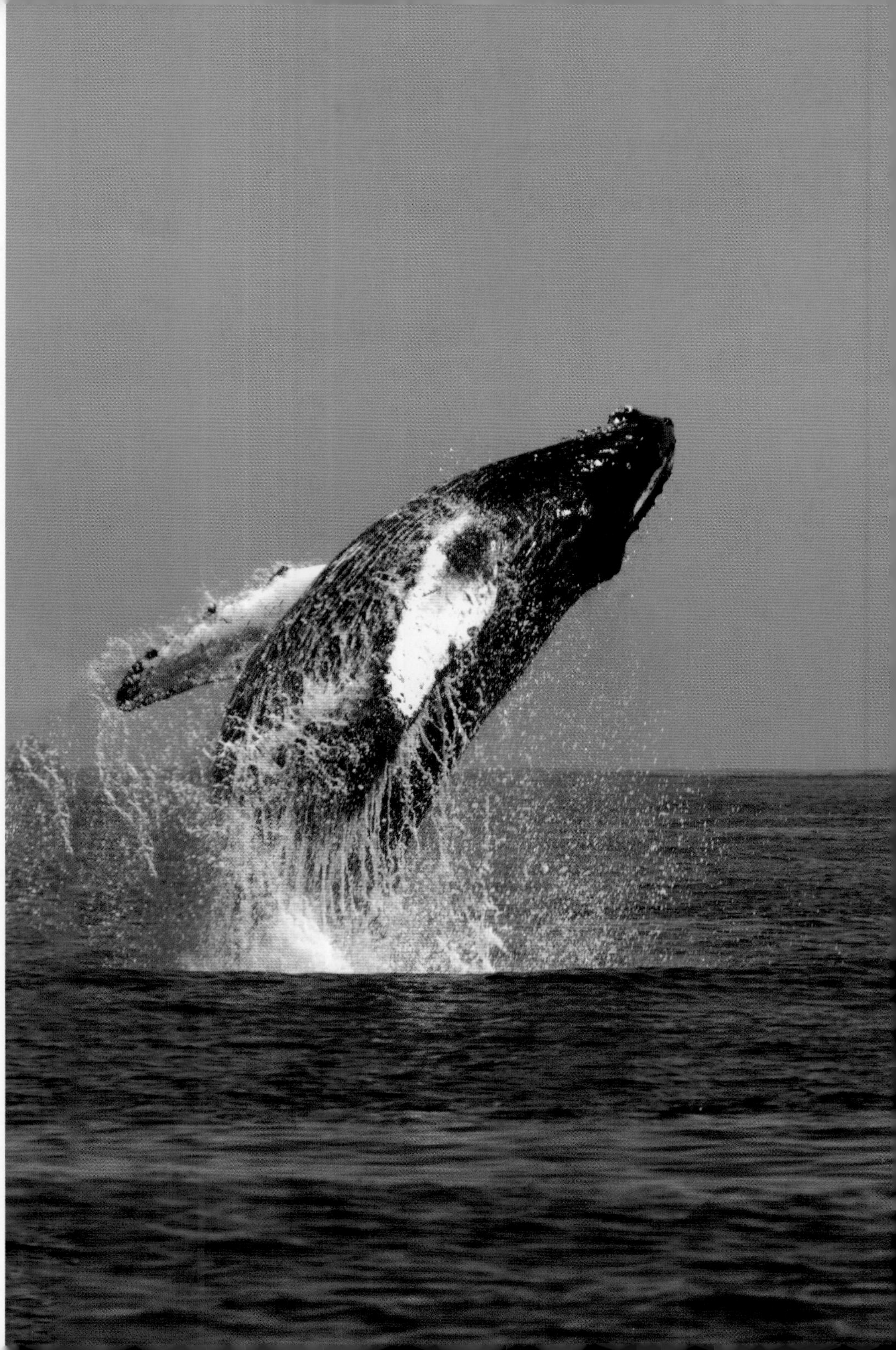

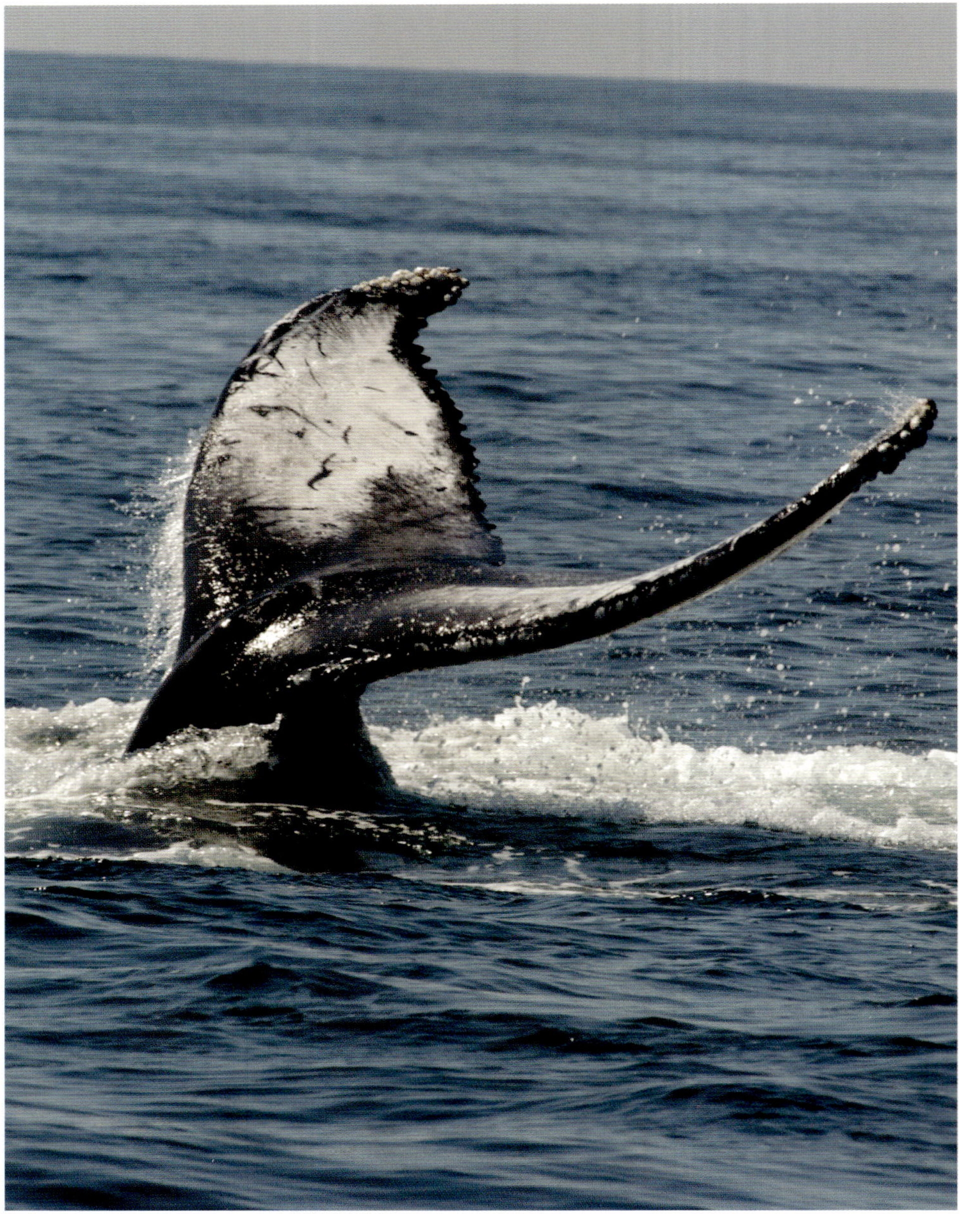

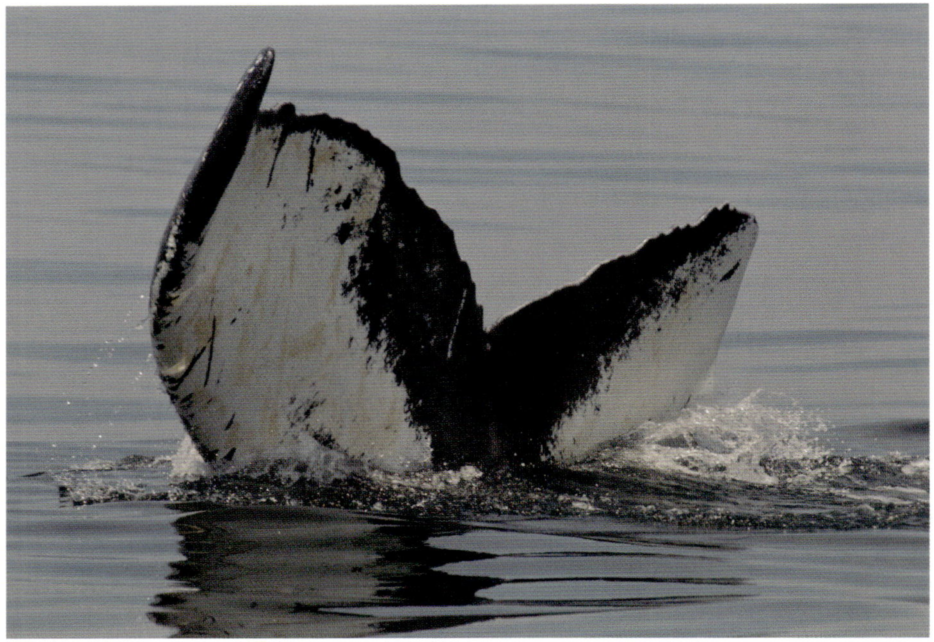

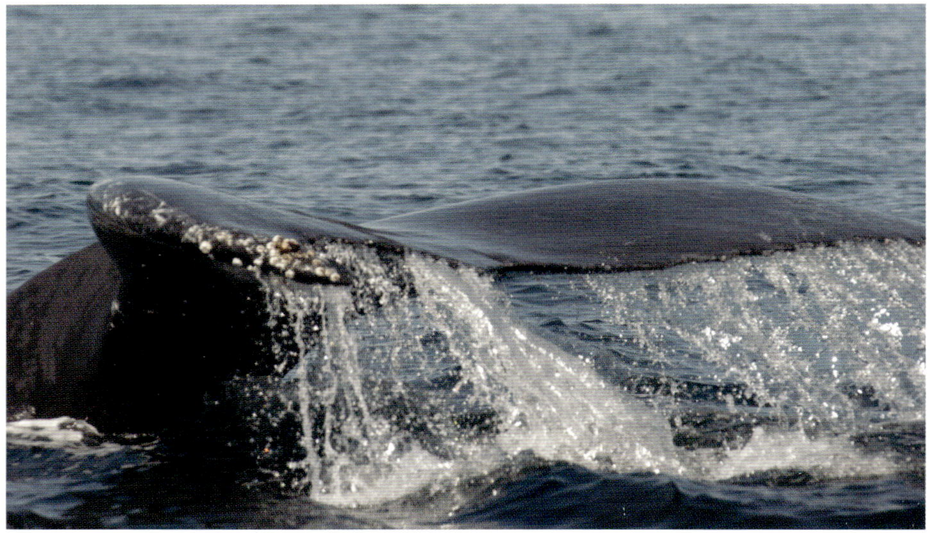

signatures

humpback flukes,
off chatham

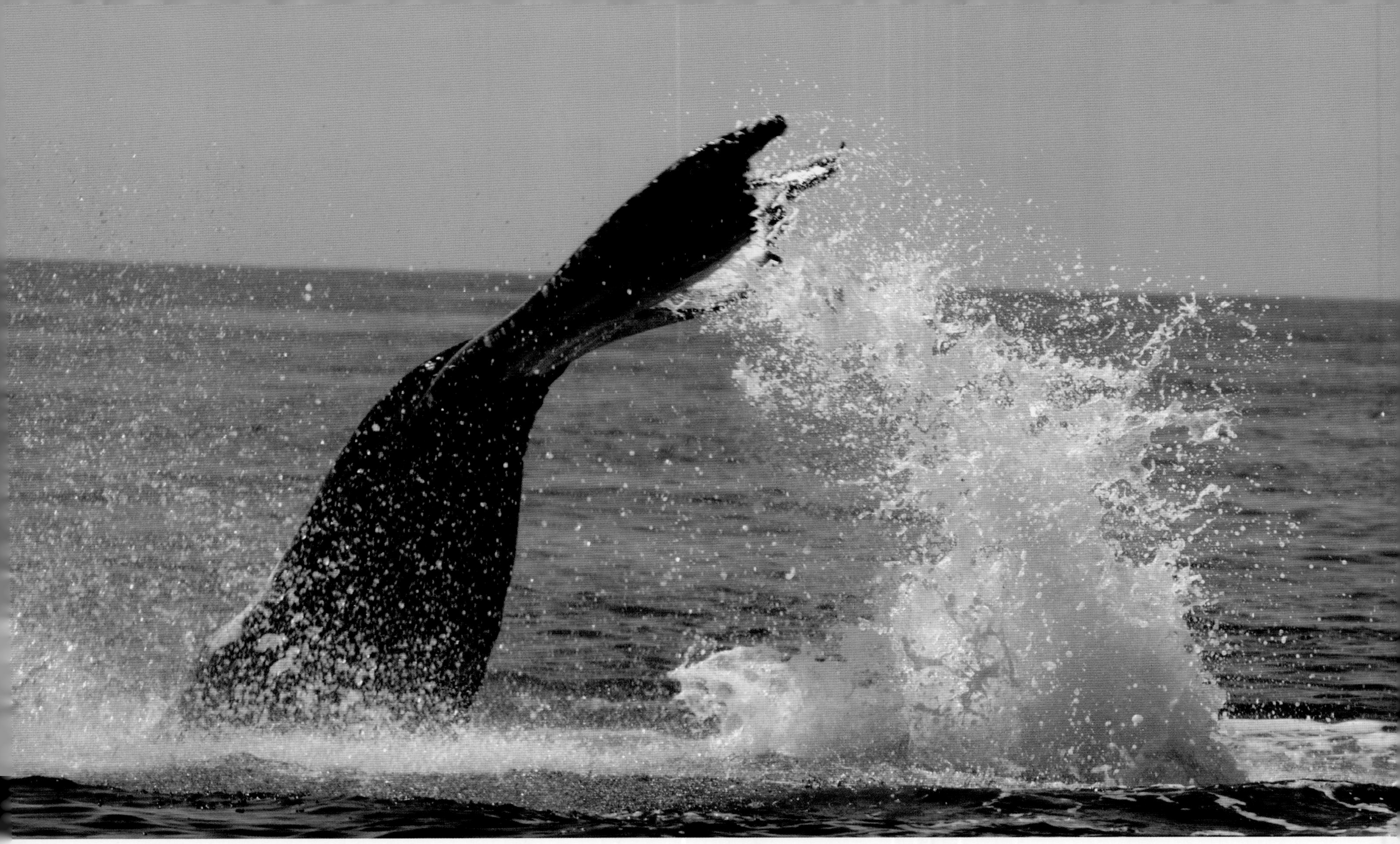

tail lobbing | humpback, off chatham

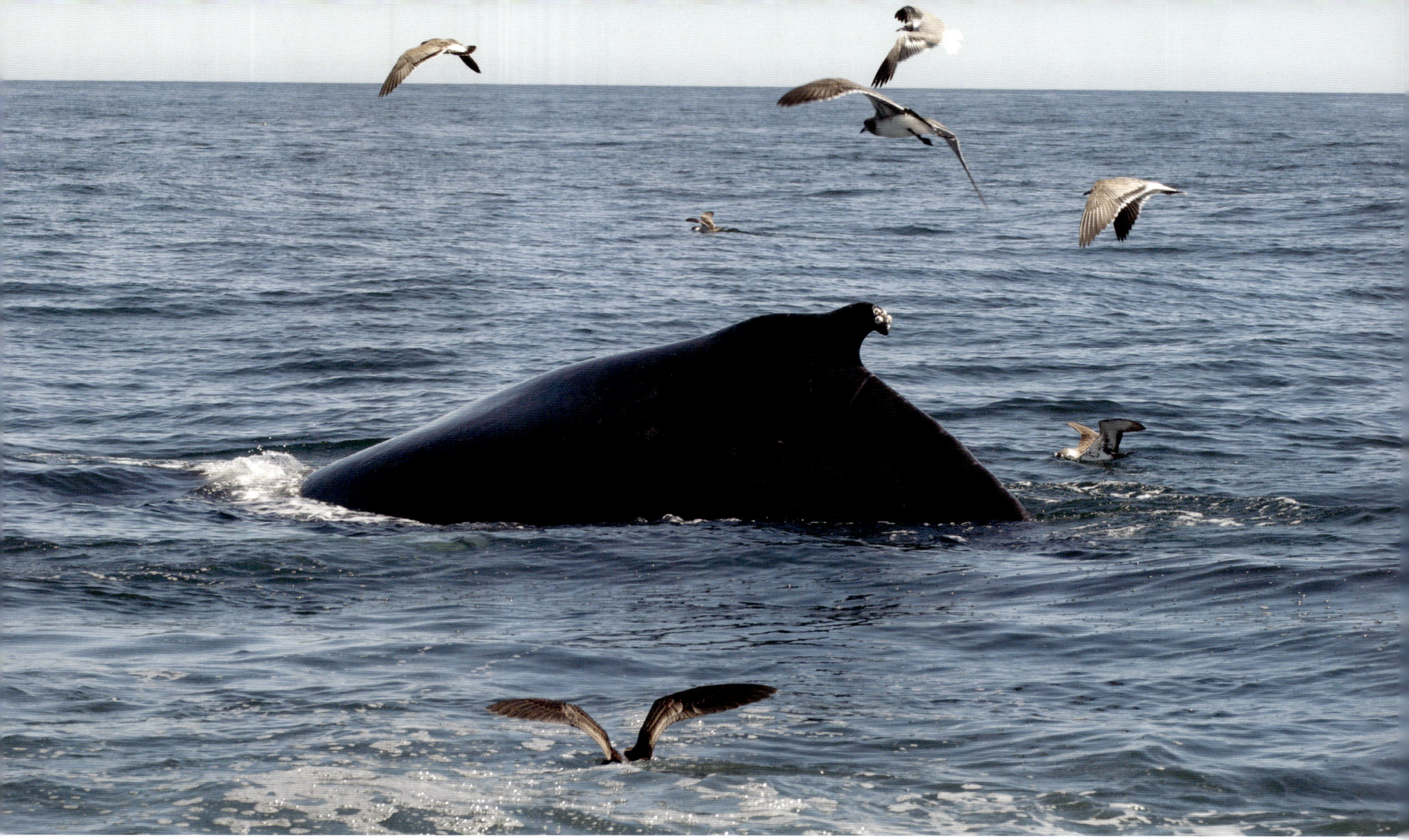

humpback whale,
off chatham

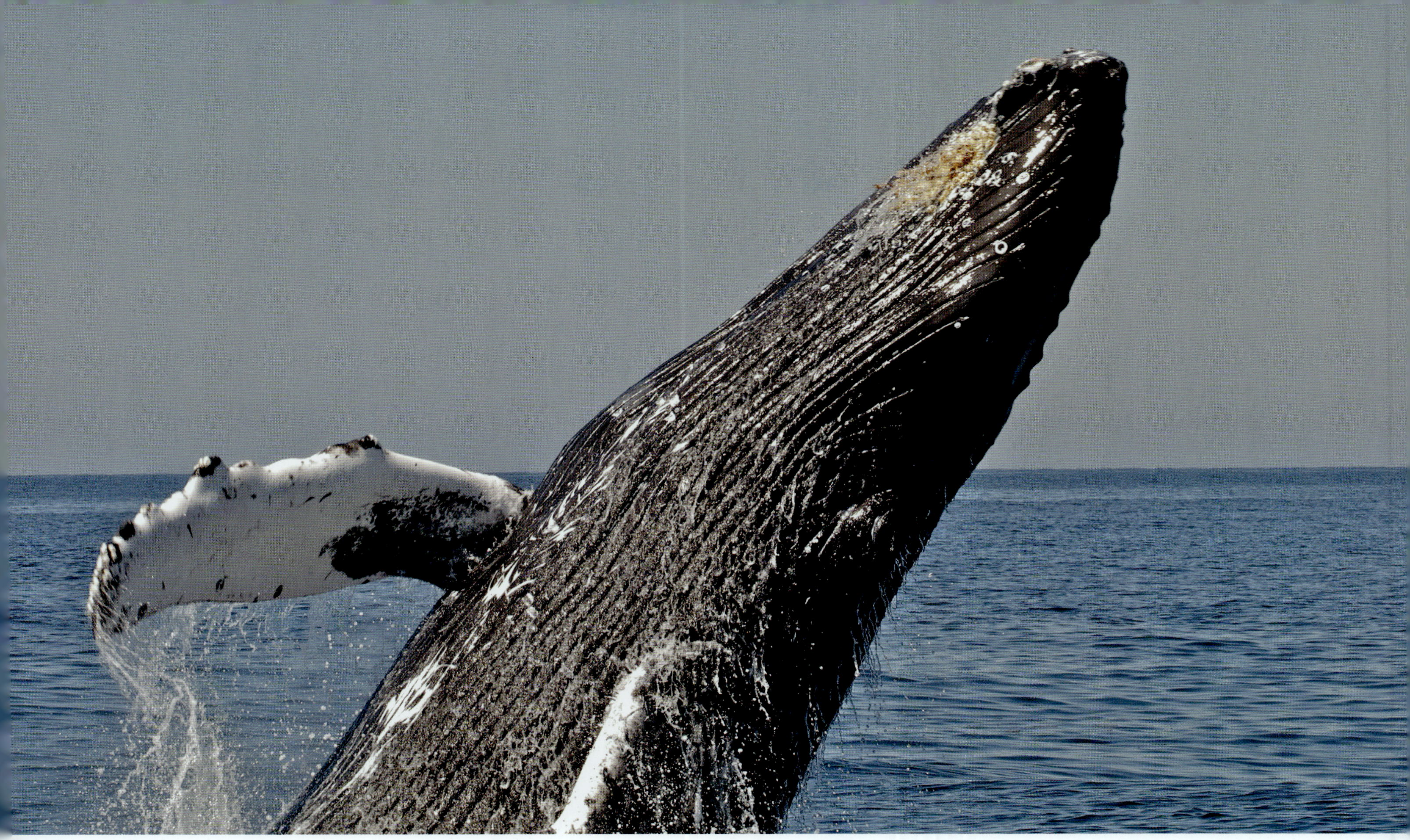

humpback whale,
off chatham

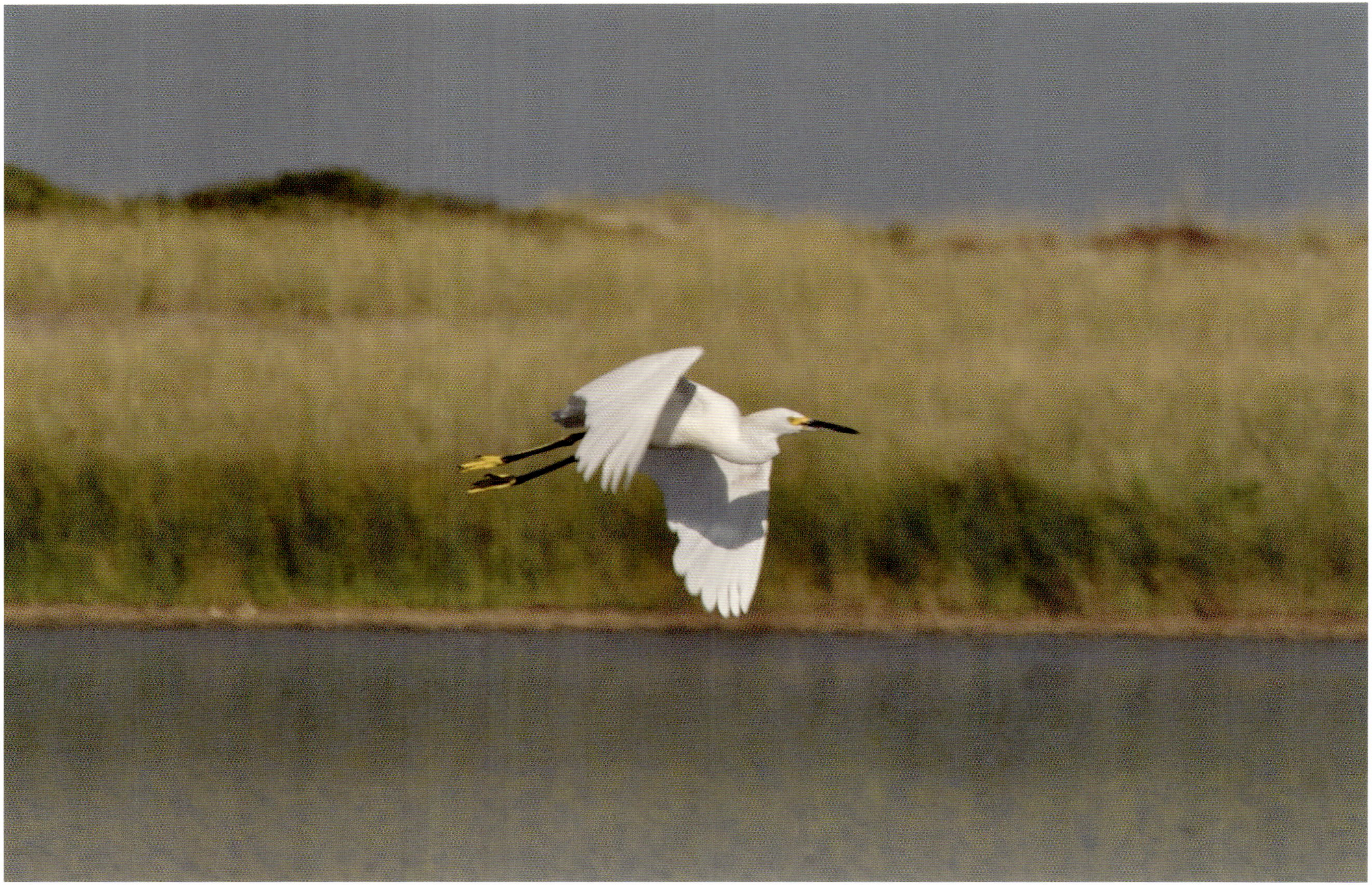

grace

snowy egret, powder hole,
monomoy national wildlife refuge

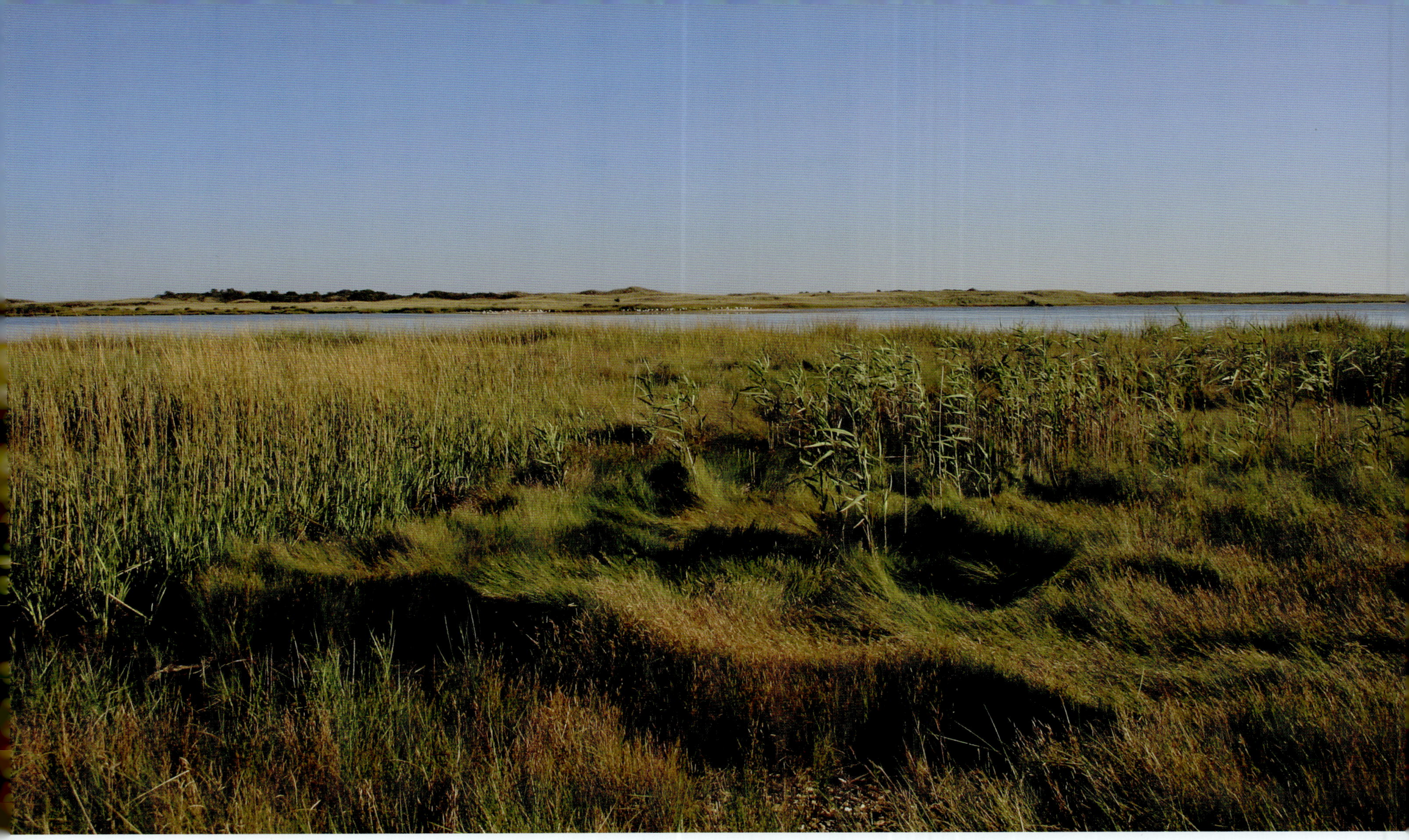

bluegrass

powder hole, monomoy
national wildlife refuge, chatham

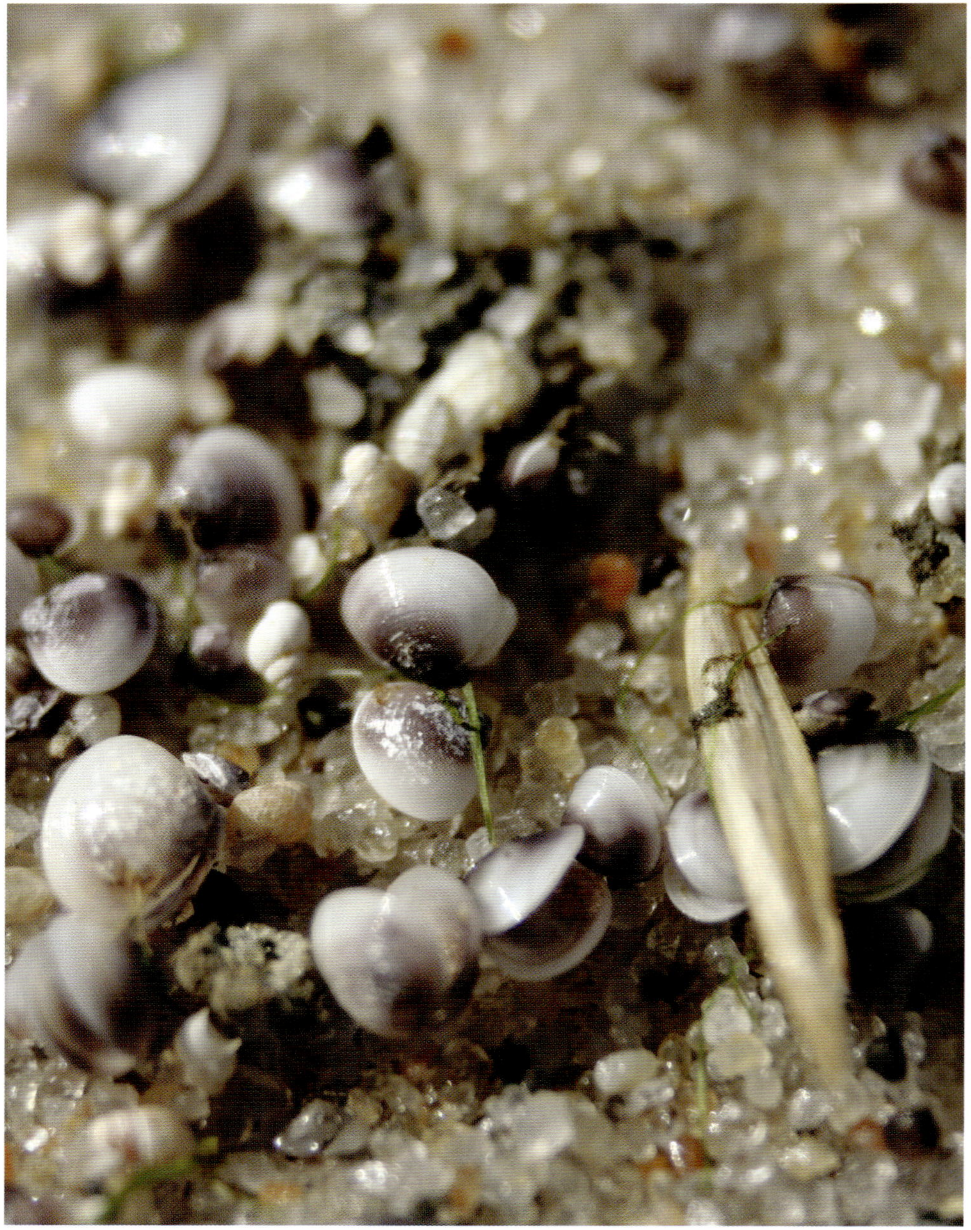

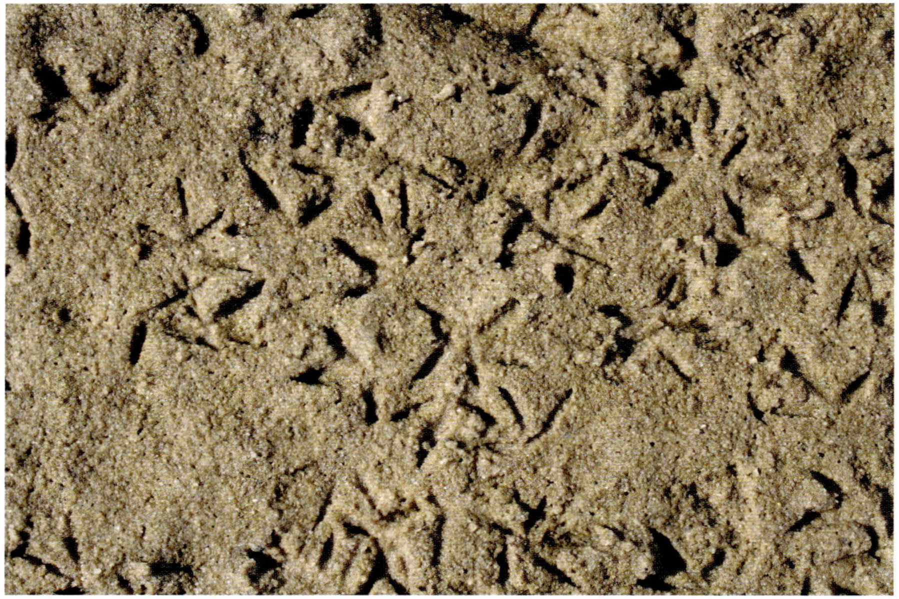

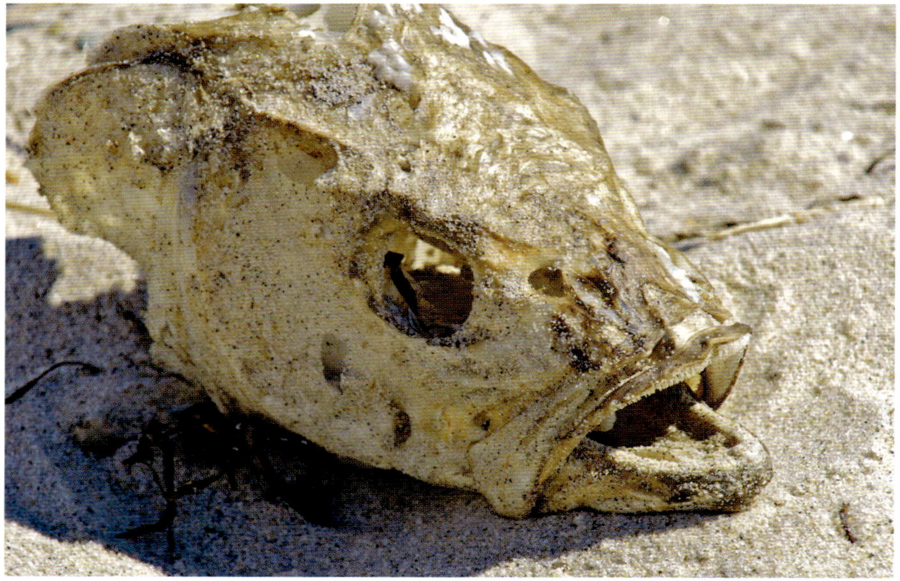

clues

shells, bird prints, and bluefish skeleton, powder hole,
monomoy national wildlife refuge

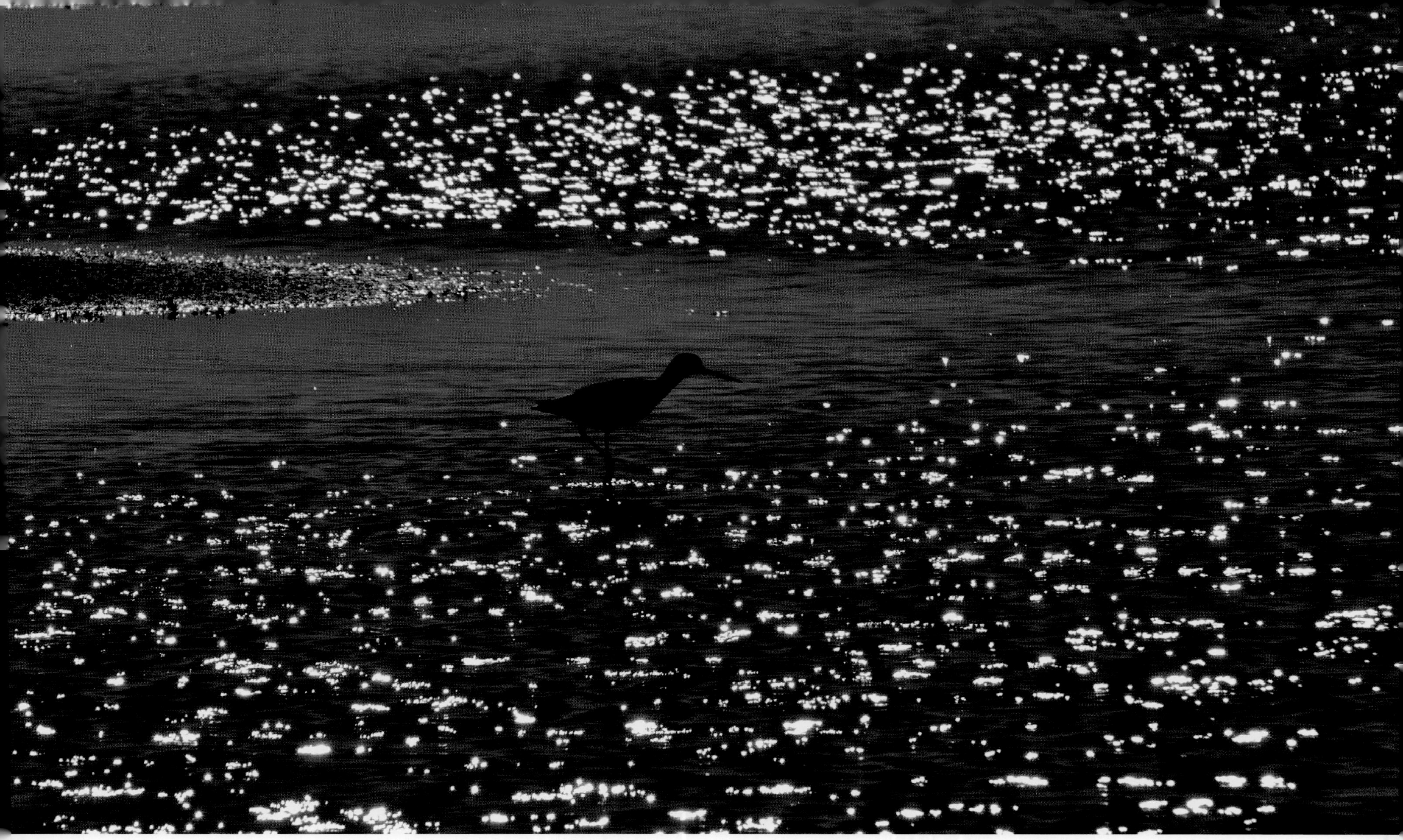

reflections | yellowlegs, powder hole, monomoy national wildlife refuge

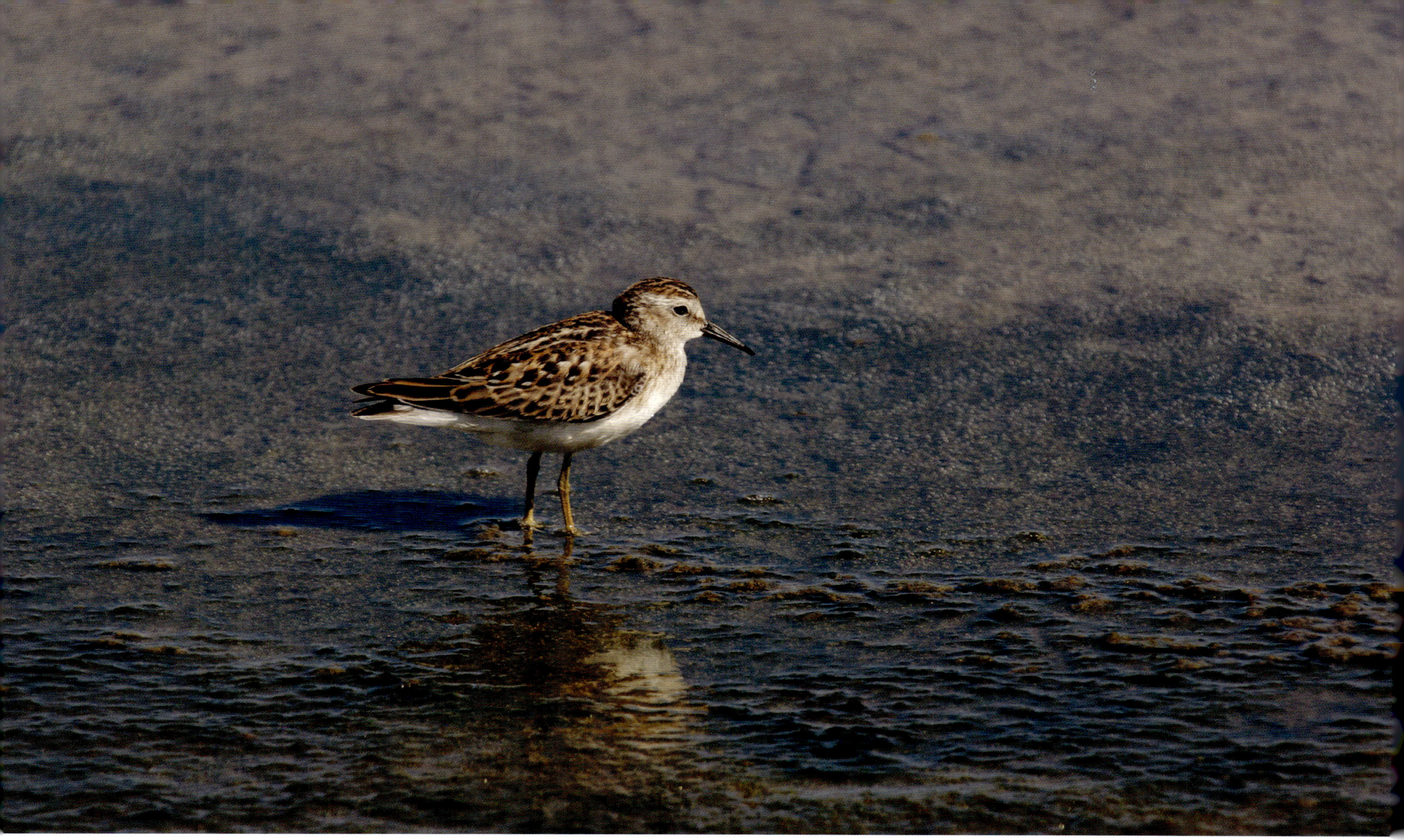

miles to go...

least sandpiper, powder hole,
monomoy national wildlife refuge

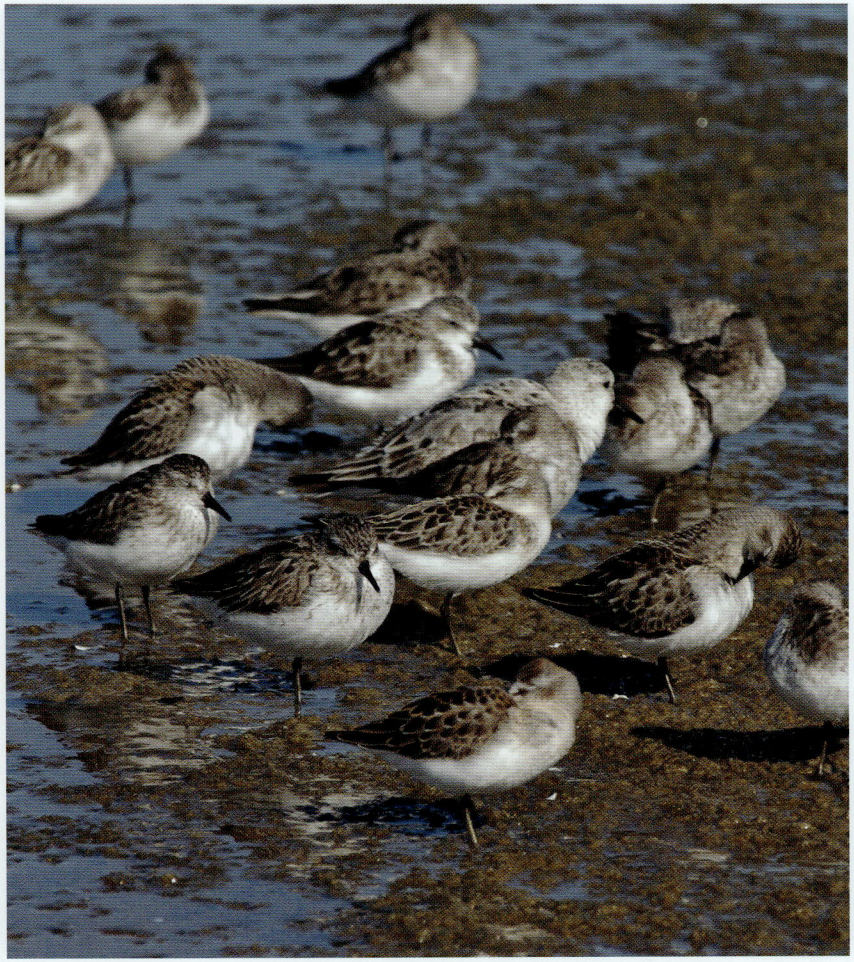

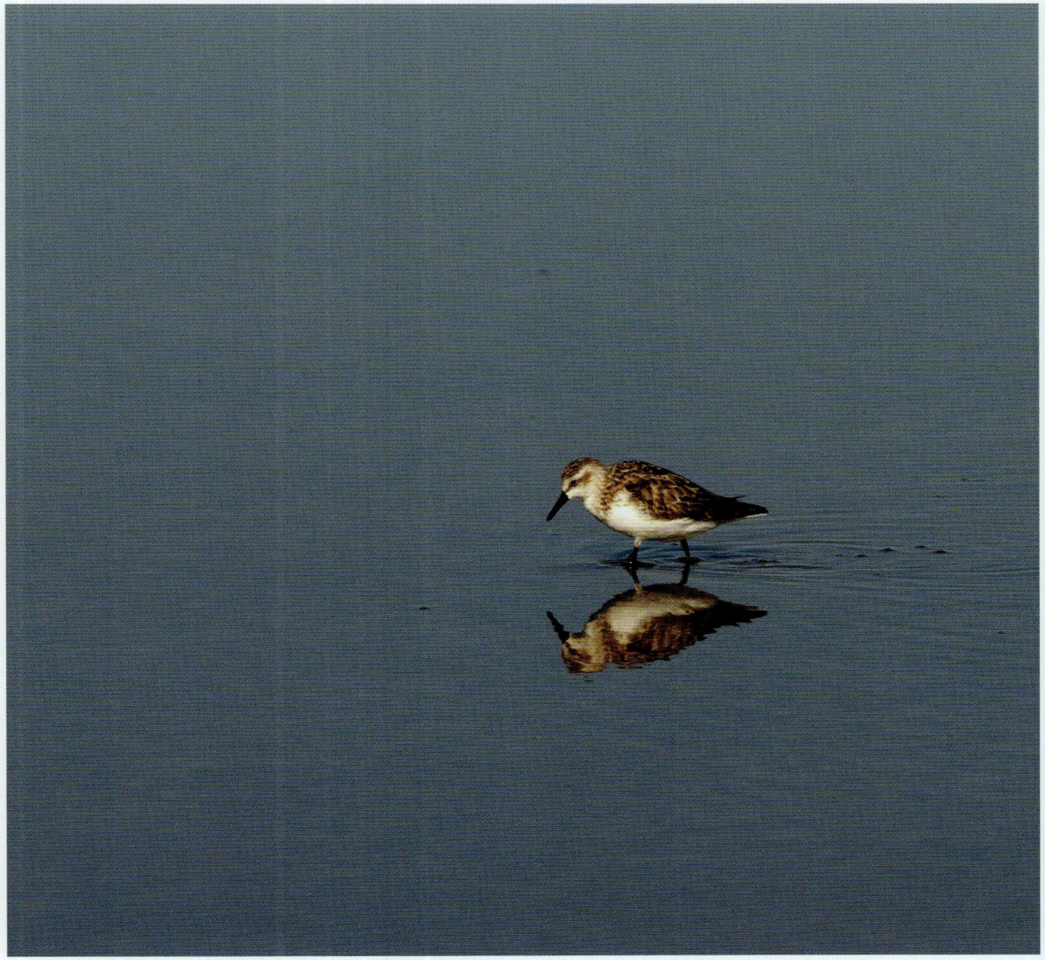

pit stop

sanderling and semipalmated sandpipers, powder hole,
monomoy national wildlife refuge

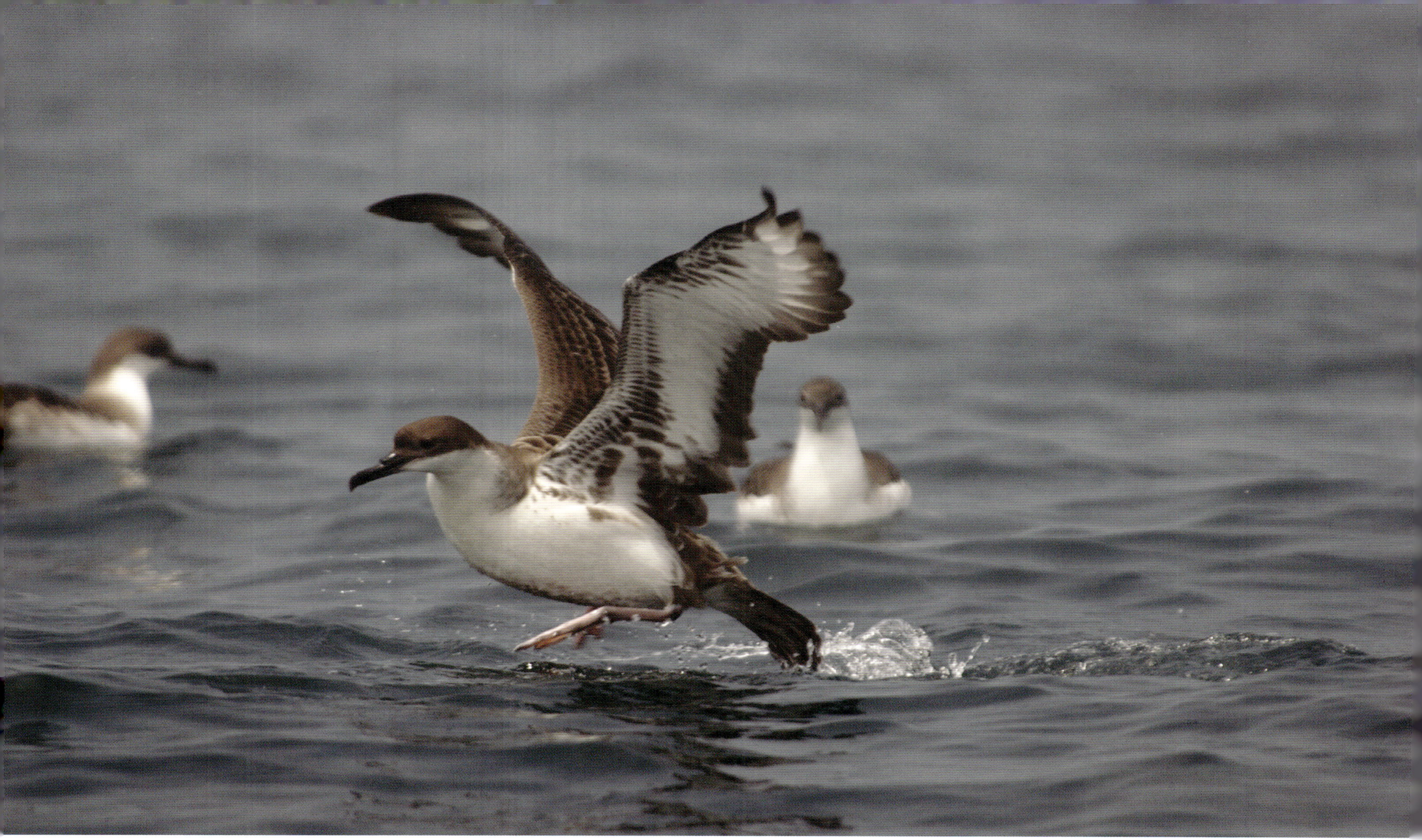

touching down

greater shearwaters at sea, off chatham

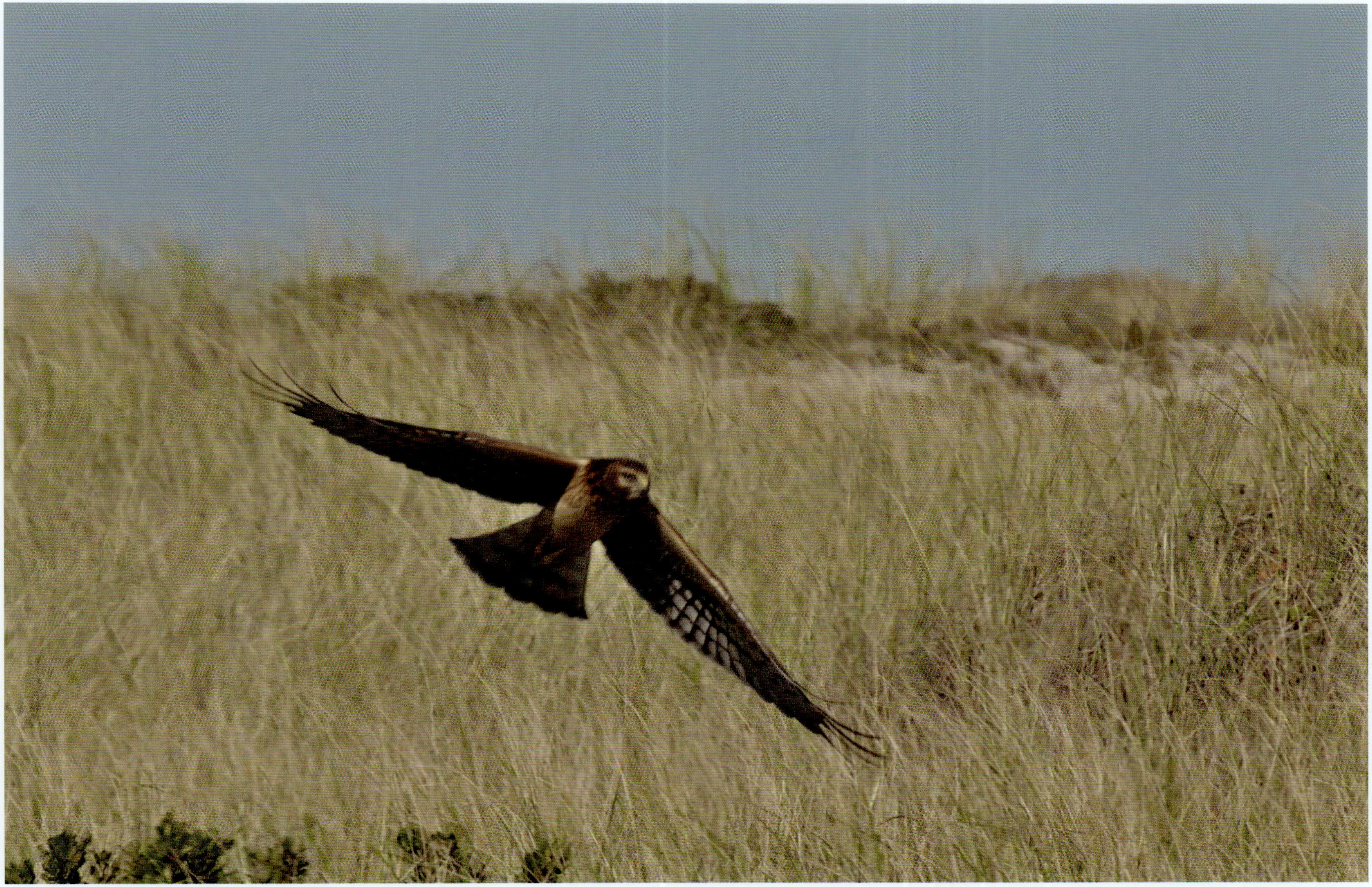

seeking prey

northern harrier, powder hole, monomoy national wildlife refuge

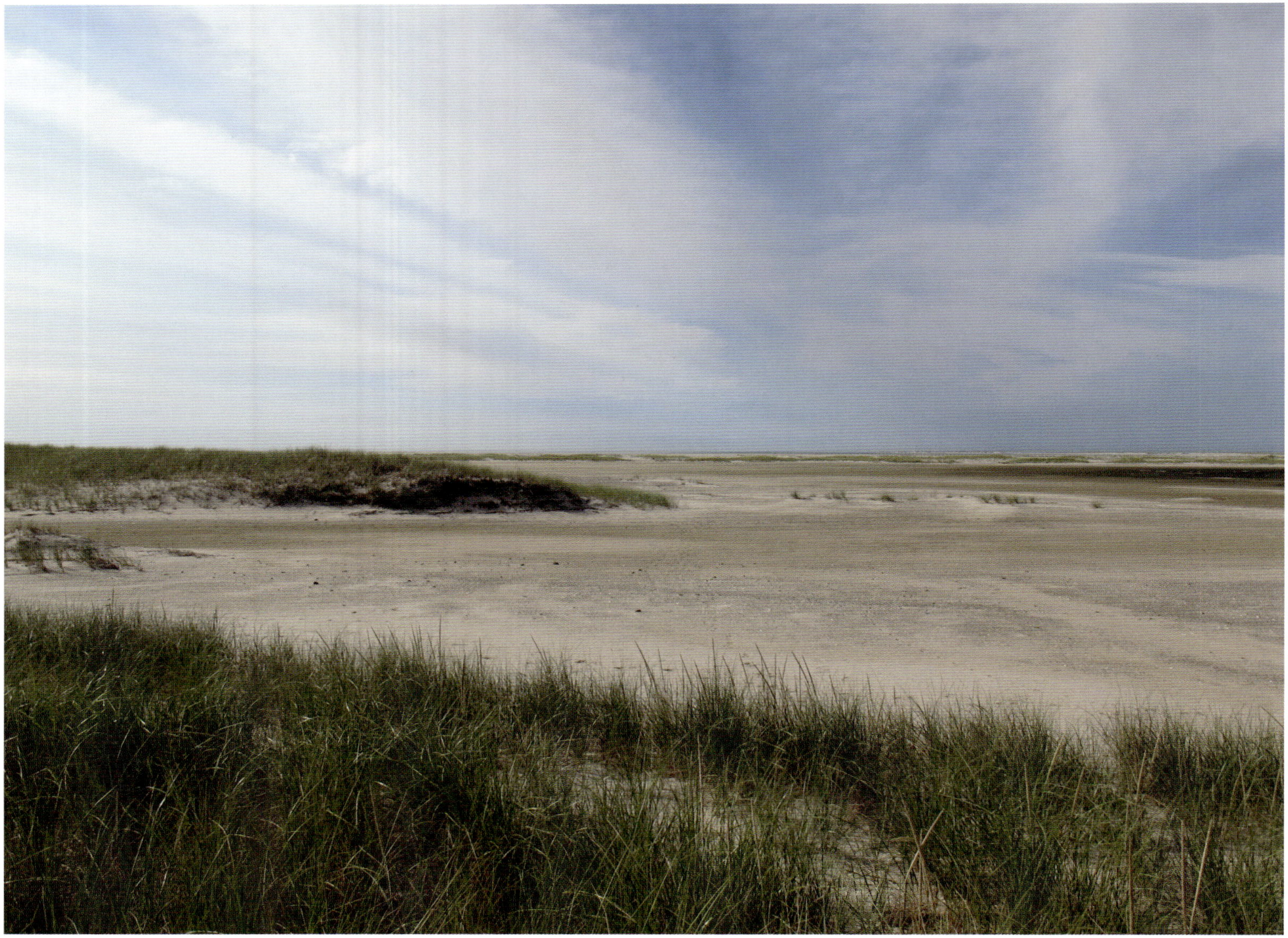

sandy green oasis

south beach,
chatham

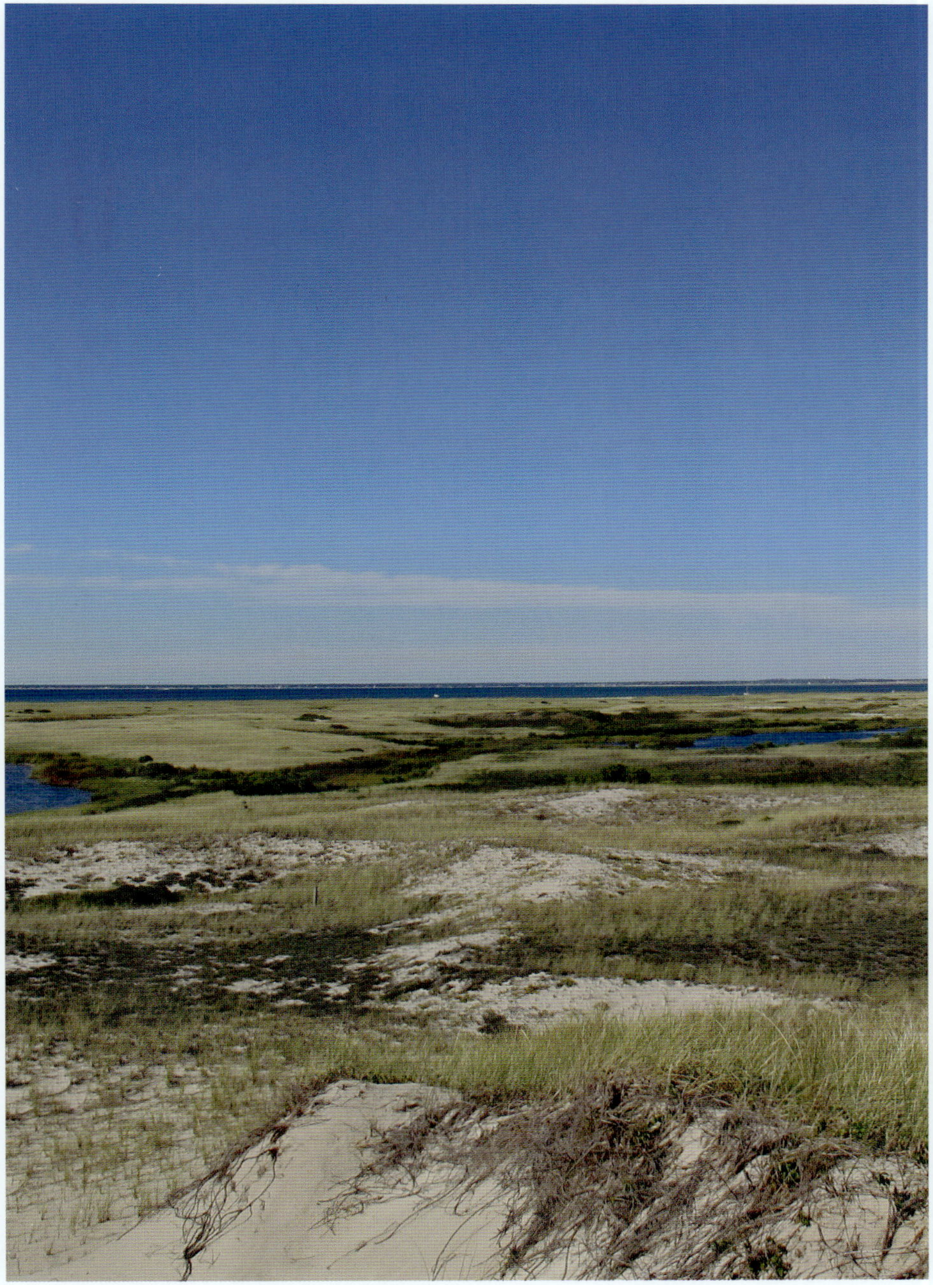

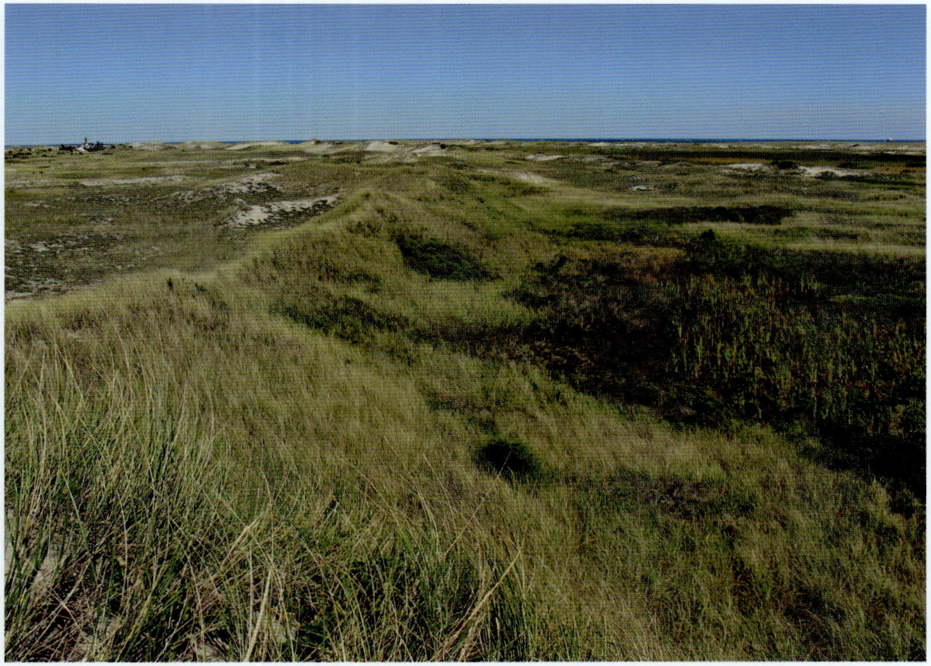

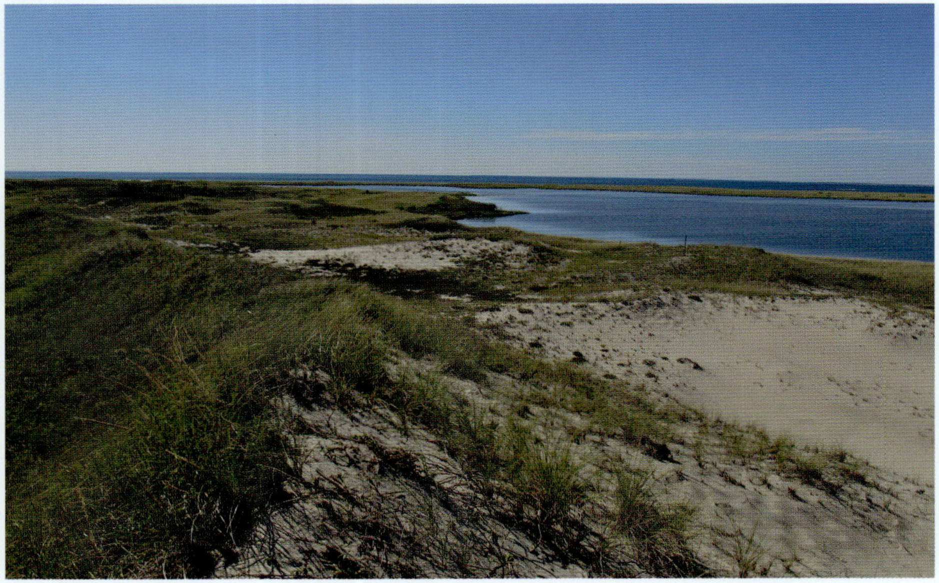

nothing but blue sky

powder hole, monomoy national wildlife refuge

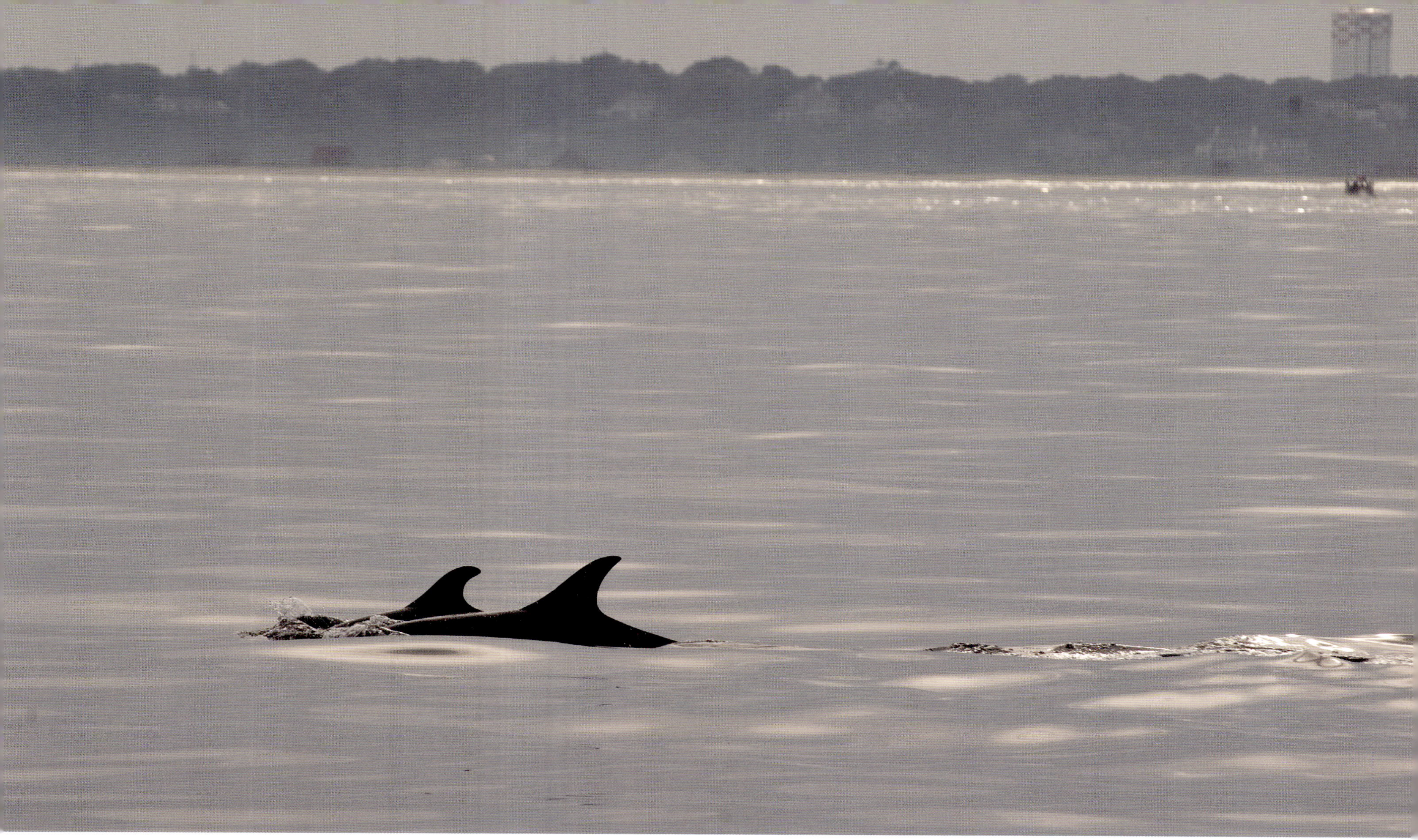

feeding at sunset

atlantic white-sided dolphins feeding with humpbacks, off chatham

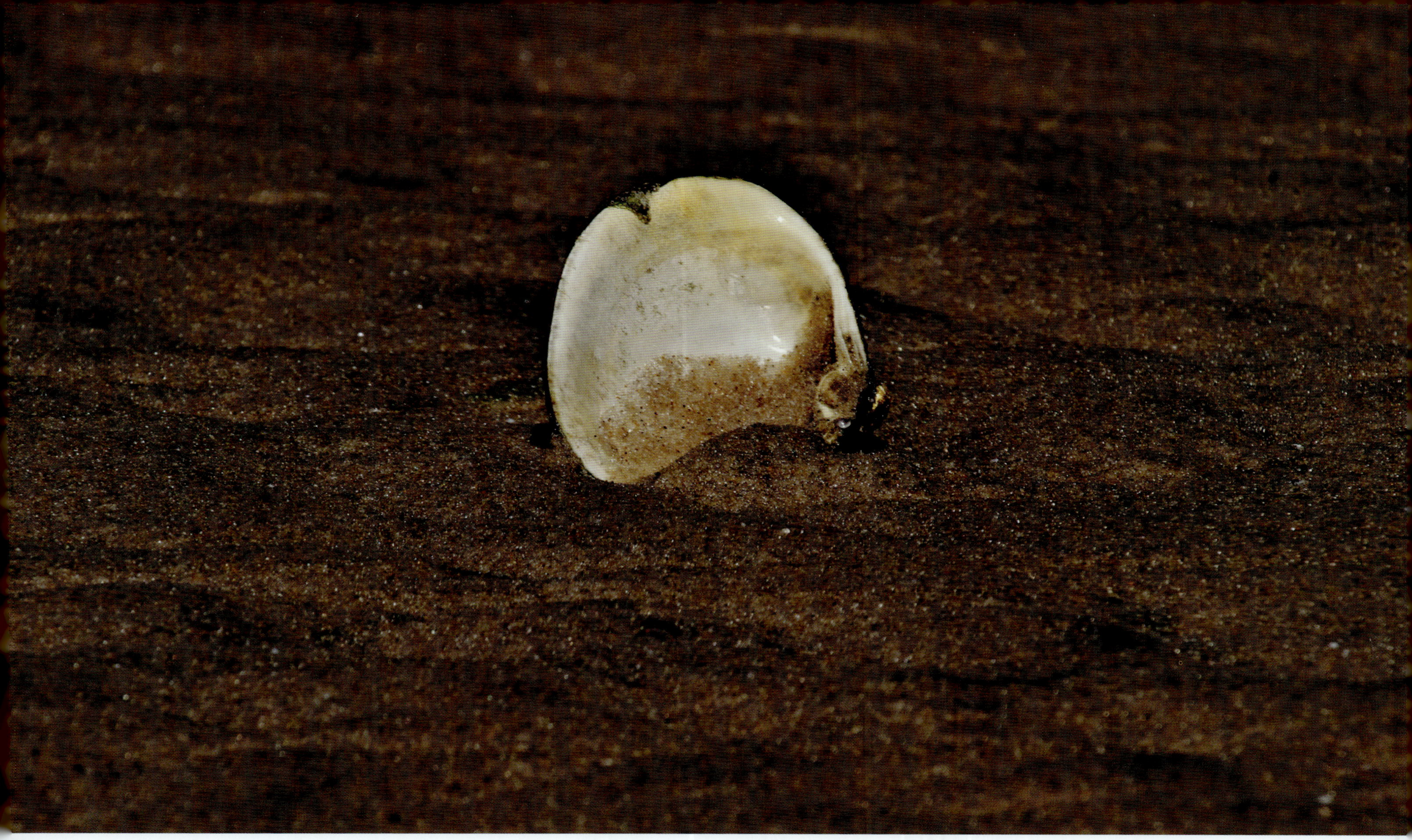

quahog shell,
monomoy national wildlife refuge

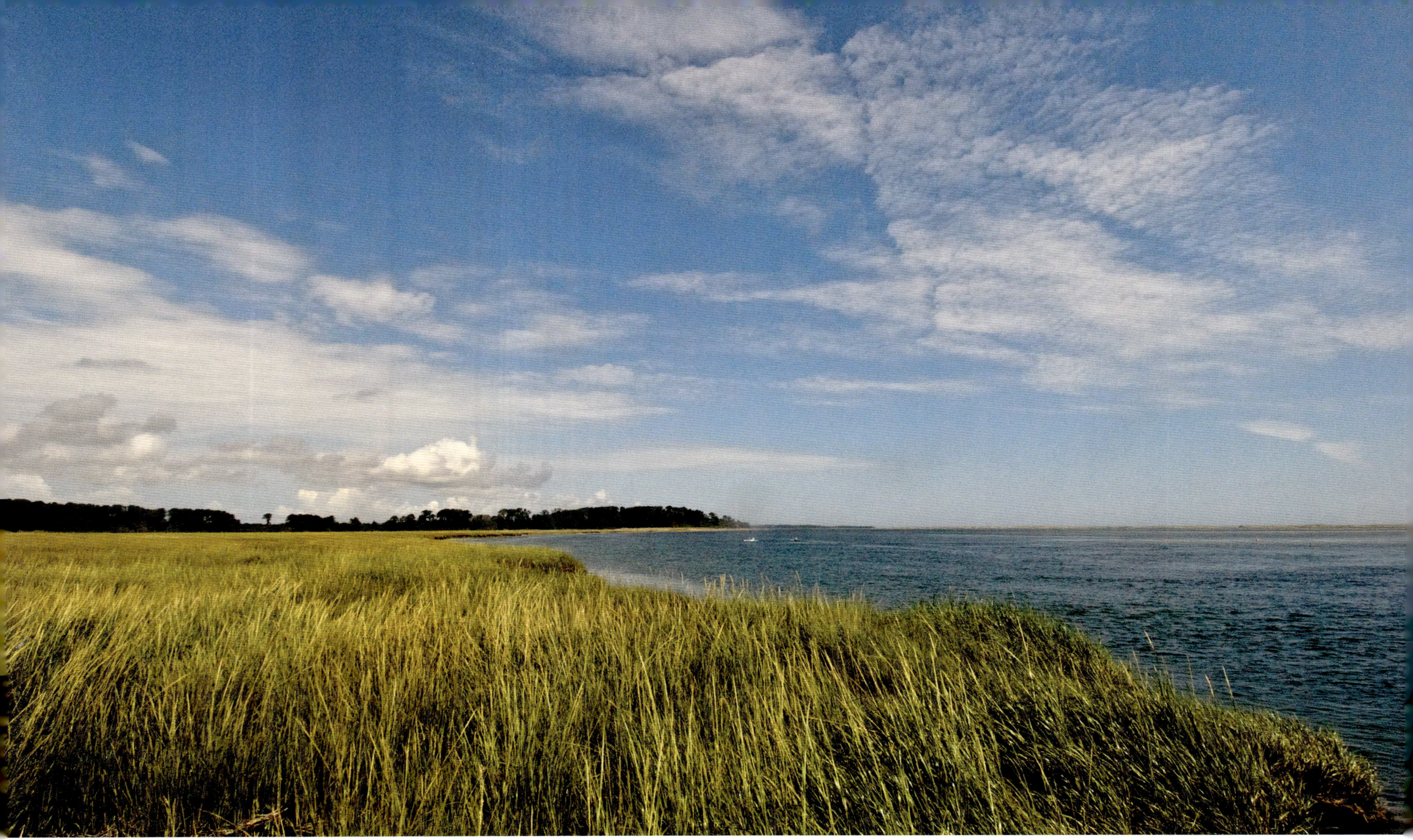

labor day

strong island, pleasant bay
chatham

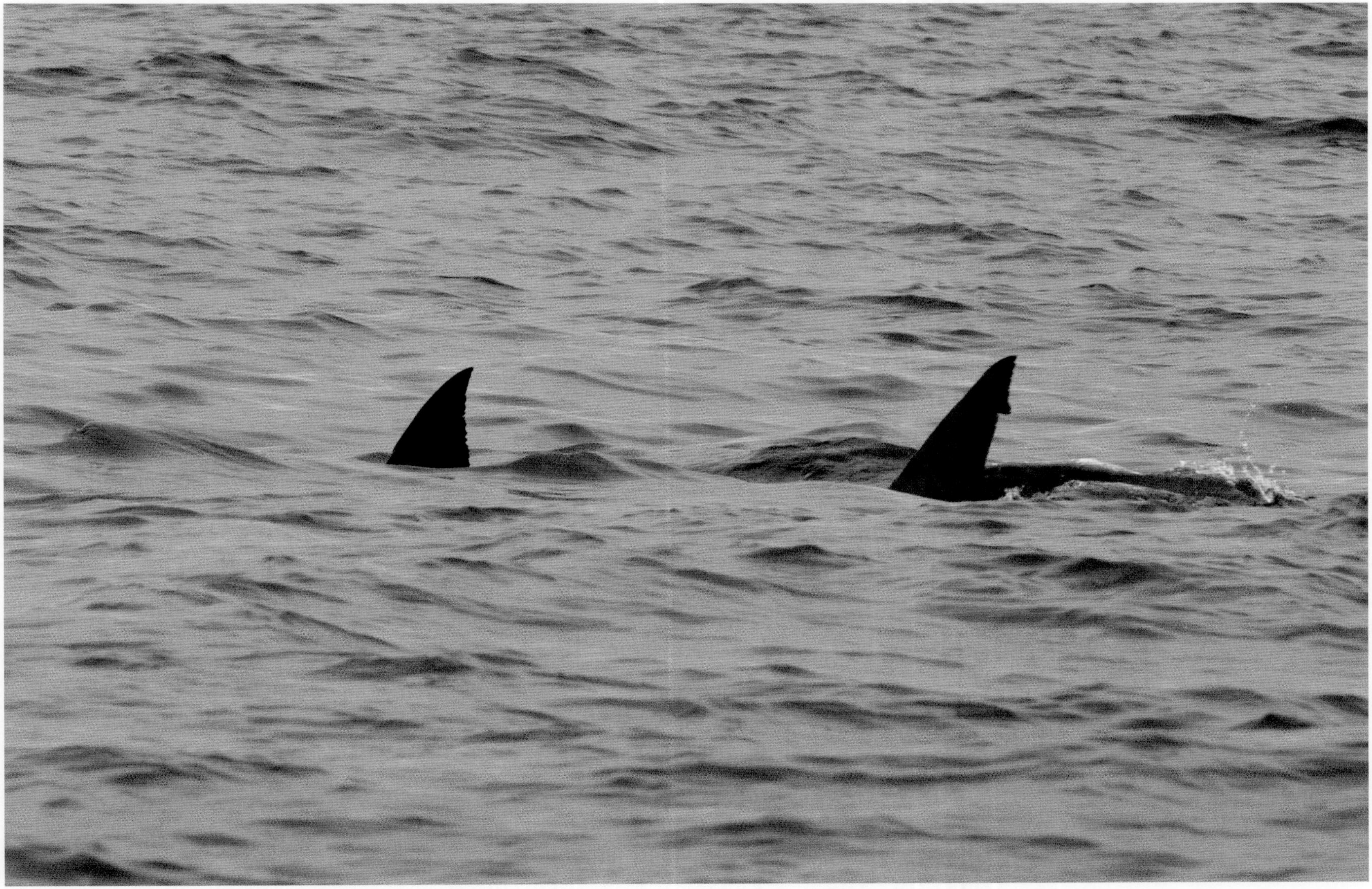

surface tension | white shark, off chatham

- long pasture wildlife sanctuary, cummaquid
- west barnstable marsh
- north beach island, chatham
- off chatham
- powder hole, monomoy national wildlife refuge
- monomoy national wildlife refuge
- south beach, chatham
- pleasant bay, chatham
- tern island, chatham
- morris island, monomoy national wildlife refuge
- chatham
- off monomoy, chatham
- chatham bar
- harding's beach, chatham
- ryder's cove, chatham
- cow yard, chatham
- chatham light
- oyster river, chatham
- chatham/harwich line
- belle's neck state park, harwich
- nauset beach, orleans
- coast guard beach, eastham
- wellfleet
- wellfleet bay wildlife sanctuary

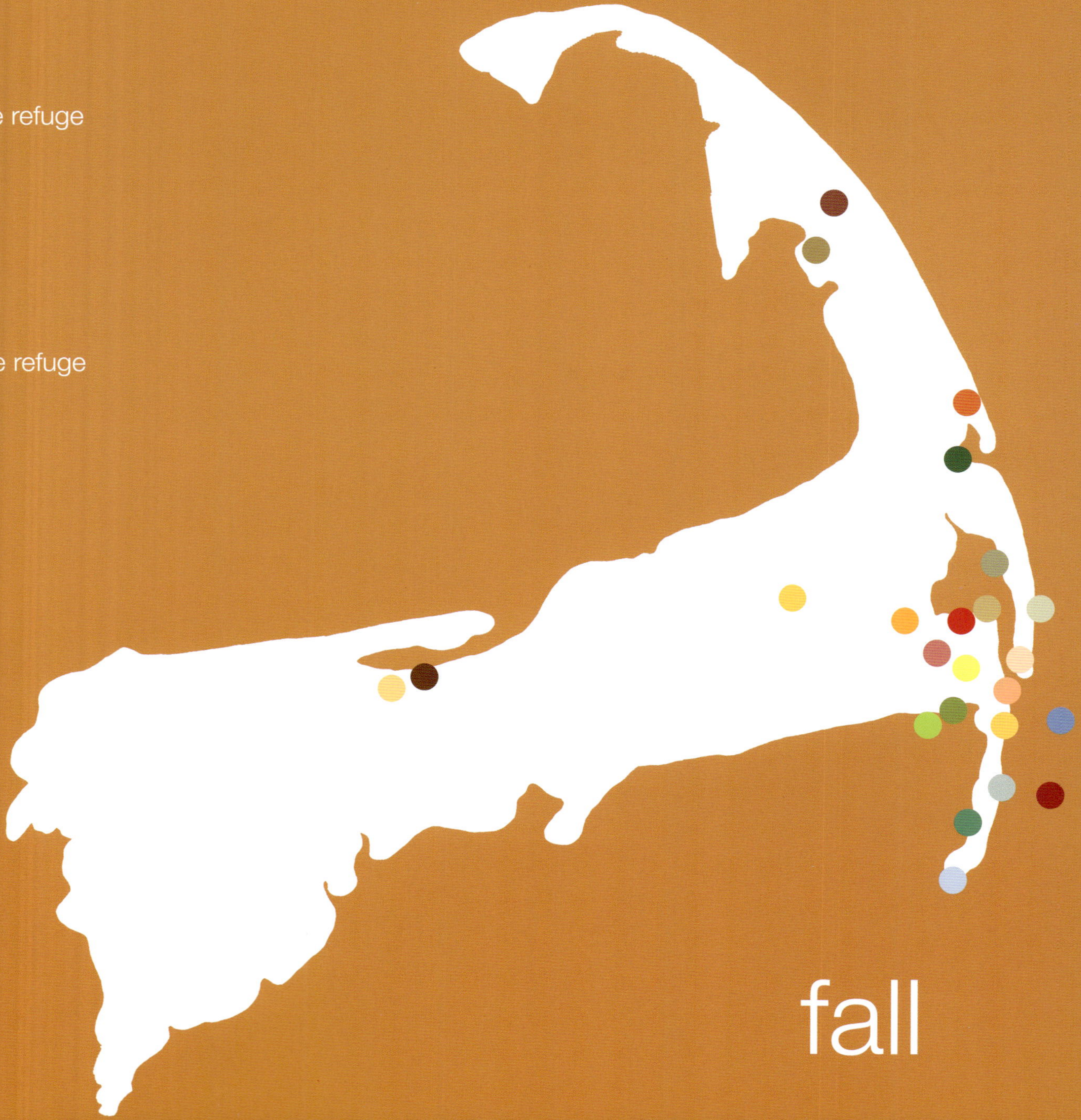

fall

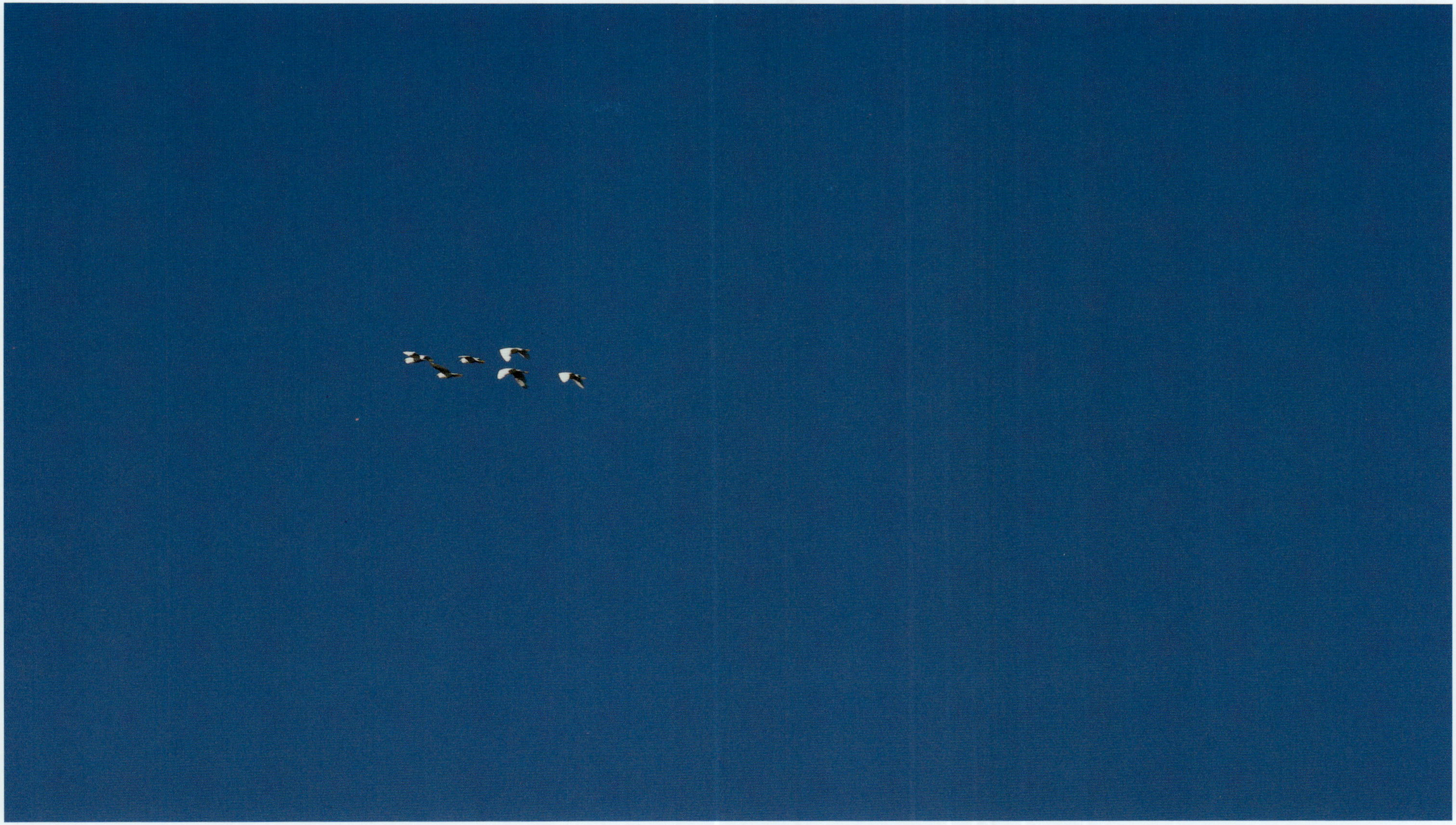

egrets heading south | monomoy national wildlife refuge

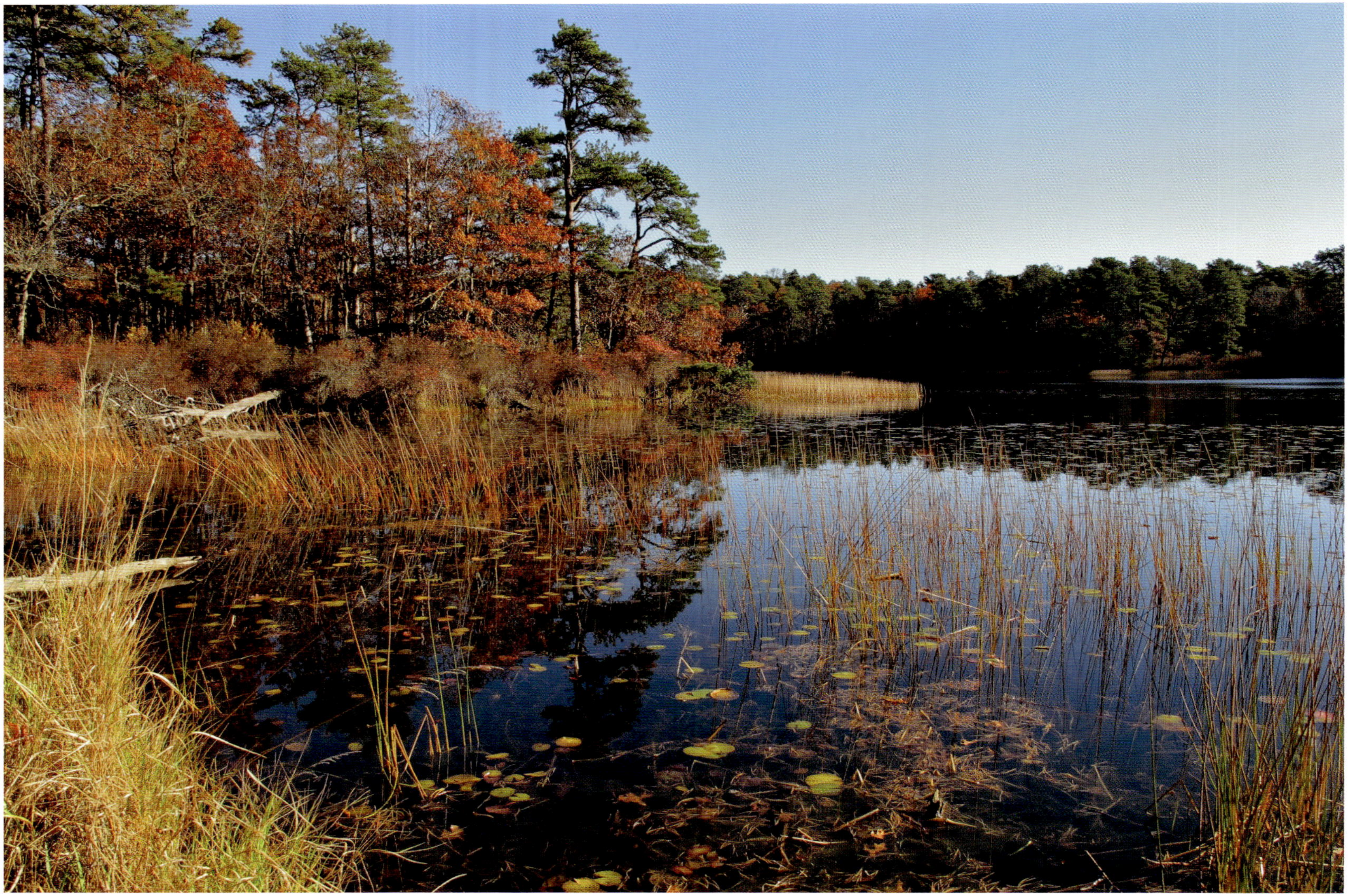

fall colors

fresh water pond,
orleans

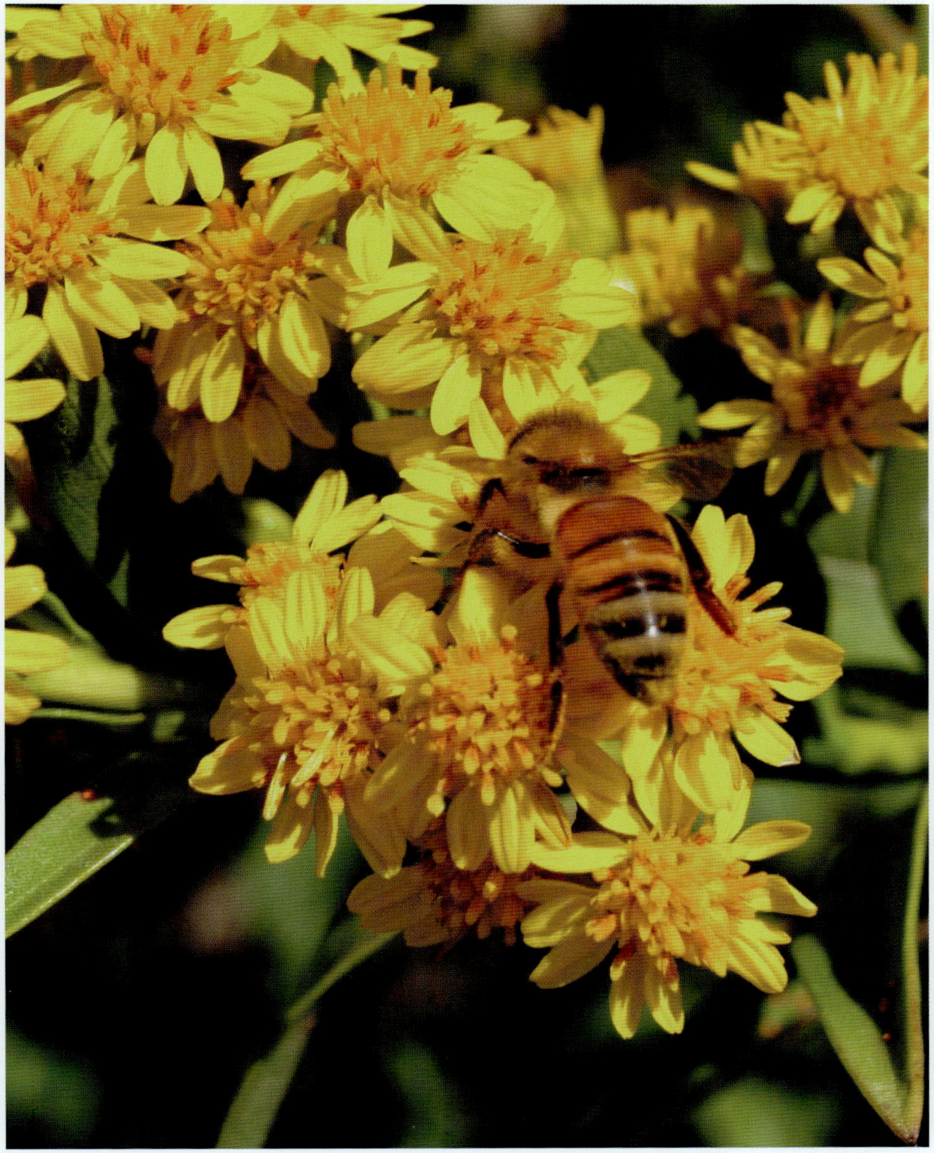

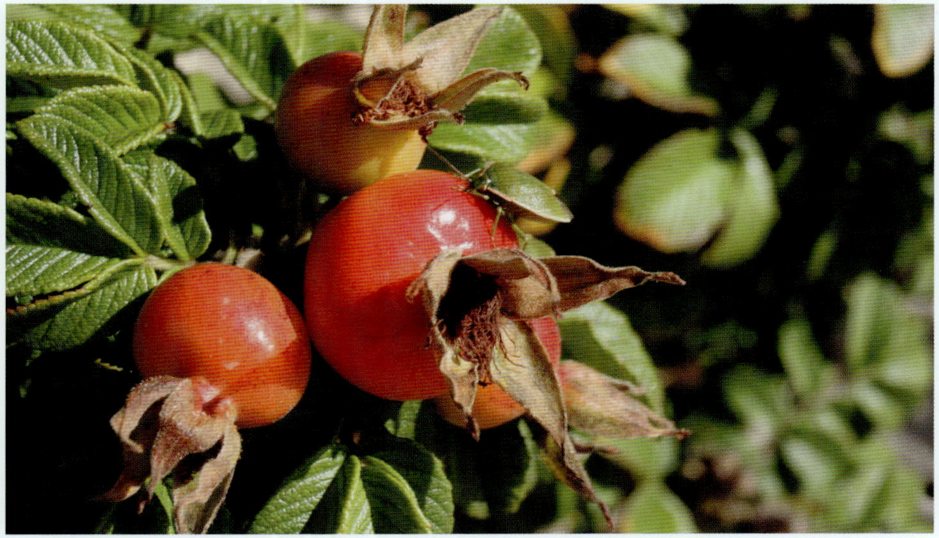

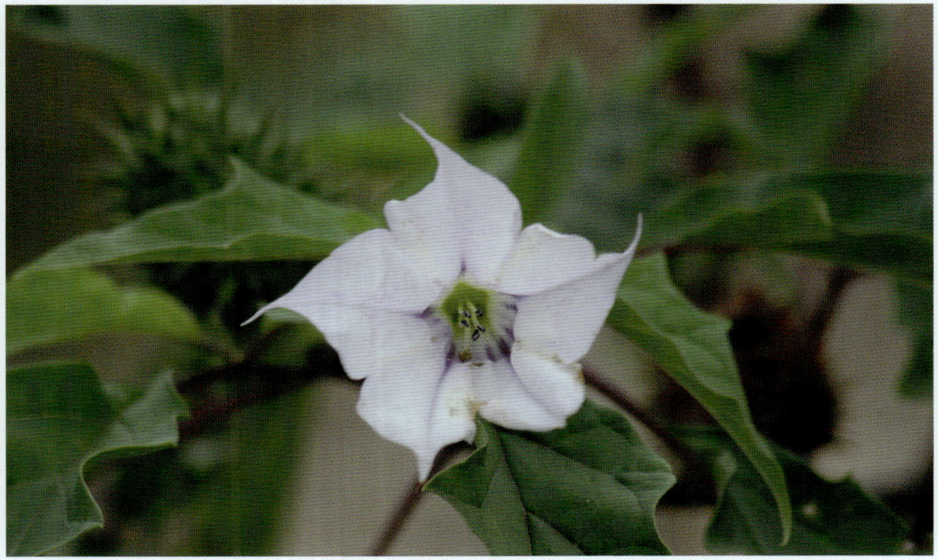

bee and blossoms

clockwise from left: seaside goldenrod, salt spray rose hips, and jimson weed, monomoy national wildlife refuge

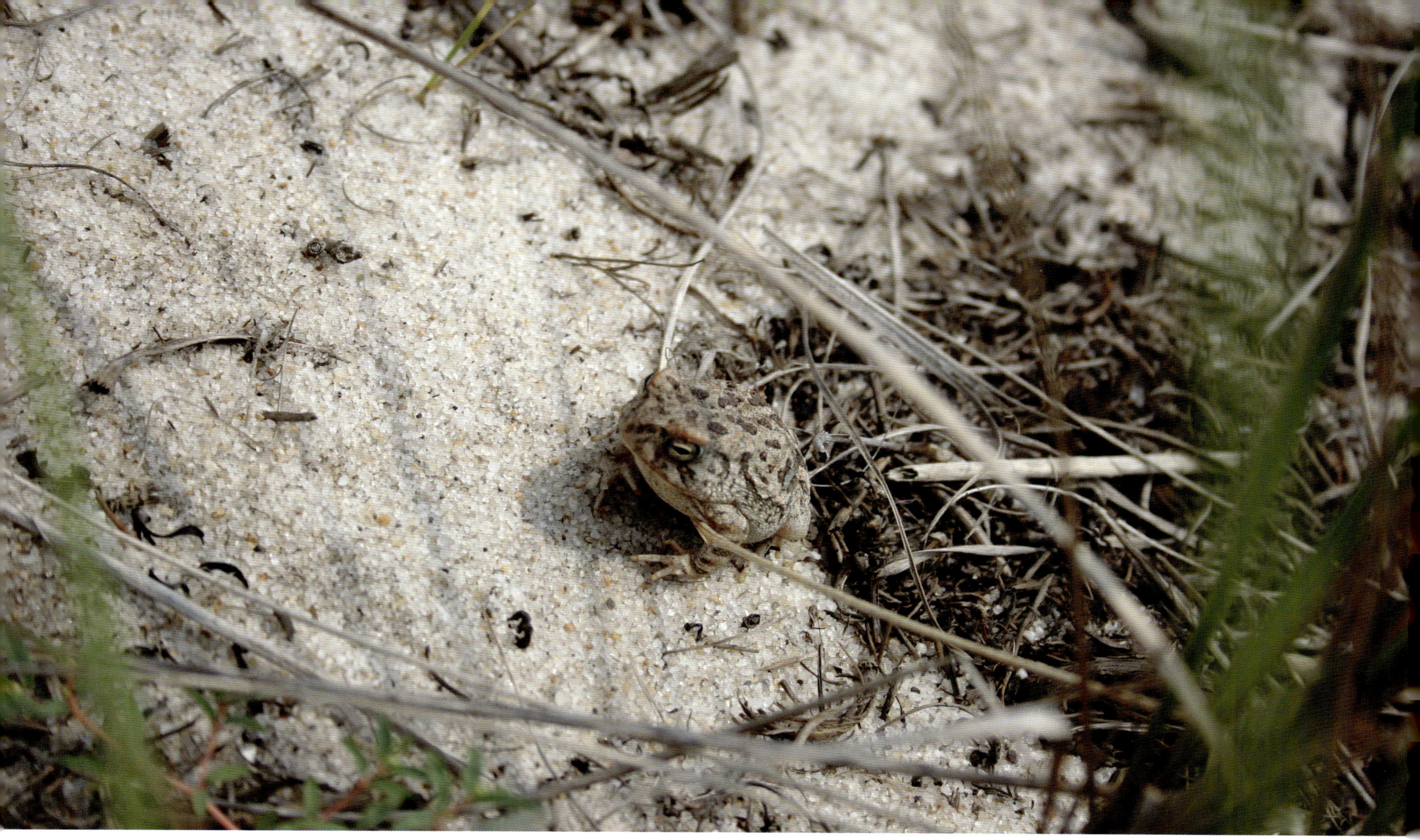

hoppin' on the sly

fowler's toad,
nauset beach, orleans

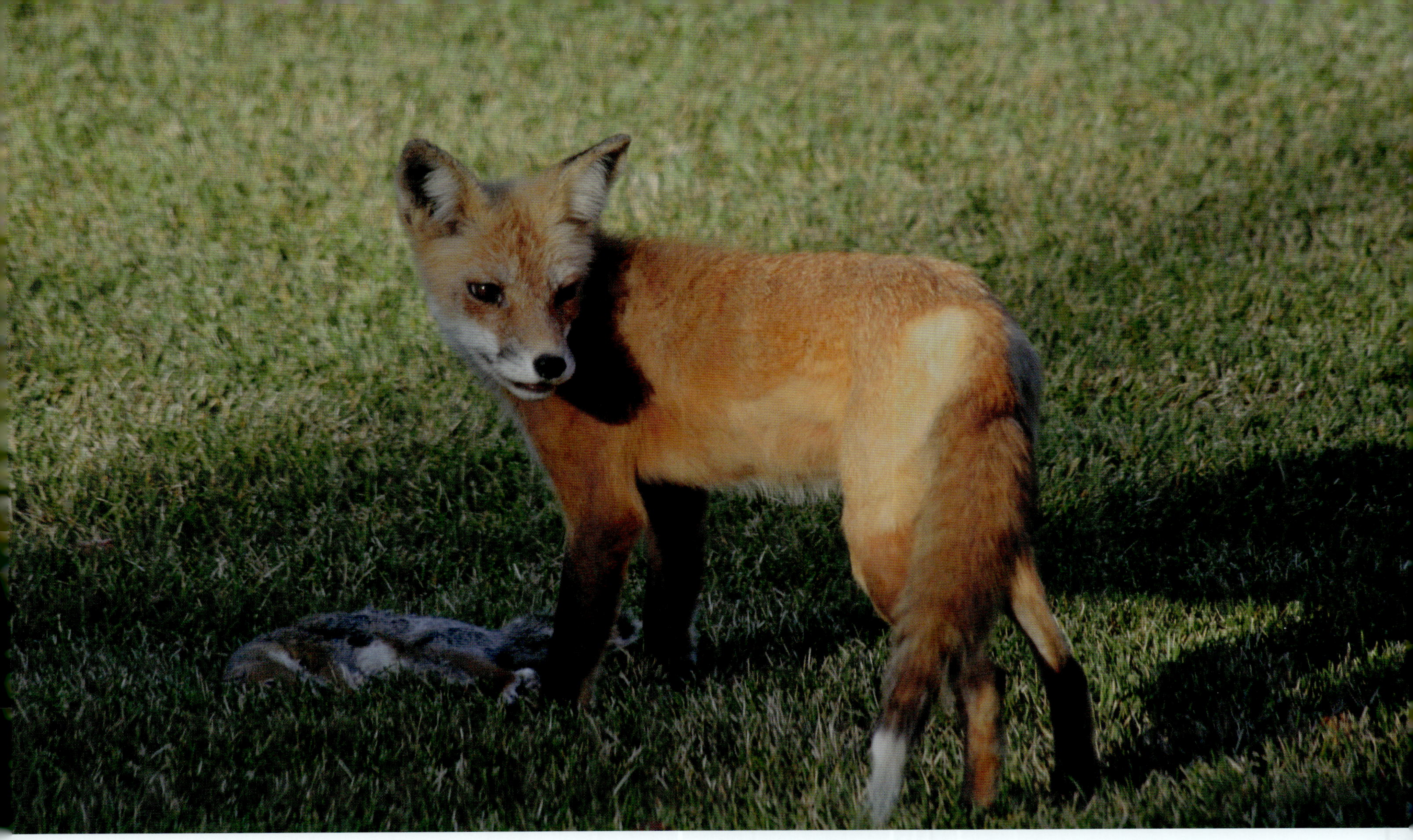

caught in the act

young male fox with squirrel, chatham

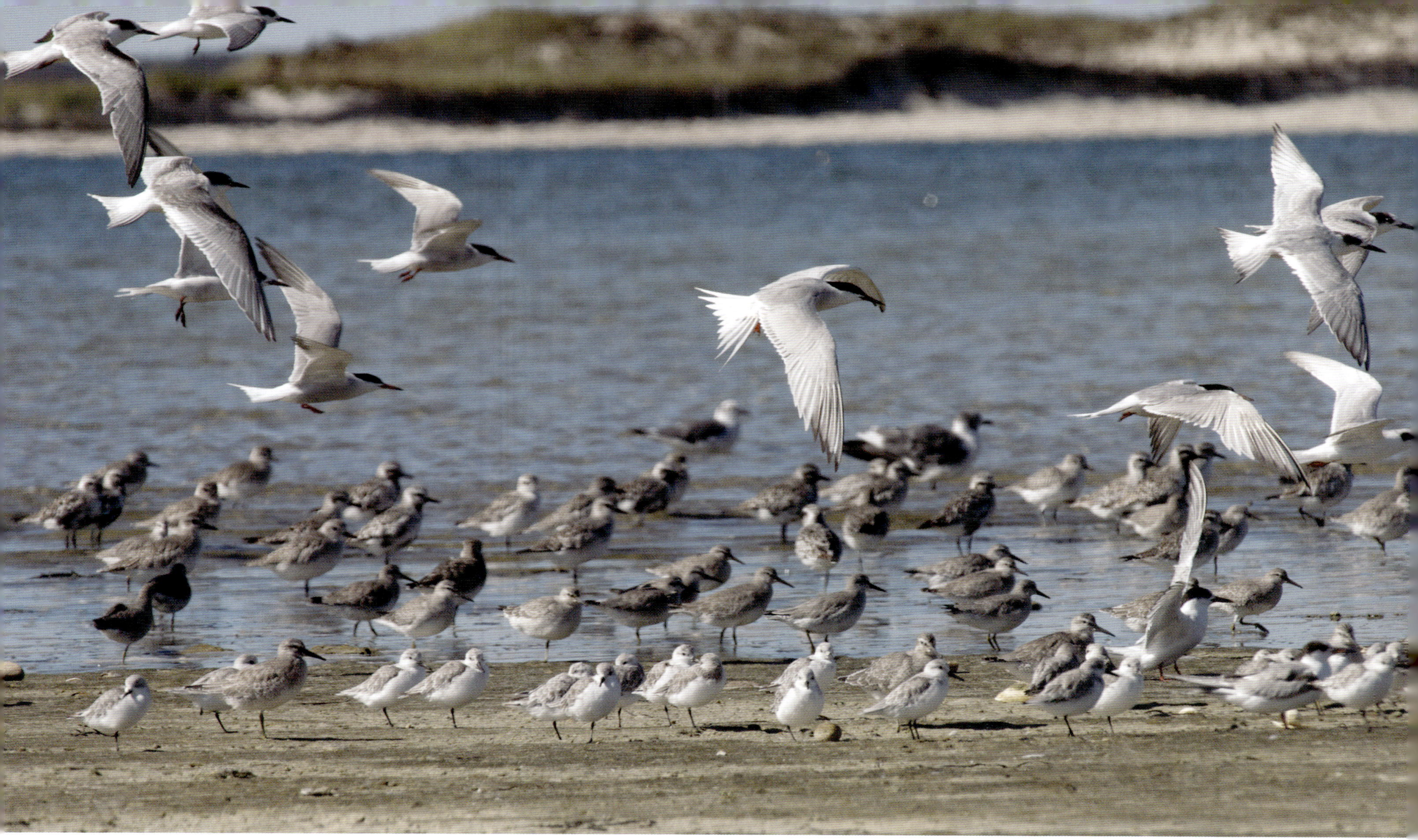

southern compass

terns, plovers, and knots gather to head south, monomoy national wildlife refuge

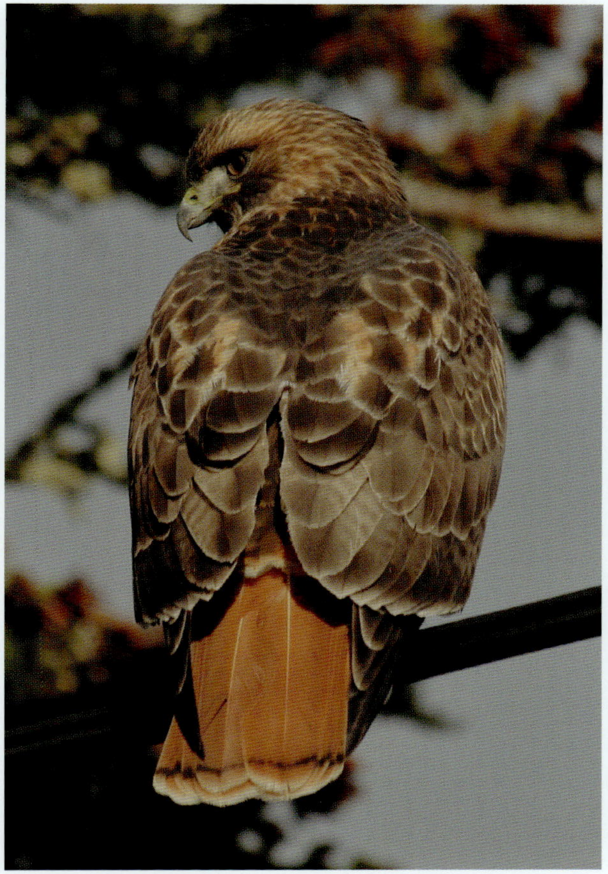

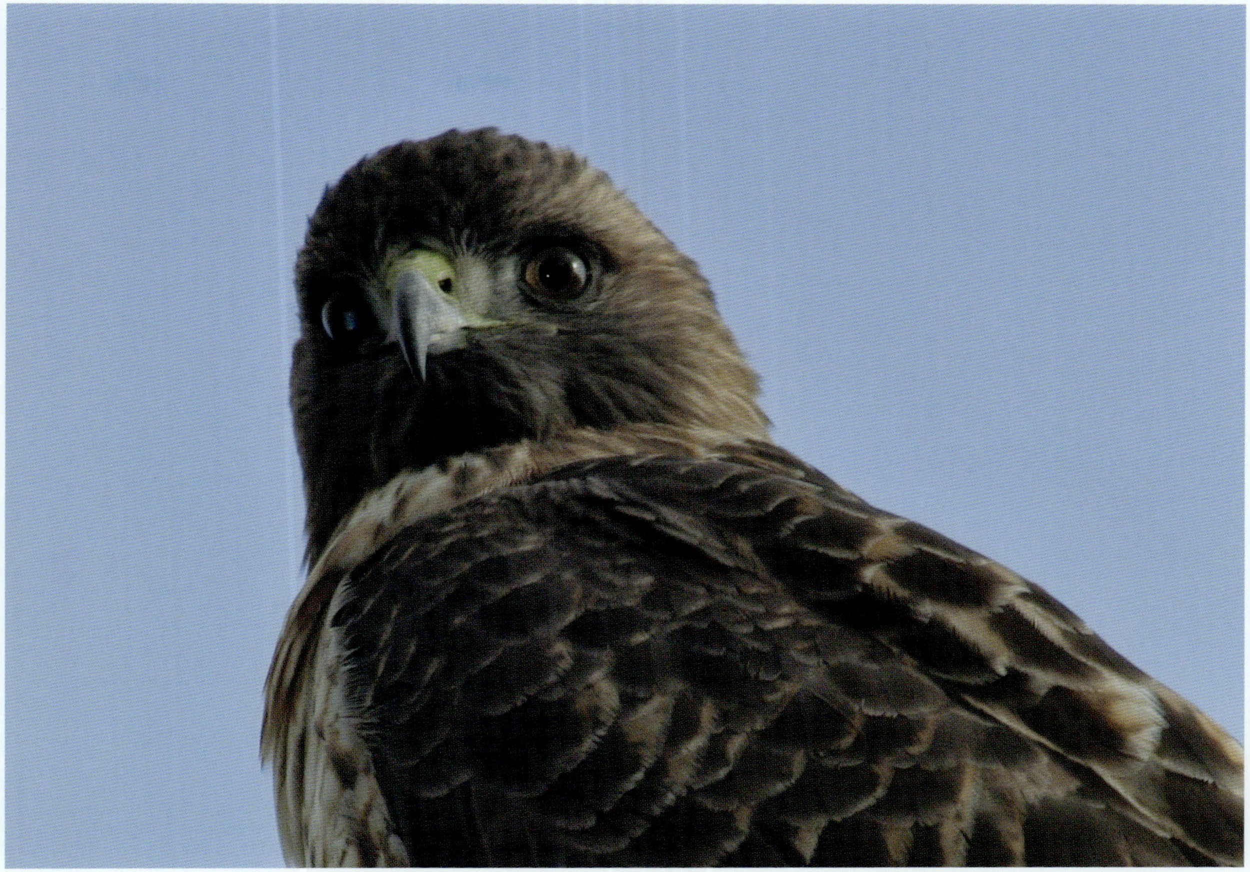

about face

red-tailed hawks,
chatham

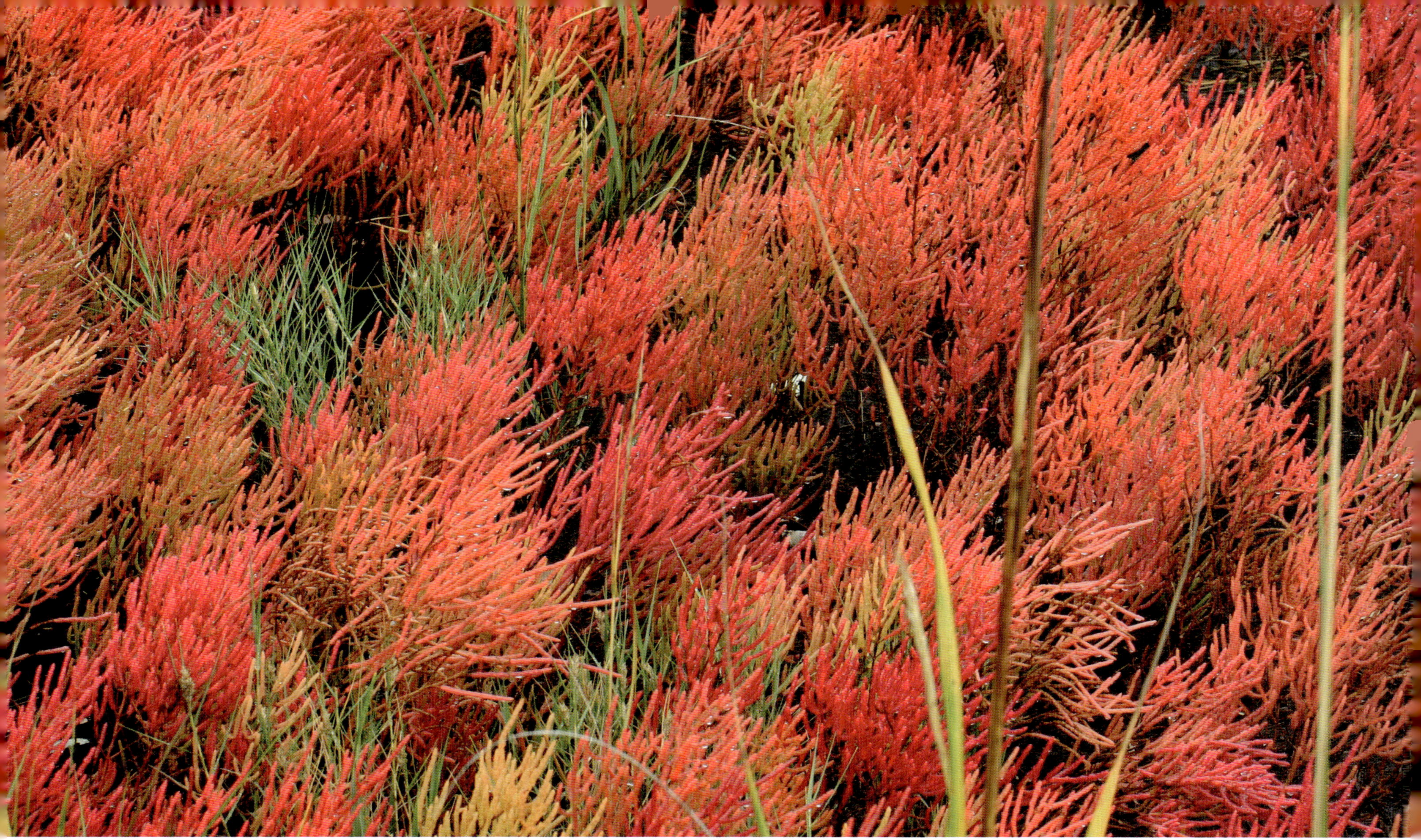

fired up

fall foliage,
belle's neck state park, harwich

sleepy by day

snowy owl,
coast guard beach, eastham

photo courtesy of tim vorhees

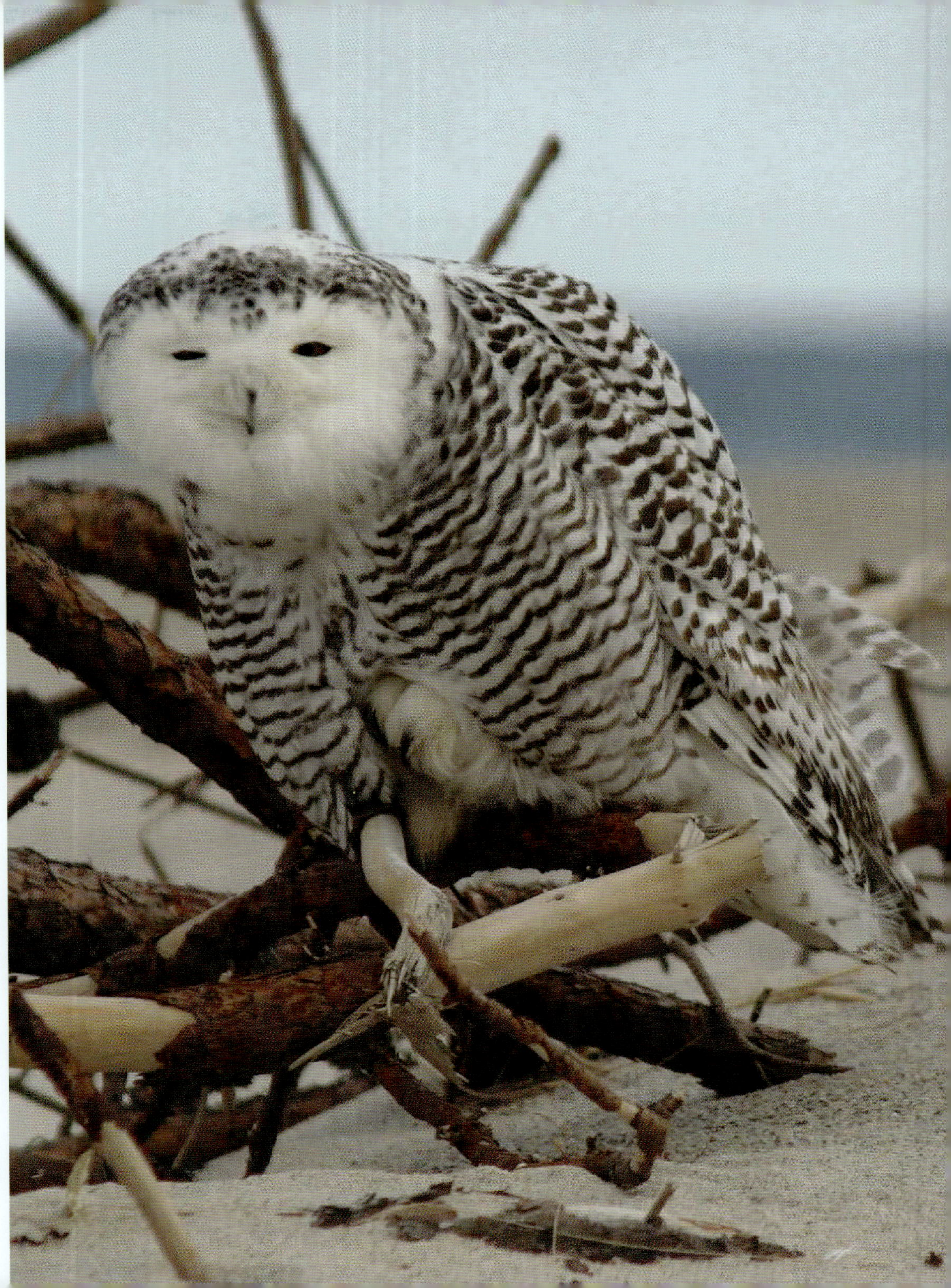

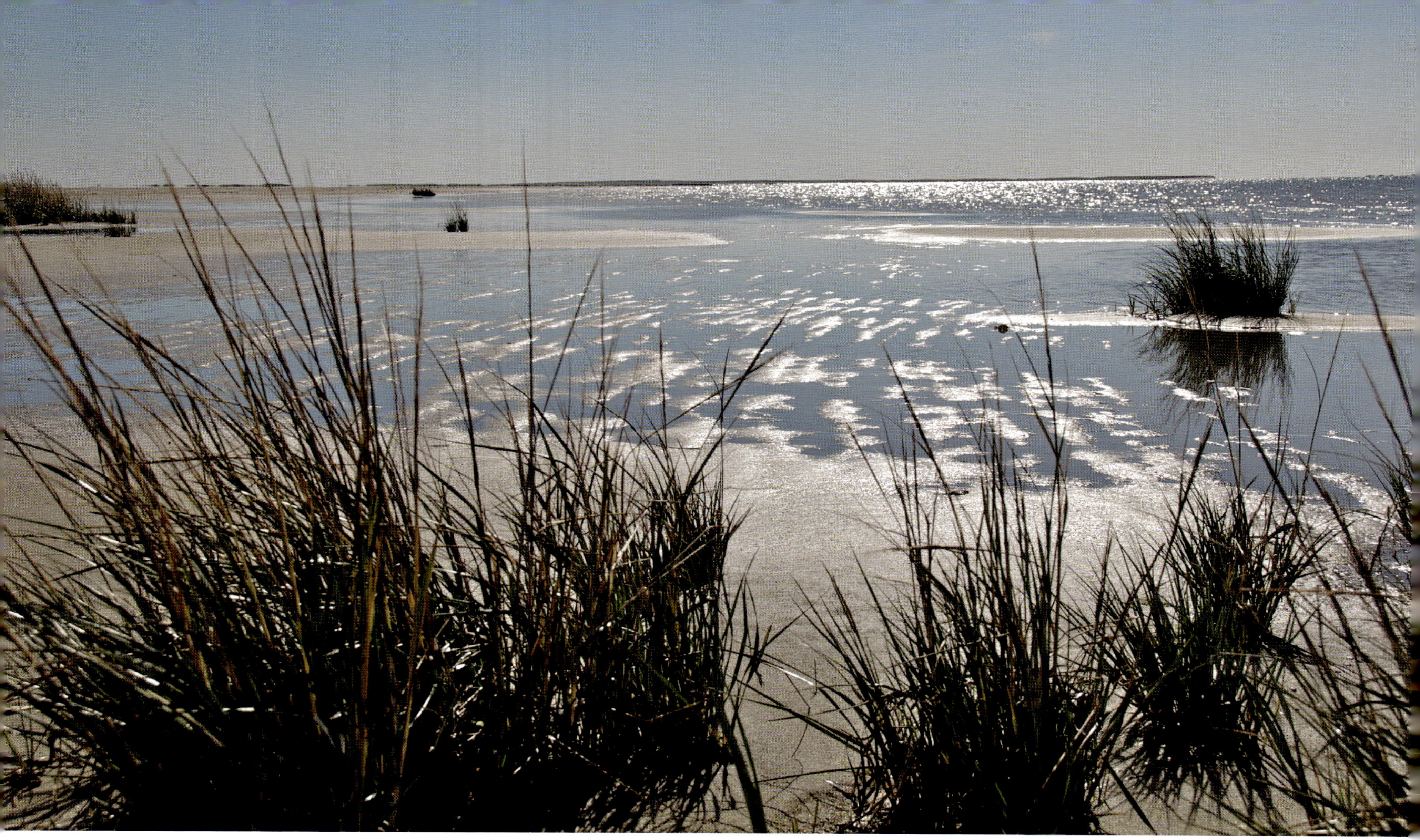

monomoy national wildlife refuge

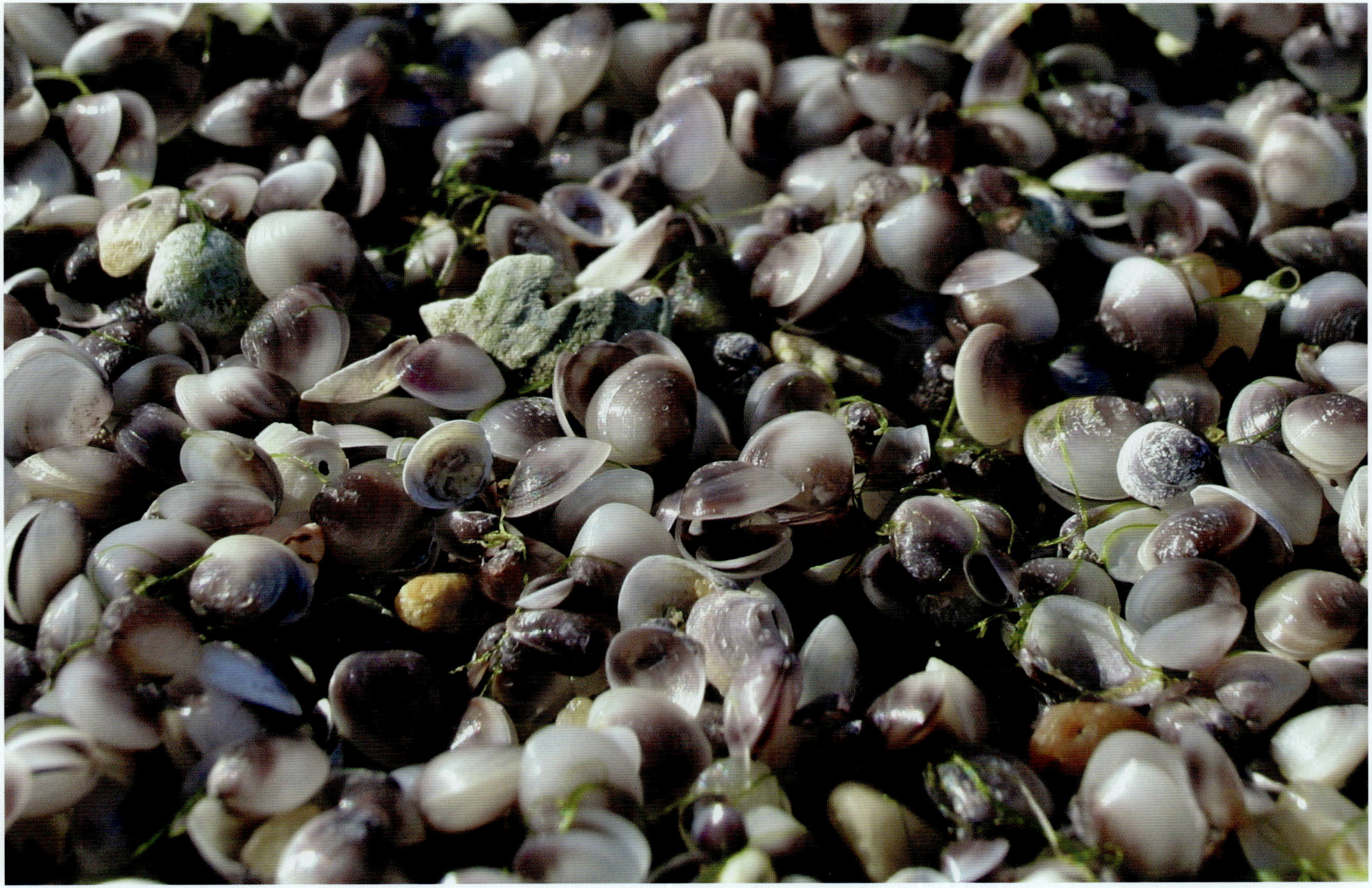

monomoy national wildlife refuge

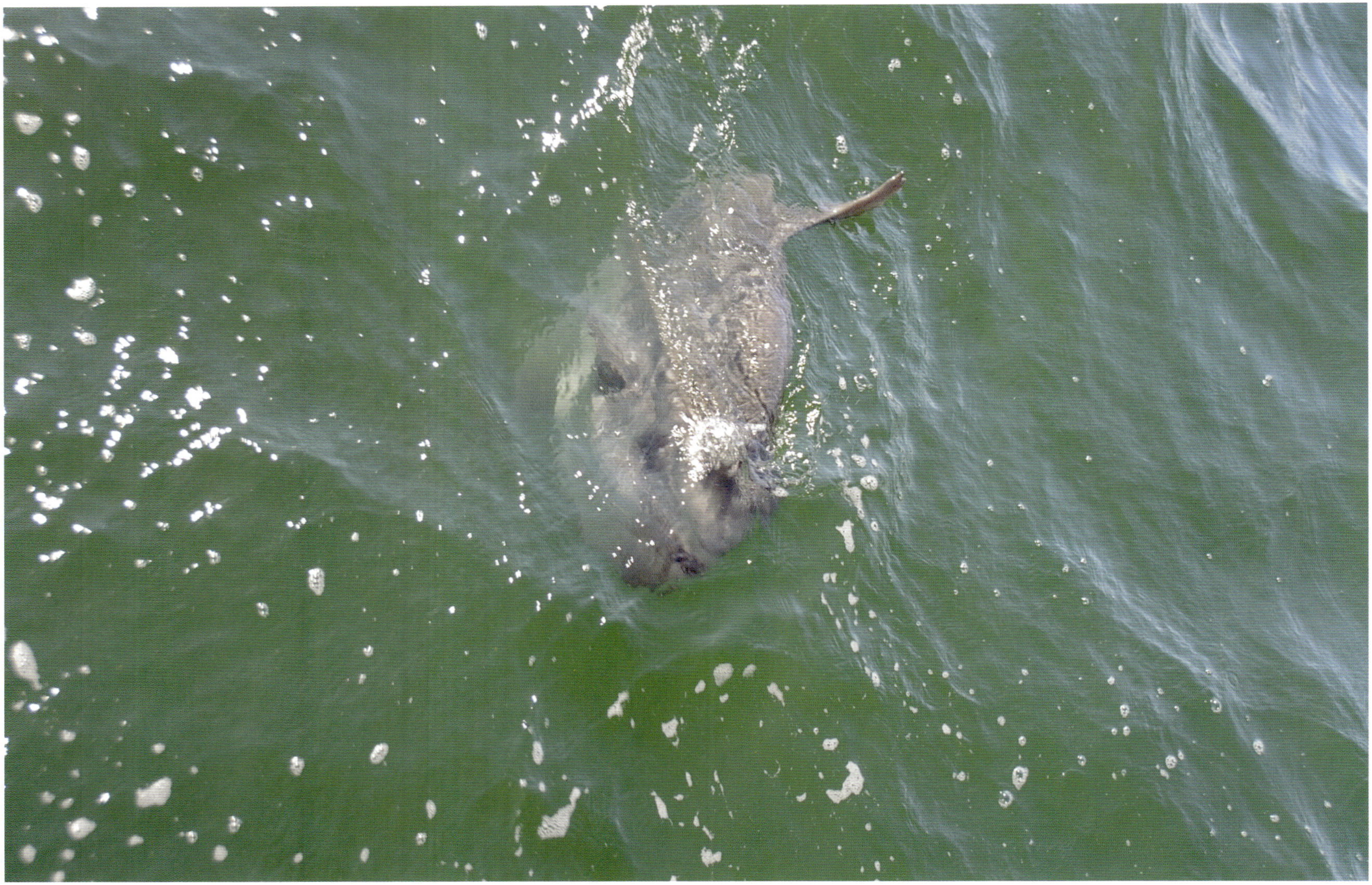

eye of the beast

mola mola,
off monomoy, chatham

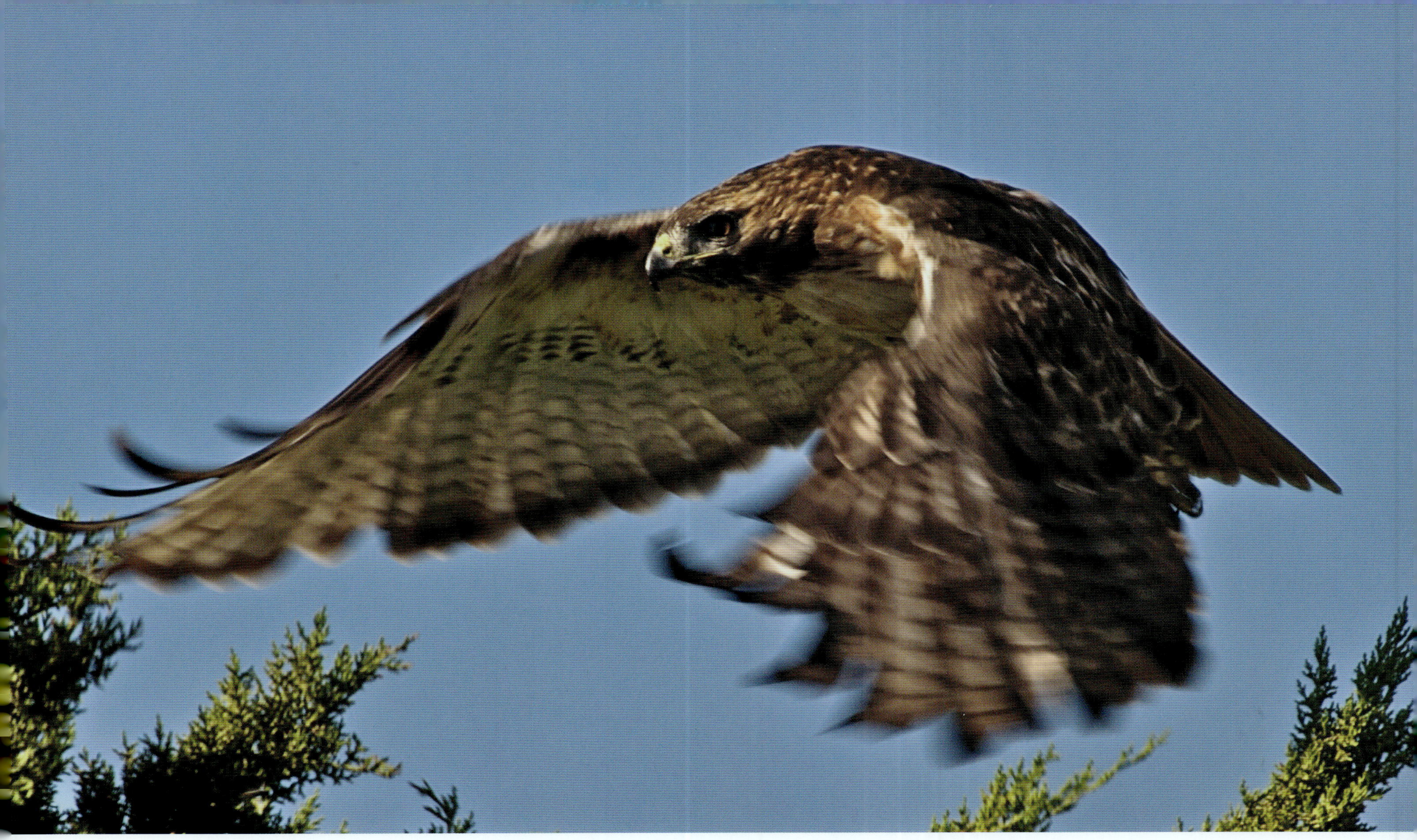

predator

red tailed hawk,
chatham

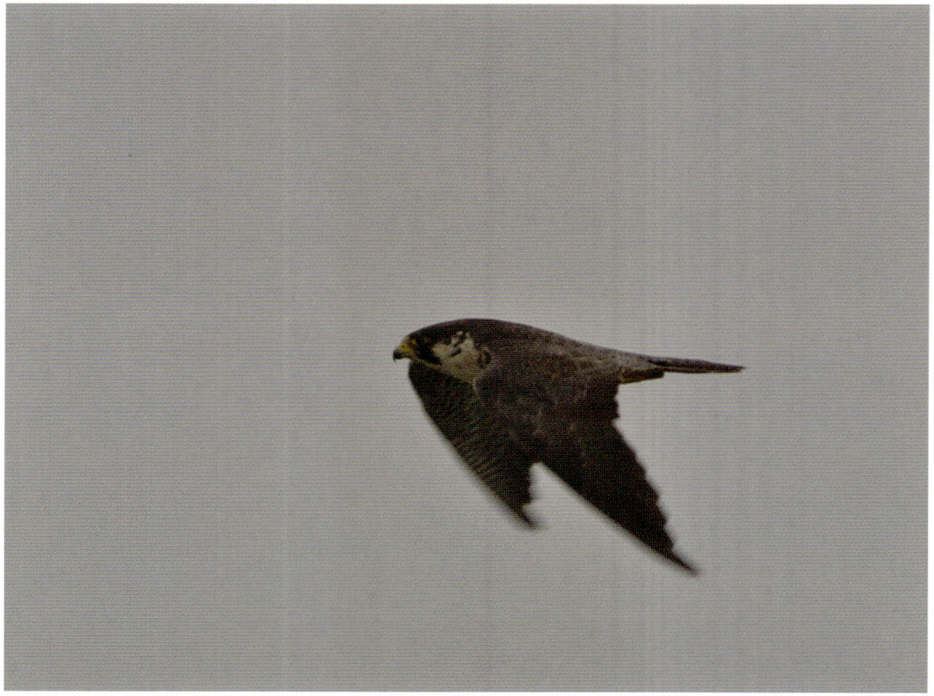

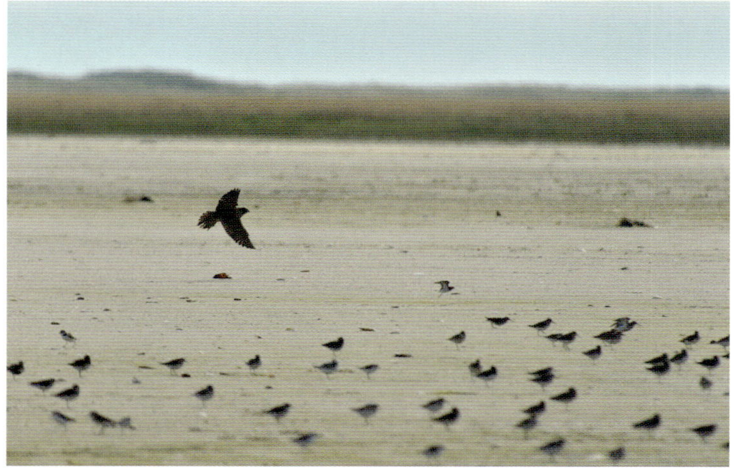

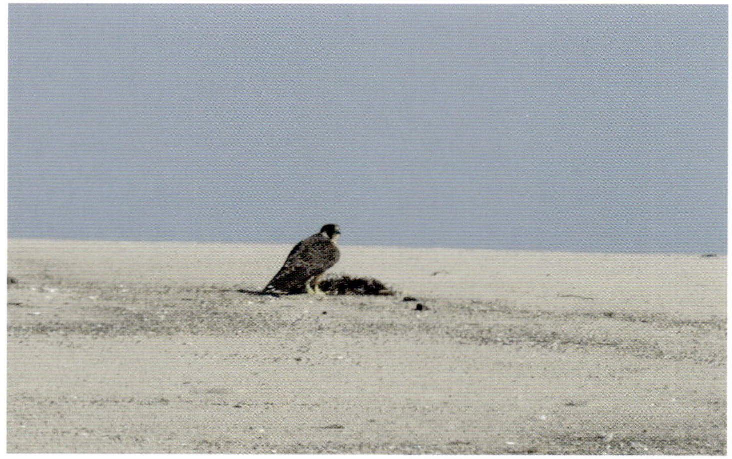

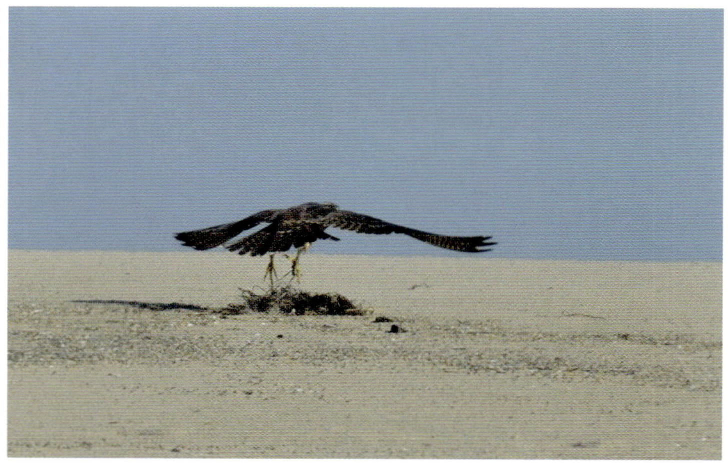

hunt and gather

peregrine falcon,
south beach, chatham

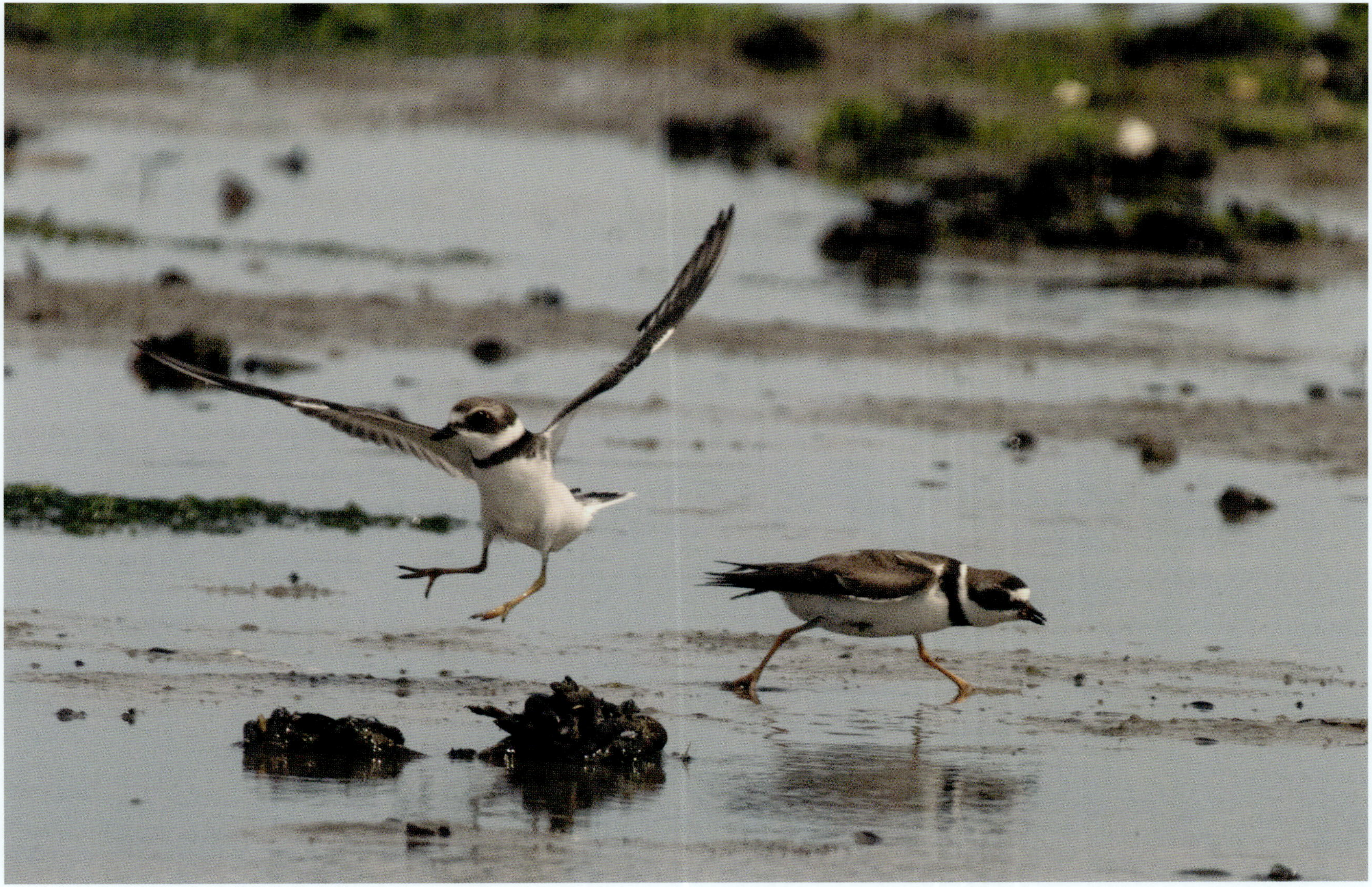

outta here!

semipalmated plovers,
tern island, chatham

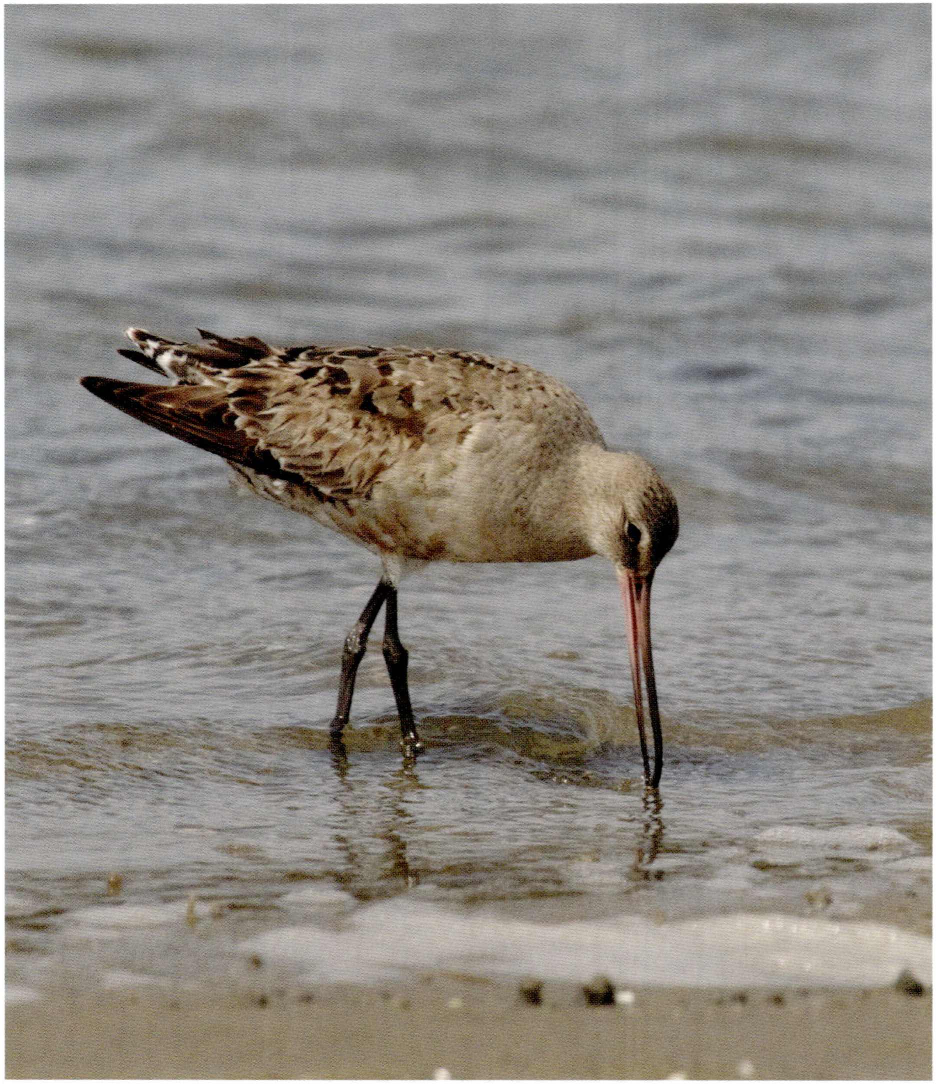

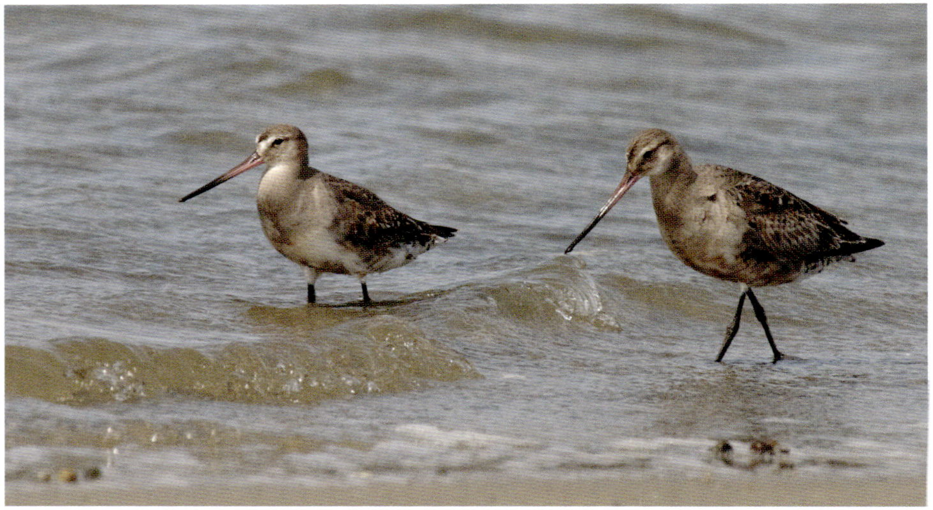

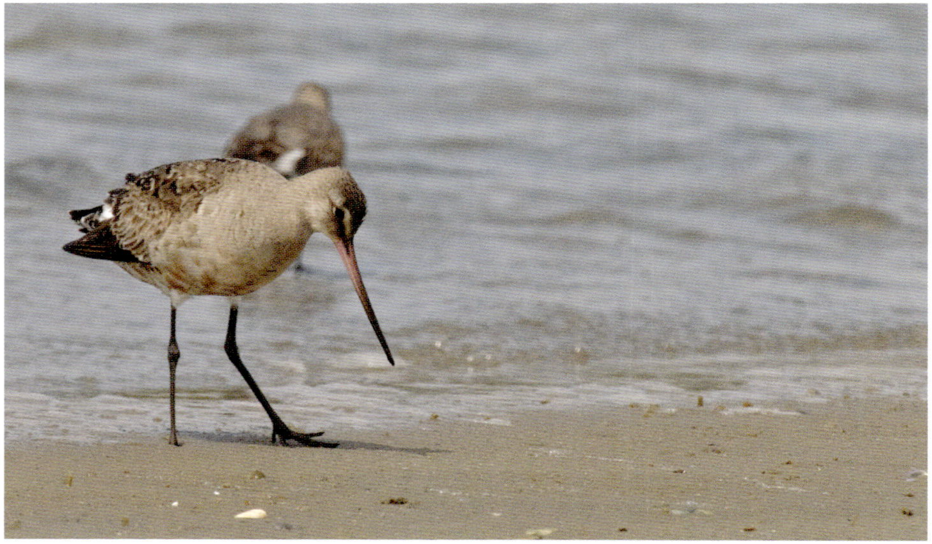

coastal forage

hudsonian godwits,
tern island, chatham

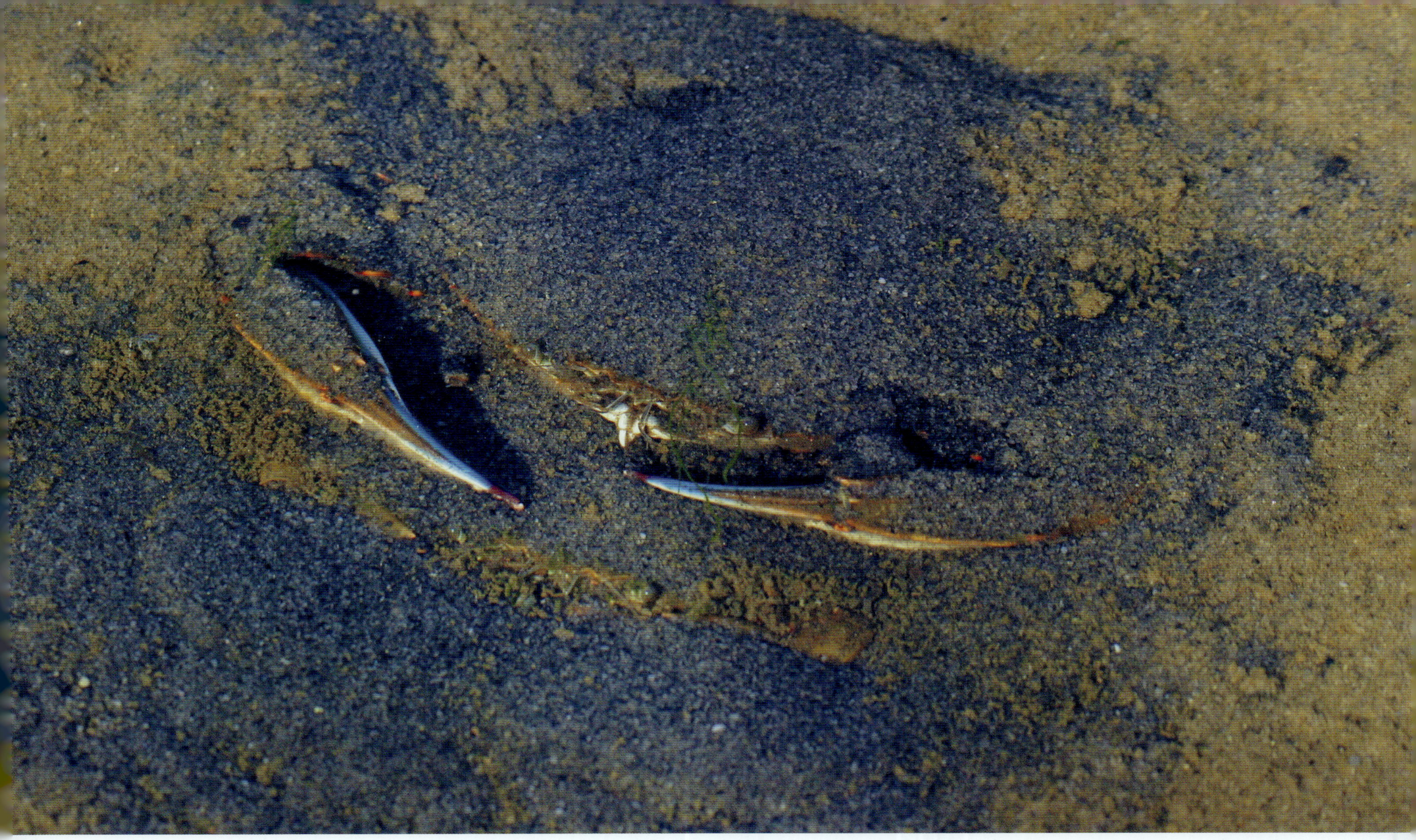

concealed in cobalt

blue crab, powder hole,
monomoy national wildlife refuge

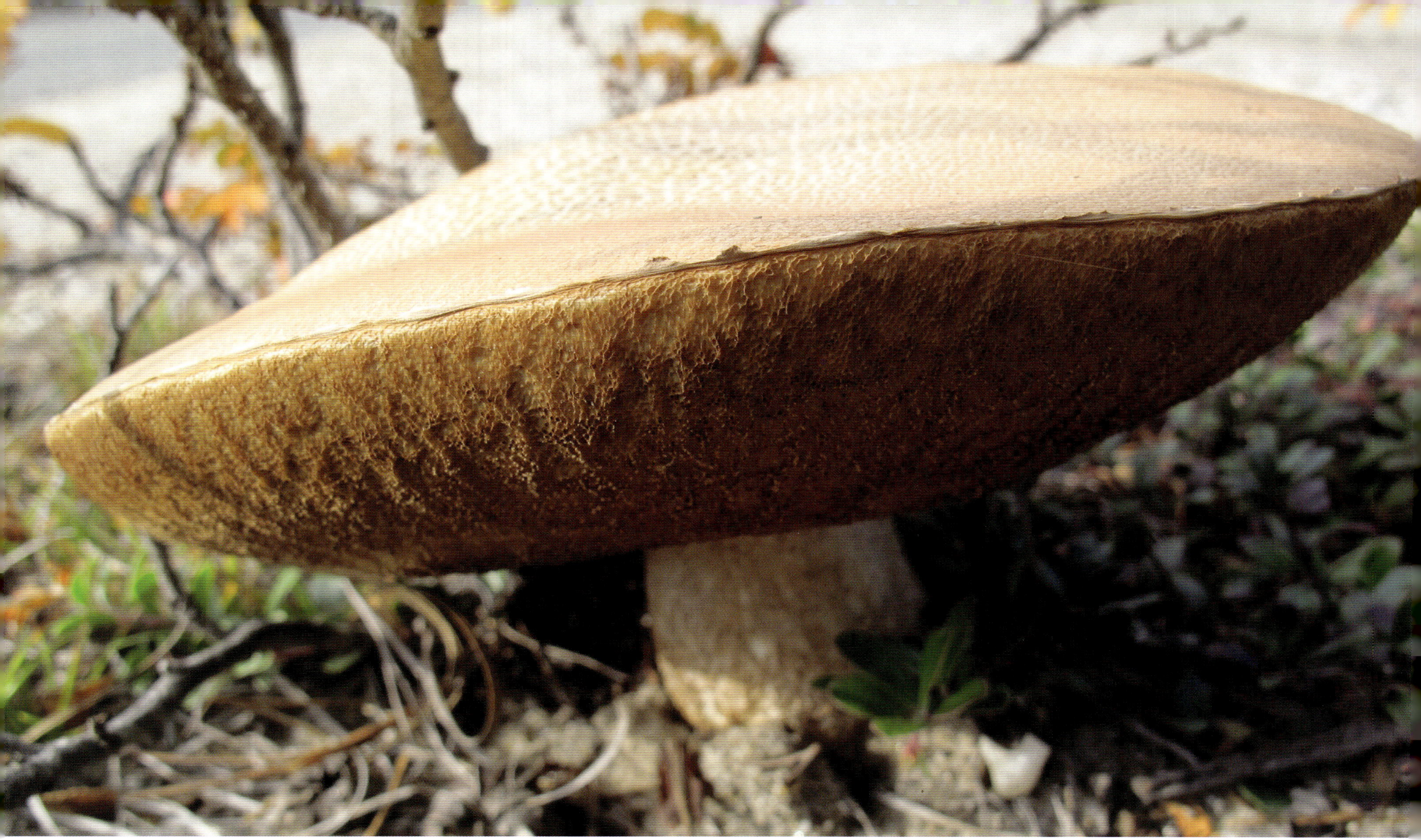

fungi, morris island,
monomoy national wildlife refuge

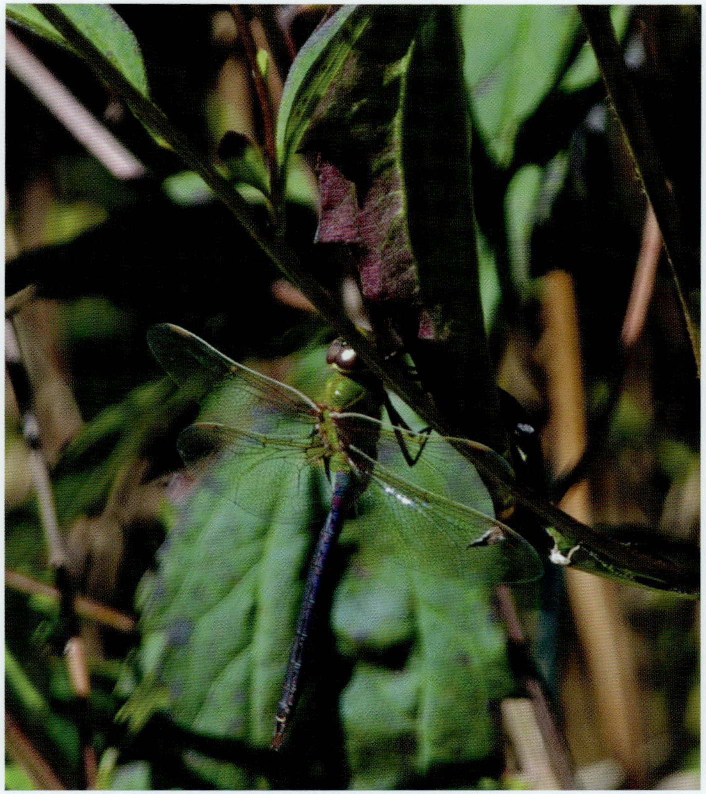

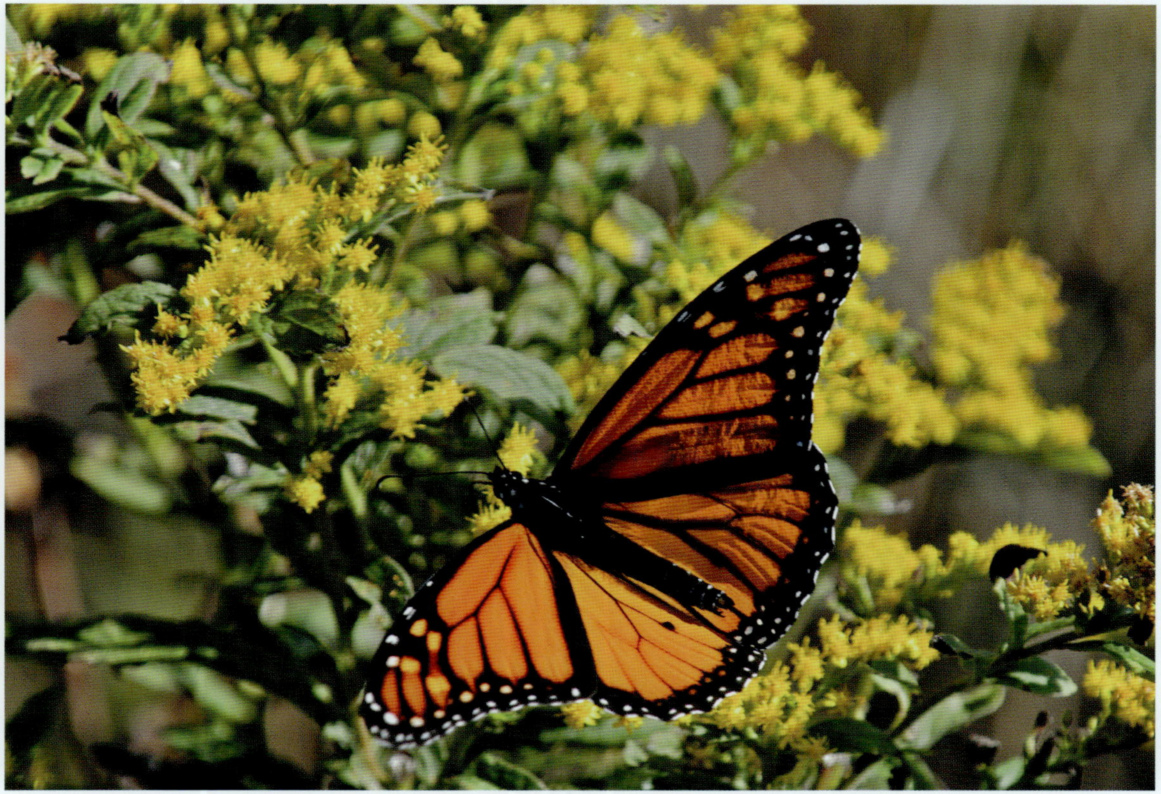

connecting flight

dragonfly and migrating monarch, powder hole,
monomoy national wildlife refuge

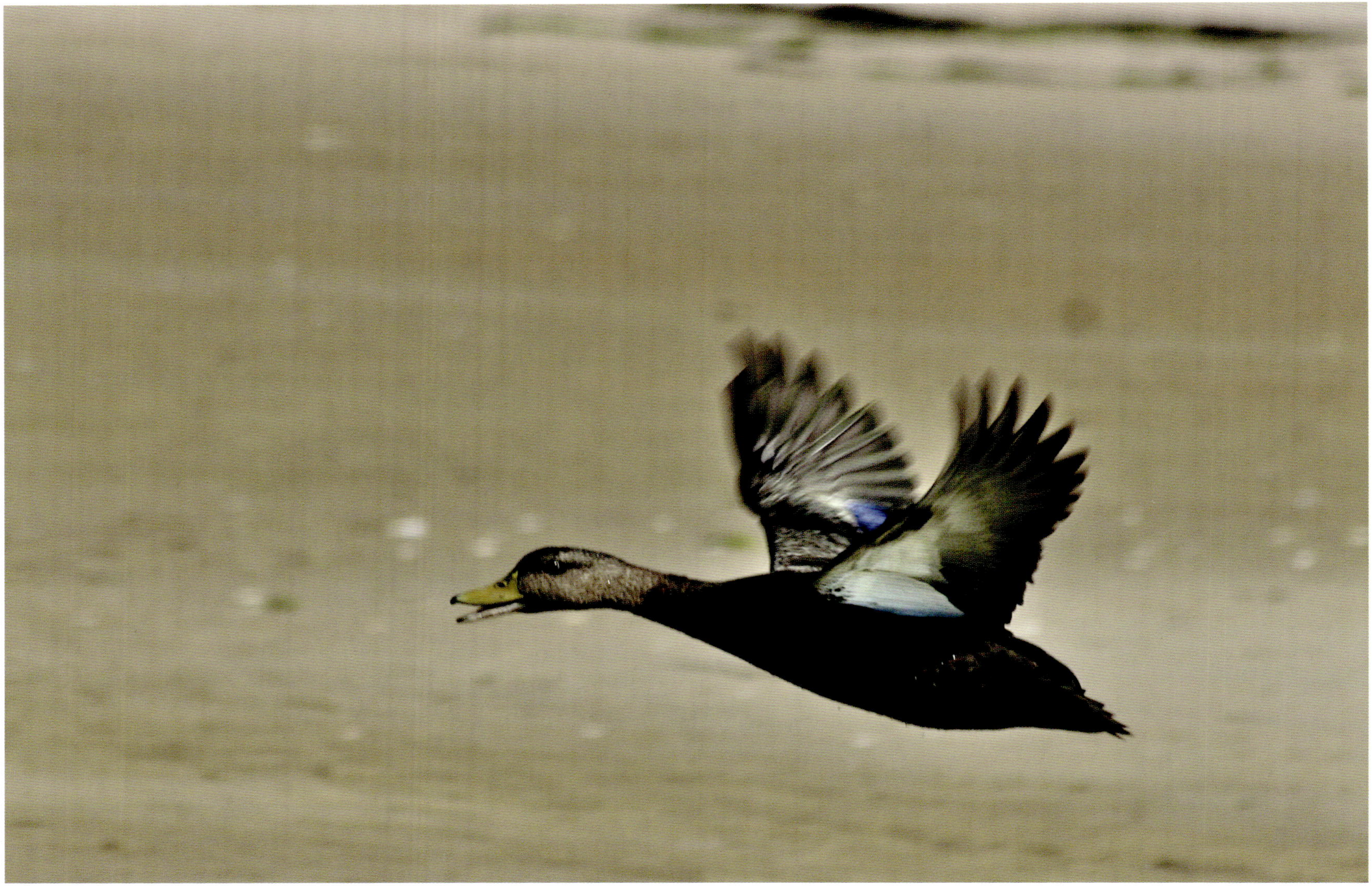

black duck,
tern island, chatham

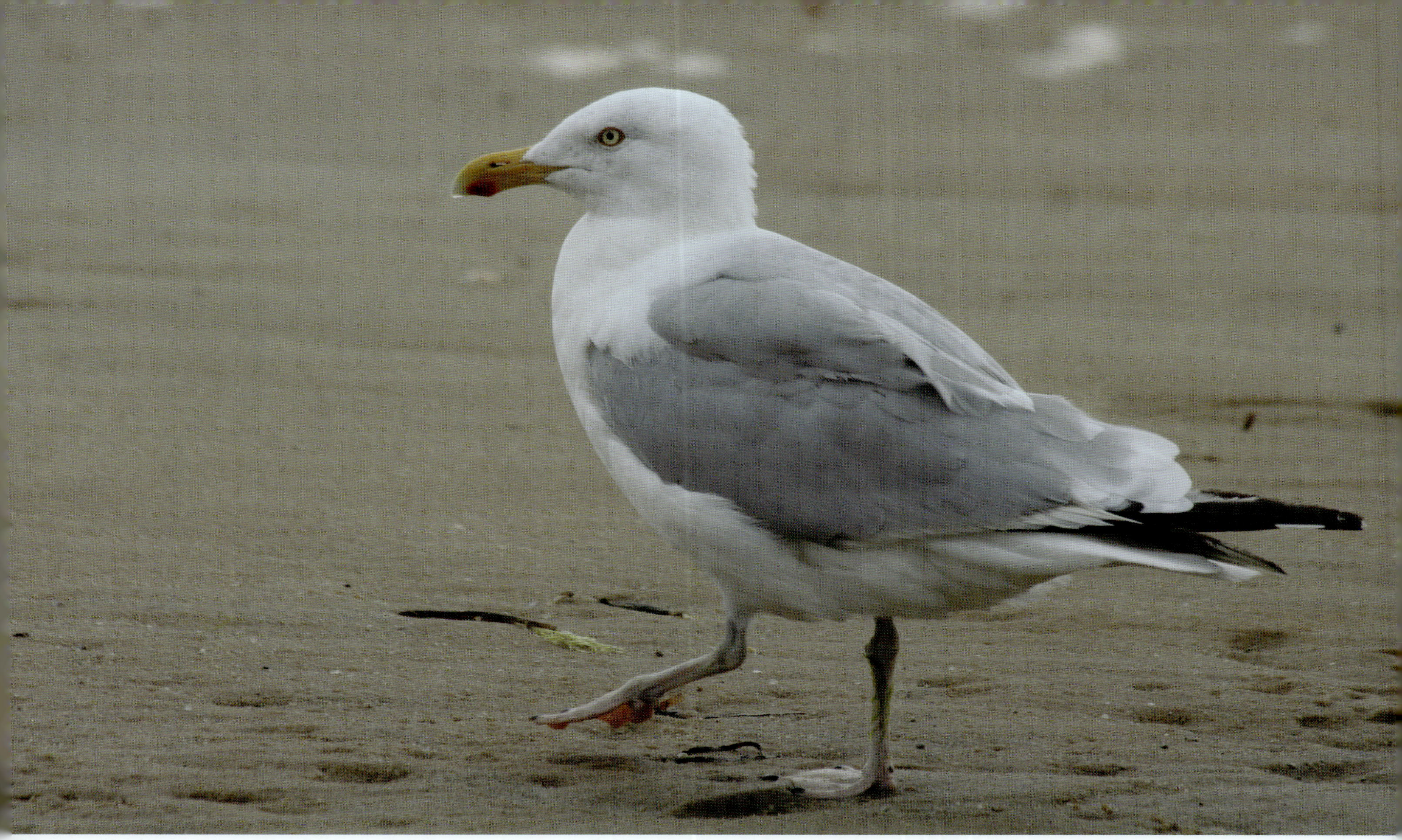

herring gull,
monomoy national wildlife refuge

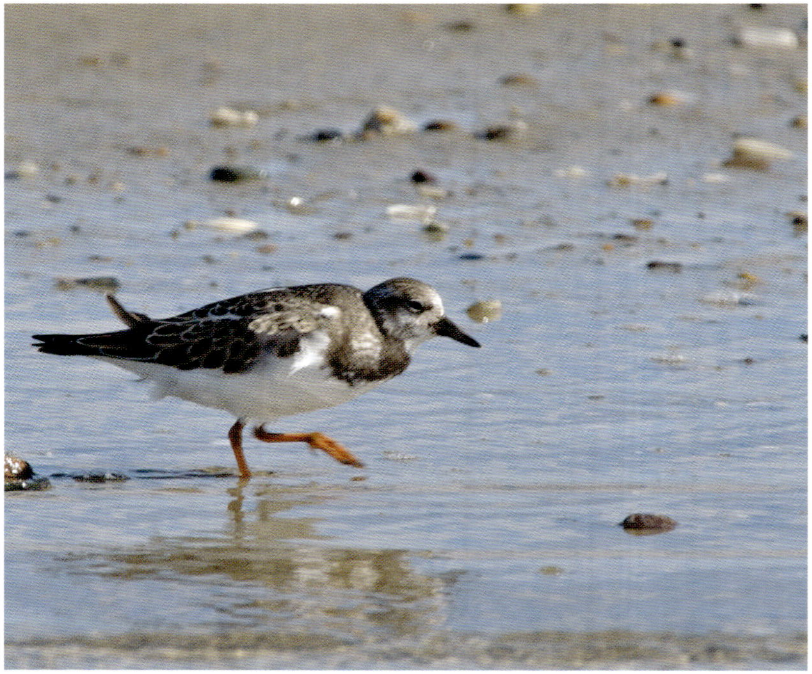

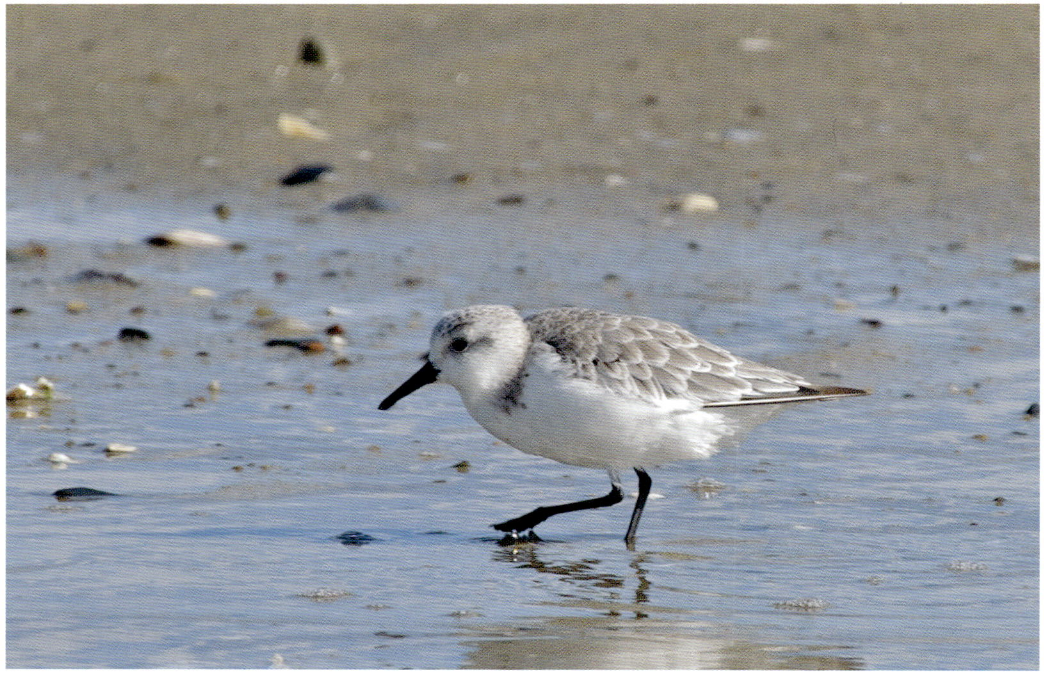

food bank

ruddy turnstone and sanderling,
monomoy national wildlife refuge

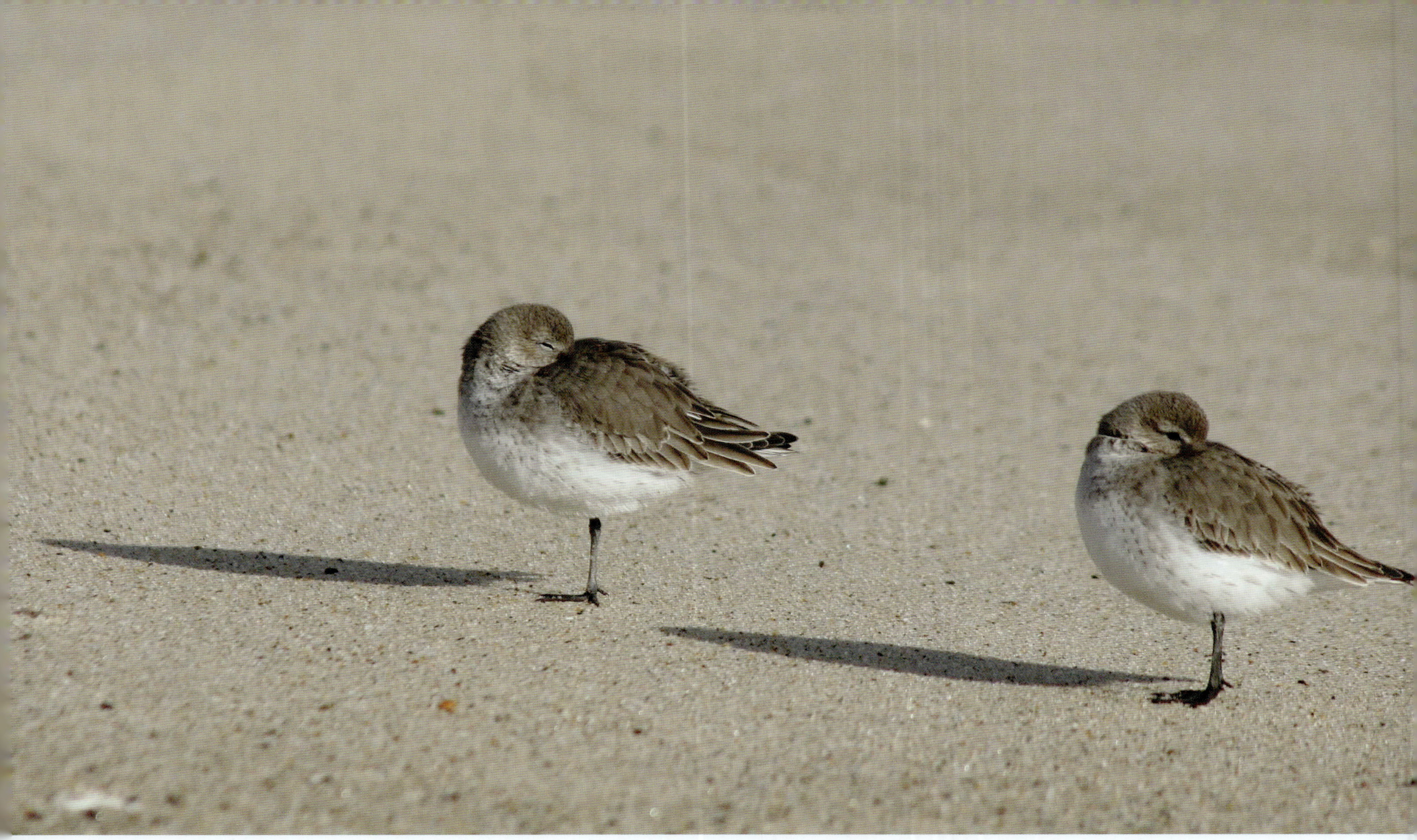

me and my shadow

white rumped sandpipers,
north beach island, chatham

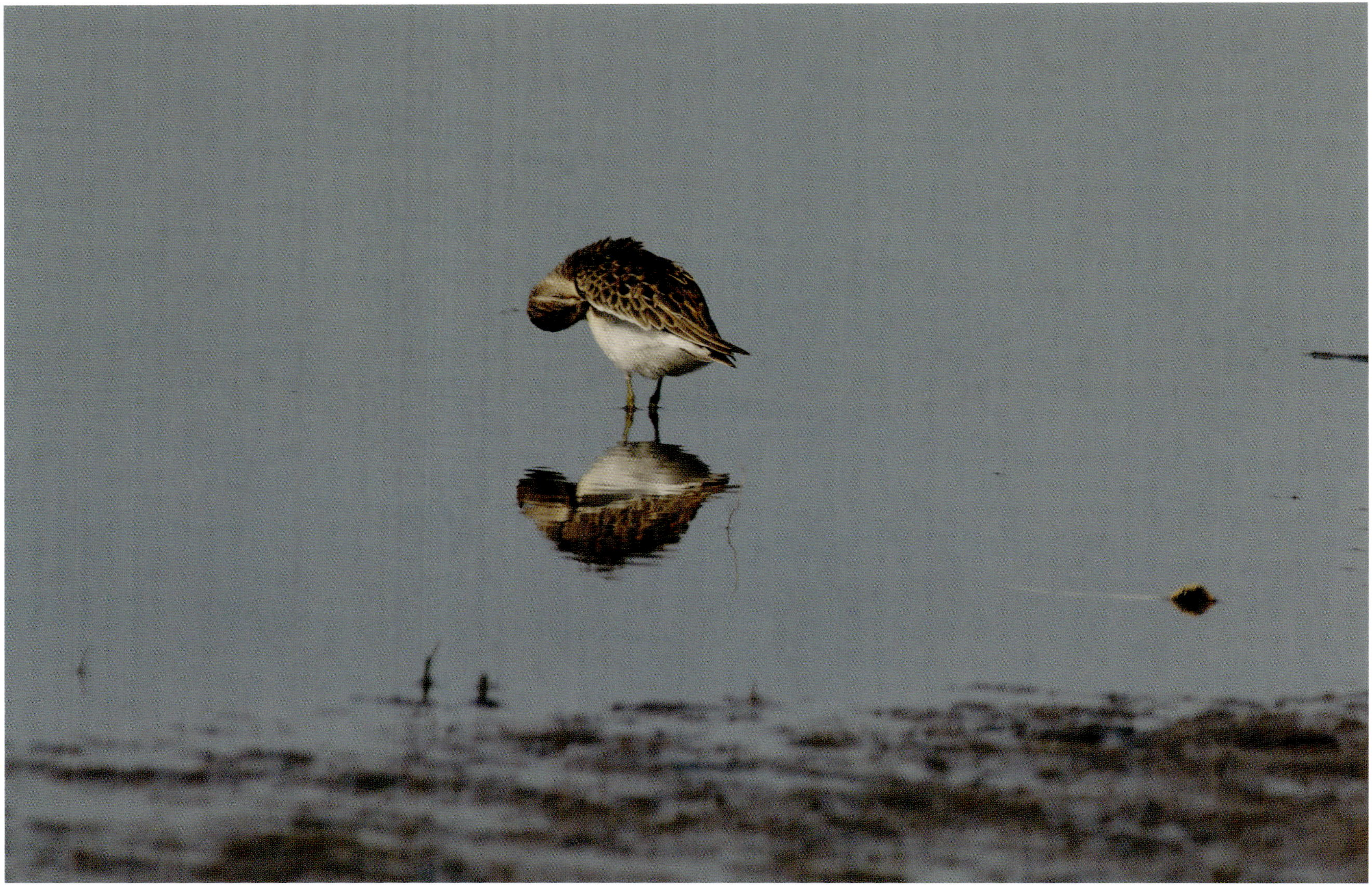

quiet moment

semipalmated sandpiper, powder hole, monomoy national wildlife refuge

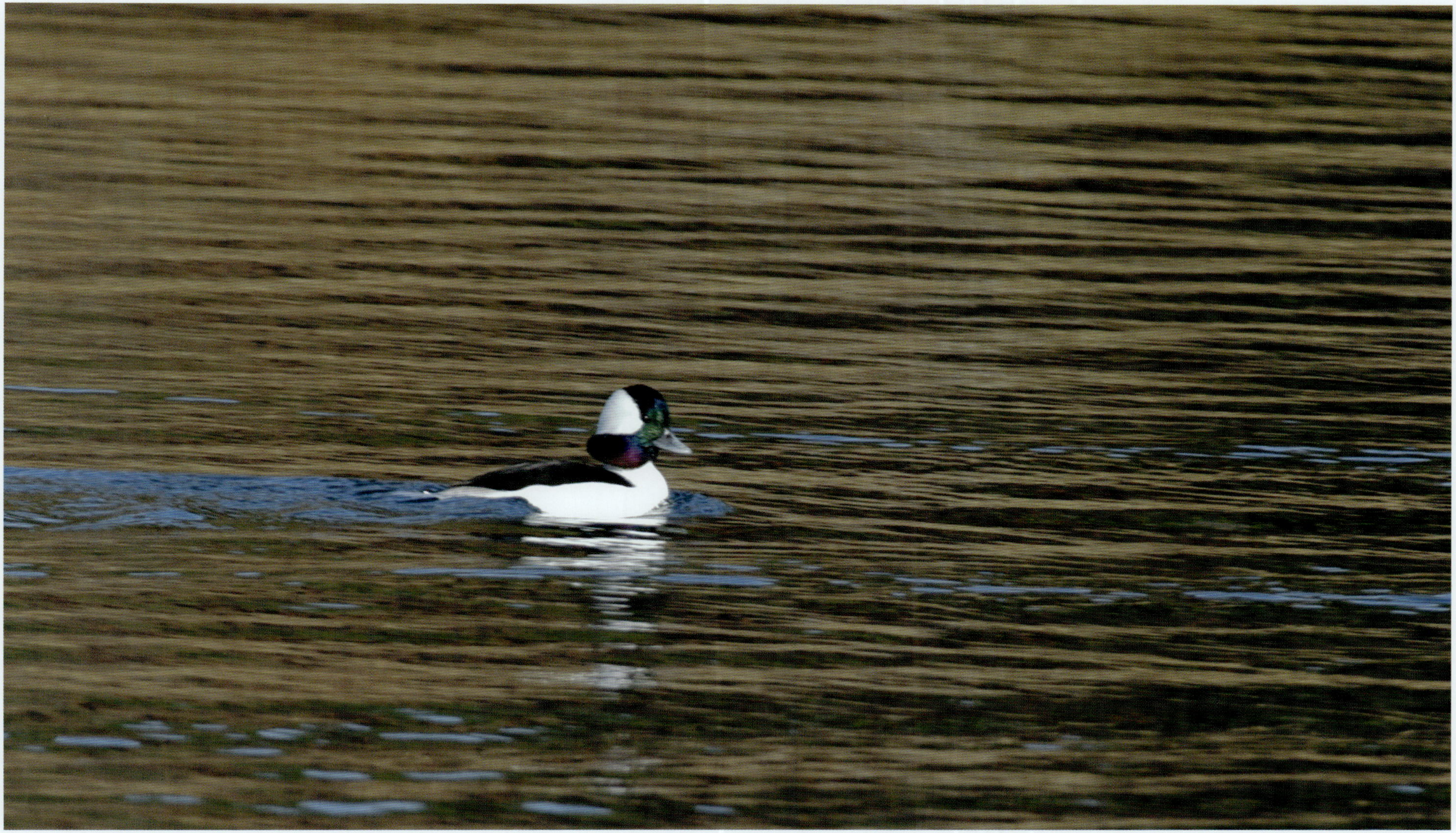

smallest sea duck

bufflehead drake,
ryder's cove, chatham

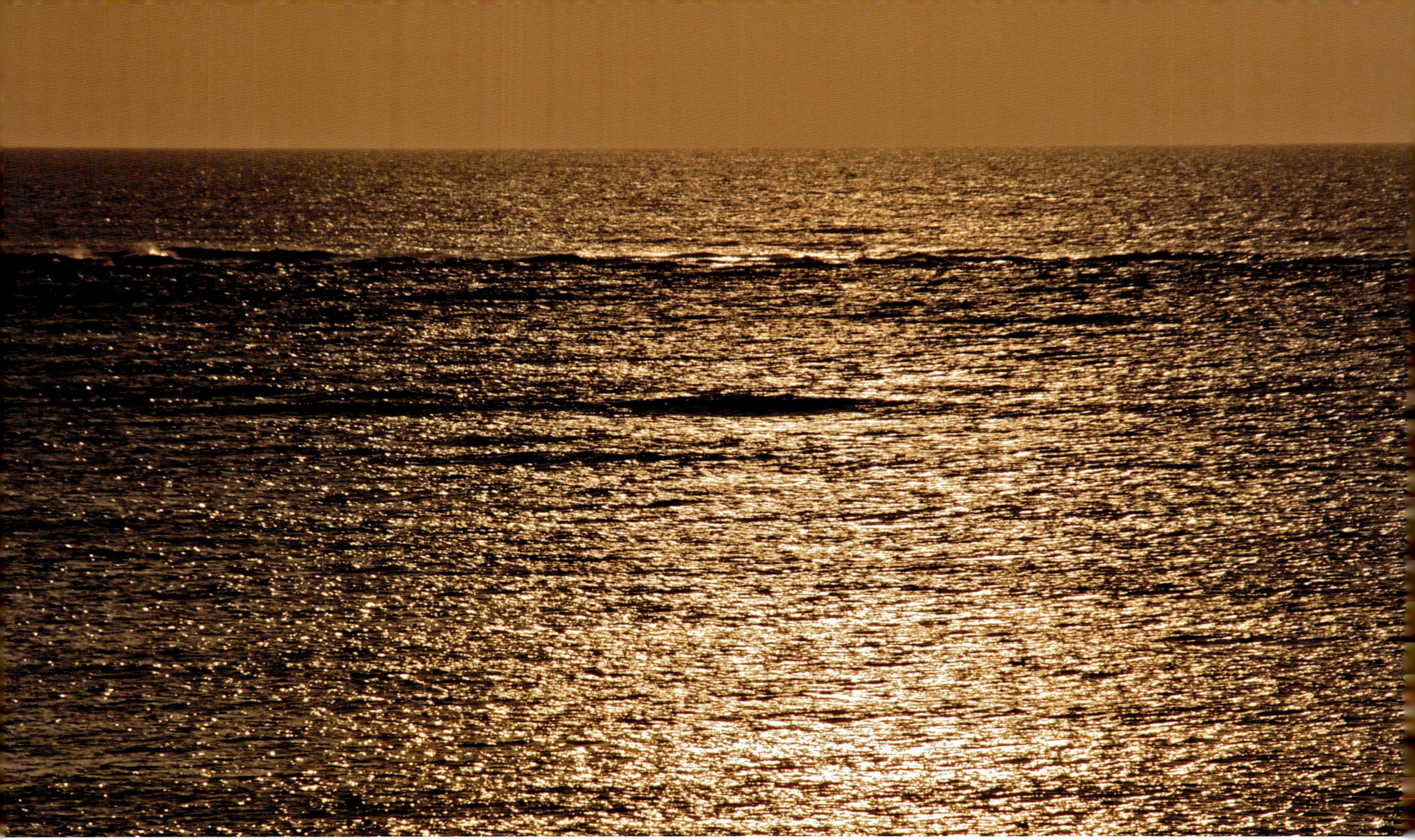

copper dawn

halloween sunrise,
chatham bar

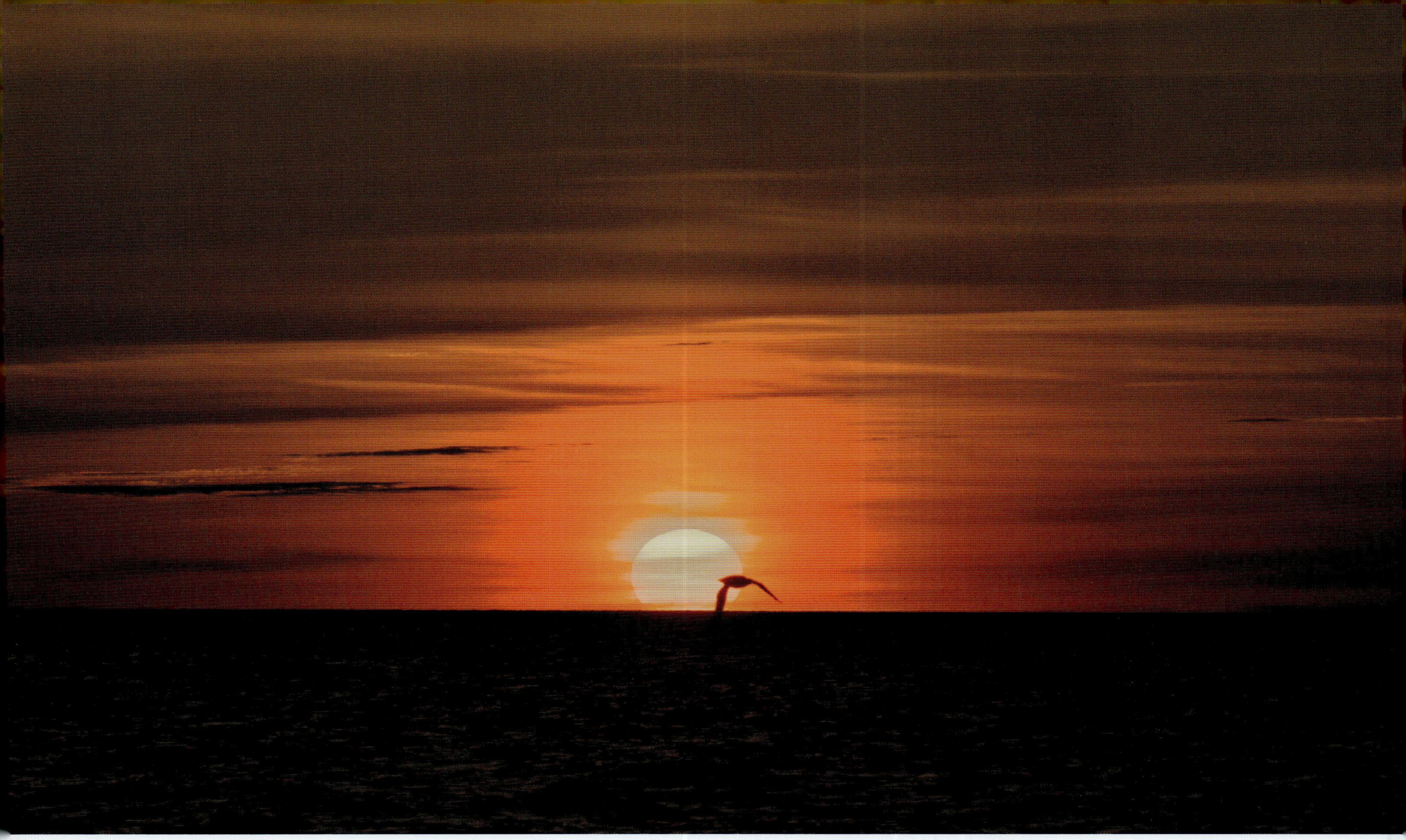

morning routine

northern gannet at sunrise,
off chatham bar

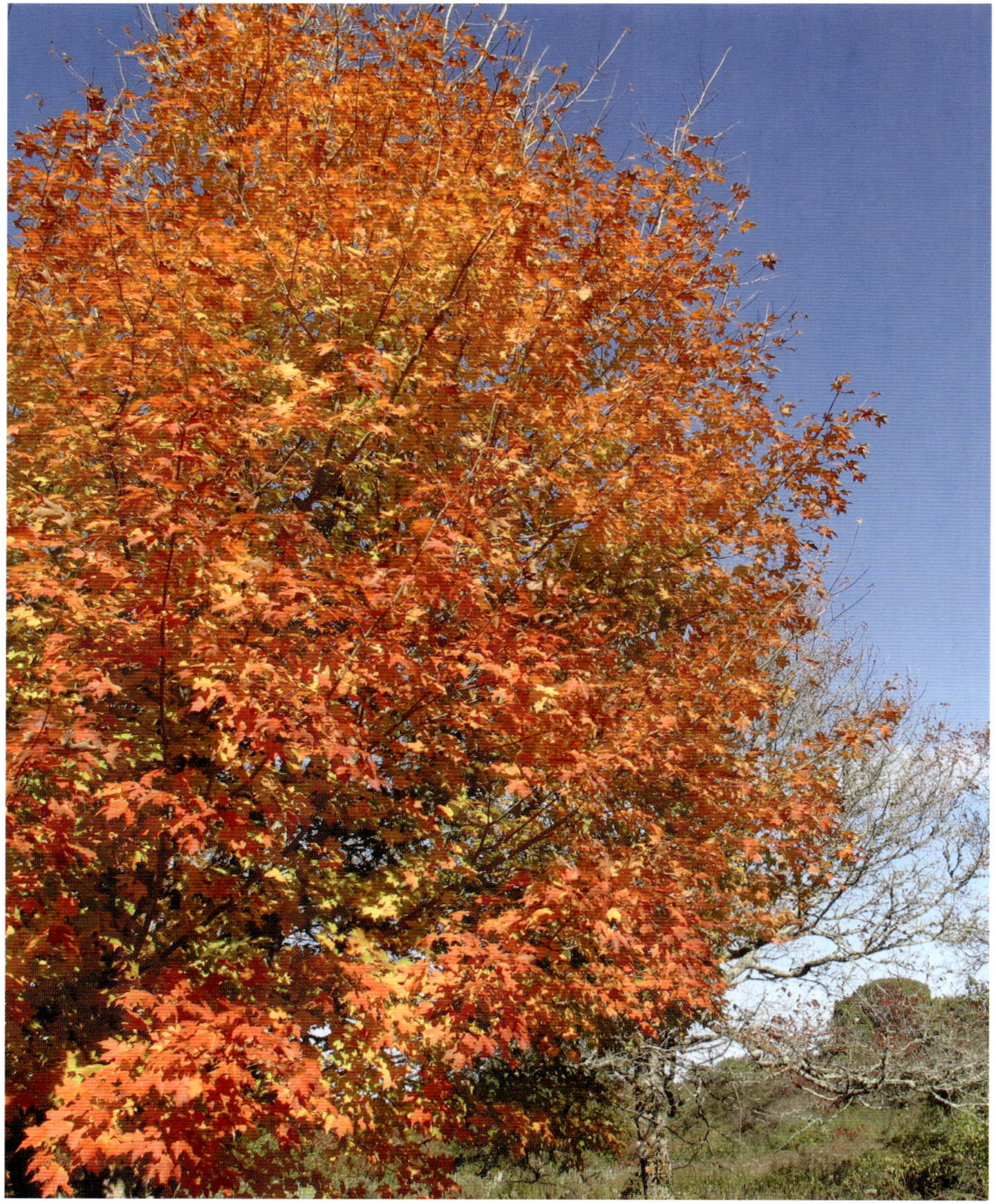

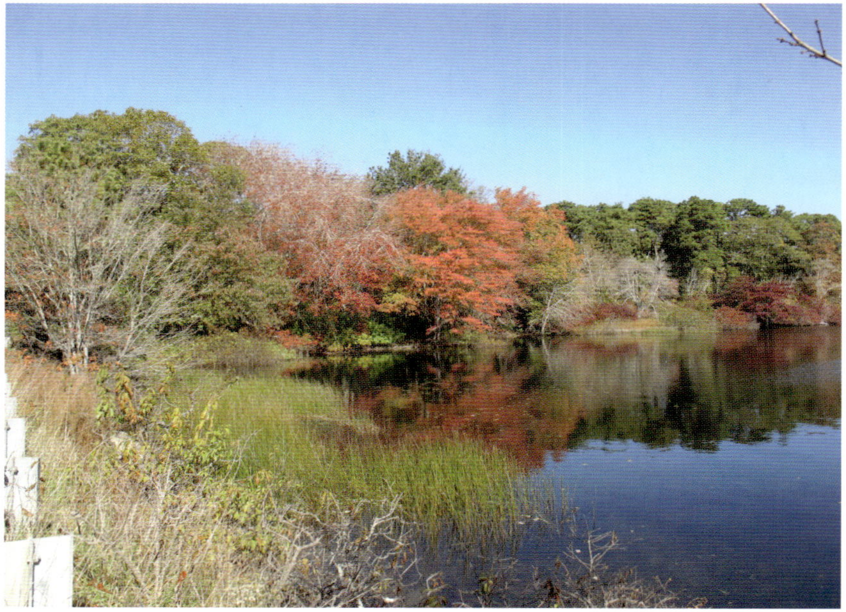

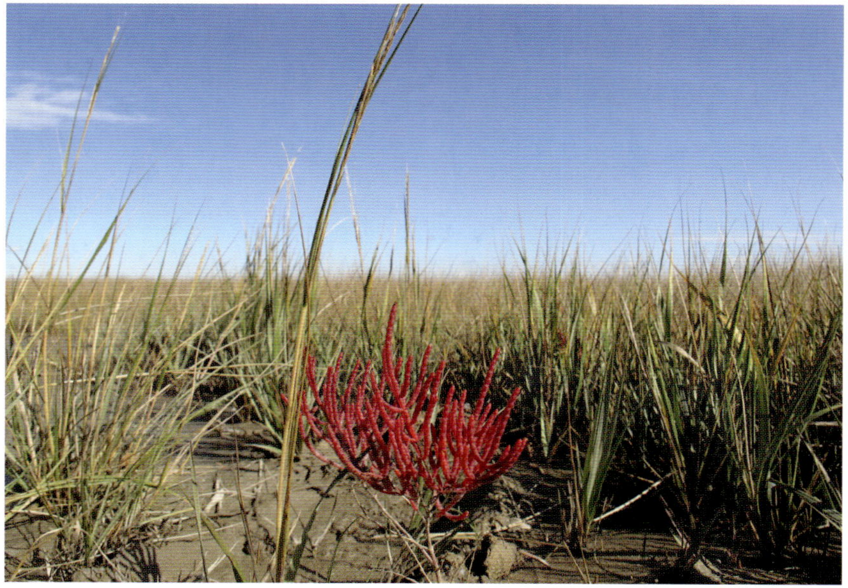

autumn hues

fall foliage,
long pasture wildlife sanctuary, cummaquid

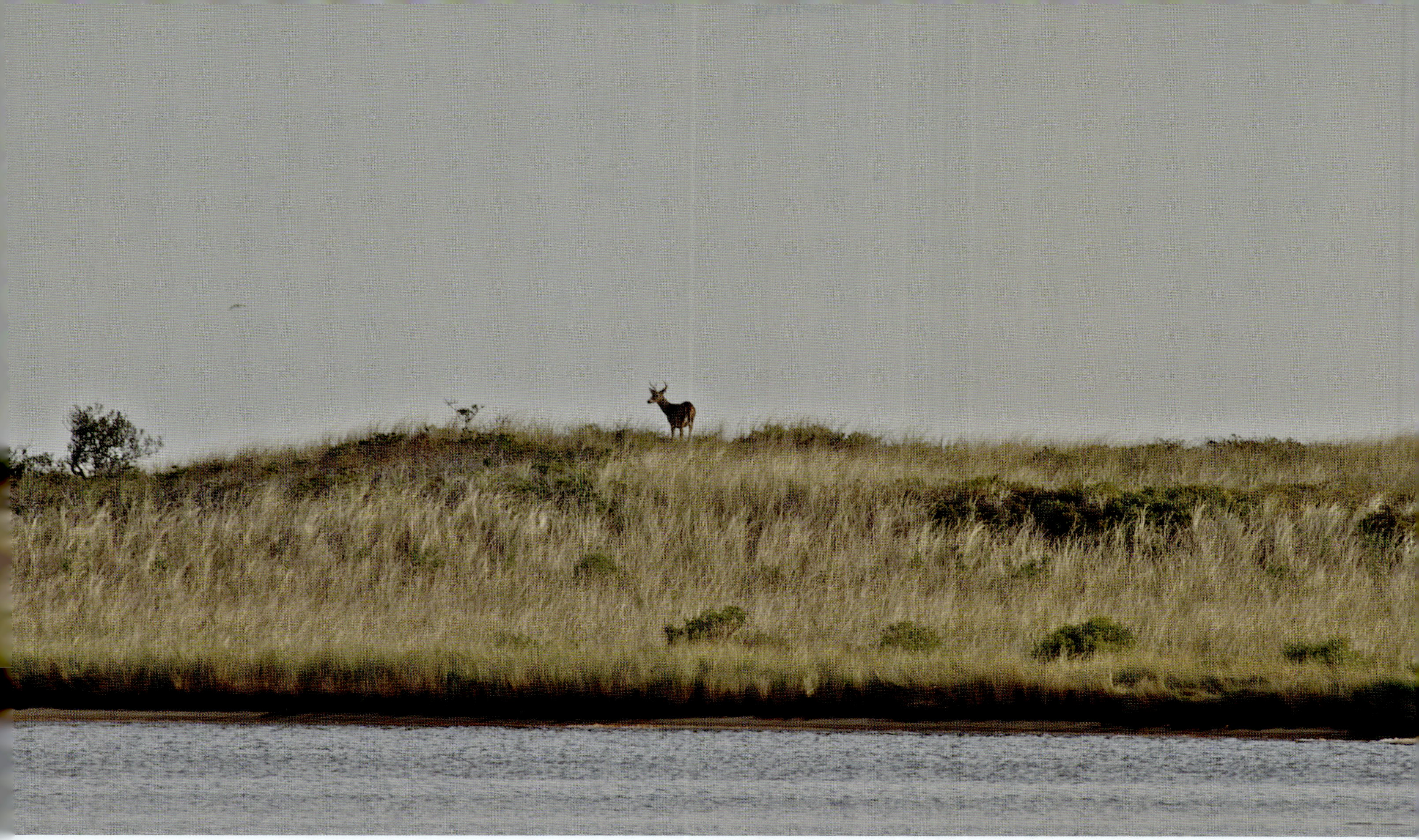

longshot

eight point buck,
powder hole, monomoy national wildlife refuge

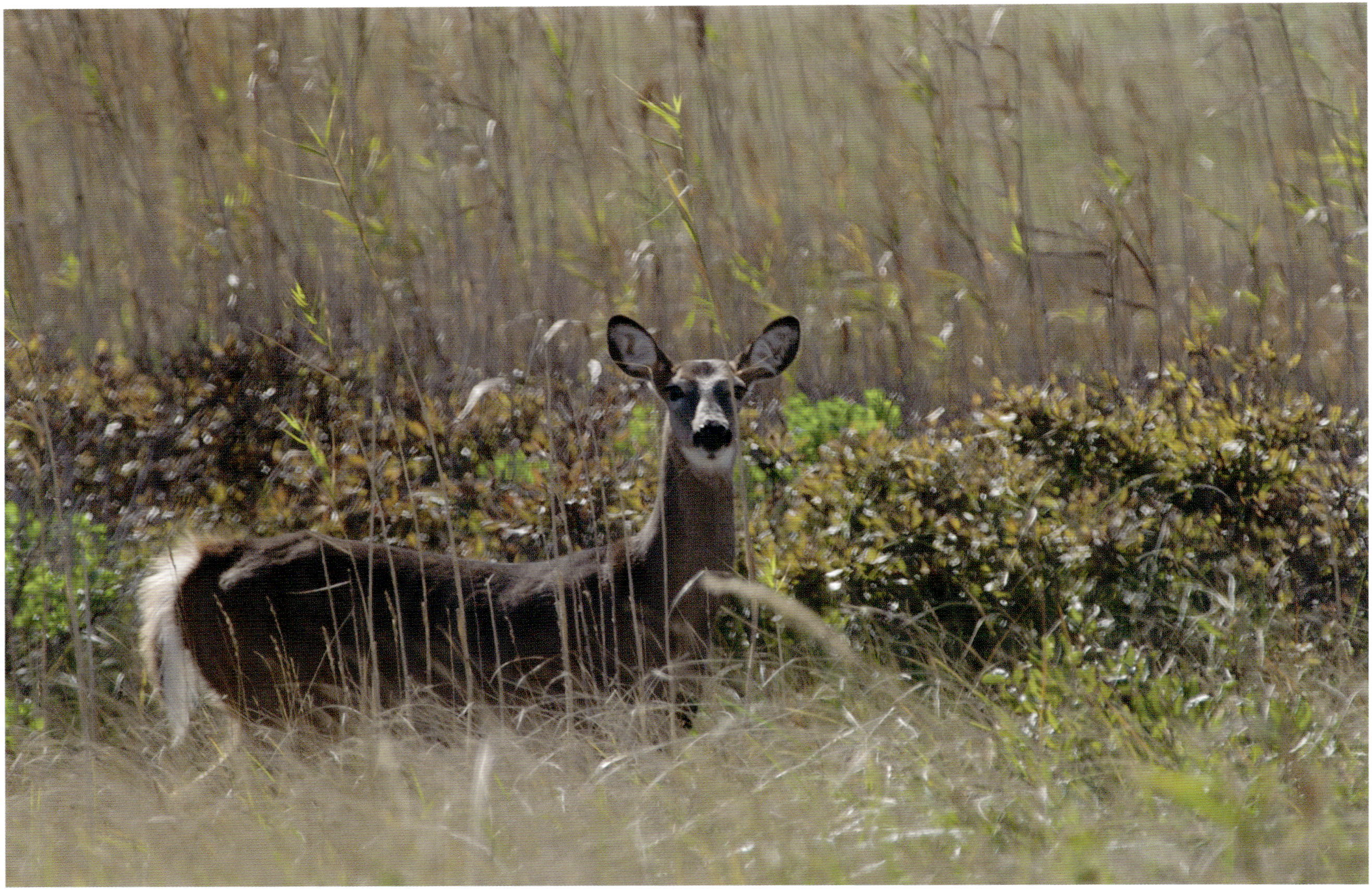

marsh haven

female white-tailed deer, powder hole, monomoy national wildlife refuge

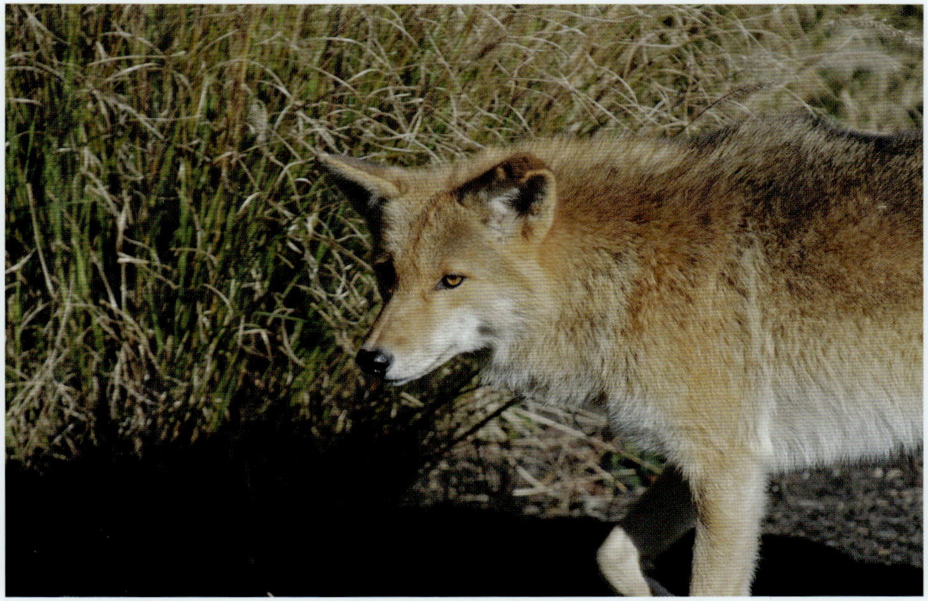

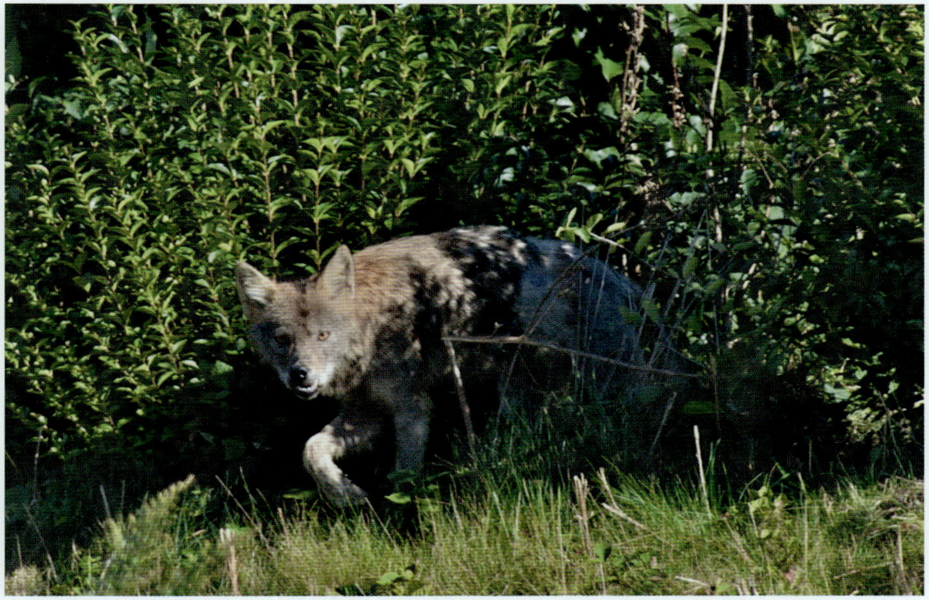

changed with age

senior and young coyote,
chatham

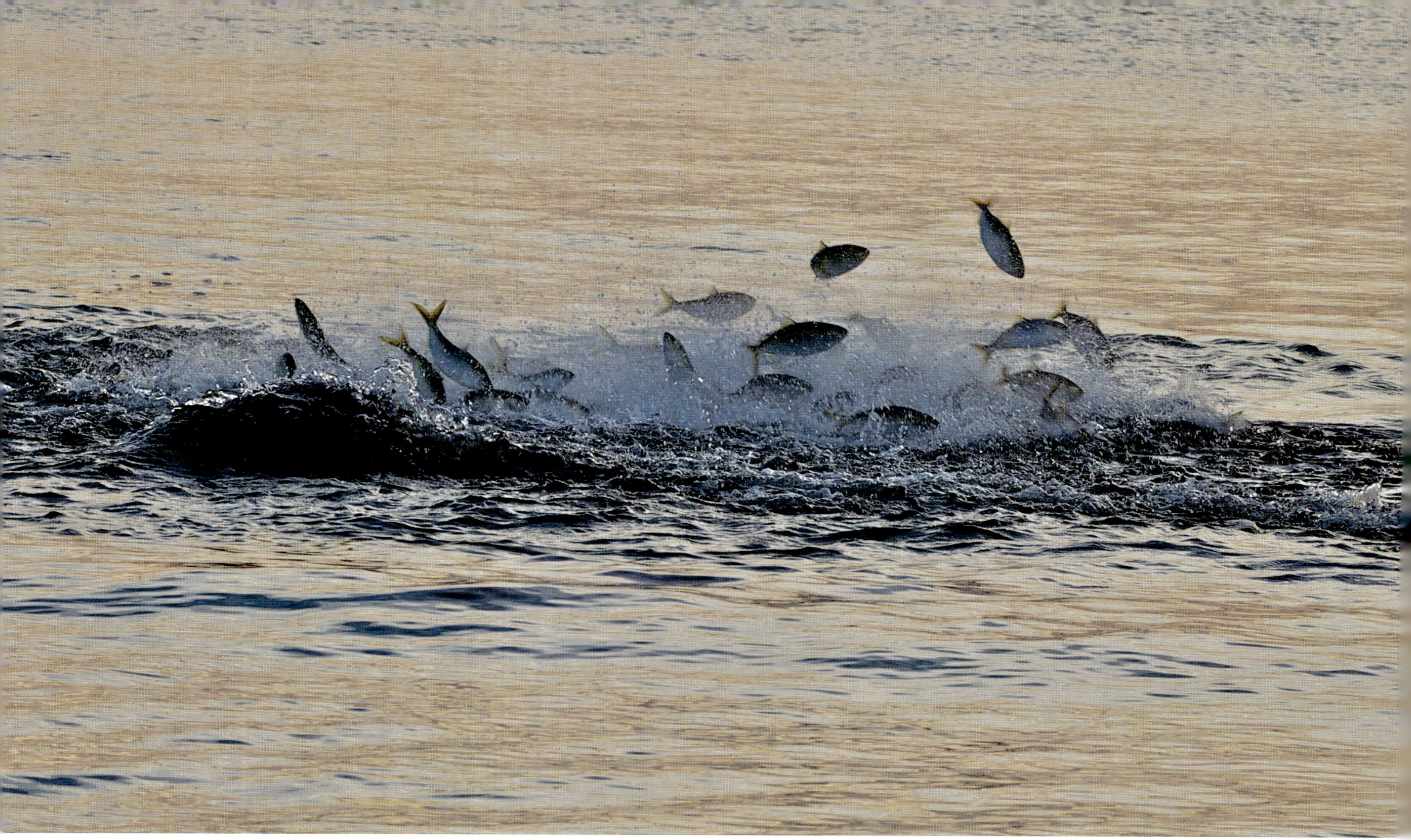

fisherman's platter

grey seal chasing poagies,
hardings beach, chatham

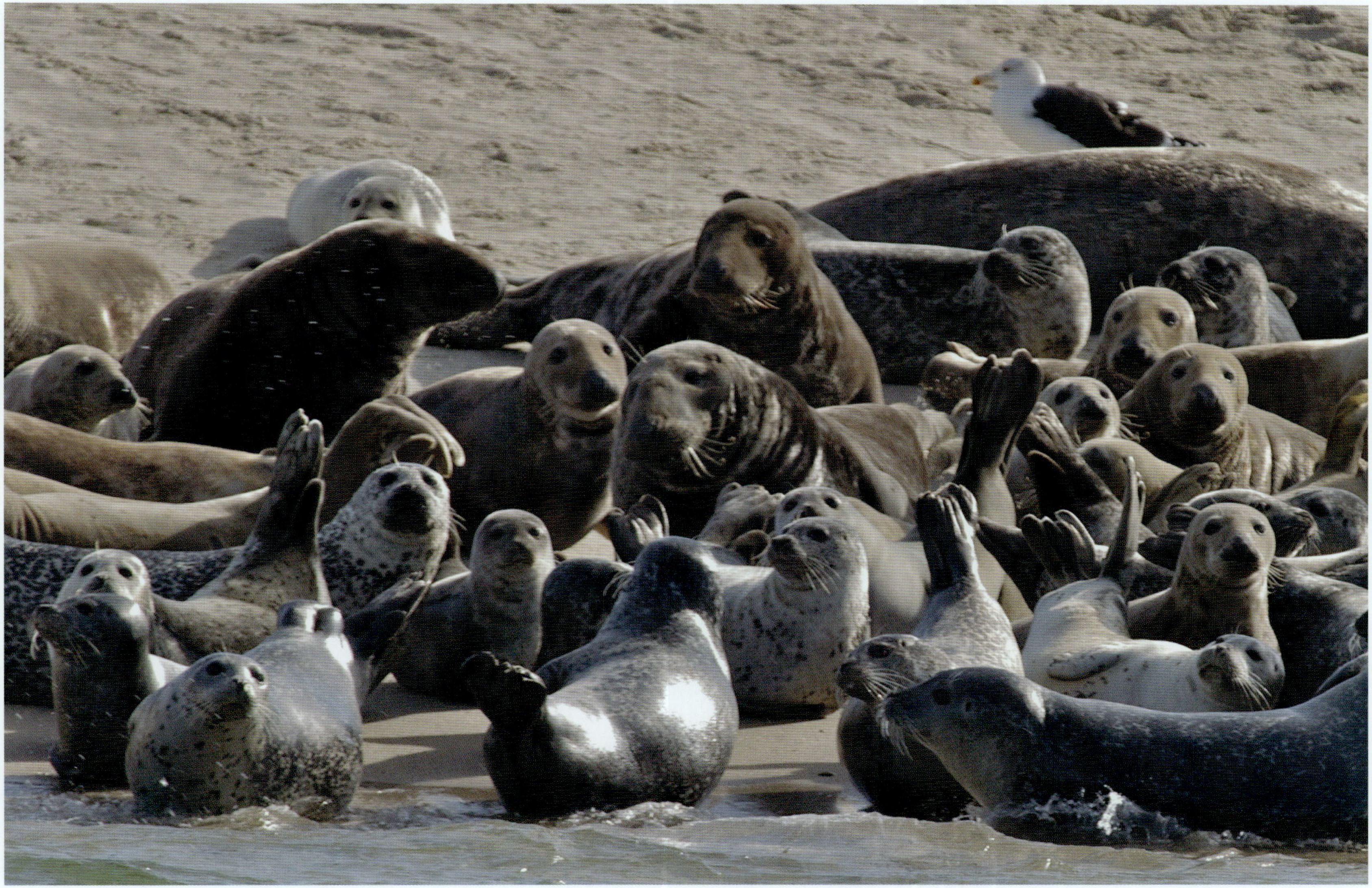

melting pot

grey and harbor seals,
north beach island, chatham

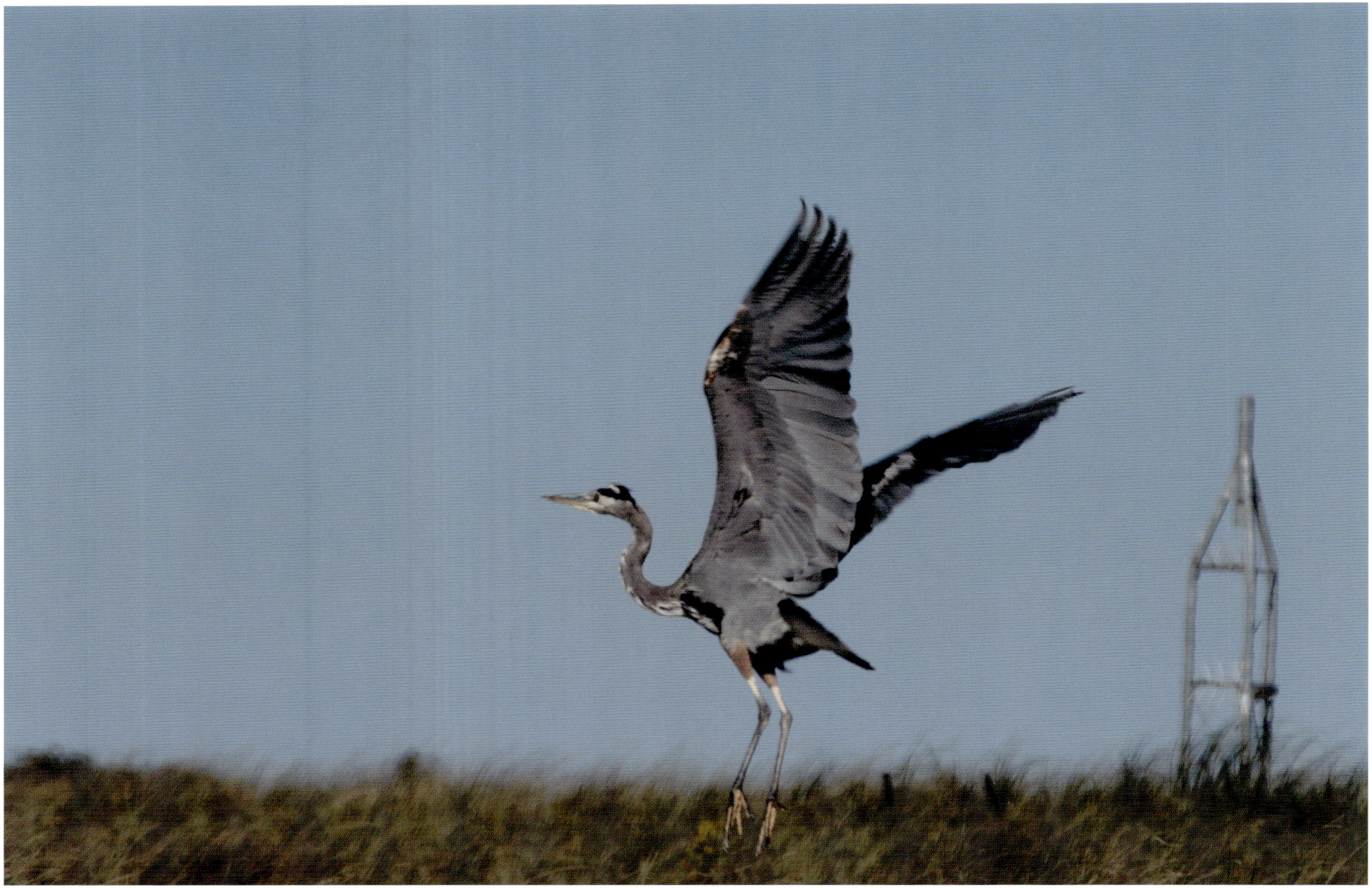

great blue heron,
tern island, chatham

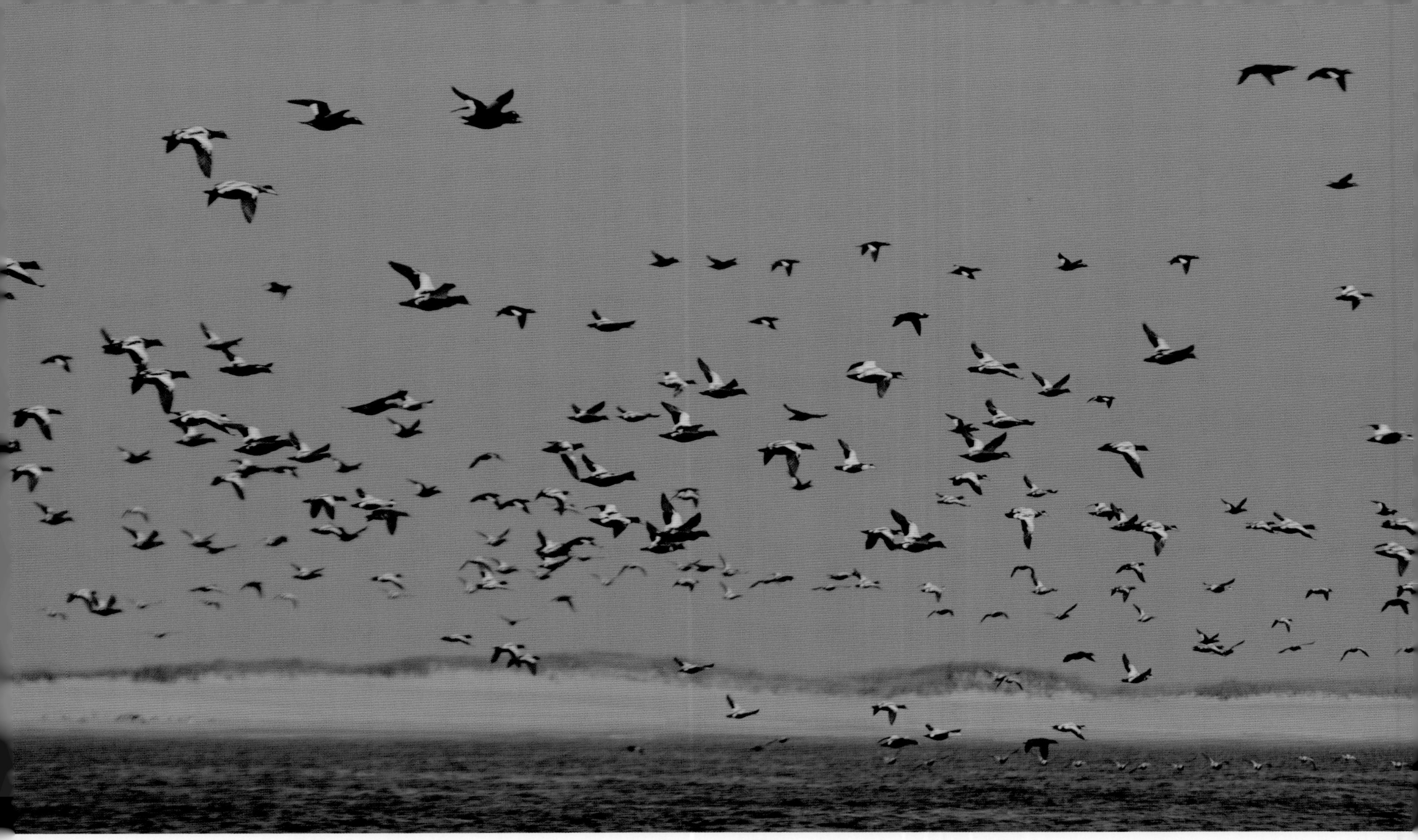

winter home

returning sea ducks,
off chatham

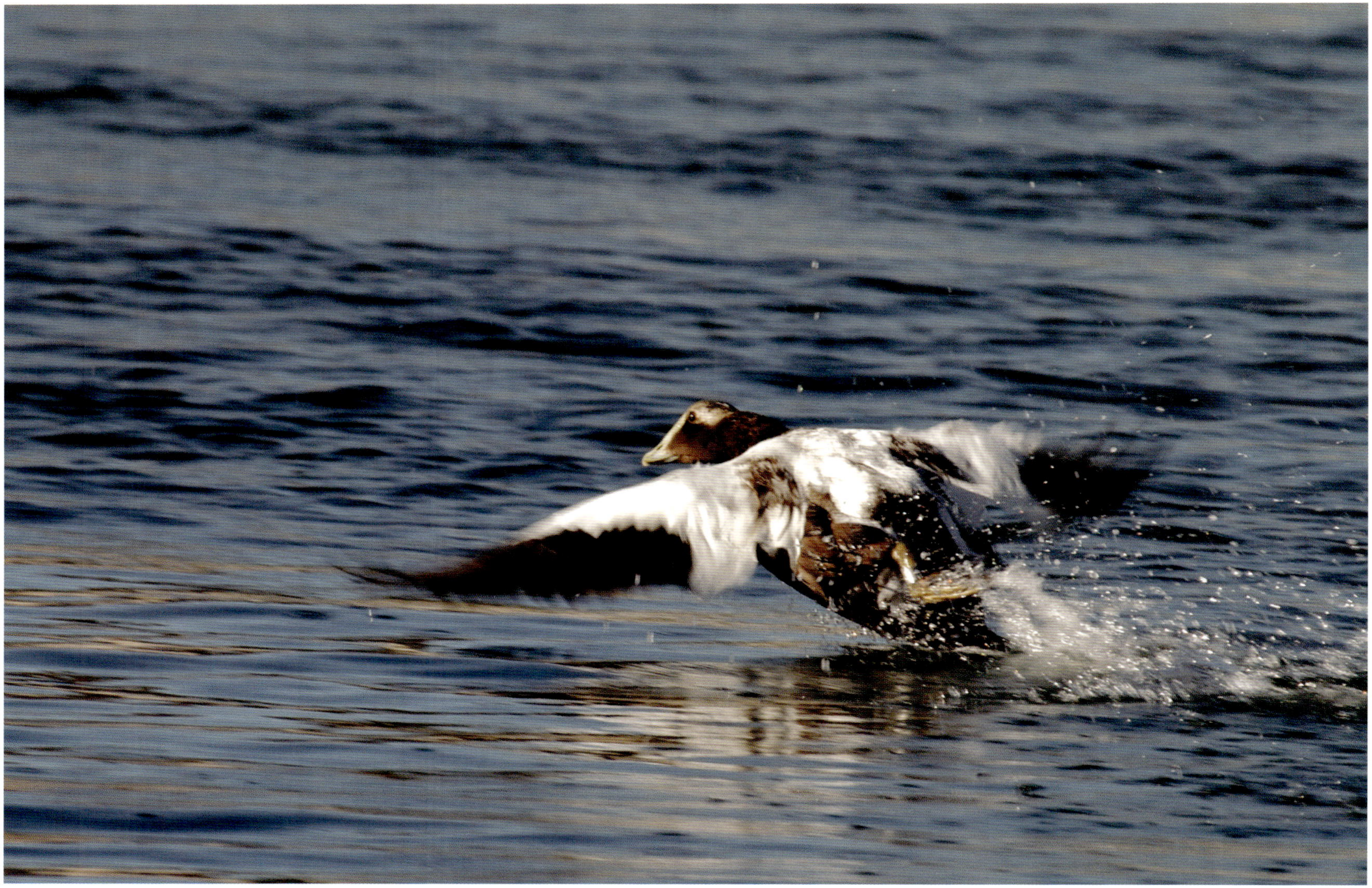

young common eider drake,
off chatham

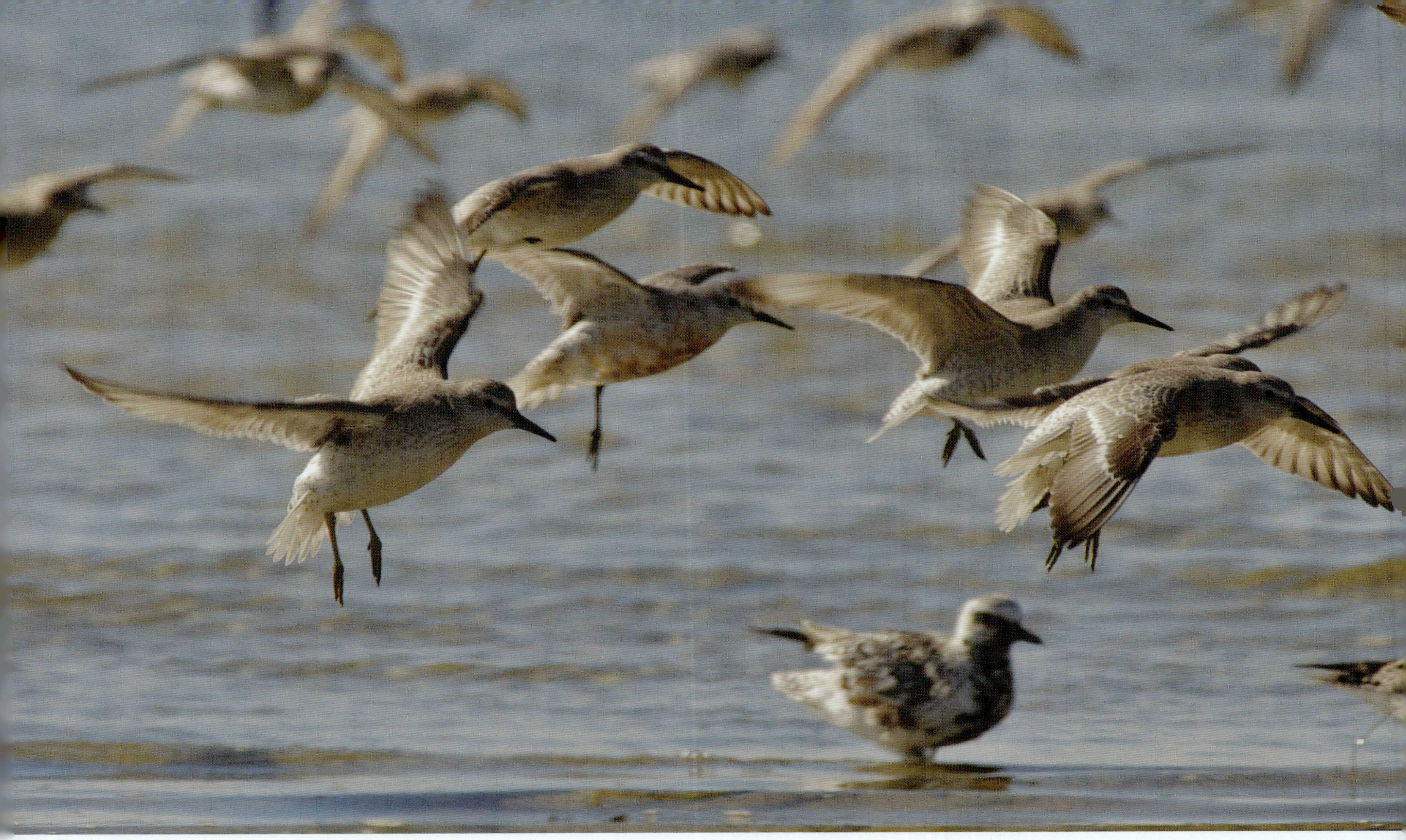

red knots,
south beach, chatham

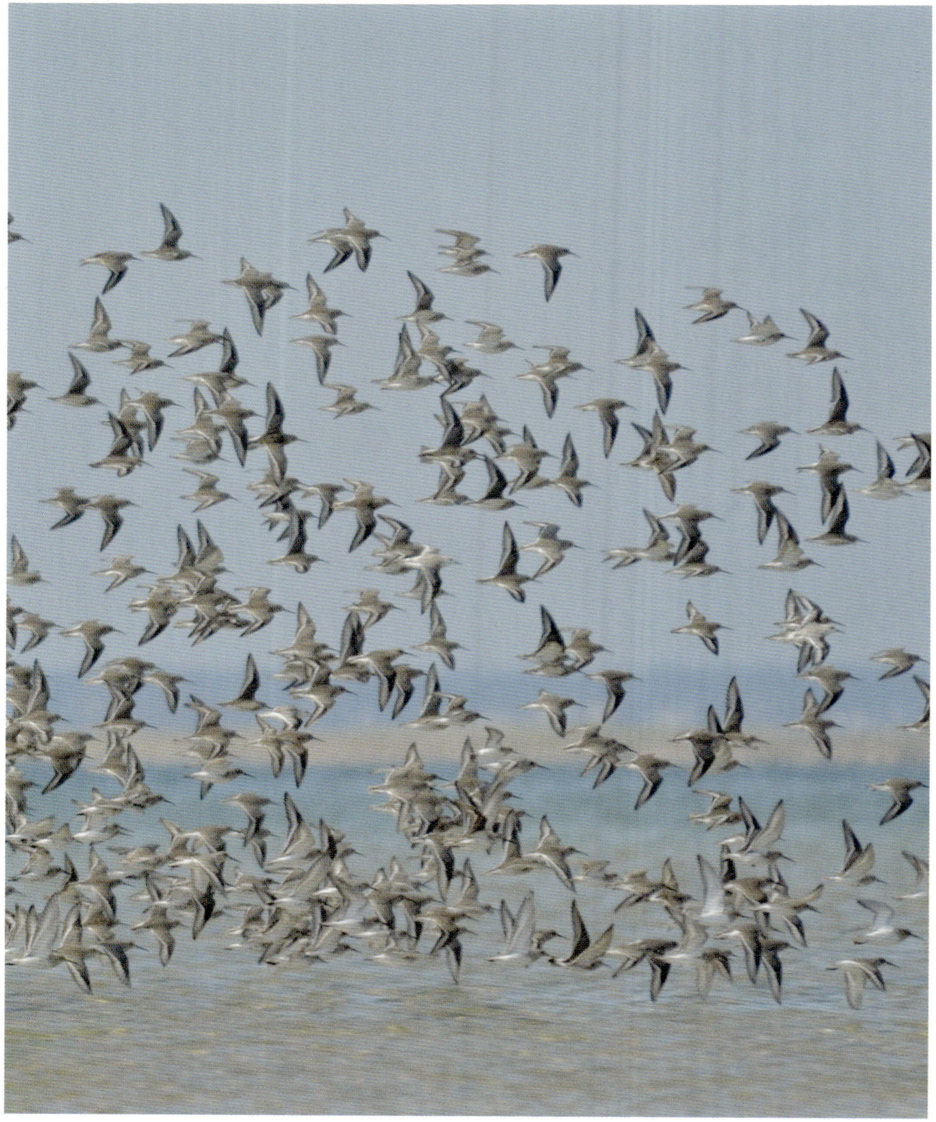
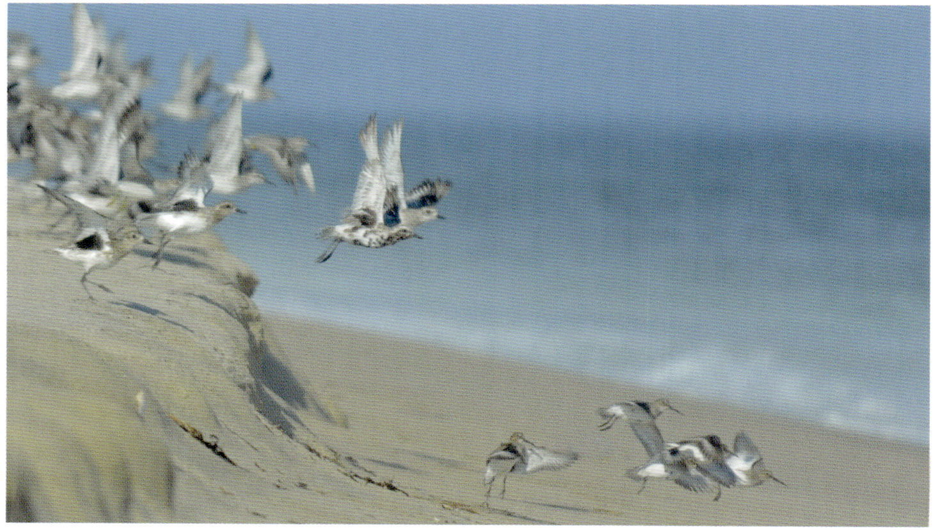
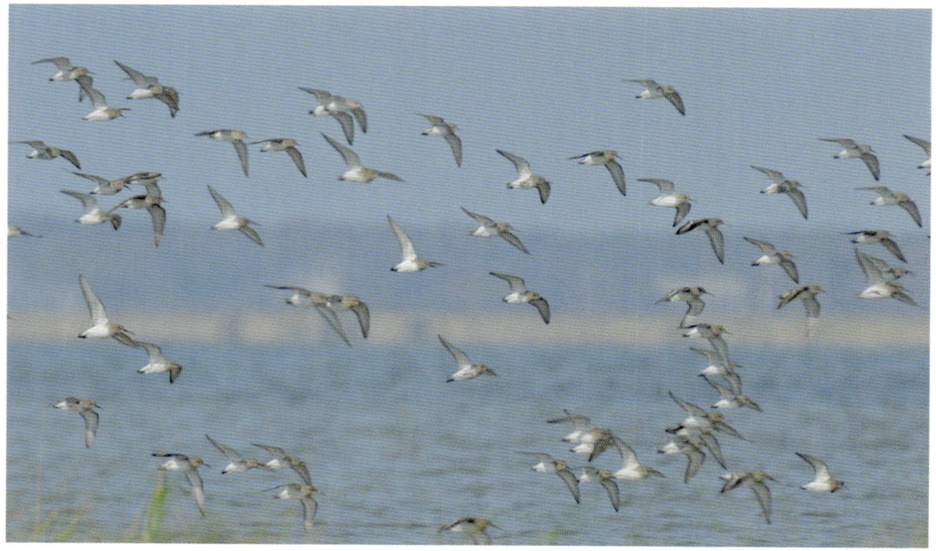

dunlins,
south beach, chatham

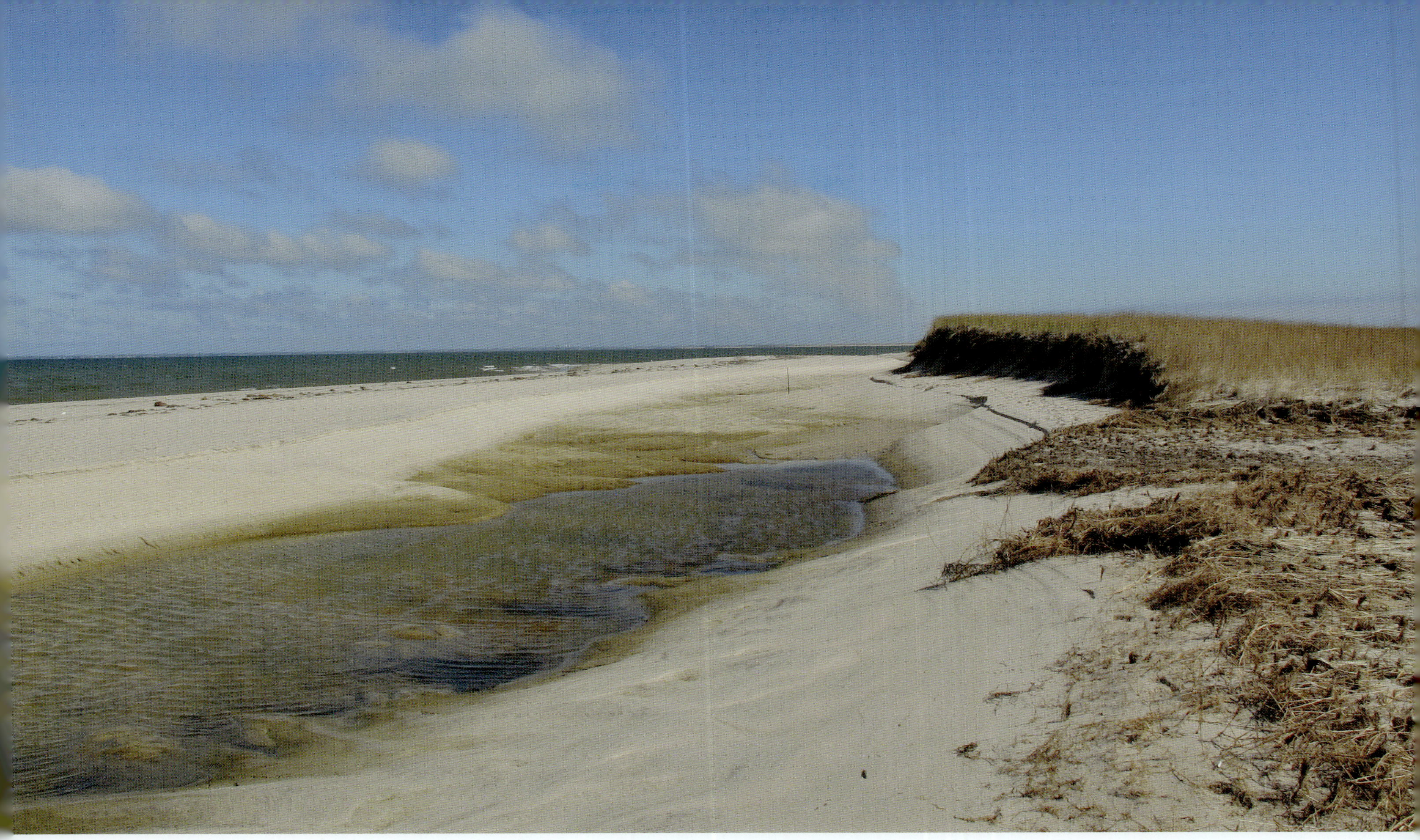

seaside pool

powder hole,
monomoy national wildlife refuge

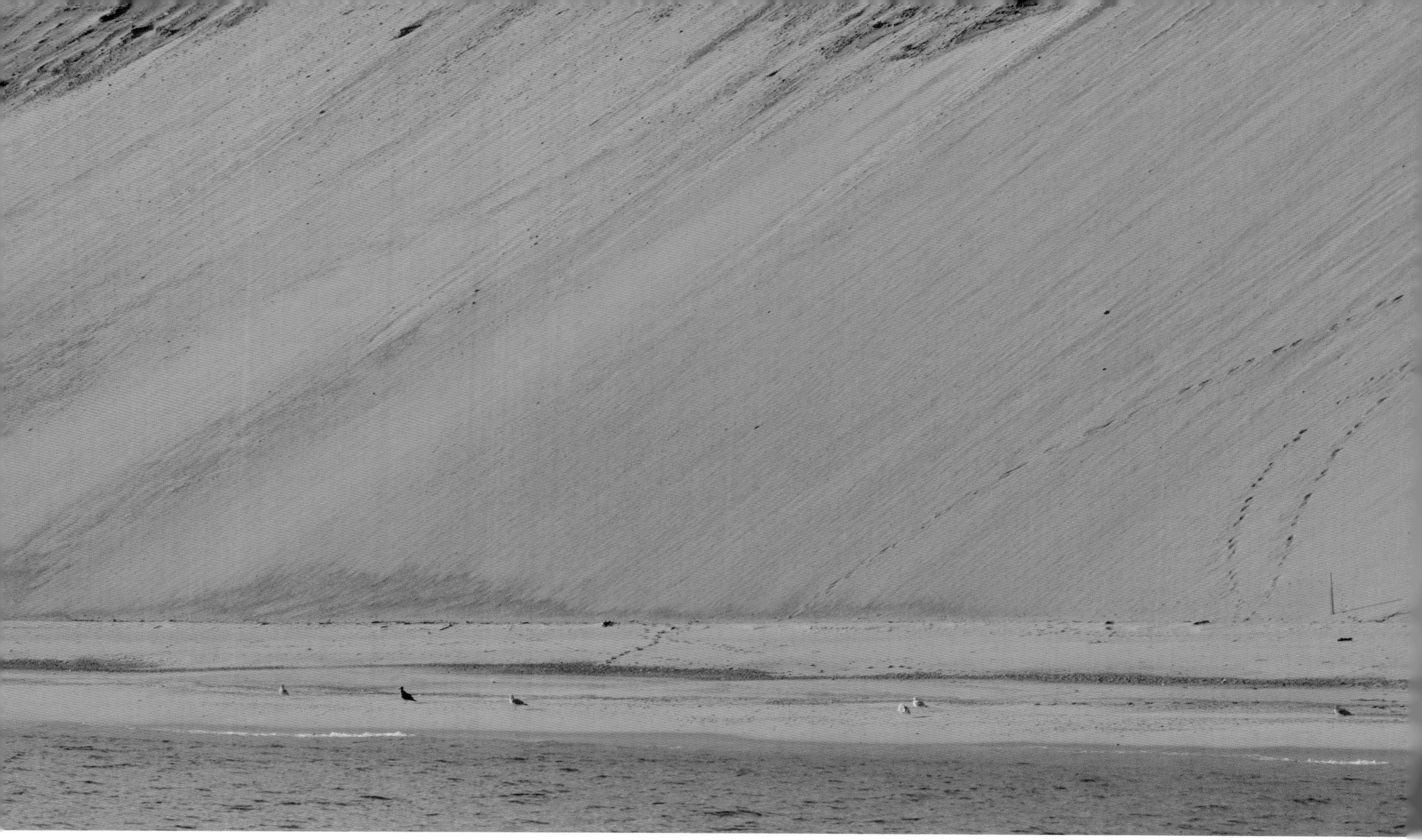

sandy barricade | giant sand dune, wellfleet

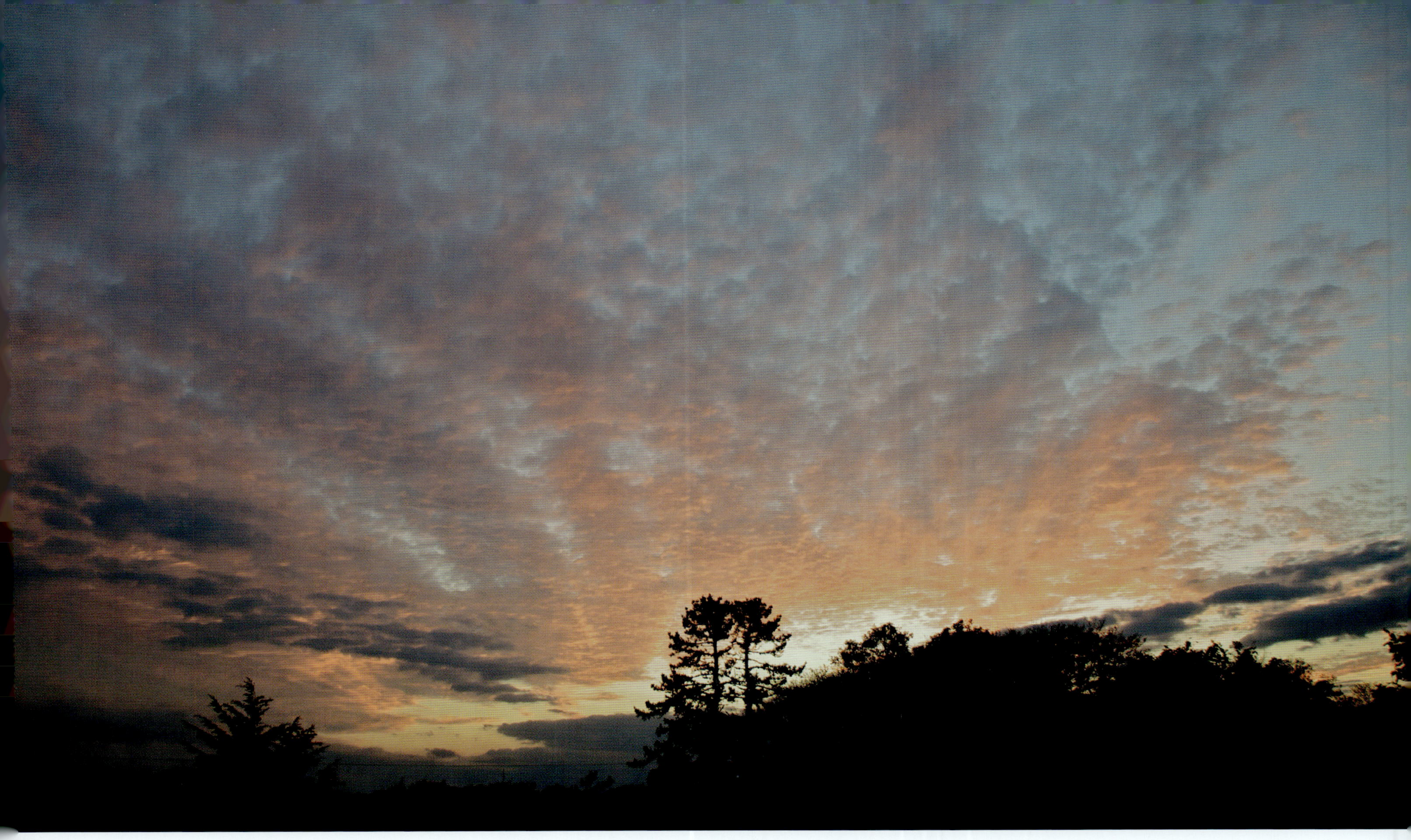

happy hour | sunset, chatham

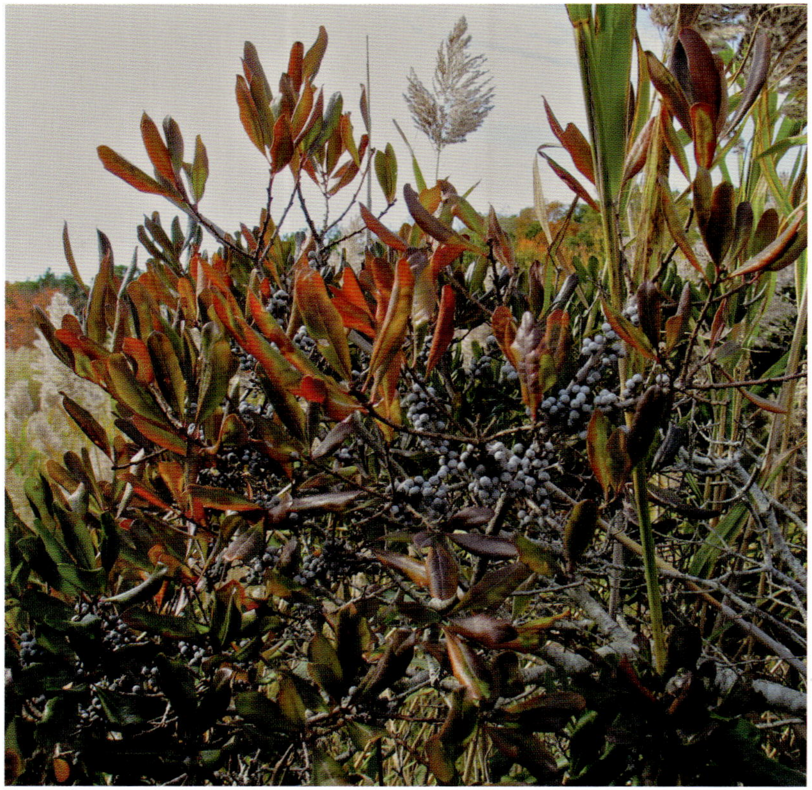

harvest tones

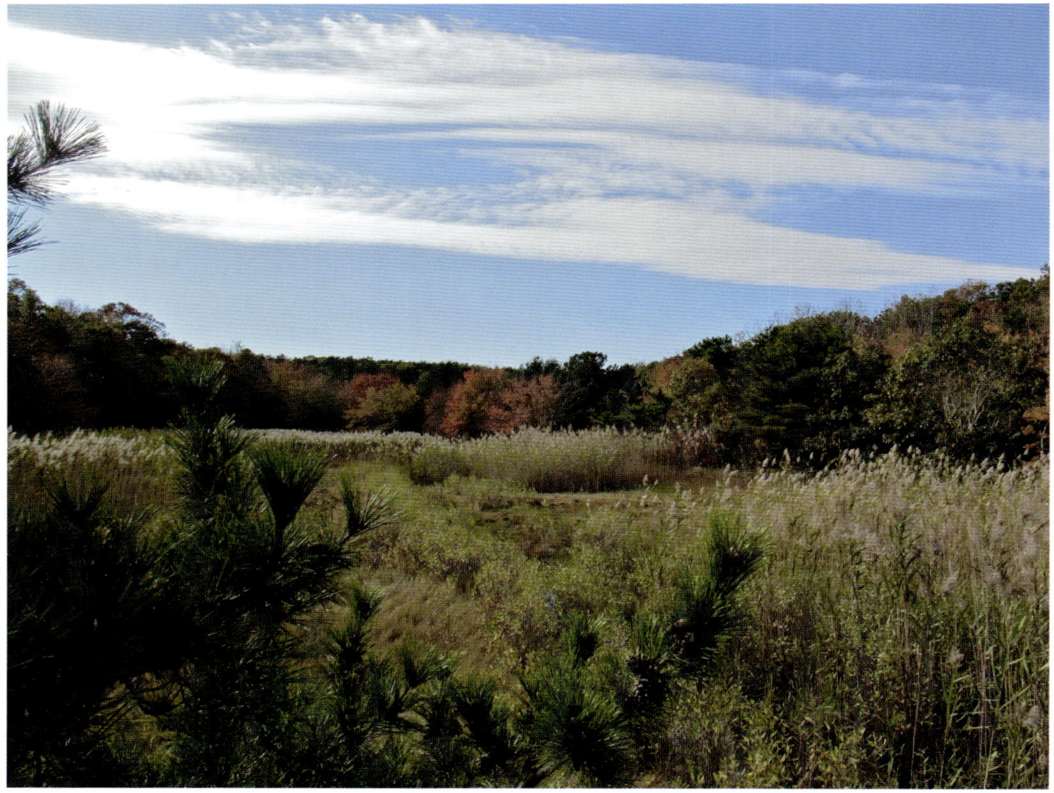

west barnstable marsh

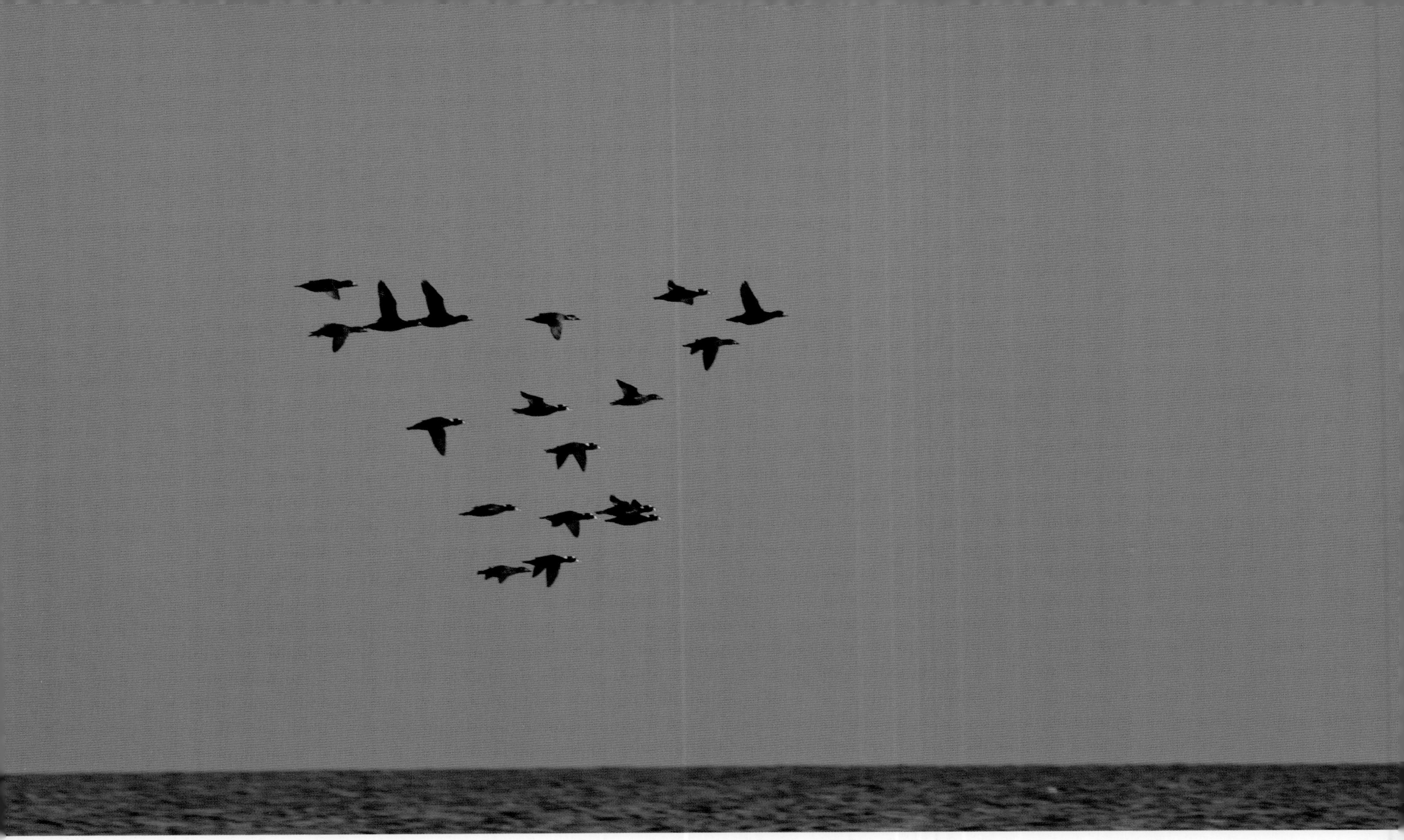

arctic arrival

scoters migrating south, wellfleet

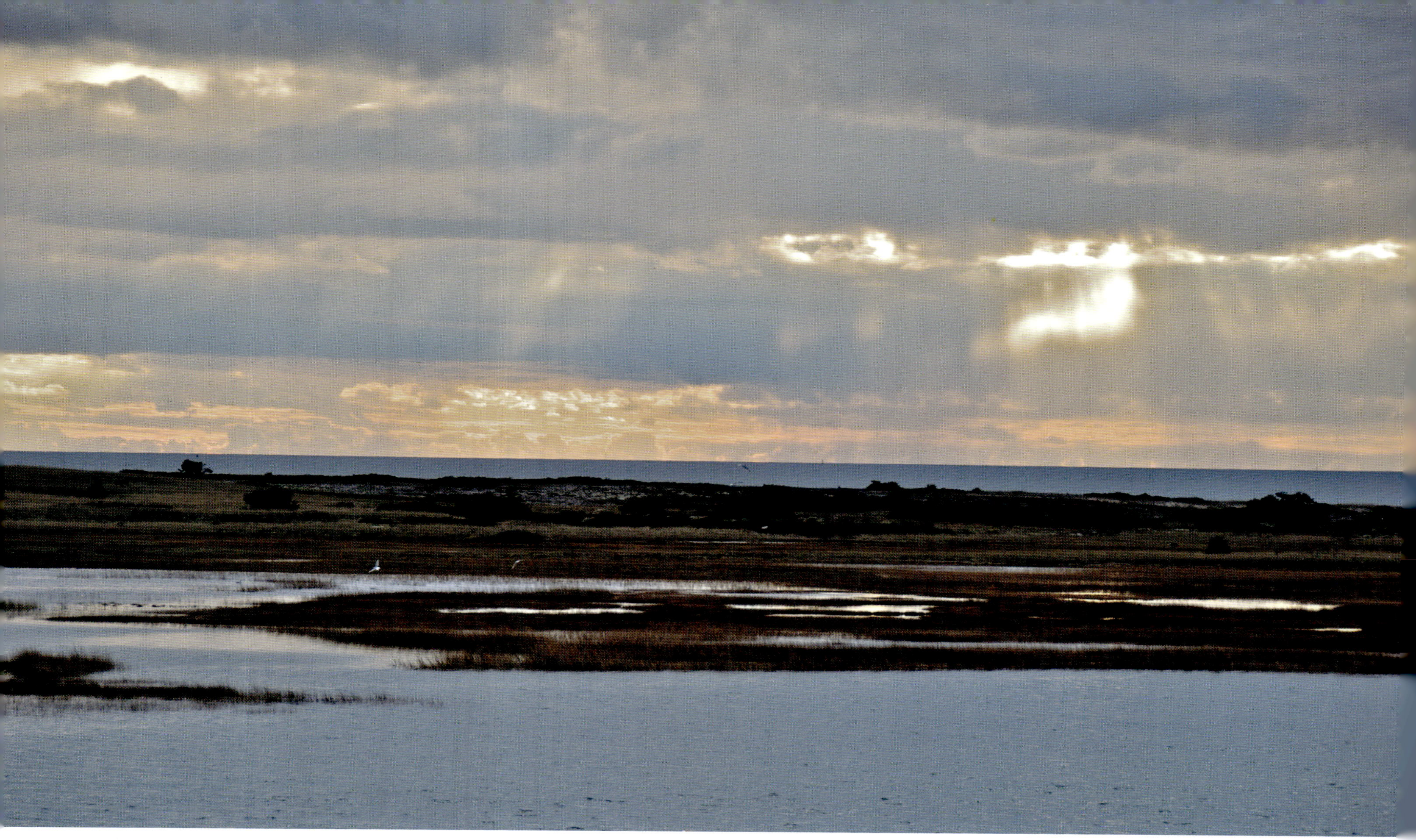

a river runs through it

oyster river,
chatham

anchor tenant

ancient basswood tree,
chatham

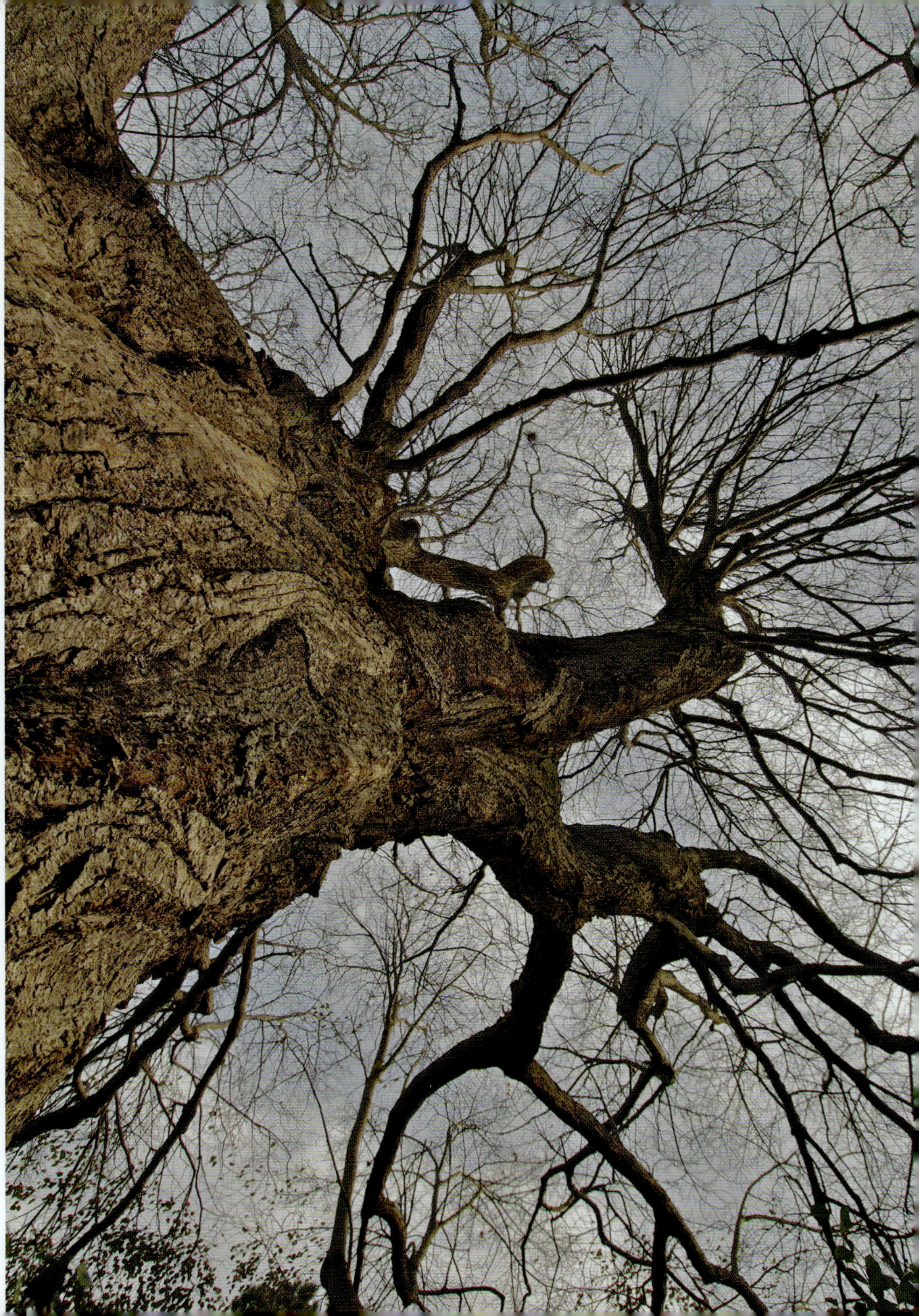

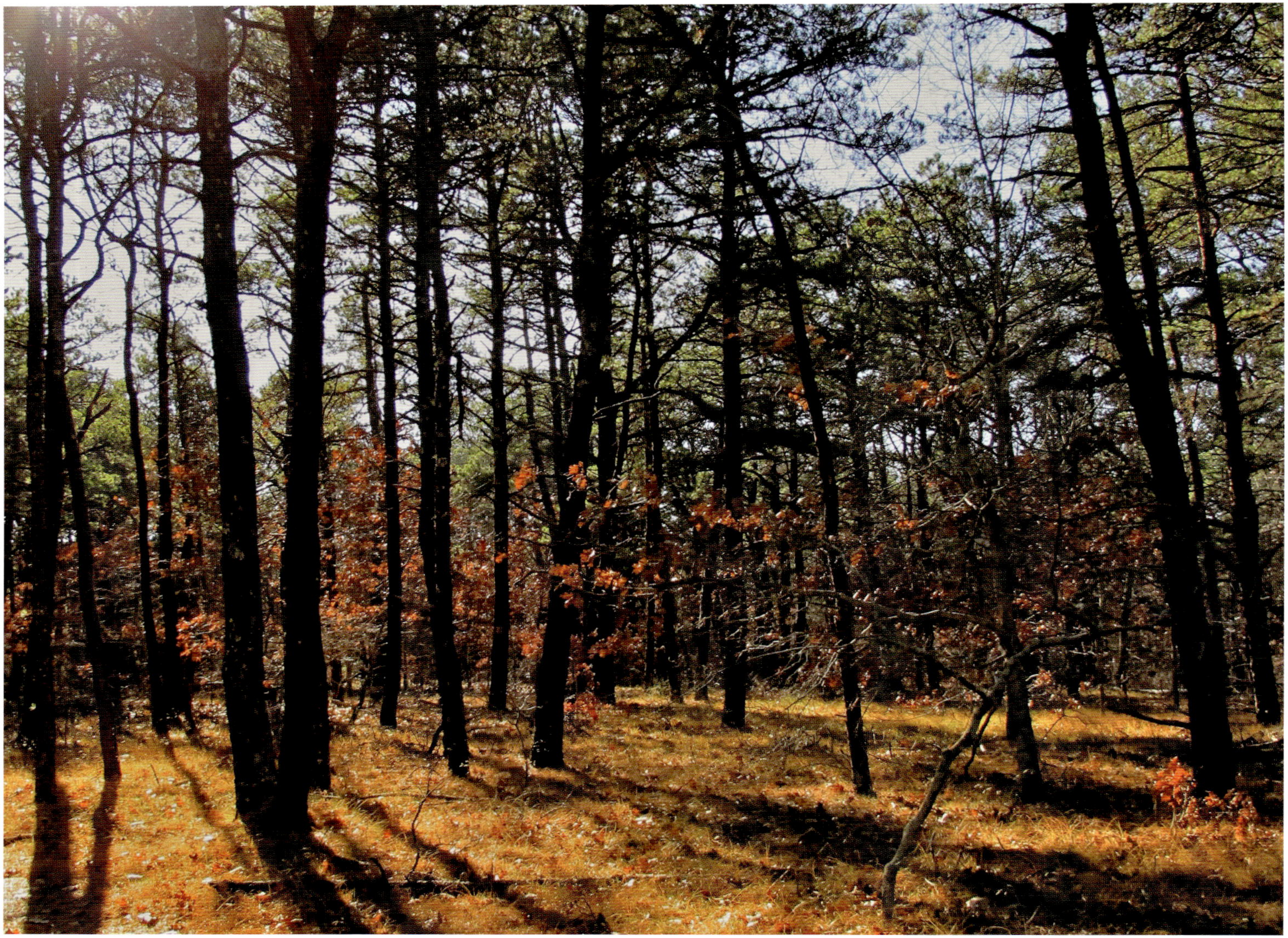

fall forest | wellfleet bay wildlife sanctuary

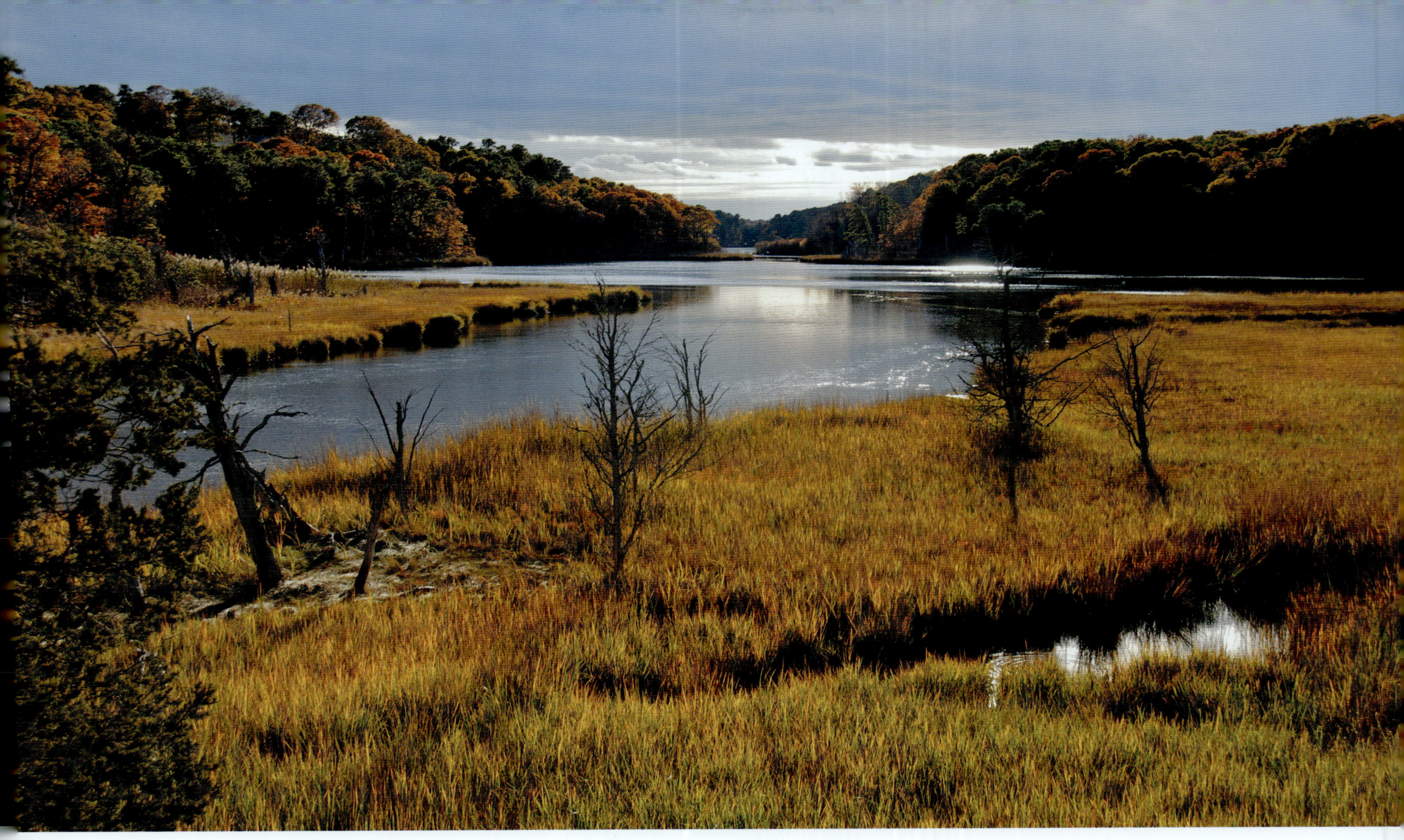

quiet place

monomoyick river,
chatham / harwich

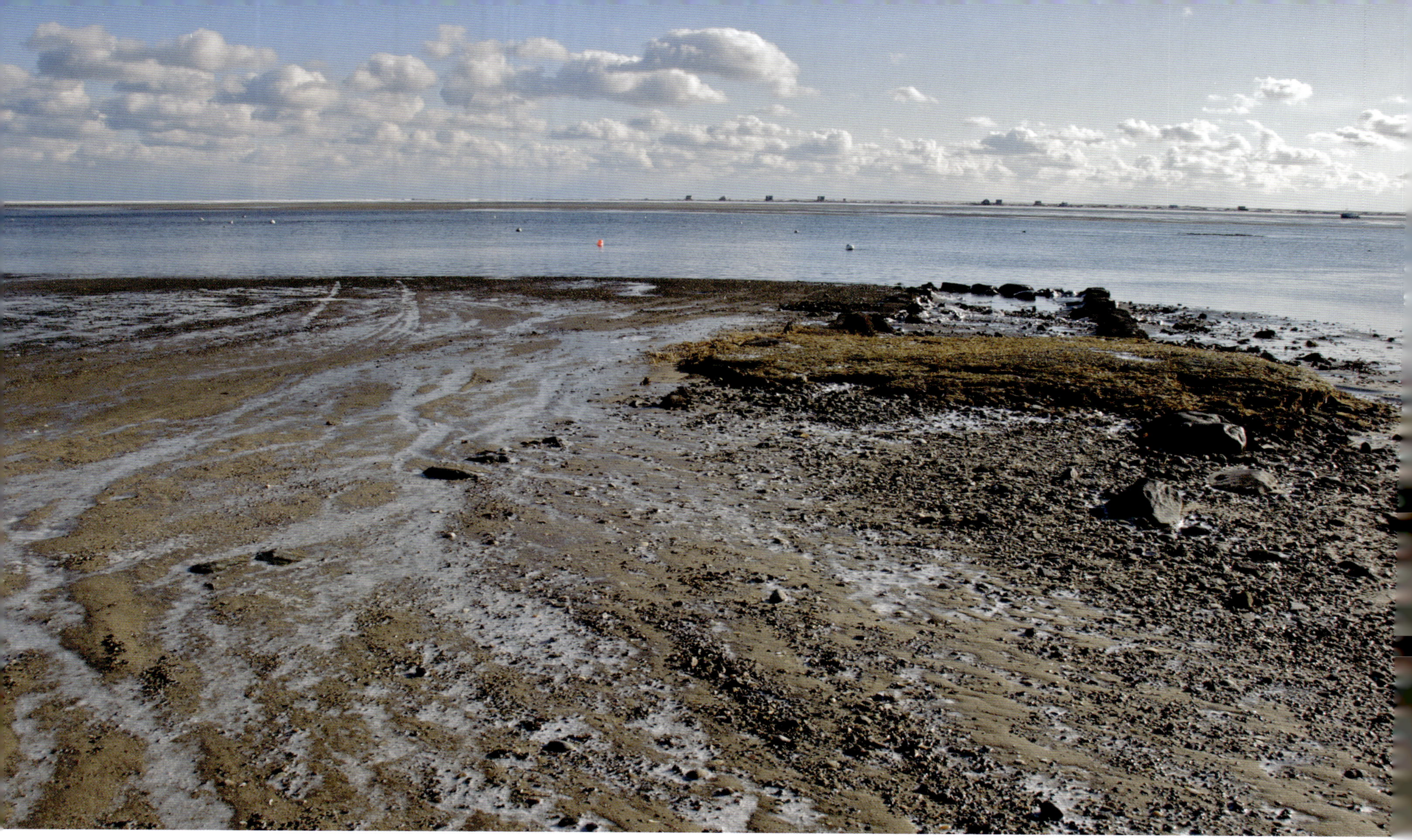

winter on the horizon

cow yard,
chatham

resources and bibliography

Everett, Roger. ***Birds of Cape Cod and the Islands.*** (Schiffer Publishing, Ltd., 2006).

Flock, Gretchen and Ann Prince Hecker, eds. ***Birding Cape Cod***. (Massachusetts Audubon Society, 1990).

Massachusetts Audubon Society. ***Monomoy Wilderness.*** (Massachusetts Audubon Society, Wellfleet Bay Sanctuary, 1972).

Sargent, Bill. ***Sea Level Rising.*** (Schiffer Publishing, Ltd., 2009).

Schwartzman, Beth. ***The Nature of Cape Cod.*** (University Press of New England, 2002).

Trull, Peter. ***A Guide to Common Birds.*** (Shank Painter Publishing Company, 1994).

Trull, Peter. ***Closer to the Great Whales.*** (Schiffer Publishing, Ltd., 2010).

Ward, Nathalie. ***Stellwagen Bank, A Guide to Whales, Sea Birds, and Marine Life of the Stellwagen Marine Sanctuary***. (Center for Coastal Studies, 1995).

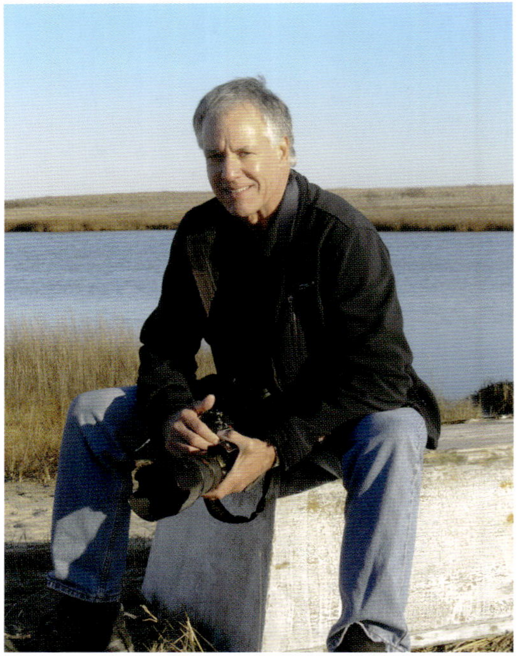

John King (photo by Shareen Davis)

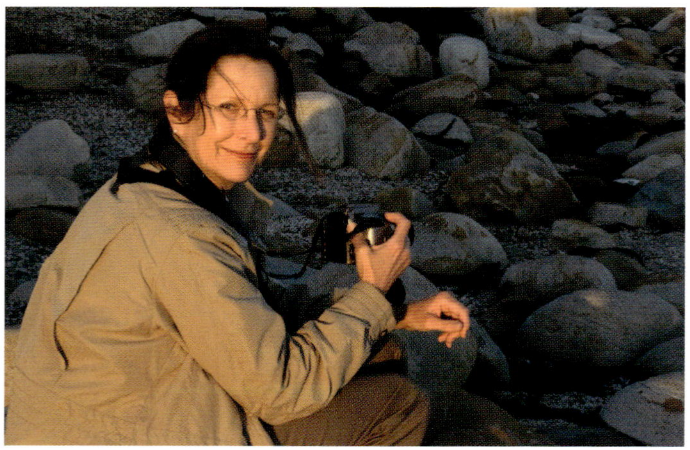

Pamela King (photo by jjking2)

about the authors

Raising a family and building businesses requires partnership, and John and Pamela King have taken that journey together since the 1970s. Initially working as commercial fishermen in Alaska, they both learned the value of hard work and an appreciation for the many moods of "mother nature."

John is an entrepreneur with a diverse resume who has strong ties to Cape Cod that span many generations. After receiving a BA in anthropology from the University of Pennsylvania, John spent more than seven years working as a commercial fisherman on vessels in Alaska. He earned his Masters license at the age of 27 and skippered the 180-foot crabber, *Baranof,* in the Bering Sea during the "hey day" of the king crab fishery. Following a subsequent, successful career in the biopharmaceutical world that spanned 27 years, John relocated back to his roots on Cape Cod and has been active in various pursuits, working to make a difference in the community. Among other responsibilities, John currently serves as the chairman of the board of trustees for the Atwood House Museum, home of the Chatham Historical Society.

In recent years John and Pamela have been pursuing a lifelong passion to experience and record the earth's wild places and wild things through their photography. They co-founded The Common Flat Project (www.commonflat.com) in 2011 to foster a message of conservation and raise awareness about the importance of biodiversity on our planet. *Wild Cape Cod: Free by Nature* is their first book. They have two grown children and make their home in Chatham, Massachusetts.